YEAR 1: A PHILOSOPHICAL RECOUNTING

SUSAN BUCK-MORSS

The MIT Press
Cambridge, Massachusetts
London, England

This book was set in Adobe Garamond Pro by New Best-set Typesetters Ltd. Printed and bound in the United States of America.

Library of Congress Cataloging-in-Publication Data

Names: Buck-Morss, Susan, author.
Title: Year 1 : a philosophical recounting / Susan Buck-Morss.
Other titles: Year One
Description: Cambridge, Massachusetts : The MIT Press, [2021] | Includes
    bibliographical references and index.
Identifiers: LCCN 2020015015 | ISBN 9780262044875 (hardcover)
Subjects: LCSH: Civilization—Philosophy. | Civilization, Western—Roman influences. |
    Chronology, Historical.
Classification: LCC CB245 .B835 | DDC 909/.09821—dc23
LC record available at https://lccn.loc.gov/2020015015

10 9 8 7 6 5 4 3 2 1

Contents

Acknowledgments

An academic book is a collective project. Past inquiries make new interpretations possible. I am grateful to the many authors cited here, whose careful labor, condensed between covers, is a gift to those who come afterward. I honor the research libraries that conserve their work, and the online sources that provide for the social distribution of ideas, valuing accuracy and public access over profits. My deep thanks go to those colleagues who have welcomed me into their domains of expertise with hospitality and good will. At Cornell: Annetta Alexandridis, Benjamin Anderson, Jonathan Boyarin, Jill Frank, Andrew Hicks, Jeffrey Rusten. And elsewhere: Daniel Boyarin, Honora Howell Chapman, Souleymane Bachir Diagne, Erich Gruen, Bonnie Honig, Mesut Ilgum, Jonathan Price, David Runia. At the CUNY Graduate Center, I have benefited greatly from interdisciplinary discussions at the Committee on Globalization and Social Change, directed by Gary Wilder.

This book crosses the established boundaries of scholarly disciplines, and consequently confronts the existence of multiple conventions as to how ancient texts are cited, written, and referenced. Because boundary crossing is precisely the goal of the project, scholarly conventions could not be followed exclusively, and compromises needed to be established. Regarding the question of orthography for words in *koine* (first-century Greek), I have written in italics the direct transliteration in English of *koine* words (with Greek letters in parentheses) when these words, standing alone, are used in multiple contexts. In general, I have worked with the NIV Interlinear Greek-English version of the Christian Bible.

The material object that you hold in your hands calls for thanks to Ian Wallace and Milo Ward for their help in preparing the manuscript. Thanks to Senior Acquisitions Editor Marc Lowenthal at the MIT Press for his nurturing patience. The work benefited immeasurably from the extraordinary knowledge and skill of Senior Editor Matthew Abbate. My thanks to him, and to the entire team at the MIT Press.

YEAR 1 is dedicated to my partner of 36 years, and even more to his grandparents born in Sicily, my maternal grandmother born in Austria and grandfather born in Greece. The diaspora has been kind to us. May it be so for others.

Introduction

YEAR 1 is a project in the reconfiguration of knowledge. The focus is on the first century. All of the schemata of modernity—time, space, conceptual differentiations, and categories of collective belonging—are put to the test of comprehending this alleged beginning, and none survives unscathed. The epistemological apparatus that modernity calls history was supposed to hold the past in place in an order leading to the present in coherent narrative form. But history writing itself provides knowledge that overturns this ordering presumption, freeing the past to speak otherwise.

Beneath the headlines of digital learning and data banks, a quiet revolution has been under way. Scholarship is transforming the very structures of knowledge, those conceptual frames that divide and order the record of human experience. In regard to the first century—this is why focusing on this moment in time is so revealing—the three most fundamental categories of historical narratives—Hellenism, Christianity, Judaism—distort the evidence. Conceptual distinctions between religion and politics, science and aesthetics, Athens and Jerusalem, or East and West do not make sense of the first-century world. The conventional approach of allotting historical material to the separate disciplines of classics, theology, and the modern secular humanities is seriously misleading. The search for origins of distinct groups leads, not to a purified source, but rather to the disappearance of the separations themselves.

Our main sources are three first-century authors who are seldom grouped together, indeed seldom even included in the usual stories told:

Flavius Josephus, historian of the Judaean War; the neo-Platonic philosopher Philo of Alexandria; and John of Patmos, author of Revelation (*Apocalypsis*), the last book of the Christian Bible. Readers may not be familiar with any of them, and those who know one may be ignorant of the others. Yet taken seriously on their own terms, they lead in surprising directions that contradict profoundly what we think we know, providing keys to a radical overturning of the epistemological preconceptions of our time. When this occurs, an abundance of interconnections becomes possible as temporally dispersed characters are drawn into the vortex of historical rearrangement. Antigone and John Coltrane, Plato and Bulwer-Lytton, Nicholas of Cusa and Zora Neal Hurston, al-Farabi and Jean Anouilh all make an appearance, not to mention Descartes, Kant, Hegel, Kristeva, and Derrida.

Owning Time

It is possible to colonize time as well as territory. It happens when particular collectives claim a specific, vertical slice of history, set upon it a flag of national or religious belonging, and control the production and distribution of the meanings that are mined within it. This clearly has been the fate of the first century. Contemporary anthropology has led the way in exposing the violent distortions in knowledge that colonization of space entails. This critique applies as well to colonized time. In exploring the distant past, we are foreigners entering alien territory. The natives share understandings not accessible to us without translation. Even if, linguistically, we know their words, we cannot assume proprietary rights over the meanings they convey. Even if we can trace the erratic path by which they have been rescued throughout time and come down to us, the privatizing laws of inheritance do not apply.

The conceptual landscape that we call globalization is forcing the transformation of historical understanding. Pollution, climate change, and viruses spread promiscuously, but so do ideas. People escape all the time from assigned containers. Humanity really is one. An educated public cannot afford to have its knowledge bound at the edge of a nation, or culture, or religion, or civilization. We are encouraged to see the noisy clashes of tribalism that dominate our media as rearguard sniping from defeated forces. It is increasingly difficult to deny what experience, on all sides, teaches: the borders between us are too porous to be defended without violating the very values for which we fight. The binary logics of us-versus-them no longer make sense of our world. Geopolitical hierarchies of difference cannot be defended.

Spanning Audiences, Spanning Sources

The research for this project spans archives that are conventionally presumed distinct. Wikipedia entries take their place alongside the most specialized academic publications. The project would have been impossible without this spanning of sources. I am indebted to the dedication of those many contributors to highly reliable, open-access sources, provided by both academic scholars of history and religious organizations of various denominations, including intertextual, word-for-word translations of many of the texts that matter for this project. But I have relied even more heavily on hard-bound books, including the invaluable holdings of Cornell University's research library, the continued relevance of which has only been enhanced in the digital age.

It is a task of this book to share with the wider public some of the recent research findings of experts and specialists. The goal is not popularization—books on the historical Jesus abound; Roman imperial foibles are the stuff of Hollywood cinema; sensationalist critiques and partisan positions in the narrating of first-century events are ubiquitous. Histories that rely on easy differences of civilization or religion are an impoverished picture of the field of historical scholarship, while theorists (my own academic specialization), due to selective readings of past texts, have not aided us in overcoming these limitations. Meanwhile scholars of the first century have been busy at work, tearing down walls between categories with explosive consequences for conventional understandings. The achievements of the very best of them, precisely because they do not underscore existing prejudices, are not sufficiently informing public debate. But whereas new knowledge of the past fundamentally challenges the premises upon which modern theories have been constructed, the converse is true as well. The very word "history" is a theoretical construct, indeed the fundamental armature by which modernity has ordered time, connecting the past in a linear, causal path to the present that projects its own reality, uninterrupted, into the future. Within this model, any break in the linear trajectory must appear as catastrophic. The possible benefits of newness are foreclosed.

Philosophy and History

Chapter 1 begins the epistemological critique by challenging the modern model of time and space that has become second nature in our time, reminding us that if the material life of history is transitory, then so too is our conceptual ordering of it. Chapter 2 initiates the historical investigation from the midst of the first century with Flavius Josephus' account of the Judaean War (66–70 BCE). This event splits open the trajectory of Roman political power as a narrative of imperial succession. Chapter 3 moves backward in time to Philo of Alexandria, contemporary of Augustus Caesar, hence part of the generation that ushers in the originary point that we call the "first" century. Its focus is Philo's commentary on a different point of origin, the book of Genesis, the beginning of time in a cosmological sense, which he interprets through a philosophical science of aesthetics. Chapter 4 considers John of Patmos' book of Revelation that dates to 96 CE, at the century's close. With this scathing critique of the Roman imperial order and its self-declared eternal verity, John envisioned the fulfillment of creation, not, as apocalypse today is defined, its physical end.

The ancient Romans had a word for the span of time considered here: a *saeculum*. It denotes the lived memory of a collective, beginning from an event such as the founding of a city, that ends when all the people who were alive at that moment have died—roughly 100 years. The organization of *YEAR 1* moves through the middle, beginning, and end of this *saeculum*, so that lived time and reflections *on* time are analogically aligned. Only then (chapter 5) is it possible to construct new constellations of past and present, in which the material is freed from modernity's ordering constraints, demonstrating the philosophical potential of a transformed relationship to the past. This structuring of the material allows a constant shifting of registers between history and philosophy. At the same time, it avoids subsuming one under the other as the history of philosophy or, alternatively, the philosophy of history. Something new is being proposed therefore: philosophy *and* history, present *and* past, in simultaneous arrangement. This task is difficult to describe in the introduction. It needs to be shown.

Historical Commons

Global humanity deserves a common history, but of what kind? There is general awareness that a different pedagogy is called for. This book is written as a contribution to its development. Here is the wager: If the first century can be reclaimed as common ground rather than the origin of deeply entrenched differences, then its very remoteness in time has the potential to lift modernity's self-understanding off existing foundational constraints, allowing a repositioning and reorientation of intellectual labor. And such a reorientation is necessary. Modernity does not have the power to transcend entrenched differences on the basis of its own resources, as the ways it describes differences are modernity's own inventions. The names of recent theoretical initiatives, postmodern, postcolonial, postsecular, are indicative of the inadequacy of this attempt to leave the recent past behind.

It may not be an exaggeration to say that the entire history of twentieth-century philosophy—mainly, but not only, in the West—can be brought in as evidence of the attempt to save modernity through its own means, as well as the frequency of its failure. Some of the best philosophers have been aware of the situation. Theodor W. Adorno, on repeated occasions, compared the modern philosophers' predicament to the marvelous tale of the Baron von Münchausen who, having fallen into a swamp on his horse, tried pulling himself out by his own pigtail.

Now, this did not stop Adorno from trying, committed as he was to the rescue of modernity's recent past. But it may also account for the fact that Adorno's own philosophy finds its contemporary effects more limited than those, for example, of the ubiquitous Martin Heidegger, who showed no compunction when he moved about in time as if all of it *belonged to him*, as if all that was required was the reading of a historical text, a book,

0.1

Illustrations of Baron Münchausen's remarkable leap (as told in the 1785 *Baron Munchausen's Narrative of His Marvellous Travels and Campaigns in Russia*, by the German writer Rudolf Erich Raspe). From left to right: by Theodor Hosemann, 1840; by Gustav Doré, 1862; unattributed.

ready at hand, to enable his personal encounter with Plato, or Duns Scotus, or Lao Tzu, from which he could take what he wanted without any sense of temporal or cultural barriers to entry, or any awareness of *not* being at home. The approach taken here is antithetical to this form of appropriation. The deeper one immerses oneself in first-century material, the more respectful one becomes of its integral complexities and the more critical of such methodological presentism that, to extend the aquatic metaphor, merely swims on the surface of time.

The Project

YEAR 1 concerns the relationship between the tasks of the historian and the philosopher. It argues for a transformed conception of just how these terms are linked together. And because it refuses to remain within any pre-given conceptual context, its approach to history, more than an immanent critique, is an approach to truth that can properly be called philosophy. It need be no secret that my lifelong relationship to the thinking of Walter Benjamin is behind this endeavor, specifically his insistence that historical objects have a metaphysical import that can be brought to legibility in the present. Benjamin described this as the "task" of the "historical material-ist." His friend Adorno wrote to him that such a project was situated "at the crossroads between magic and positivism," and warned, "this place is bewitched."[1] I make no claim of succeeding where Benjamin failed, or even trying to accomplish what he intended. I am a different sort of thinker. My research is in and about a different historical moment than those that concerned him. But I have long considered as objectively compelling the precarious positioning that he took, and that Adorno shunned, of reading the fragments and details of history as vital to the philosophical endeavor. I make no apologies for opening up this project to its dangers. The question is: Can the discovery of historical facts transform philosophical presupposi-tions, and can it do so in such a way that rescuing the past, by overcoming the narcissism of the present, provides an experience of epistemological liberation?

While the focus of this book is the first century, the event for which it receives this originating rubric is marginal to the account. Its geograph-ical location is the eastern Mediterranean, but its philosophical interest is skewed toward western Europe. It focuses on Jewish thinkers, but not Jewish identity. It deals with theological writings, and yet the religious story is not our main concern. Is this, then, a secular book? Not quite. As philosophy, the book extends hospitality to pre-Kantian, pre-Cartesian metaphysics. The modern philosophical claim that immanence—staying within the bounds of subjective experience—is the litmus test of truth is judged as unduly narrow, and very possibly unwise. A transcendent realm is acknowledged as vital for philosophy's work, even as its truth remains beyond our grasp.[2]

The collective addressed in this project is generational. Just as those who lived in the first century experienced a reality that all of *us* do not share, so we alive today have our own time in common. In the context of the stance taken in this book, all of us are descended from survivors who have witnessed, suffered, and perpetrated history's horrors. We have that in common. One way or another, the mothers who bore us escaped annihilation, giving to each of us a Year 1. And that is no small legacy to share.

0.2
Village of Geyre (Turkey), photo from the early 1970s, before the unearthing of the first-century city of Aphrodisias that lay beneath. Photo by Ara Guler. © Ara Guler/Magnum Photos.

1 COUNTING TIME, CHARTING SPACE

First . . .

The First Century. Already we have problems. This is no innocent nomenclature. It marks a claim to ownership of time. For whom was it the first
century? Presumably the Christian West. And yet even that is not a given,
as no Christian called this the First Century for at least 500 years, and it
took until the eighth to eleventh centuries for the A.D. form of dating
(*Anno Domini*, Year of the Lord) to catch on, finally sparing chronologists
the need constantly to revise their own positioning within the prescribed
6,000 years of biblical time.[1]

Because of miscalculations along the way, even Jesus was born, it
seems, as early as 7 years before his birthdate of Year 1, or perhaps 6 years
after.[2] And he, of all alive then, would never have considered making this
claim on time his own.[3] There was a kind of Year 1, indeed many of them
during this period, as the form of dating that counted the years of rule
of the Roman emperors. (Our) first century's year 1 was the 28th year of
rule of Rome's first emperor, Caesar Augustus (né Octavius), who held
the position for 40 years until his death in 14 CE. His years of rule were
publicly noted, but not in the straightforward sense, 1 through 40 of his
years in power, as had been done earlier and elsewhere in the lists of kings.[4]
Rather, the time was noted in terms of the number of times of renewal
of the multiple titles that the emperor held, as tribune (an office renewed
annually), consul (a two-year, two-person term as head of the Senate, not
always held by the emperor), imperator (commander), a titled renewed

1.1

Augustus Caesar, silver denarius, Lyons mint, n.d. (between 2 BCE and 13 CE). Obverse: laureate head with the inscription: "Caesar Augustus Divi F Pater Patriae" (Caesar Augustus son of a god [Julius Caesar, posthumously divinized] and father of the country). Reverse: Gaius and Lucius, grandsons of Augustus whom he adopted as his sons and heirs (they did not outlive him), each with a hand resting on a shield, with the inscription: "Augusti F[ilii] Co[n]s[ules] Desig[nati] Princ[ipes] Iuven[tutis]" (sons of Augustus, designated consuls, first among the young). The British Museum, IOC.1235. © The Trustees of the British Museum. All rights reserved.

with significant military victories, and princeps (the first, most eminent), Augustus' name for himself. No standardized chronology emerges from these multiple, renewable titles with varied lengths of office.[5] They appear sometimes, but not always, on the minted coins, sometimes, but not always, followed by the number of times an emperor held them.

On the coin of Augustus shown in image 1.1, there is a reference to consulship ("Cos") but no date.[6] But even when coins indicate the number of terms an office was held, for us these are not easily legible.[7] Dating of the coins by the numbers *on* the coins is incredibly difficult. Transcription tables are required.[8] Year 1 returns to date the first year of various title-holdings of Augustus' successors: Tiberius (14–37 CE), Caligula (37–41 CE), Claudius (41–54 CE), and Nero (54–68 CE), all of whom minted coins with multiple dating systems, claiming their personal ownership of time. Then it gets complicated.

68–69 CE was a year of civil war fought over imperial succession that followed the forced suicide of Nero, last of the Julio-Claudian line. During that Year 1, four emperors claimed power.[9] All of them issued coins with differing strategies of identification. Galba, for example, first issued coins continuing dates of the Claudio-Augustan emperors, and then switched to his own year 1. Otho's rule was so brief—a matter of months—that no reckoning of time appears on the coins. Vitellius, the third emperor, was captured and killed by Vespasian (69–78 CE) who, returning from military victories against rebels in the Judaean War, established a second (Flavian) imperial line through his two sons, Titus (78–81 CE) and Domitian (81–96 CE), the latter of whom was assassinated and died without heirs. Nerva (96–98) and his adopted son Trajan (98–117) rounded out the first century of first years of imperial rule. That makes an even dozen—far more on the coins, given various titles held. With regard to inscriptions on the coins, however, it is victories in war, concern for one's heirs, or promises of peace throughout the provinces that are more significant concerns than mere chronology. Events are celebrated, titles appear, but how these relate to sequential dates cannot be determined.

The point of relating these convoluted numismatic details is to provide estrangement from any easy appropriation of the past. Historical time is not self-evident. Our continued use of the calendar of 12 months and 365¼ days, developed during the Republic by Julius Caesar (Augustus' father by adoption), provides a false sense of security.[10] It obscures how much work historians have had to do to fit not only the coins but all the recorded events of antiquity into our present-day temporal grid. In his study devoted to the complexities of Roman time, Feeney writes: "The centuries-long work on constructing a coherent historical chronology on an axis of B.C.E./C.E. time has been absorbed and naturalized so thoroughly by all of us that we can take it completely for granted, and forget just how much synchronistic work our predecessors going back to the Renaissance had to do in order for us to be able to say something like 'Xerxes invaded Greece in 480 B.C.E.'"[11]

Stone tablets called *fasti*, set up in the city forum, provided Romans with annual calendars of monthly dates of public significance, including

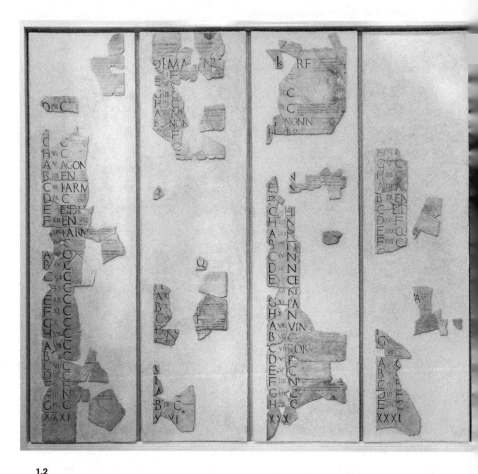

1.2

Fasti Praenestini, calendar of Verrius Flaccus. From Palestrina, between ca. 6 and 9 CE. Photo by Jastrow / Wikimedia Commons / CC BY 2.5.

market days, legal dates, sacred rites, and festival events.[12] In the Republic, they were paired with consuls' names, so that their terms of office identified the year. As emperor, Augustus changed their nature by using the solar regularities of the Julian calendar to mesh its time with civil time, superimposing on both an imperial "language of power" by crowding onto them the "various doings" of the imperial family, including "[b]irths, deaths, apotheoses, assumptions of power, accessions to priesthood, comings of age, dedications of temples, victories in battle."[13] This assemblage provided

1.2 (continued)
Detail of the Fasti Praenestini. © Marie-Lan Nguyen / Wikimedia Commons / CC BY 2.5.

the appearance of a harmonious confluence between the imperial family's personal events and the collective rhythms of social life. Feeney (speaking of the Roman orator Cicero) notes: "What to us is a matter of numbers is to Cicero a matter of personal relationships—fathers and sons, uncles and nephews, junior and senior friends."[14]

We need to understand our abstract time schema as itself historically specific. For the first century, the uniformity of abstract numbers was not observed as meaningful. The hours of day were read off sundials, hence their lengths varied with the seasons. The twelve hours of daylight were shorter in the winter, longer in the summer, and the inverse was true for night—a perfectly rational system, but for us disorienting in the extreme. Histories were told by analogies with distant and mythical events. Rome and Carthage were twinned reaching back to Troy as their model, linking

1.3

Great Cameo of France, second quarter of the first century. Bibliothèque Nationale de France. "In the upper level are [the imperial family's] deceased or deified members, including Divus Augustus. The surrounding figures may be Drusus the Younger (son of Tiberius), and Drusus the Elder (brother of Tiberius) flying on Pegasus. In the middle level appear the emperor Tiberius flanked by his mother Livia; standing in front of them are Germanicus, Tiberius's designated heir, together with his wife Agrippina the Elder, behind [whom are] the future emperor Nero and the figure of Providentia (Foresight); behind Livia and Tiberius are Claudius, emperor if the cameo was made in ca. 50–54 AD, and his wife Agrippina the Younger. Agrippina the Younger's hairstyle seems to confirm a date for the cameo between her marriage to Claudius in 49 and the accession of her son Nero as the fifth emperor of Rome in 54. Alternatively, the cameo was commissioned to celebrate Tiberius' adoption of his grandchildren, the sons of Germanicus, as heirs in 23 AD, and the dynastic stability it ensured, comparable to the earlier adoption of Germanicus by Tiberius in 4 AD, also referenced on the cameo. . . . In the lowest level are captive barbarians." (From "Great Cameo of France," Wikipedia.)

Julio-Claudian Family Tree

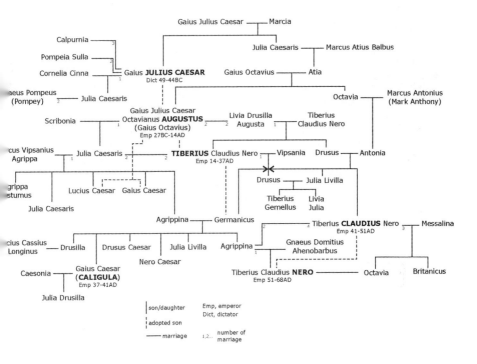

1.4

Modern time chart of the Julio-Claudian emperors (27 BCE–63 CE). ("Julio-Claudian Family Tree," Wikipedia.)

present and past events in a series of correspondences.[15] Multiple time orientations were the rule, without the overarching grid that holds them all in place.[16] The very proliferation of number series indicates that the inhabitants of what we call the first century had a different idea of how to orient themselves in time than we do today.[17] We could not have known the time by means of our chronological method, and they, having the *fasti* as orientation, would not have cared.[18]

Revolt Coins

Consider another example: Two years before the Year of Four Emperors, in 66 CE, Jews in the Roman province of Judaea became involved in a different kind of civil war, when groups rebelled against the Roman presence and

1.5

Silver shekel, revolt coin using Paleo-Hebrew alphabet. Obverse: omer cup (for Temple ritual) with smooth rim, pearl on either side, base with pearled ends; dotted border. Reverse: stem with pearled base and three pomegranates; border of dots. Roman Empire, 66–67 (year 1). The British Museum, 1875,0503.9. © The Trustees of the British Museum. All rights reserved.

the Judaean king endorsed by Rome. The rebels captured Jerusalem and the Jewish Temple; for four years until their devastating defeat by Titus, son of the emperor Vespasian, which led to the destruction of the Temple, coins were issued with a date for each year, 1 to 4, suggesting not a new imperial reign but a new historical era, which within the Jewish context might be presumed to have had a specifically messianic significance.[19] But we would be wrong to move too quickly in interpreting their meaning by projecting onto their appearance more familiar practices of our time.

The coins, known as the "revolt coins," have been studied in depth by historians. We have a detailed accounting of their number and nature. Silver coins bear the slogan "holy Jerusalem" (*yrwšlm hqdwš*) and indicate their weight, "shekel of Israel"; the bronze coins of the second and third year bear the motto "freedom of Zion"; the fourth-year coins have the words "for the redemption of Zion."[20] No names of political authorities or rebel leaders appear. The designs are of objects connected with Jewish cults and festivals: a chalice, perhaps the one that was on the shewbread table in the Temple, and a three-pronged object that has been identified as either a pomegranate stem with three buds or perhaps a priestly staff.[21]

It is easy for us to infer a similarity between the dating on these coins and similar dating systems used during the revolutionary struggles of modernity, when both Jacobin-revolutionary France and Dessalines-led Haiti began to issue coins dated from year 1.[22] This enactment of time's meaning is seen as prototypical of Western modernity, marking an event's significance as a temporal rupture in history. However, in the case of the Judaean rebel coins, these numbers are not future-oriented: "The use of palaeo-Hebrew script and ancient biblical names ('Israel,' 'Zion') seem to hark back instead to a mythical distant past."[23] A long-standing claim of cultural difference connects Jewish culture with linear time; however, scholarship on the first century does not bear this out: "the Greek 'circular' conception of time, as opposed to the 'linear' or teleological conception for the Hebrew Bible . . . is a misconception as far as both the Greeks and the Jews are concerned, mistaking occasional or circumscribed or dialectical usages for some holistic mentality."[24]

Are the rebel coins evidence of an anticolonial revolt, a proto-nationalist struggle? That would presume solidarity among Judaeans during this war, which was not the case: "No single leader was accepted by all the different factions; quite the reverse, many of them were actually engaged in fighting one another."[25] Regarding a messianic reading, "Messianic ideas and leaders with Messianic aspirations were flourishing under Roman rule in Judaea. . . . A climactic atmosphere of eschatological expectation was felt up to the last moments of the burning of the temple."[26] Nonetheless, there is no coherent messianic narrative to construct on the basis of the groups who rebelled, certainly not one that would tie to the issuing of the coins. The inscription of the bronze year 4 coins, "for the redemption of Zion," had possible eschatological meaning, and may have been minted by a specific leader, Simon Bar Giora, who entered Jerusalem with his forces and took control in the last year of the war, and was taken as prisoner to Rome and executed there as part of the victory celebration.[27] However, what strikes scholars as remarkable is the degree of consistency in the coins over the four years of war despite these multiple factions, which might instead suggest the desire to avoid a radical break in the Temple traditions.[28] The experts admit, "the work of attributing the first revolt coins is emphatically incomplete. . . . Neither numismatists nor historians have been able to agree who struck the coins: who were the minting authorities among the many factions competing for control of Jerusalem during the revolt."[29]

This book will not answer the question of the meaning of the coins. We resist the tendency to project onto historical objects any one of a number of narratives familiar to present-day readers. This is not the point, but rather to point *out* how deceptive the subsuming of the past under modern categories can be, and how easily historical fictions then take over. There is no reason to protect the general reading public from the lack of assurance that we as scholars have. On the contrary: much is to be gained by disrupting the complacency of existing understandings that can be called the narcissism of the present, which sees in the past only the origin of ourselves.

Von Ranke's idea of history writing as a struggle to discover the past as it *really* happened *remains the task*. But paradoxically (impossible to realize!) it cannot be the goal. Disagreement and dissent are to be expected. However, the polemics of the partisan are unwelcome. History writing is not a rhetorical construct of good guys and bad that can be manipulated for current propaganda. The uniquely human ability to learn beyond the limits of the present opens historical time. The goal is to liberate the objects—in this case, the quite beautiful coins—to speak to us in another way, rather than mirroring our own reflection.

Chronology Unlimited

So how did chronological dating from Jesus's birth come about?

Muslim dating of time from the Hijra (622 CE) occurred within decades of the event.[30] This was a period when Christians still conceived time in biblical terms.[31] Indeed, as Garth Fowden notes, the "initial concept" of Hijra dating "had not a little to do with the perceived shortcomings of Christianity," whereas Christians taking note of Islam's elegant solution were in turn disposed to accept a proposal for Anno Domini dating as an alternative (although at widely varying times within the

1.6
An example from 'Abd al-Malik's reformed coinage (which previously had included figurative imagery), Umayyad Dynasty, ca. 696 CE. Muslim coins took several decades to evolve their distinctive style. They name the year in AH dating, indicating that time begins with the event of God's prophecy to the Prophet Mohammed—not the Prophet's birth date, nor the year of reign of any Islamic ruler. The British Museum, 1846,0523.14. © The Trustees of the British Museum. All rights reserved.

Greco-Latin world).[32] For us today, the overarching, abstract chronology of Western time is the dominant form, a fact that embodies the history of modern imperialism.[33] "For us" here is an inclusive category. The Muslim who today can translate readily from hegemonic Western century dating into the Hijra system, based on the lunar year (of a different length and with a different first day), is increasingly rare.[34] Still, we can appreciate the fact that Islam's intelligent system of dating forward, finally emulated by the Christians, allowed them to escape the threat of running out of days before the end of days, and needing constantly to move the temporal goal post further forward due to the lack of punctuality of the end's appearance.[35]

This book sustains the hegemonic mode of Western dating, while mitigating the universal Christian claims of AD (Year of the Lord) by the more modest delineation preferred by scholars, CE (Common Era). With a nod to the world's indebtedness to Islam for the inventive institution of a rational chronological system, and also in appreciation of the fact that CE dating adopts the use of the Hindu-Arabic decimal system (the spread of which allowed the medieval West to abandon the cumbersome Roman and Greek numbering systems by letters), and further in full recognition that there have been multiple other indigenous dating systems in the world, we affirm that no pure dating exists no matter how abstractly conceived. All are historically evolved with no universal status but convenience, the fact that, in our time, the system is commonly shared. Arguably, all are indebted to one another.[36] We cannot separate out the strands of our shared past—nor should we try. Yielding to a common chronology is a technological necessity demanded by global systems today. Rather than reversing the power relationship by privileging another form, or attempting to eliminate dominant grids completely, we need to keep in mind that CE dating is a (quite wonderful) convenience, nothing more.

Owning Time

Let us consider the *Res gestae divi Augusti* ("Things Accomplished by the God Augustus"). It is the life testimony of the first Roman emperor,

1.7
The replica, created during the Fascist period, of the text of the *Res gestae divi Augusti* (the self-celebratory autobiography written by emperor Augustus), engraved along the base of the Ara Pacis museum in Rome. Photo by Giovanni Dall'Orto, March 29, 2008 / Wikimedia Commons.

describing in the first person and in great detail the events and accomplishments of his reign, listing the "firsts"—his favorite word—achieved by him.[37] Augustus speaks explicitly of his years as emperor as "my era." Time belongs to him, although, as with the minted coins, there is lack of concern for chronological sequence, so that the political narrative of the events listed is extremely difficult for modern historians to reconstruct.[38] The *Res gestae* was written by the emperor in the years before his death, and was intended for public display (the divine title was bestowed upon him posthumously by the Roman Senate).[39] This autobiographical description of the emperor's rise to power and virtuous actions, including military conquests, financial largess, festivals, games, public building projects, and the bringing of peace and prosperity, is one of the most famous primary sources of Roman imperial history. But is the document known?

Certainly it is seen—not the original, an inscription set in bronze at the site of Augustus' mausoleum shortly after his death that has long

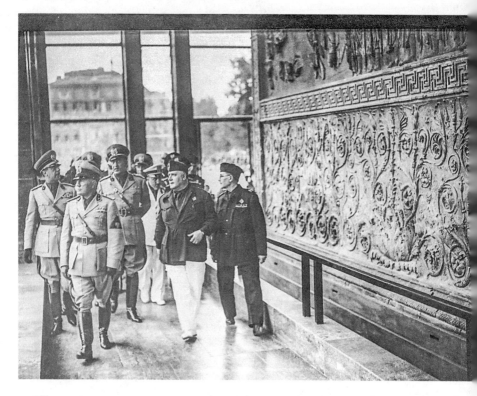

1.8
Photograph of Mussolini at the opening of the Roman pavilion for the Ara Pacis (Altar of Peace), September 1938. Deutsches Archäologisches Institut, Rome.

since completely disappeared, but a twentieth-century copy erected close by, cast in bronze on a travertine wall, that marks a compulsory stop on the well-worn path of today's tourists in Rome. It was constructed under Mussolini in 1938, as part of a year-long Augustan Exhibition of Roman-ness (*romanità*), in celebration of the bimillennium of Augustus' birth (63 BCE), and it served as the podium for a glass pavilion to house a second Augustan monument, the then-recently excavated Ara Pacis (Altar of Peace, 9 BCE), that was visited by Hitler during the festival year.[40]

The pavilion was finished quickly and cheaply to meet publicity dead-lines, as the image, not the object, was supreme.[41] Today the *Res gestae* wall provides the foundation of an important new museum built to replace the glass pavilion. Designed by the architect Richard Meier, it opened in 2009 on April 21, which is the customary birthdate of the city of Rome. Meier's construction, a classic example of 1980s International Style, was rent with controversy from its inception. What, the traditionalists asked, was a modern construction doing in the city's historic center, and why was a non-Italian architect commissioned to build it? One critic compared it to a Texas gas station.[42]

While visually integrated into the natural site, historically the monument's high-modern profile is noncontextual in the extreme. It seems at home anywhere precisely because it obliterates the specific history of any particular place.[43]

Now, the abstract universality of Meier's contemporary architecture that claims a global at-home-ness might suggest that the way to avoid such misplaced chauvinism as Mussolini's is to ignore history altogether. What better way to found the Year 1 of a new global order than simply to erase the past? The present study is a sustained argument against such historical amnesia, because it builds the future on faulty foundations. Moreover, it cannot even see that this has happened. The surest way to intensify the political dangers of a mythic construction of the past is to foster ignorance of the historical truth about it.

Temple to the God Augustus

If the original Roman tablets of the *Res gestae* have disappeared without a trace, if the Latin primary sources provide only general references to the text, how is it that we know its exact wording? A largely intact copy of the *Res gestae* has been preserved. It was carved into a temple wall in the ancient city of Ancyra—today's Ankara, the city chosen to be capital of the modern Turkish nation by its founder Mustafa Kemal Atatürk. The wall was made fully visible as part of Atatürk's program of glorifying the country's ancient cultural heritage.[44] Within a frame of national histories, this double appropriation (by both Italy and modern Turkey) appears as a contradiction. But if we focus on the materially persistent, physical object itself, then an entirely different history opens before us. Here, very briefly, are the salient facts.

1.9
Museum of the Ara Pacis (Museo dell'Ara Pacis), 2009, designed by Richard Meier. Photo by Antonella Profetta. © Antonella Profetta / CC BY 2.5.

1.10
A Texas gas station. Photo by David B. Martin, II. © David B. Martin, II.

1.11
Ancyra temple to the worship of the god Augustus with the *Res gestae divi Augusti* inscribed on the walls of the cella, Ankara, Turkey. Photo: Carole Raddato / Wikimedia Commons. CC BY-SA 2.0.

The original founder of Ankara was Augustus himself. The city of Ancyra, capital of the Roman province of Galatia, was colonized by veterans of Augustus' army in ca. 25 BCE, and its public buildings were constructed by the enslaved prisoners of his wars. Two other copies of the *Res gestae* have been discovered in Galatian cities of Asia Minor, one at Antioch (near Pisidia) and a third in Apollonia (today's Uluborlu).[45] In 2012 a further fragment of a copy of the *Res gestae* was identified in the city of Sardis in the neighboring Roman province of Asia.[46] These appear to be the only copies. Nowhere else in the Roman Empire have even partial inscriptions of the *Res gestae* been found, indicating that initiative to erect them in public view came from local interests in cities practicing the emperor cult in these Roman provinces of Anatolia, not from imperial decree.[47]

Augustus was worshiped here as a god in his lifetime. The Ancyra temple predates the *Res gestae* inscribed on it (in 14–19 CE) by several decades, and was constructed as a place for worship of the living god Augustus

1.12
Detail of the Ankara *Res gestae*. Photo by Marie-Lan Nguyen. © Marie-Lan Nguyen / Wikimedia Commons / CC BY 2.5.

and the goddess Roma, the city that bore him. The temple exemplifies the emperor cult that was broadly extant, not only in Galatia but in the adjacent, coastal province of Asia to the west.[48] The cult fused Rome's imperial present with the past of Greek mythology. These eastern provinces shared with Rome the Hellenic panoply of gods; they shared as well the mythic hero, Aeneas, who migrated to Italy in the diaspora caused by the Trojan War. It was from Aeneas, offspring of the goddess Venus-Aphrodite and a princely cousin of King Priam of Troy, that Augustus claimed descent. This hero's story was retold by the first-century BCE poet Vergil, whose Latin epic, the *Aeneid*, allegedly sung to the emperor by the poet himself, gave heroic legitimacy to the Julio-Claudian line.

The *Res gestae* inscribed on the wall of the Ancyra temple was bilingual. Next to the Latin text of the Roman original is a close translation in Greek.[49] This first-century language is called *koine*/κοινή, the word that in Greek means "common." It was not the Attic Greek of Athenian philosophy (Plato and Aristotle), or the Ionic Greek of Homer (the *Iliad* and *Odyssey*) but rather the Greek whose usage had spread across the East through trading networks now thought to have preceded, and thereby facilitated, the conquests of Alexander the Great, whose empire adopted this shared idiom as its own. By the time of Augustus, *koine*, the "common language," had become the lingua franca of the post-Alexandrian world.

The central role of *koine* in multiple histories—Jewish, Christian, Roman, Greek—is an indication of the entanglements of the past with which this book is concerned. It takes its lead from the geographical shift in recent scholarship from Western Europe to the Middle East in the burgeoning field of what is called late antiquity, which stretches from the empire of pagan Rome to that of Christian Byzantium, and continues on

1.13
Temple of Roma and Augustus, Ankara, Turkey, exterior wall (southeast) inscribed with the Greek version of *Res gestae divi Augusti*, view from the east. Photo: Klaus-Peter Simon / Wikimedia Commons / CC BY-SA 3.0.

to the political rise of Islam. In this period the complexities of cultural and religious intertwining simply cannot be captured by the categories and concepts of history as traditionally told in the West. Cooley's detailed study of the *Res gestae* recognizes that "this broad inclusion of geography shifts things," transforming our mental mapping of the past.[50] Her book juxtaposes Latin and Greek versions on facing pages, a format that attests to the double nature of the Roman imperial era, providing a visual balance between east and west, Ancyra and Rome, rather than a nationalist-centered story of either side. It is not that Rome was "unoriginal" compared with the Hellenic styles that it adopted.[51] In the first century, which despite the political rupture of civil war in 68–69 CE is coherent as the first era of the *Pax Romana* (Roman Peace), Hellenic history cannot be pulled apart from Roman history, certainly not along national lines.

The reason we have such a good copy of the *Res gestae* in Ankara is the fact that the structure of the wall on which it was inscribed was first a pagan temple, then (ca. sixth century CE) a church, and then a fifteenth-century mosque. In the history of the temple's survival, all of these layers of belonging must be included. The building's preservation has been ensured precisely by the historical entanglements that interest us. A focus on the material, historical object demonstrates not only the arbitrariness of exclusionary claims to ownership of time, but also the necessity of shared work among scholars if accurate knowledge of our common past is to be achieved.

The ancient history of Europe is a history of marginality. The center of civilizational gravity was farther east. Moreover, this "center" was in motion. The economic base of the Roman Empire was long-distance trade. The people who engaged in it lived in scattered locations along its routes— that is, they lived in diasporas that were not excluded from imperial power but situated at its base. Roman imperial history is part of the commingling of three continents. This last point needs elaboration.

A Sense of Place
We have no maps of the first-century world in the modern sense of the term.[52] Descriptions given in primary sources are verbal. Mountains and

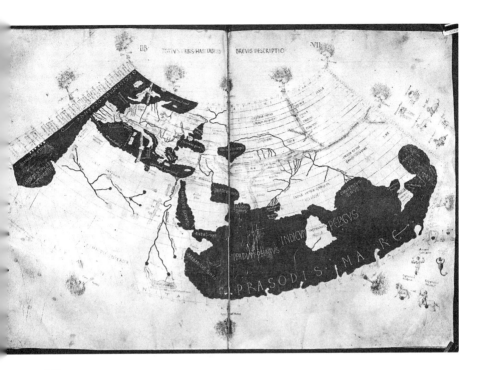

1.14

A mid-fifteenth-century Florentine map (attributed to Francesco di Antonio del Chierico) from an illustrated edition of the second-century *Geography* written by the Alexandrian geographer Claudius Ptolemy, showing the world as Ptolemy knew it through the written descriptions available to him. It indicates Ptolemy's mistaken understanding of the Indian Ocean as a land-surrounded sea. The island of Sri Lanka ("Taprobana") is huge in comparison to the neighboring Indian peninsula, signaling its trading importance. The Southeast Asian (Malay) peninsula ("Aurea Chersonesus") is sketched roughly. The seasonal reversing west/east monsoon winds were known in the first century (called the Hippalus after the navigator who discovered them), enabling cross-ocean sailing long before longitudinal measurement on open waters was possible (not until the eighteenth century). In the public domain.

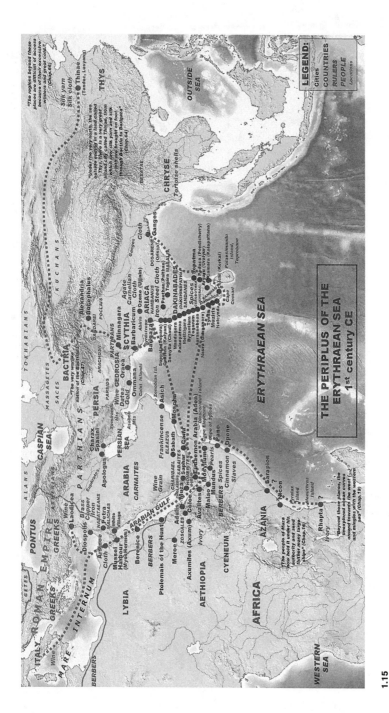

1.15

Modern map derived from descriptions in the sailors' manual *Periplus of the Erythraean Sea*, securely dated to the mid-first century CE, that served a vital purpose of practical knowledge for the Arabian, east African, and Indian Ocean trade. The *koine* term *Erythrās Thalássis* (Ερυθράς Θαλάσσης) means "Red Sea," and is applied in the manual to this entire maritime area. In the public domain.

valleys, rivers and seas were visible markers and maintained their names despite changes of rule. Among written itineraries was the first-century sailors' manual *Periplus of the Erythraean Sea* (Περίπλους τῆς Ἐρυθρᾶς Θαλάσσης), which provided a compendium of information on the whole area of the northwestern Indian Ocean, including the Red (Arabian) and Persian Seas. It functioned as a geography text, noting ports, coastal landmarks and distances between them, trade routes, monsoon winds, and other information vital for travel from east Africa to the Persian Gulf, and from the Kushan kingdom in the Indus valley to the south Indian and Sri Lankan kingdom of Chola, as well as the goods that were transported and the people who engaged in the trade. Its verbal descriptions, when superimposed on a modern spatial mapping, allow us to construct an image legible to us of first-century trade.

Trading cities within this network had relative autonomy, and multiple ethnicities called them home.[53] Nomadic peoples crossed several geographies; some settled permanently in cities as merchants. Those whom Herodotus named Scythians, located between the Black and Caspian Seas (today's Georgia and Iran), migrated south through Bactria to the Indus valley (today's Kashmir and Pakistan), an area that in the first century CE became the Kushan Empire.[54] Such migration paths served trading caravans moving along intersecting routes, extending westward from the silk producers ruled by the Han Dynasty of China to Aleppo and Palmyra in Syria, or through the Khyber Pass and Kushan Empire into south Asia. Lines of trade connected the frankincense groves of the Hadramawt (today's Yemen) and pearl producers of the Gulfs of Aden and Persia to multiple locations: Palmyra in Syria, the Nabatean city of Petra (in today's Jordan), and Caesarea Maritima in Judaea.[55] The Red Sea routes connected, via the monsoon winds, to the ivory and spice-producing areas of east Africa (today's Somalia, Tanzania, and Mozambique),[56] and to the Chola kingdom (south India and Sri Lanka) that was ruled in the first century by the Tamils, who traded further by sea with southeast Asia and China.

This was the already existing world into which imperial Rome inserted itself. From Augustus to Domitian, the determining factor of foreign policy on multiple occasions was access to this eastern trade. Land routes of trade were effectively blocked by Parthia that ruled over lands of the former Persian Empire. Parthian royal armies on horseback defeated Roman foot soldiers on multiple occasions.[57] Armenia was strategically important not only as a passageway into Parthia during invasions, but also as a connecting link to the silk route across the (Iranian) plateau to the northern route (through today's Afghanistan) into China.[58] Despite collaboration when mutual interests were involved, Parthian resistance to Roman penetration was constant. A text from the Han Dynasty of China comments: "Znxi (or Anxi [安息], i.e., Parthia) wishes to control the trade in multi-coloured Chinese silks and so blocks the route to prevent (the Romans) getting through."[59]

Given Parthian control over land routes, Roman acquisition of Egypt was crucial, because Egypt's Red Sea ports (specifically Berenike and Adulis) gave them access to the Indian Ocean trade in luxury goods.[60] When in 31 BCE the future emperor Augustus defeated queen Cleopatra VII and her consort (his rival) Marc Antony, he seized this trade, her source of wealth, and made it his own.[61] Multiple traders were already active in this commerce—Palmyrenes, Nabateans, Sabeans, Jews, Aksumites, Indians, and Tamils[62]—and they remained active as middlemen after the coming of the Romans. But Augustus was able to dominate, if not the transport of luxury goods from Arabia, east Africa, India, and China, then a massive share of the profits that accrued from this trade because of the Roman chokehold over Mediterranean access.[63]

The eighteenth-century historian Edward Gibbon dismissed the Indian trade in luxuries as located at the fringe of Roman life, and not crucial for Roman imperial success. The topic has received renewed attention. Not only has the seminal importance of this trade for Roman imperial wealth been reevaluated.[64] The trade is now appreciated because it "opens windows wide on the long history of the Indian Ocean itself, putting in perspective later moments of the relations between the 'West'—be it the Roman Empire, Islamic West Asia, or Atlantic Europe—and South Asia."[65] When maps of the Roman Empire are focused on the Mediterranean Sea, this crucial economic network disappears from view. It was peopled by

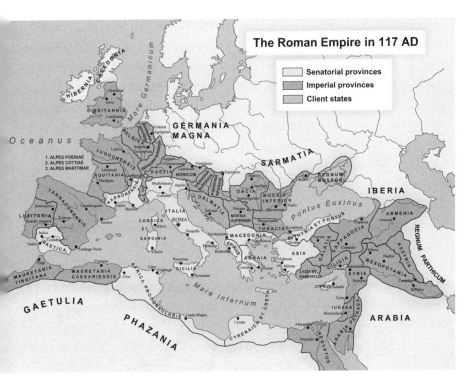

1.16
The Roman Empire at its greatest extent (in the reign of Trajan, 117 CE) included provinces only loosely integrated, and the lands of "friendly" kings. Map by Andrei Nacu.

multiple diasporic groups, whose spatial arrangements comprised the economic infrastructure of the first-century world.

Diasporic Consciousness

Diasporic consciousness that connects the fragments of history, rather than cosmopolitan universality that mistakes hegemony for wholeness, is celebrated in this book. The works in *koine* discussed here were written by people of multiple belongings. Philo of Alexandria, port city of Egypt, drew analogies between ancient Jewish and Greek philosophers. Flavius Josephus of Judaea, who lived and worked in imperial Rome, was influenced by ancient Greek authors, and wrote his first text in Aramaic with a Parthian audience in mind. John of Patmos was familiar with Judaean sources, including Hebrew texts found in the Dead Sea Scrolls, while writing in and to the Roman province of Asia where the emperor cult dominated urban life. Situated at points along the eastern hub of the Roman Empire, these thinkers lived the diaspora, discovering analogies across lines of difference as an enrichment of particular identities. Today such perceptiveness is sorely needed. Modernity's universalism has as its underside a frightening discourse of identity that builds walls against outsiders. Diasporic commonality connects the dots of surviving data in different constellations, forming patterns that evoke the cohabitation of the earth. The historical appearance of such consciousness has been evanescent and, like the *choral* χώρα, "difficult to catch,"[66] yet visible, it seems to me, in the openness to diverse humanity that lies embedded in image 1.17.

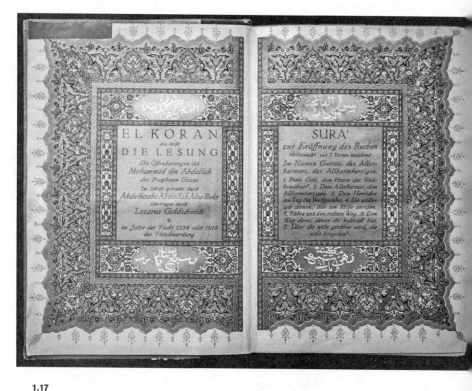

1.17

Folio pages 1–2 of *Der Koran*, new translation, edited and translated by Lazarus Goldschmidt (Berlin: Brandus, 1916). Photo © Manu Bruckstein. Courtesy Taswir projects.

It is a folio page from a book of translation.[67] The book is the Holy Qur'ān, newly edited and translated from Arabic into German by Lazarus Goldschmidt, the Lithuanian-born scholar of Ethiopic (Ge'ez), who also translated the Babylonian Talmud from Hebrew into German. It was published in Berlin in 1916, that is, in the second year of the First World War, a conflict that was global in scope. The right folio page introduces the Holy Qur'ān. The left describes the book's printing. Striking is the intellectual breadth that infuses both words and dating with a diasporic accuracy that defies the extreme nationalism of the times:

El Quran / that is / THE READING / The Revelation of / Mohammed ibn Abdallah / the prophet of God / laid down in writing by / Abdelkaaba Abdallah Abu Bakr / translated by / Lazarus Goldschmidt / in the year of the Flight 1334 or in the year of the becoming flesh 1916.[68]

Diaspora simply means scattering. In the Bible (Gen 11:1–9) the story of the tower of Babel speaks of the origin of multiple languages and scattering of peoples as God's response to humans' hubristic attempt to build a tower to the heavens. In the Qur'ān this multiplicity of languages is not punishment but rather obligation. It defines God's charge to humanity:

O People. We created you all from a single man and a single woman, and made you into races and tribes so that you should come to know one another. (Sūrah 49:13)

Diaspora is not a culture but a condition, one that grounds the epistemic necessity of translation.

2.1
Lapith fighting a centaur. South Metope 27, Parthenon, ca. 447–433 BCE. Photo © Marie-Lan Nguyen / Wikimedia Commons / CC BY 2.5.

2 TRANSLATIONS IN TIME: ON FLAVIUS JOSEPHUS

Method

We are in need of a method. How might the relationship between history and philosophy work against the conventions of ownership of time? Philosophy tends toward universality. History is wedded to particularity. How can their collaboration inform an idea of universal history that does not sacrifice differences of historical experience, but honors them?

Combining the Incommensurable

Let us begin with a phrase from the nineteenth-century historian Jacob Burckhardt: "The philosophy of history is a centaur." This description appears dismissive, perhaps a warning, not a formula for success. The centaur, animal in lower body, human in the head and heart, is an impossible beast, a liminal fusion of spirit and matter, not only mythical but monstrous. Here is the longer quotation: "Above all, we have nothing to do with the philosophy of history. The philosophy of history is a centaur, a contradiction in terms, for history coordinates, and hence is unphilosophical, while philosophy subordinates, and hence is unhistorical."[1] How, then, are these two forms of knowledge, history and philosophy, to be connected without subordinating one to the other? Can coordination itself produce philosophy? Two traditions will need to be avoided because they have not served us well. One is the Hegelian hierarchy that subsumes history within a concept of philosophy as Spirit or Reason (*Geist*), and views this concept as actualized in the course of historical events. The other is modern phenomenology that considers historical conjunctures as contingent and reduces the status of history to mere historicity, a lived experience of temporality making no more than existential claims. In both cases, the critical power of the encounter between present philosophizing and the historical past is blunted. If instead the tension between history and philosophy keeps both in play, if these knowledge procedures are horizontally rather than hierarchically arranged, can the difference between them be made fruitful? The philosophical significance of linguistic practice suggests a comparison: can history writing be a way of doing philosophy if philosophy is understood as a task of translation?

Walter Benjamin's description of the "task" (*Aufgabe*) of the translator suggests a possibility. He uses as metaphor an image that anticipates his later description of the "task" of the historical materialist: "For if the sentence is the wall before the language of the original, wordliness [*Wörtlichkeit*] is the arcade."[2] The century-old urban arcade is a passageway that pierces through the street façade of the present, providing an entry point into the past. The translator, similarly, treats words as entryways. Words, rather than sentences, are the "primary element."[3] Benjamin creates a noun (*Wörtlichkeit*) from an adjective (*wörtlich*). It is translated officially as "literalness" but I prefer a calque, "wordliness," to mark a procedure that relies on the word's illuminative power. The juxtaposition of original and translation does not eliminate the distance between them. "A real translation is transparent; it does not cover the original, does not block its light."[4] There is no attempt to smooth over the difficulties in finding equivalences. Rather than focusing on the semantic meaning of the text, the translator treats each word as a "fragment" of language as a whole.

For the translator of fragments of *history*, the "wordliness" of the temporally distant original is the specific detail, while the wall might be understood as the established narrative that the present tells about itself. The detail that counts is the one that arrests the reader because it does not fit that narrative. It will be evident that recognizing the marginal, the overlooked, the inappropriate demands expertise. The specialist is indispensable. One has need of a certain antiquarian instinct to trace such details down. The scholarly rigor of disciplinary adherence thus demarcates the

2.2
Photograph of the street wall of the entry to Passage Vivienne. Photo: Mbzt / Wikimedia Commons / CC BY 3.0.

ground of knowledge—but not the gaze. The latter, as Benjamin showed us, is a philosophical procedure.

There is the word, but there is also the historical object, the Paris arcade itself. If the sentence remains caught in the text, the arcade provides an escape. It is not text but image, indexing a historical object named by the word and experienced by particular human beings at a historically transient moment in time. At issue is not historical contextualization as a relativizing epistemological move that is said by philosophers to rob the experience of truth, as if transience and truth were philosophically incompatible. Rather, the object is indispensable for establishing the *Wörtlichkeit*, the wordliness of historical translation, and hence its truth.

Philologically, we can push this idea further. Benjamin's neologism *Wört-lichkeit* can be compared with his repeated attempt to utilize the suffix *-barkeit* (-ability) for philosophical gain. Weber has written a book on "Benjamin's -abilities," his uses of this suffix on multiple occasions, famously in the essay "The Artwork in the Age of Its Technological Reproducibility [*Reproduzierbarkeit*]."[5] Not quite the same is happening here. The suffix "-ability" forms nouns from verbs, whereas "-liness" denotes an adjectival quality. But if we consider word (*Wort*) as expression, then this early formulation by Benjamin, *Wörtlichkeit*, might be thought of (although he did not) as a pair with *Wört-barkeit*, the express-ibility of the material world, its capacity, in human language, to be named.[6] The aim here is not an exegesis of Walter Benjamin's texts. Rather, it is to recognize a philosophical understanding of translation that allows us to bring philosophy and history into a different relation than those that have dominated in (and over) the past.

The word, as the expression of objects, pulls away from subjective intent. Whereas speakers of English tend to define a "literal" reading as reductive, perhaps equivalent to a fundamentalist interpretation of Scripture, as if its truth were fully accessible within the text (the correlate in German is *buchstäblich*), Benjamin's idea of "wordliness" moves interpretation in the other direction. When in his philosophical text "On the Concept of History" he describes the "task" (*Aufgabe*) of the historical materialist, he has a materialist metaphysics in mind: words draw us away from the present toward the transitory objects, the historical particulars they have named.[7]

But this also means that to speak of historical objects, and more, to speak afterward about what is written of them, is to deal with ghosts, icons, avatars, monuments, fetishes, afterimages, ruins, and not the historical object itself. If the word or the image is the ghostly residue, the dead metaphor, of a sensory, transitory nature, the experience of which truly disappears, how is philosophy to acknowledge this severe limitation to its capacity to tell the truth? Philosophy as historical translation would then strive to bring to life the residues of a still-distant past, to resurrect them or, if theological language is to be avoided, to bring their *wordliness*

2.3, 2.4

Interior, Passage Vivienne, Paris, nineteenth century / Wikimedia Commons / CC BY 3.0; ruins of the agora in Aphrodisias (now Geyre, Turkey), first century CE, photo: Jonathan S. Blaire.

back into circulation, transforming knowledge of both past and present in the process.[8] It follows that subsuming the past under contemporary logics and categories—even those of radical contemporaries like Foucault or Agamben—is insufficient. For them, history is the starting point for the development of concepts, but history as temporal distance is superseded. The historical object is a means to an end, not itself the philosophical goal. The concept, as method, then takes on imperial airs, subsuming potentially every concrete case. (Governmentality or bare life, genealogics or states of exception, are discovered in every corner of the globe.)[9]

How to move forward, then, in moving backward to the first century? Consider the confession of that excellent historian, Fergus Millar: "Those who study and teach the history of the ancient world suffer from a great disadvantage, which we find difficult to admit even to ourselves: in a perfectly literal sense we do not know what we are talking about."[10] A seemingly insurmountable constraint! But now consider Souleymane

Bachir Diagne's formulation, when speaking of his participation in the *Dictionary of Untranslatables: A Philosophical Lexicon*:[11] "Translation is the impossible task that in the end always succeeds."[12] Translation is impossible. And we do it anyway.[13] Moreover, the translation process is intrinsically philosophical, defined by what Diagne refers to as lateral universality: "Philosophy can *only* be universal if it moves across differences."[14] And: "it is distance that constitutes philosophy."[15] Diagne is speaking of linguistic distance, but the claim might apply to temporal distance as well.

Words do not hang on the façade of the present, advertising their availability. They are embedded in history, which forms no continuous tradition. Modern German philosophy has thought otherwise. What has been called, rightly, Heidegger's "ontological nationalism" congeals in his declaration that philosophy has only one language, Greek yesterday and German today.[16] But what if the Greek of yesterday has been *mis*translated by the Germans of today, precisely because the task of *historical* translation was ignored?

> The only way to reach universality is horizontal, never pretending to abandon the realm of particularity; the way leading through [translation] . . . making various languages clash, marry, meet, befriend, mingle with, and confront one another.
>
> —AGATA BIELIK-ROBSON[17]

The Mimetic Capacity

We are inquiring as to what happens when the task of the historian is understood as itself philosophy, a task of translation that crosses the chasm between a distant past and our time without exclusionary appropriation by the present, without present categories of knowledge reigning supreme but, rather, in a way that transforms knowledge on both sides of the temporal divide.

Consider Marx on the ancients, the comments with which he concludes the introduction to the *Grundrisse* (1857). In asking why differences in modes of production and, correspondingly, in forms of consciousness do not lead to historical solipsism, but allow for our appreciation of another era, he turns to the ancient Greeks. He asks why it is that Greek art and epic poetry, grounded in myth and "bound up with certain forms of social development," still afford us aesthetic pleasure and indeed, "in a certain respect, count as a norm and as an unattainable model." He answers:

> A man cannot become a child again, or he becomes childish. But does he not find joy in the child's naïveté, and must he himself not strive to reproduce its truth at a higher stage? Does not the true character of each epoch come alive in the nature of its children? Why should not the historic childhood of humanity, its most beautiful unfolding, as a stage never to return, exercise an eternal charm? There are unruly children and precocious children. Many of the old peoples belong in this category. The Greeks were normal children. The charm of their art for us is not in contradiction to the undeveloped stage of society on which it grew. . . . [It] is inextricably bound up, rather, with the fact that the unripe social conditions under which it arose, and could alone arise, can never return.[18]

Contrast Marx's approach with Walter Benjamin's very different orientation with regard to the same issue, the connection between phylogeny and ontogeny, in the 1933 text "The Mimetic Faculty."[19] Children's play, Benjamin observes, preserves a mimetic capacity to perceive the world analogically that extends to nonsensuous similarities. He writes: "The child plays at being not only a shopkeeper or teacher but also a windmill and a train." He continues:

> It must be borne in mind that neither mimetic powers nor mimetic objects remain the same in the course of thousands of years. Rather, we must suppose that the gift of producing similarities (for example, in dancing, whose oldest function this is), and therefore also the gift of recognizing them, have changed with historical development. The direction of this change seems determined by the increasing decay of the mimetic faculty. For clearly the perceptual world [*Merkwelt*] of modern man contains only minimal residues of the magical correspondences and analogies that were familiar to ancient peoples.[20]

The implication in Benjamin's text is this: what the nineteenth-century European Karl Marx can only see as "childish" about ancient mimetic arts (despite their incomparably skillful, mimetic productions of human forms) is due to the undeveloped, hence still-childhood stage of Marx's own mimetic faculty.[21] The difference between them lies in Benjamin's concept of history. Marx's conflation of ancient Greece with humanity's childhood was in full accord with the attitude of Hegel.[22] In contrast, Benjamin's rejection of history as progress was logically consequent, leading him to challenge the entire schema of history within which this metaphor of humanity's "childhood" was inscribed.[23]

Benjamin believed that the training of children's innate mimetic capacity had been stunted by bourgeois education. Imagistic cognition had been sacrificed to the pedagogy of written texts. Repetition, learning by rote, diminished human mimetic skill, reducing it to mere mimicking, eternal repetition rather than inventive play. (The rhythmic improvisations of dancing retain this playfulness of bodily translation.) In the Paralipomena to the text "On the Concept of History," he writes: "The basic conception in myth is the world as punishment—punishment which actually engenders those to whom punishment is due. Eternal recurrence is the punishment

2.5

Max Ernst, frontispiece for Paul Éluard, *Répétitions*, 1922. © 2020 Artists Rights Society (ARS), New York / ADAGP, Paris.

of being held back in school, projected onto the cosmic sphere: humanity has to copy out its text in endless repetitions," and he refers in parentheses to Paul Éluard's book of Surrealist poems, *Répétitions*.[24] The frontispiece of Éluard's book, an image by Max Ernst (image 2.5), provides the historical object of his words.

This image is in striking contrast to all of the other illustrations by Ernst both on the cover of *Répétitions* (Repetitions) and throughout the small book, printed by the avant-garde publisher Sans Pareil (literally, "without equal"), that pointed to the newness of the poetry and images the book contained. Its position as frontispiece, an image to which Benjamin referred on several occasions, suggests that Benjamin experienced Surrealism as a critique of, and escape from, the cognitive stunting that the bourgeois upbringing of his generation had entailed.[25]

In the 1933 text on the mimetic capacity, Benjamin considered "whether we are concerned with the decay of this faculty or with its transformation," and surely he hoped for the latter.[26] Not only the work of the Surrealists, but silent cinema and specifically the gestural figure of Charlie Chaplin, might provide a new kind of schooling in the mimetic faculty.

If our understanding of a distant past demands a mimetic capacity to recognize similarities across temporal expanse, the method is uniquely relevant to the first century. For if we are searching for a way to tie together the most diverse forms of the surviving sources, then the fact that their creators were extremely sophisticated in the development and deployment of their mimetic faculty means that studying them can provide a schooling for us and potentially a transformation in this capacity itself. The problem of historical translation then becomes: how to expand our understanding of the past to embrace the then-existing capacities for recognizing similarities for which we have lost the ability, rather than wipe out their traces in our presentation of history, as if they were not a necessary attribute of history's truth.

When applied to writers in the first century considered here, the capacity to present thought analogically unites figures as seemingly diverse as Flavius Josephus, Philo of Alexandria, and John of Patmos. Each of these three forms one—the more marginalized one—of a pair of thinkers, the other

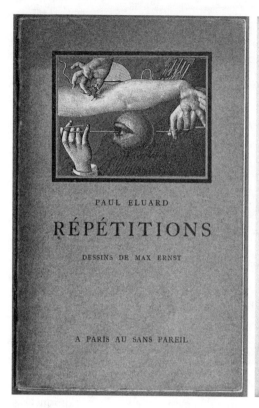
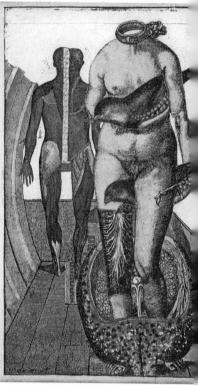

2.6, 2.7

Max Ernst, cover for Paul Éluard, *Répétitions*, 1922; Max Ernst, "The Word (Woman Bird)," 1921, illustration for *Répétitions*. © 2020 Artists Rights Society (ARS), New York; ADAGP, Paris.

of which is more accessible to present discourse. So: Josephus, not Tacitus, the more acceptable historian; Philo, not Seneca, favored by philosophers today; John of Patmos, writer of the book of Revelation, not Saint Paul, the darling of Marxist postsecularists Badiou, Žižek, and others.[27] Now, if we apply to them *our* privileged category of Identity, it will be said that they were all Jews. But Philo and John were appropriated by Christians, and no group has been eager to claim Josephus as its own. The ways they make advocates of identity categories uncomfortable, their diverse ways of *being* Jewish, blur the boundaries of these categorical distinctions.[28] Metaphor, mimesis, the pairing of nonidenticals: such analogical constructs abound in ancient texts, providing keys to a method of juxtaposing philosophy and history across fields now segmented by vertical divisions into separate histories organized by categories of difference: Christian, Jewish, Hellenic, Roman.

We turn now to Josephus.

Flavius Josephus

Flavius Josephus (born Yosef ben Matityahu, 37 CE)[29] names the author of the *Bellum Judaicum*, a history of the Judaean War in which he participated, first as general on the side of the rebels in Galilee, and then, after his capture, on the side of the Roman troops under Vespasian, who was sent by Nero to quell the revolt. Josephus' detailed history is an account of events that included the siege of Jerusalem, destruction of the Second Temple, final battle of Masada, and Titus' triumphal return to Rome as son of the newly installed Emperor Vespasian, whose victories in the East secured his victory in Rome and who, as last in the long Year of Four Emperors, established the Flavian imperial line to which his two sons (Titus and Domitian) were heirs. In the context of modern history, this war that ended the era of the Second Temple is legendary as the moment when, to cite Jacques Derrida, "the Jews had to renounce their national existence."[30] Derrida is hardly alone in this understanding. Legend, left unchallenged, congeals into myth. Philosophers need to know the difference.[31]

As a participant-observer, Josephus is an incomparable source for the events of 66–73 CE. Indeed, we have no other. His later, multivolume history of the Jews from biblical times to his own age, *Jewish Antiquities* (*Antiquitates Judaeicae*), is likewise unique. And yet historians traditionally have slighted the value of his work. The classicist Mary Beard considers his "bizarre treatment" by the academy as a consequence of the "disciplinary police" at the borders of knowledge divisions: for classicists, he has been "somehow off limits"; "his book is 'about' Jews and Judaea, not Rome and the Romans."[32] Yet Jewish historians, while producing "an embarrassment of riches" of works on Josephus, have had deep misgivings, claiming he is "unreliable" as a historian, a propagandist for the Flavians and at worst a "self-serving traitor."[33] A marginal figure indeed.[34] The *Bellum Judaicum*, written by a Jewish military leader who belonged to the high, priestly class, and who lived and wrote in Rome under the largess of the Flavian conquerors of Judaea, troubles both disciplinary boundaries and identity categories to the point of erasure. The misgivings of the disciplinary police are precisely what have drawn the interest of a new generation of scholars.[35] Due to his bridging of enemy divisions, Flavius Josephus allows—indeed demands—suspension of the conceptual grid of identities and categories that have held the past in place. We follow the lead of these scholars, whose innovative work represents the new actuality of international scholarship, and is now benefiting from a collaborative project to produce a new English translation, with extensive commentary, of the totality of Josephus' works.[36]

The Text as Historical Object

Why does the text of Joseph's history written in Greek bear a Latin title? Historians have simply referred to the work as the *Bellum Judaicum*, rendered in English as *The Jewish War*. The introduction to the standard English translation (by H. St. J. Thackeray in 1927) provides a clarification.[37] *Bellum Judaicum* names, not Josephus' Greek text, which we have lost, nor an earlier version by Josephus to which he refers, also lost, but the corpus of extant manuscripts that have survived in various languages— Latin and Slavonic, a Hebrew paraphrase (*Josippon*), as well as multiple Greek variants.[38] Why have these been preserved? From early on, Christian scholars found Josephus' works invaluable for their own concerns, as they provide crucially significant evidence for the historical existence of Jesus. Christians traditionally arranged Josephus' complete works, not in the order in which they were written, but with the *Bellum Judaicum* following the *Jewish Antiquities*. The latter, later-written book mentions Jesus, John the Baptist, and Jesus's brother James, and ends just before the Jewish War against the Romans in 66 CE, so that readers, turning sequentially to the account of the Jewish War, are easily led to accept the early Christian church's interpretation of the narrative that dates to the second century CE. The Alexandrian theologian Origen (185–254 CE) claimed the "entire Jewish nation was destroyed" because of the "sufferings which they inflicted on Jesus.”[39] But a justification of Christianity at the expense of the Jews is not anywhere to be found in Josephus' text.[40]

It matters, then, that the historical object named by the words *Bellum Judaicum* is not the historical event described, but a materially surviving text, a copy of a lost original.[41] Christian appropriation works its way into the process of inheritance, as the text's very survival can be attributed to its usefulness for history's later victors. Even so-called secular scholarship has maintained residues of this Christianized line of descent, the problematic nature of which recent scholarship has done much to expose. And yet a satisfactory solution cannot be reached simply by reversing the binaries in an act of Jewish *re*appropriation, because it begs the question of what "being Jewish" at this time and place entailed.[42] Nonetheless, questions of where Josephus' loyalties lay, what "side" in the various struggles he was on, and the identity of the audience for which he was writing have traditionally dominated the interpretive field, often with the implication that evidence of either loyalty or disloyalty to one or another partisan position is synonymous with proof as to the account's "accuracy" in the modern, positivist sense of the term. But given the lack of any other accounts, these arguments are circular, benefiting their own partisan positions: either Josephus has given us the facts according to today's empiricist standards (including the modern historians' fixation on the proper chronological order of events),[43] or his so-called facts are really fictions and proof of his treachery, hence useless for serious historians to engage.[44] For both arguments, knowledge of Josephus' character and motives is as indispensable as it is impossible to acquire.

The point is that the ongoing debates over where to locate Josephus along the identity axes *cannot* be resolved if the identity categories themselves are inappropriate. An alternative is possible if we keep in mind the central point of historical translation, and ask: What, as exit points within the document's language, do Josephus' words in their wordliness name? Can they lead us out of the tautological circle of partisan interpretations? This attempt takes us into the complexities of contemporary scholarship, demonstrating at a micro-level how the knotted constraints of historical tradition function and are negotiated today.

The Judaean War

There is little dispute that an earlier version of the *Bellum Judaicum* to which Josephus in his introduction refers was in Aramaic, the spoken language of Jesus and others in the Judaean kingdom, not Hebrew, a closely related language (with which, as someone with priestly training, Josephus was also likely to have been familiar).[45] Minute analysis by historians of the extant texts (which, keep in mind, are indeterminately removed from the original) begins on the book's opening pages, where Josephus says that he wrote it with a Parthian audience in mind.[46] Steve Mason describes the standard view that is now under revision: "The argument goes like this. . . . Josephus, a proven collaborator with the Romans, . . . [writes] an official account of the conflict, from Rome, it is assumed, to the nations beyond the borders of the empire. The book contains numerous passages that declare the invincibility of Rome and Rome's divine favor. . . . If we recall that the Parthians, at least, came close to war with Rome a couple of times during the first century, we might easily conclude that [citing Thackeray]: 'Josephus was commissioned by the conquerors to write the official history of the war for propagandistic purposes.' That he wrote *War* as a lackey of the Romans, retained by them to help quell any further revolutionary hopes in the East, was until recently the standard scholarly view, and it still has many adherents."[47]

As head of the Canadian Josephus Project, Mason writes profusely on all aspects of Josephus scholarship, and has gone very far to challenge the fundamentals on which this interpretation rests. This extends to the title, which, he rightly points out, refers not to the Jewish but the *Judaean* War (*Bellum Judaicum*): to a place, not a people.[48] It reminds us from the outset that people practicing the Jewish faith lived throughout the Roman imperium. In Antioch, Alexandria, Ephesus, Rome, and many places in between, Jewish communities existed as self-legislating *politeia*. Their collective "freedom" (*eleutheria*), dating with few interruptions from the time of Alexander—and of the Persian kings before that—needs to be understood as protection by a superior power rather than independence in the modern sense. Judaea, a province of Rome, was far from being the whole of the Jewish people. *Diaspora* had been for long a fact of Jewish life.

If their history is ignored, if Judaean land and Jewish people are equated, then this important distinction disappears, and with it the multiplicity of Jewish practices that did not depend on the Temple cult or the land on which it stood. At the same time, as Mason notes, Josephus is our only non-Christian source for the identifying term "Christian" in the first century CE: "[N]o other writer before 100 [CE] mentions the Christians"; the first Roman authors to do so were Pliny the Younger, Tacitus, and Suetonius, whose works date to the second decade of the second century.[49] Appropriation of Josephus by vertical inheritance as "Christian" history has thus been an *ex post facto* endeavor.

Translating Translation

One sentence of the prologue has been under particular scrutiny:

> In these circumstances [where no "accurate" (ἀκριβὲς) narrative account yet exists], I—Josephus, son of Matthias, a Hebrew by race, a native of Jerusalem and a priest, who at the opening of the war myself fought against the Romans and in the sequel was perforce an onlooker—propose to provide the subjects of the Roman Empire with a narrative of the facts, by translating into Greek [Ἑλλάδι γλώσση μεταβαλών] the account which I previously composed in my vernacular tongue and sent to the barbarians in the interior.[50]

At the start, a key word causes concern: μεταβαλών (*metabalon*). Thackeray's English equivalent is simply "translate," but the word means more: to render or adapt, hence to change or even transform.[51] Beard observes: "Whether you imagine that our text of the *Bellum Judaicum* is a 'straight' translation of some Aramaic predecessor, or a freer adaption, only loosely based on the earlier book, depends (ironically) on how you translate his Greek term μεταβαλών"—that is, whether you translate that word itself to mean "translate"![52] At stake for scholars is an evaluation of the factual integrity of the text in the process of this translation, whether Josephus' reliance on "assistants" (*synergoi*/συνεργοί) to which he refers in a later text (*Contra Apionem*) was so great that one cannot presume the Aramaic and Greek versions gave the same account of events, or whether it can even be said that it was Josephus who authored the Greek translation that appeared under his name.

Why make so much of a word? Can it matter whether Josephus "rendered" from his "native tongue" or "translated from his native language"? Well, first, it matters because a lot of interpreters make much of it, precisely to provide a certain vertical mode of interpreting Josephus, given the interested parties. But if in fact this vertical slicing of historical heritage is not relevant to the first century, as we believe to be the case, then the words can also be lines of escape that land both the texts and ourselves as readers in a space potentially free from exclusionary claims. The debates over *this* word, however, will not take us farther than Josephus' personal loyalties, a question of little interest to the philosophical inquiry that is our goal.

Second Sophistic

Now, one has to note that the quality of Greek in Josephus' text is very high. And the fact that he is known to have finished writing it after 75 CE means that Josephus was part of a movement post-50 CE named by scholars the Second Sophistic.[53] This was a literary movement among the circles of the Greek-speaking elite from Rome to the eastern Mediterranean, in protest against the prevalence of *koine*-speaking populations who, in the opinion of the elite, had vulgarized the language. The educated classes tried to counter *koine*'s equalizing force by a rhetoric that concentrated on grammatical style, a "purer" form, for which the Attic Greek of classical Athens provided the idealized model. Swain writes in his history of the language: "Atticism looked to an ideal of correct Greek within an already widely polarized language situation with clearly established differences between educated and non-educated Greek."[54]

This linguistic community was characterized by a multiethnic membership, whose schooling gave them entry into a cosmopolitan elite. Whether born Jewish or Greek, Roman or Asian, they named *themselves* "Hellenes."[55] Scholars settle for "Greek" as the name of this Atticized *koine* and we, for the moment, will follow suit.[56] It was a cultural, not a national identity, to which literacy and the leisure required for proper education provided access.[57] Swain stresses the fact that "culture" here means cohesion in an idealized, not an anthropological sense. It was belonging based on a "love of the ideal of Greece [*Hellas*] rather than its contemporary reality."[58] Constructed on an educational, not a locational divide, this non-Latin culture functioned as a form of social belonging across other differences and brought a certain autonomy from Roman hierarchies of power: "The leaders of Greek intellectual life in the second sophistic period were part of a world that did not need Rome."[59] Swain's careful description of the linguistic realities is significant for understanding Josephus' place within the Second Sophistic movement, although Swain himself does not cross disciplinary boundaries to enter the arena of Judaic history and Josephus' texts.

For that we turn to the work of those who have focused on the many allusions to ancient Greek texts that are found in Josephus' works.[60] From Homer's *Illiad* to Sophocles' *Antigone* to Pindar's *Pythian*, the echoes of Greek poetry resound. Most significant for us, the long-recognized prototype for Josephus' presentation in the *Bellum Judaicum* is the most famous of ancient Greek histories, Thucydides' *Peloponnesian War*. Josephus' analogies to Thucydides' text are not disputed. No one doubts that Thucydides resonates deeply throughout the *Bellum Judaicum*. The issue is how, and why. Scholars have focused on the politically partisan implications of these references. Here again the image of Josephus as traitor looms large.[61] And again the debate flounders because Josephus' subjective intentions are impossible to ascertain.

Chapman has recently shifted the angle of scholarly interest by emphasizing the function of ancient Greek analogies within the world of the Second Sophistic. Allusions, parallels, likenesses to ancient prototypes comprised a literary method that in Sophistic rhetoric was considered an argument for the validity of the newer text. Thus when Josephus writes in the prologue that he worked to achieve the "sound" (φωνή) of Greek, his claim extends to literary topoi, style, and form in both poetry and prose. These "time-honored pairings" are evidence of the legitimacy of the arguments made.[62] More than literary embellishments, the resonances with ancient, authoritative texts expressed "connections between people, places, events, myths, and ideas that otherwise might seem remote, yet their similarities resound through time and space."[63] In analogies discovered across these distances, the truth of historical events might be seen to appear. As a reference to the mimetic capacity that, according to Benjamin, was not a constant in history, it deserves our attention. The "accurate" (ἀκριβὲς) account of events that Josephus claims, echoing the claim made by Thucydides in his preface, would then refer less to empirical facts than to interpretation by means of analogies, those nonidentical similarities that pairings with previous, time-honored texts provide.

Thucydides as Mimetic Model

Whereas historians commonly argue that Thucydides' text is historically accurate by modern standards, his own claim to objectivity is not that of a positivist historian—nor would positivism have been the criterion for judgment during the Second Sophistic. A different kind of truth is being sought by these ancient writers of history, one that deserves to be named philosophical. Both wars, the Peloponnesian and the Judaean, are considered as manifestations of a determinate historical dynamics that emerges whenever and wherever such conflict appears. The prototype— here Thucydides' history—is the objective criterion for recognizing these dynamics. Philosophical questions that cannot be answered on the level of logical disputation turn to history to discover how times of conflict evolve in reality.

Precisely because Hellenic education extended beyond a limited ethnic perspective, it could make claims to universal validity. It was comprehensibly persuasive to the cosmopolitan elite of Rome, who considered themselves as "rightful inheritors of the classical world."[64] But the argument goes further than this. If we are right, then the criterion for judging whether or not Josephus "lied" in his account of events is not the point. We do not have to presume he was Machiavellian in his motives. We do not have to focus on inner motives at all, a pyschologistic approach that is quite impossible to make certain—for any author, indeed even for oneself. We will argue consistently that attributing subjective motives is quite irrelevant to philosophical interest in an object of historical investigation.

It is important to clarify that the approach of the Second Sophistic is not "modern" by either the historian's or the philosopher's current criteria. The modern debate has been between positivists interested in empirical facts and theorists who utilize their own concepts as interpretive keys. But if there is indeed something else going on in ancient texts, something that we have overlooked, then tending to nonmodern categories of understanding signifies the desire to rescue highly developed forms of knowledge to which modern education does not presently provide access. And if the anthropologist's sensitivity to difference does operate here, then "difference" is not the cognitive goal. Rather, it is to explore time spatially, to translate between times, and in the process to loosen our own boundedness to modernity's categories that in our own transitional moment have become a form of entrapment.

Stasis

When Josephus refers in the *Bellum Judaicum* to the events of 66–73 CE, he names them not *polemos*, the Greek word for war (Latin: *bellum*), but *stasis*. The persistence of this word in his account demands our focus, because the word *stasis* means *civil strife*—internal violence among the Judaeans, not war against the Romans, and not the Romans' own, coterminous struggles during the Year of Four Emperors (68–69 CE), which they themselves named "civil war" (*bellum civile*).[65]

Stasis echoes profoundly Thucydides' text of the Peloponnesian War, signaling the Second Sophistic mode of Josephus' interpretation. This word provides a powerful point of entry into the past which recently has received the scholarly attention it deserves. Rajak alerts us to the "predominance" of the concept of *stasis* in the *Bellum Judaicum*: "In seeking to understand the fall of the Holy City and the Temple, [Josephus] offers one general explanation repeatedly: they were destroyed by *stasis*."[66] *Stasis*, writes Mason in his commentary to the new translation of Josephus' *Bellum Judaicum,* is the account's "*Leitmotif.*"[67] In discussing Thucydides as key to Josephus' method of *imitatio/mimesis*, Price refers to a Greek text, *Concerning Mimesis* (Περι μιμήσις) by the first-century CE historian and rhetorician Dionysius of Halicarnassus.[68] This was a handbook of the rhetorical technique of mimesis that was current in the first-century Sophistic literature, and it named the fifth-century BCE historian Thucydides as leading among suitable models for emulation.[69] As we have noted, allusion to ancient Greek texts was a form of argument, an appeal through the older, authoritative texts for the newer text's legitimation. It is here that we may find a way out of the solipsism of our present preoccupations into a space of history that is otherwise obscured by the linear reception of it.

Acknowledging the importance of *stasis* in Josephus' work breaks definitively with the traditional line of interpretation based on the *in*appropriate appropriation of Josephus by Christianity. The sin of the Judaeans is not their treatment of Jesus.[70] Nor, in fact, is it the action of any particular Judaean group. Josephus makes no defining distinctions as to which party is playing the leading role in initiating strife. Rajak notes significantly that the occasions of his use of the term "zealot" do not form a fixed reference to a particular group. Whereas Jewish nationalist histories have tended to glorify the Zealots as Judaea's defenders against imperial Rome, in Josephus' account the word describes not an identity but an action, "a way of responding in a situation."[71] He uses multiple terms in this way, not only "zealots" (*zelotai*) but "brigands" (*lestai*), "assassins" (*sicarii*), "insurrectionists" (*neoterizontes*), and also the "tyrants" (*tyrannoi*) who lead them, as "fomenters of civil strife" (*stasiastai*).[72] He thereby condemns generally those who threaten the established order.[73] Josephus writes in opposition not to this or that faction named—much to the frustration of present-day interpreters for whom the categories of identity are paramount—but to the fact of factionalism itself.[74]

Taking Josephus at His Word

Rajak does "not want to make too much of this vocabulary, for it is quite probable that Josephus deployed those words and not others partly because they were the ones which happened to spring readily to mind and looked appropriate to a Greek history."[75] For precisely this reason, however, we will focus on Josephus' vocabulary, because *stasis* is not just an appropriate Greek word. It is a central analytical idea in Thucydides, whose account of the Peloponnesian War provides the model for the mimetic practice that Josephus's text employs.[76] There are rhetorical parallels in the *Bellum Judaicum* to Thucydides' account: claims of "accuracy" in method, first-person speeches of the protagonists, the pairing of opposing speeches, elements of tragedy as dramatic form. But *stasis* as the defining term within which these

2.8

First-century CE fragment of a papyrus bearing a passage from Thucydides' *Peloponnesian War*. In the public domain.

names are deployed is *mimesis* of another dimension. It applies the model of historical events developed by Thucydides, most clearly in his analysis of events in Corcyra that demonstrate the utter destructiveness of *stasis* to civic life, exceeding any intention of the actors involved. The sections of *Peloponnesian War* in which Thucydides, rather than narrating events and speeches of others, comments reflectively on *stasis* are as celebrated as they are brief: two short chapters, 82 and 83, in book III. Glossed with renewed interest in the post-Cold-War era (for reasons that will become clear), their dense and difficult language develops, from the specifics of the Corcyran case (3.69–81), a model of *stasis* that becomes key to his analysis of the war as a whole, as *stasis* breaks out in multiple cities caught up in the dynamics of the conflict.

When compared with Josephus' account of the Judaean War, the parallels are striking and the influence of Thucydides "unmistakable."[77] In both accounts, factional loyalties supersede familial ties as *stasis* engulfs the whole area. Josephus writes: "The most intimate relations broke all connections with each other and attaching themselves to those who shared their political views formed up into opposing camps. *Stasis* was everywhere."[78] Civil strife spreads like a sickness. Indeed, in Jerusalem (as in Athens during the Peloponnesian War) an actual plague results. Famine results in loss of food supplies that intensifies the misery. A state of *nosos*—madness, suffering, disorder—inflicts both physical and psychological harm upon the Jewish people.[79] Josephus, like Thucydides, recounts the degeneration of ethical life that this civic anarchy produces. Chaos and fear prevent families from burying the plague's victims, acts of impiety lead to disregard of burial rites and customs that are described as well by Thucydides—and that bear affinities to the moral plight of Antigone in Sophocles' fifth-century drama, except that in *Bellum Judaicum* it is Titus who, when viewing the unburied dead, responds with a "manly" groan.[80]

A central element of Thucydides' analysis of *stasis* is its effect on language. Josephus, similarly, recognizes "perceptual refraction and re-naming as typical symptoms of the general convulsion."[81] In the course of civil strife, the deployment of words is distorted. In an atmosphere of extreme polarization, attributes name their opposite: boldness is called courage, and desire for peace is treason.[82] Josephus describes the behavior of those perpetrating the violence: "In short, they boasted of their crimes."[83] Oaths are broken in Corcyra, and this is true in Jerusalem as well.[84] With the destabilization of meaning, fear and hatred escalate. Even the Temple of Jerusalem is not safe as a place of refuge (as was true of the Corcyran temple of Hera in Thucydides' account). As a consequence, the carnage is terrible. *Stasis* rips the city apart: "[B]etween them the people, like some huge carcase, was torn to pieces. Old men and women in their helplessness prayed for the coming of the Romans and eagerly looked for the external war [τόν ἔξωθεν πόλεμον] to liberate them from their internal miseries."[85]

In both accounts, civil strife merges with foreign war, as partisans rely on the aid of outsiders and the line between internal and external conflict, *stasis* and *polemos*, breaks down. In Corcyra, Spartans and Athenians are brought in to aid the conflicting parties. In the Judaean War, "zealots" appeal for aid to the Parthians and Idumeans. Josephus describes the factions opposed to war as bringing in Roman aid because they long for the peace that a Roman victory would reestablish. This parallel in particular has elicited strong reproach from commentators, because it obscures both Roman misgovernance before the war and the role of the Roman troops in perpetuating and intensifying the violent conditions.[86] Clearly, Josephus (who owed his freedom to Vespasian and Titus)[87] does not find in the Romans' behavior justification for those who fought against them. He insists that Titus did not want to destroy the Temple, but due to the continued *stasis* in the city he was left no choice. Josephus recognizes that those he calls zealots considered Roman domination the ultimate source of the conflict. But for him what matters is precisely *stasis*, violent disunity among the Jews themselves.[88] "For not even when the Romans were encamped beneath the walls did the civil strife [*stasis*] slacken within."[89]

Of course, Josephus' descriptions, "consistently against the insurgents," amount to a refusal to grant to any of those "revolutionaries" who act against the Roman imperial regime a legitimation for their violence.[90] In Josephus' text, the war appears "in no way, therefore, a Judaean *national* revolt against Rome."[91] Among historians, this is where the controversy lies. According to Price, when Josephus, adhering closely to the Thucydidean prototype, uses *stasis* as "a kind of one-word mimesis" for all of the fighting, as if it were only a question of internal violence, he obliterates the inextricable overlay of the anti-Roman struggle that comes to dominate: despite the multiplicity of groups involved, Price argues, at stake is ultimately one issue, war against Rome.[92] Hence, what Josephus describes as civil strife between "pro-war" and "anti-war" parties is not factionalism in the classical, Thucydidean sense, but an insurrection (*apostasis*/ἀπόστασις) against imperial control.[93]

The debate, again, falls back on Josephus' motives. Mader claims that Josephus' "gross distortion" of Thucydides is nothing but a deception—the more he argues, the more of a liar he becomes. Thucydides, argues Mader, provides Josephus a cover-up for his own, antirevolutionary sentiments. Mader warns us that we are foolish to be taken in.[94] Rajak, less vituperative, still acknowledges that Josephus is biased in a political sense on the side of the Romans. Price considers Josephus' "ambivalent" annotation of the word *stasis* as an indication of his awareness of the "double nature of the rebellion," and because of his own personal involvement, "he was of two minds as to how to portray it."[95] Mason argues that Josephus' intent was to speak to a Roman audience, and that as a "master of oblique discourse," his representation of events uses "figured speech" ironically to produce a desirable effect.[96] In any event, Josephus' history, a partisan account, is a far cry from the objectivity for which Thucydides has for centuries been praised.

Scholarship risks tearing apart Josephus himself, waging civil war against him by making his words mean their opposite, psychologizing his intent, and discrediting his warnings. Of course, Josephus is not Thucydides. The latter is the prototype to emulate, not the mimetic copy. Moreover, Josephus tells us from the very beginning that his will be a passionate account, allowing him to "lament the calamities which befell my country."[97] And yet he claims simultaneously that it is written for "those who love truth."[98] Can it be both? Can mimesis as a method and Thucydides as a model provide insight into a kind of truth, one that historical parallels reveal? If we stay with Josephus on this level, which can properly be called philosophical, then the text has truth effects of a different order that does not reduce his rhetorical practices to manipulative authorial intent.

Keeping Our Distance

Philosophy distinguishes itself from contemporary historical debates by reflecting on the unspoken assumptions of those engaged within them. In the particularly fraught case of the Middle East in our time, silent assumptions speak multitudes. On the face of it, the debate over Josephus' text has no justification for taking place at all. As our only written account of the war, it cannot be critically evaluated by comparison with others.

The author's inner motives are not available to us. If these are unknowable and authorial integrity is doubted, then historians are caught in the paradoxical project of making the text bear witness against itself. All of its data substantiate the reality of the Judaean War as a historical event. The fall of the Second Temple of Jerusalem is its cornerstone. Josephus, and Josephus alone, gives us names, places, battles, and scenes of this event. Modern Israel justifies itself historically, retrospectively, by the moments of its destruction: it begins with its disappearance. History becomes the long road of historical retribution for this injustice, or at the very least its sympathetic narration.

The dynamics of historical interpretation—either in Josephus's time or in our own—do not hold themselves apart from the world in which they take form, raising the question of what, indeed, is the historian's task. The assumption that history belongs only to those collectives that possess a territorial nation is a Hegelian prejudice that extends with a long reach in time. Were it not for this deeply entrenched prejudice within the very concept of history as it emerged in the West that makes national histories the litmus test for collective realities and, moreover, endangers the physical survival of those who are denied a land-based nation-state, the urgent need for a uniquely "Jewish" history would not exist.[99]

Unraveling the issue of identity as it relates to the *Bellum Judaicum* and the destruction of the Second Temple has been a central concern of scholarship. It is a textbook case of the pitfalls of scholarly work generally, which thinks it knows where it is going before research actually begins. In 1853, Heinrich Graetz launched his writing of a multivolume history of the Jews that plotted out eras in advance of the research in ways that became problematic as the writing went forward. Schwartz explains: "What engendered Graetz's difficulties was his original *a priori* framing of Jewish history as a neat triad that characterized the Second Temple period as the era of *a religious community in its land*."[100] What he discovered instead was not only the vast expanse of the diaspora—the first-century world was "chock full" of Jews elsewhere[101]—but the complicated history of Jewish rulers in Judaea, who represented multiple power factions and were in no way synonymous with a religious community. Nationalist historians have emphasized the latter, writing histories of a territory that became the land of Israel, wherein the destruction of the Temple appears as a watershed event. Schwartz explains the error of "those many who write as if 70 meant the demise of a Jewish state—which is simply not true."[102] The end of the Jewish state had already happened. Judaea was made a vassal state of the Roman Republic in 63 BCE and became a Roman imperial province in 6 BCE, hence loss of political sovereignty was an accomplished fact.

The history of Jews and Judaism is not the same as the history of Judaea and the Temple cult.[103] Diasporic Jews were perhaps the majority in the first century; their communities were centers of local governance, local synagogues, and literary expressions of "extraordinary breadth and vitality."[104] But it would be wrong to place the onus of responsibility on scholars of Jewish history for the prejudice of privileging *national* stories of the past. Of relevance, precisely to the writings of Thucydides, is the fact that the text of his *Peloponnesian War* has been marked by mistranslations with a bias toward epistemological nationalism, which has obfuscated readings ever since. Before returning to our comparison of Thucydides and Josephus, a consideration of this historical inheritance is called for.

City-States and Thomas Hobbes

The first translation of Thucydides' *Peloponnesian War* into English was by Thomas Hobbes in 1629 (it was his earliest publication). He based his work on Lorenzo Valla's fifteenth-century Latin version, which Hobbes knew in an edition that had the ancient Greek on the facing page.[105] For his translation, Hobbes confronted a cluster of words from fifth-century BCE Greek that he considered it his task to bring up to date. Among the key words relevant to us here are these: *stasis, polis, koinon, nomos, demokratia,* and *arche*. For none of these terms is there a precise English equivalent, certainly not in England in the time of Hobbes; by bringing this text into contemporary readability—this is my point—he takes control of its meaning. So: *polis*, which means in ancient Greek urban center, or town (of tens of thousands to a few hundred thousand inhabitants), is translated as city-*state*.[106] *Koinon*, which implies common or shared, is translated as alliance of such states.[107] And *stasis*, which means taking a stand—but also, a partisan stand, and consequently to act in a way that can lead to civil strife—is translated by Hobbes as sedition, i.e., treason against the state;[108] *nomos*, which means not only law but customary practices in general, is translated simply as "law" with the implication that law is a state function, while *demokratia*, which means literally "people power," is equated with a particular state form, and *arche*—which means "rule," and in this sense causal origin or beginning as it relates to present dominance or hegemony —is translated, problematically, as "empire."[109]

You see what is happening here. In transferring Thucydides' ancient language into the political discourse of seventeenth-century England, with its civil wars that Hobbes opposed as treason, its issues of absolute sovereignty of the nation that he theorized, and its colonial acquisitions that produced a maritime empire from the Americas to Asia, Hobbes ensures that the terms become immediately applicable to the emerging, modern, imperial nation-state.[110] Hobbes' later book *Leviathan* (1651) became the founding theoretical treatise on the sovereignty of this new nation-state. In our present neoliberal order, his theory is still considered the *locus classicus* for understanding the structure of nation-states in their modern Western form.[111] As a consequence, the transhistorical, quasi-universal status of this form is substantiated by the foundational documents of the fifth century BCE—so that democracy cannot be thought without nation-state sovereignty.

Hobbes is the bridge from Thucydides' *Peloponnesian War* to the influential realist school of international relations, which views sovereign states as rational, self-interested actors pursuing hegemonic ends.[112] The realist school claims transhistorical validity for its theory by equating universality with abstraction. Purified from contamination by the specifics of historical occurrences, the model of rational self-interest appears (like modern architecture!) to be appropriate anywhere it is applied. For those schooled in the classics, however, this reading of Thucydides is "a dangerous over-simplification."[113] Not only does it ignore the historical contingency of events. While purporting to be "objective," it is in fact "ideologically loaded," silencing its critics from the "high ground" of reasoned truth.[114] By treating states monolithically as quasi-individuals whose reasoned actions are determining, it cannot account for the existence of dissent *within* the state based on the "deep social divisions" that lead to *stasis*.[115] In the context of the Cold War, the realist school established itself as the rightful heir of Thucydides. We are proposing a different line of descent. With an eye to historical detail and the illuminative power of words, we return to our discussion of Thucydides and Josephus.

Nomos

Examining more closely the arguments of contemporary historians regarding Josephus' motives, it becomes evident that they depend on a disaggregation of categories into distinct realms of social life: politics as separate from religion, prophecy as separate from law. Hence, for example, Mader accuses Josephus' account of "secularization" that "psychologizes" the revolutionaries who, he claims, were piously motivated.[116] As for Josephus' own appeals to "religion," Mader considers them crude "political" manipulation.[117] Rajak concurs with Mader that a "religious" motivation is lacking: "throughout Josephus treats the rebels, in all their guises, simply as political adversaries."[118] In contrast and as an argument against political partisanship, Spilsbury takes this priestly and prophetic side of Josephus' character seriously, acknowledging his self-understanding as an inspired prophet.[119] What are his motives? What are the facts? Did the Jews really do the horrible atrocities that were predicted in the Bible: even starving mothers eating their children (*Bellum Judaicum* 6.210–212)? Is this not a self-serving exaggeration, and should we not therefore dismiss the "truth" of the account that he gives?

These analyses assume a binary division between politics and theology, the secular and the religious, that is not relevant to the philological argument, or to the *philosophical* argument on which the philology depends. Each of these terms is presumed by historians in its modern meaning. Josephus is considered suspect because he allows categories to converge that we hold apart: politics, religion, prophecy, law. However, as we shall see, they cannot be isolated in the case of Thucydides' Greece either. Price says that, of course, Josephus' world is not the same as Thucydides' own. "His historical vision could not have been more different than that of Thucydides."[120] But precisely on this point, there is a world of difference between our assumptions and the ones that these two writers shared.

This convergence of categories is the concern of a new study by Daniel Boyarin, who has consistently demonstrated his capacity to think outside of the accepted conceptual divisions, paying attention to what the words speak as we listen across the centuries. His reading of Josephus leads him to understand the key term *nomos* against the grain of European historical understandings. The simple translation of *nomos* (νόμος) is "law," which, according to legal positivism, is the given, written legal code. The counter-school of law is based on historical hermeneutics, a leading spokesperson for which, in the twentieth century, was the judicial historian Carl Schmitt. The latter has dominated debates by his resounding insistence that *nomos* is the sovereign act of territorial appropriation that precedes the law and legitimates its violent enforcement. First and foremost, *nomos* presumes jurisdiction over land: "In the beginning was the fence."[121] Schmitt traces this meaning back to the ancient Greeks, a classic case of creating a linear, historical continuity as proof of the argument made. But when historians do their work without a Schmittian bias, their findings do not substantiate this overarching claim.

Boyarin has examined closely the entire corpus of Josephus' writings, including his later, multivolume history of the Jews, and discovers in the word *nomos* a terrain of meanings far greater than scholars like Schmitt have assumed:

> Contrary to the frequent stereotype that Greek Judaean writers reduced the Torah to "law," it is clear from Josephus that he, at any rate, understood *nomos* in a way far more expansive than our notion of "law" would predict. For him, it incorporates civil and criminal law, the organization of government, plus cultic practice including Temple and private observance, and also beliefs about God, much more than "law," "politics," or "religion," incorporating, one might fairly say, all of them and thus demonstrating the falseness of all these terms as categories [we use] for describing his world.[122]

And what of the world of Thucydides? The word *nomos* and its derivatives appear 61 times in the *Peloponnesian War*, similarly naming a set of practices that enters into religious belief, cultic practice, political discourse, ancient custom, ethical life—and even language. For the disruption of language characterizing *stasis* in Thucydides' account that was Josephus' model is described as a disruption of linguistic laws (*nomoi*/νόμοι).

The "Laws" of Language

The lethal threat of *stasis* to societal existence is the unhinging of words from their connection to citizen action. Verbal conventions, the linguistic "laws" of the *polis*, require a degree of constancy if they are to name the situations of life that citizens share.[123] Factionalism fractures the public use of words. As *stasis* intensifies, the rapidity of change causes a "breakdown in linguistic *nomoi*," destroying the very basis of social communication.[124] Thucydides signals such a breakdown in his description of civil strife in Corcyra.[125] The details of his wording in this section (3.82–83) have been scrutinized by recent scholars who share a philosophical interest in the grammatical eccentricities, neologisms, and examples of *hapax legomenon* (one-time usage) that Thucydides employs.[126] The intensity of this focus corresponds to that of Benjamin, who described the *wordliness* of language as its *capacity to name*. Here is the crucial passage from Thucydides' text:

> Men assumed the right to reverse the usual values in the application of words to actions [ἀξίωσιν τῶν ὀνομάτων ἐς τὰ ἔργα]. Reckless audacity came to be thought of as comradely courage, while far-sighted hesitation became well-disguised cowardice; moderation was a front for unmanliness; and to understand everything was to accomplish nothing.[127]

The "application of words" here is a process of evaluation (*axiosis*/ἀξίωσις). Note that the term Thucydides actually uses is "name" (*onoma*/ὄνομα), not "word" (*logos*/λόγος), and it is the process of evaluative naming (ἀξίωσιν τῶν ὀνομάτων) that has been disrupted: reckless deeds are named courage, those who act with prudence are named cowardly, and acts of moderation named unmanly.[128] "Simply, the words are different—the atmosphere certainly is—but, and this is critical, the words have *not* changed their *meanings*. Nothing happened to them. . . . That same act in saner times, when *stasis* was not ravaging the cities, would have fallen under the concept of *irrational daring* and been so called."[129]

In normal times, the words used are taken to be identical to their referent; the unhinging of this connection disturbs what is presumed as an ontological relationship between an action and its name. But in *stasis*, names are shown to be transient in the truth of their referent, and evaluations of being are destabilized (courage/irrational daring), with fundamental philosophical implications. Ontology becomes history: not eternal, natural law, but the naming law (*nomos*) of practices that undergird ethical life.[130] This customary use of words is open to change.[131]

What changes historically is therefore neither the word nor the action but, rather, the evaluation of actions, how they are named and thereby the judgment (*dikaiosis*) that is made about them.[132] Without the shared naming of values, the practice of public ethics becomes disrupted, confounded, contradictory. The passage in Thucydides continues: "Wild aggression was a mark of manhood, while careful planning for one's future security was a glib excuse for evasion. The troublemaker was always to be trusted, the one who opposed him was to be suspected. The man who devised a successful plot was intelligent. The one who detected it still cleverer; but the man who thought ahead to try and find some different option was a threat to party loyalty" (3.82.4–5).

Public actions appear in language that expresses the values attributed to them. What we are calling *wordliness* is the relationship that occurs in this naming process. But in *stasis*, when "the constraints or customs of the community" that "set the background" for evaluating actions are disturbed, upholding communal values becomes impossible. Thucydides writes: "As a result, neither side behaved with any higher scruples [*eusebeia*/εὐσέβεια], but those who found a good-sounding explanation for their dreadful deeds enjoyed the better reputation."[133] The word *eusebeia* means literally piety, that is, "high scruples" as recognized publicly by pious actions. In this passage, piety includes conformance to social norms for which proper naming is the precondition.[134]

Loraux notes that the word *eusebeia* appears in Thucydides' text only once.[135] But it is crucial, because at stake are not mere words, not just fights over what to call things, but the very legitimate, the binding oath that founds the city, into which its present residents are born, and by the customs of which they are raised. Acts of piety link citizen *trust* to shared *belief*. The word *pistis* [πίστις] names them both. In this passage of Thucydides, *nomos* encompasses the expanded meaning (law, custom, religious rites, binding oaths, ethical norms) that is found in Josephus' use of the term in the *Bellum Judaicum*. Their shared idiom provides a model of civil strife that is lost within the epistemological nationalism of modern understanding.

Philologically related to both *nomos* and *onoma* is the verb *nomizein* (νομιζείν), used for "evaluative reasoning"—not formal reason, and not mere subjective opinion, but judgment mediated by the *nomos* of public life.[136] Allison notes: "*Nomizein* does not possess absoluteness or finality; it is a reasoned observation considering the fact(or)s presented to the recipient. It is an act which occurs in the realm of what are reasonable, conventional, and socially recognized phenomena. This is categorically different from pure thought."[137] We may note that the word "to think" (*noein*) in the sense of pure thought is how Carl Schmitt understands thought (*noos*), which he therefore refuses to connect to *nomos*.[138] But *nomizein* is a different verb, which needs to be translated "consider to be," "consider convention"; as the public use of thought, *nomizein* holds the speaker responsible for judgments made.[139] That responsibility demands a process of evaluation: *axiosis*. The English word *axiomatic* registers the social embeddedness of the evaluating name, which to the community of speakers is self-evident, accepted; it goes without saying.[140] So there is something collective, a public perception, that has a claim to the naming of truth, one that may be loosened and altered by the force of rhetorical persuasion.[141] In *stasis*, however, it becomes totally undone. The force of history overpowers the judging process.

Diagnosis of Change

Thucydides' approach to the effect of *stasis* on language is modeled on medical knowledge.[142] We have already spoken of the parallel between *stasis* and plague that appears in Josephus' account as well. Here we need to emphasize that the medical parallel of disease—which deals with symptoms rather than causes, processes rather than identities, bearers rather than agents of change, and moving situations rather than eternal states—opens up a philosophical possibility for history that is not available to ontology. To explain: because ontology is concerned with the meaning of *being*, transitoriness is a threat to its truth. Hegel believed he could resolve the antinomy between being and change by a philosophy of historical *becoming*. But with the rejection of the Hegelian metaphysical principle that truth appears historically, the study of history becomes philosophically imperiled: historical change, while making it impossible to sustain permanent statements concerning "being," loses its claim to be meaningful in itself. The unavoidable consequence is relativism: ontological claims are relativized by historical contextualization, while historical outcomes are left to contingency and chance. But what Thucydides is able to achieve in his analysis of *stasis* is a grasp of the dynamics of change itself. The situation of *stasis* is a historical contextualization that can be generalized—not by (ontological) claims regarding human nature per se, but human nature as it is shaped and affected by the tumultuous changes brought about by civil strife.

Contingency, the aleatory element in human events, does not make all comprehension impossible. Rather, just as a doctor may not know the historically specific *cause* of the plague, nonetheless the symptoms, course of the fever, its side-effects and inevitable spread to others—these can be known. They yield to descriptive generalization. In *stasis*, the socially destructive consequences that follow the unmooring of "proper nomic behavior" are predictable, even if historical outcomes (whether the afflicted patient lives or dies) cannot be known in advance.[143] Unlike the abstract rationality of realist theories, this is a science of the historical situation. As in medical practice, the objectivity of diagnosis is nonpartisan. It does not begin by taking sides. The analysis focuses on the generalizability of the coincidence of factors in which human beings lose control.[144] "The focus is on circumstances as historically effective factors, not on individuals. The individuals are subsumed in the circumstances."[145] Clearly, what is being generalized is a historical condition. "The quality of human beings is only of interest if it has influence on the events and is therefore an element in the events."[146] The situation as such becomes an object of history; the human quality *as actualized* is the "object of historical consideration, not the individual qualities of any old man."[147]

The dynamic of both history and disease has a name: *kinesis*.[148] The word means: motion, movement, change. Historical events, like the course of an illness, take on life of their own.[149] Humans are powerless to control the process. And this powerlessness feeds into the crisis of naming. Prudence is called cowardice, because it has the effect of cowardice given the situation, and reckless daring is turned by the situation into bravery. The destabilizing motion of *stasis* overcomes the laws of the *polis*, hindering purposive action and damaging collective life.

Stasis can be seen as the prototype for this process due to the internal dynamics of the word itself. The name resists reification. It is unstable, containing its own *kinesis*. For *stasis* has a double meaning, incorporating movement at its very core. On the one hand, *stasis* refers to a posture or position enacted in word and deed: taking a stand. As such, when applied to Athenian democratic practice, it names, as the very essence of citizenship, responsible participation in public life. Writing on Athenian democracy, Finley notes that *stasis* was "the prerogative of free men"; Solon's law made it mandatory for citizens to take a stand on issues under debate.[150] But this same practice, when it becomes extreme, destroys the city. Citizen action falls under a dynamic whereby civic debate leads to factionalism and the public expression of dissent turns violent.[151] The question is whether *stasis* as citizen debate will allow the airing of contesting views within a context of shared values, or whether *stasis* as civil strife becomes war.

Stasis as Polemos

In Corcyra, both "factions" engaged in civil strife invite opposing sides of outsiders, Athens and Sparta, into the *polis* to aid their cause. When this happens, it becomes impossible to sustain the division between "us" and "them," the crucial ideological distinction of war as a defense against the outside, the foreign, the other. The enemy within is then not aberrant to the dynamic of civil life but unavoidably entangled with it. Loraux recognizes the "intellectual boldness" of Thucydides when he rejects "the dichotomy between *stasis* and *polemos*, between the sedition which ruins the *polis* and the external war which enhances its glory."[152] Described by Thucydides "with the same vocabulary as *polemos*," *stasis* is inseparable from it: "internal struggles are in league with external conflict, where the divided citizens, the better to tear themselves into little pieces, introduce Athenians and Spartans inside the walls of their city."[153]

Loraux names this a "double mimesis," whereby "civil war imitates foreign war" as the merging of language testifies.[154] Moreover, between *polemos* and *stasis*, "it is not clear which of them causes which"; at first it appears that war is the "triggering moment," producing factionalism within the *polis*; but "then it happens that this initial shock is also the 'pretext' seized by 'those who desire revolutionary change.'"[155]

"In the beginning was the fence," writes Schmitt, asserting with this spatial claim the foundational distinction between friend and enemy, well suited to the epistemological nationalism for which his theory of sovereignty is well known.[156] But no, not so, according to Thucydides, whose *Peloponnesian War* begins with the simultaneous presence of inner and outer struggle. In book I relating archaic history (known among scholars as the "Archaeology"), *polemos* and *stasis* are present together.[157] Loraux comments: "In the beginning was stasis. But also: in the beginning, war."[158] When the "ideological boundary between them has vanished," when war and stasis flow into each other, the party-faction "occupies the place of the city," obfuscating a fundamental distinction of collective existence.[159] It leads to the "most generic of perversions" that characterizes civil war.[160] Civic virtue (*arete*) is forced into an impossible conundrum when two names of one and the same action cross into each other: the valiant, "beautiful death" of the warrior defending the *polis*, and the murder of a fellow citizen—*phonos*, the greatest crime.[161]

How could the Judaean War among brothers, sons of Abraham, have been otherwise than *stasis* in its most tragic form? When loyalty to a faction that poses for the city takes the place of loyalty to the network of families and kin of which the *polis* as a whole is composed, Jew kills Jew and in so doing, in the name of defending *nomos*, violates *nomos* at its very core. How to judge the situation otherwise than that *stasis* as the dynamic of civil war *is* terrible? Like Thucydides, Josephus reports rapes, killing, looting, and every kind of sacrilege. When the practices of war invade the city and brother kills brother as an act of bravery, when armies of occupation intensify the strife through a confusion of outer and inner dangers, when actions of war and actions of civic life become entangled, when even the most noble intent of an act is judged as unworthy by the situation, people are forced into responses of mere survival. Destroyed trust strips civic life of everything other than private interest, because any other possibility means death.[162] And the most terrible aspect of *stasis*—then as now—is the erasure of the difference between beautiful death and criminal act—martyr and murderer. Between two names, hero and assassin, the act of killing is the same.

The partisan sides that fight against each other in civil war must ultimately be reconciled. Loraux describes in moving terms, with reference to the Altar of Lethe in the center of Athens, how the Greeks coped with this very difficult task of collective forgetting. It demands a public ceremony. After the barbaric treatment of fellow citizens in civil war, one must forget the past—more accurately, one must remember the necessity of forgetting. And the Greeks expressed this in the most profound fashion: they dropped a day from the calendar: "The month has barely begun and it is already amputated . . ."; a wound, a scar, the first day is followed by the third—to remember, you delete, and still you have to explain the deletion—this is remembering to forget.[163] It is a sensibility lost in Hegel's justification of violence as history's motor force, whereby the brutalities of temporal unfolding are redeemed under the name of progress.

Antigone as a Tragedy of *Stasis*

Sophocles' *Antigone* was first performed at the festival of Dionysia in Athens (441–438 [?] BCE) at the close of the First Peloponnesian War.[164] If the Corcyran *stasis* occurred a decade later (427 BCE), and Thucydides' account of it a few years later still, then the tragedy is anticipatory, and may well have been Thucydides' model for understanding the ambiguities of *stasis*, with its tragic convergence of war among kin and war against an enemy outside the *polis*.[165]

For in the drama, the enemy leader against Thebes is the brother of Thebes' defender. In war, they have killed each other, rivals for the Theban throne that, as sons of the Theban king Oedipus, they were meant to share. Creon, their uncle, now king, honors the death of Eteocles, the brother who defended Thebes, and denies burial rites to the other, whose very name Polyneices (*poly-neikis*), means "much strife."[166] Antigone, who is the sister of both, wills to bury Polyneices in defiance of the king's merely human decree. She insists on "justice enacted" against an unjust human command, honoring through customary burial the age-old law of the city—that divine *nomos*, law of a higher sort, which began one knows not when.[167] She holds fast to an evaluation of justice that King Creon names treason. When Creon orders her buried alive, she hangs herself.[168] Her suicide absorbs from the *polis* the poison of *stasis*, a deed of civic rescue memorialized and commemorated with every performance of the tragedy that bears her name—a political act if there ever was one.

Modernity's Misreading

This is not the way Hegel interpreted the tragedy, and Hegel's appropriation has dominated all subsequent debate. For him, the Athenian context of Sophocles' writing is not the confusion of *stasis* and war, enemy and kin, but the historical unfolding of self-consciousness whereby men move from familial relations and mythic law to the political realm as citizens under the human-made, rationally justified laws of the state. With this move, the Greeks are at the threshold of self-consciousness.[169] The *nomos* that Antigone sees as sanctioned by the gods is for Hegel *mere* custom (*Sittlichkeit*), the family form of recognition, superseded by a dialectical temporal progression that replaces the diagnosis of *kinesis*. Each level of social life is sustained in this progression, but it is trumped by the higher one. The lowest, closest to nature, is the realm of immediacy, the concrete universality of kin relations, the place of women that brothers (and not their sisters) leave behind.[170] Within the higher levels of abstraction and (male) individuation, the earlier level is "sublated" (*aufgehoben*, assimilated and overcome). It goes to ground, as Hegel words it in the *Logic*. History according to Hegel belongs to the victors. But the ground, the earth in which hero/assassin and enemy/brother are buried, is not silent. Hegel's schema of historical progress walks over these dead, the warring brothers and women who mourn them.[171] Antigone, whose actions are immortalized in dramatic form, will not let us forget the tragedies of which historical progression is composed.

Sophocles creates no Hegelian hierarchy. Both forms of law, and the inevitable tension between them, reign over his tragedy: the human law of the ruler that determines the present life of the *polis*, and the customary *nomos*, the ethical ordering of the gods, of Dionysus whose festival *Antigone's* performance celebrates, and Athena who gives the city her name.[172] The Athenian *polis* is constructed physically to honor divinities as the scene for the enactment of public life. Dionysus names the city's open theater where *Antigone* plays (to an audience in which women are included)[173] in the shadow of the Acro-*polis*, the high-up, protected citadel, where a new temple to Athena (constructed ca. 447–438 BCE) is just then being completed to celebrate the earlier Athenian victory over the Persians. It bears the name Parthenon. The word means "virgin, unmarried woman," as is Antigone at the time of her death.[174] Again we observe that there is no division in Greek antiquity—or in the first century CE—between "religion" and "politics."[175] Our meaning of both words is historically shallow, grounded in the hierarchies of power that culminate in the modern, land-based nation-state.

Hegel's Mistake

What model of history writing is appropriate here? Shall we historicize Hegel? *Antigone* played in Berlin during Hegel's youth. His friend Hölderlin produced the new translation. The classicist Heinrich Voss's savage criticism of Hölderlin's lack of conventional philology precipitated the poet's mental breakdown. Hegel had a sister, Christiane Luise, who cared for their widowed father, was jealous of Hegel's marriage and perhaps also of his life. In close accord with bourgeois conventions and Christian teachings (the public *nomos* of his time), Hegel believed a sister's duty was in and to the family.[176] Christiane Luise never married, lost her position as a governess, spent time in an asylum, and throughout her life was mentally unstable. One month after Hegel's death, she committed suicide, but not for Antigone's reasons.

Shall we, rather, historicize the complexities of the reception of Hegel over two hundred years, most markedly Nietzsche's anti-Hegelian appropriation of Dionysus against Apollonian reason, or Hegel's hierarchy of the state over social life that was vulnerable to Nazi appropriation, or the French postwar attempt to redeem Hegel by halting the dialectic and returning to Antigone's tragedy as an ever-existing struggle between the ethical and the political, when the political subject is the unwitting speaker of an ideology of power and ethical life is privatized and individualized as existential choice?[177] In this reception, philosophical reason that acknowledges history is constrained to critical negation, while Lacanian psychoanalysis psychologizes the law.[178] The subject-as-citizen is replaced by a split subject, who cannot act on principle without being undermined by the ambivalence of individual desire.[179] The point is that our understanding of the classics is blocked by Hegel's epistemological frame of nation-state and privatized ethics that adheres to a divide between religion and politics, and a faulty sense of being at home with the ancients. Hegelian Hellenism is an obstacle. It stops thought. Shut up in the post-Hegelian bubble, the central dilemma of collective life that is expressed by the word *stasis* leads into dead ends of interpretation. *Anthropos* as a political animal is chased into a cave of the unconscious by the depoliticizing approach of psychoanalysis.[180] If s/he tries to escape, the entry is blocked by "ideology," the (post-)Marxist suspicions of political discourse *tout court*.

For Hegel, Hellenes were proto-Christians; their universality *belonged* to him, and not to the Other, the Oriental, the Jew.[181] Derrida understood the situation most clearly: "We will never be finished with the reading or rereading of Hegel, and, in a certain way, I do nothing other than attempt to explain myself on this point."[182] But Hegel has made a mistake. (There may be no progress in history, but there is progress in history writing.) Misunderstandings of the central word, *polis*, translated by Hobbes and affirmed by Hegel as "city-*state*" and seen as proto-national in its historical form, have missed the relevance of *stasis* for *Antigone* and reduced the ancient meaning of the political to the statist aspect of social life. However, just as *nomos* implies no separation of religion from politics, so *polis* cannot be reduced to *citizen* life.

The ancient name *polis* slides in meaning, referring at times to the citadel as the focal point of the city, at times to the public sphere of citizen action, and at times is used as an inclusive term, embracing all those within its boundaries, of which only a minority are active as citizens (*politai*) who perform their roles in public for the entire city to view, to hear, to gossip over, and ultimately to evaluate (*axioo*/αξιόω). In *Antigone* the anonymous chorus passes judgment on Creon. At first they agree that Antigone has transgressed the king's promulgated laws: "[T]he presumption is always that [Creon's] will reflects the united will of the city."[183] But in the course of the drama Creon changes from king to tyrant before their eyes. When Antigone tells him: "The citizens are on my side, but fear has closed their lips," and Haemon confirms it, Creon protests: "Will the city tell me what commands to give?"[184] His outburst "completely contradicts his constitutional stance," subverting his claim to be the city's savior as he tyrannically separates his own sovereign power from the will of all.[185] It is Antigone, then, who embodies the public will, and Creon who privatizes power as his personal domain.

Here is the irony: Hegel made history central to his philosophy of Reason, wherein the course of history converges with the latter's realization. And yet historical knowledge at the time that he wrote was in its infancy. Spurred on by Hegel's thinking, history writing has flourished over the last two centuries, increasingly exposing the inadequacies of his own conceptual and philosophical tools, which when applied to antiquity are especially problematic.[186] The limited realm that we call politics was not the pinnacle of life in the ancient *polis*. Ober makes a clarifying distinction: the "politico-*polis*" is a "subset" of the more inclusive "*polis*-as-society."[187] They are inextricably bound together in the "*politeia*"—for moderns, a confusing term in Aristotle's *Politics*, because it is not identical to the actions of the citizens and the laws that they make. Rather, it expresses the larger *polis*-as-society, "including the 'ideological' system of norms, beliefs, and practices on the basis of which social goods were distributed."[188]

Ober rightly places the word *ideological* here in quotation marks as, again, a modern rendition of ancient reality. For the ancient Hellenes, ideology was no mere superstructural phenomenon. In divine law, *nomos* as custom, "natural" to each city even when differing from the *nomoi* of others, was the fundament of political life. How is it, then, that this distinction between *polis*-as-citizens and *polis*-as-society gets inscribed onto a

Hegelian public-private division that sequesters women from civic life as politically insignificant? No, they were not citizens, but citizen power was a "subset" of urban life. Antigone's act is political within the wider web of law and kinship of which the *polis*-as-society is composed. That is what Hegel gets wrong.

Stasis as Systemic

Unity in the ancient *polis* depended on a form of agreement that Ober calls "consensual inequality."[189] "[N]either the *polis* nor the *politeia* will be preserved intact if the *politeia* qua social contract is regarded as substantively unjust by any social group capable of bringing destabilizing force to bear."[190] Hence the ever-present danger of civil war. *Stasis*—taking a stand in the "political" *polis*—threatens the founding law, the divine law that provides the legitimacy for every kind of difference of which the *polis* is inevitably composed.[191] And yet so long as the conditions of social inequality in which this founding law persists have not been reconciled with social justice, political instability remains the case not temporarily, not contingently, but essentially.

Contained within *stasis* is a terrifying ambiguity between an act of honor and an act of crime, indistinguishable but for the names we give to them. Both Josephus and Thucydides have been read as supporting the status quo of power against those who claim justice in rebellion. Such a conservative reading is too simple. Rather, the fundamental ambiguity of collective life is grasped in the dynamics of *stasis*, which refuses to divide protagonists into heroes or villains on the simplistic basis of who wins. The other side of this analysis is recognizing the capacity of a demagogue to *produce* the conditions of *stasis* by ripping the names of civic virtue apart from the actions to which they apply, and then reversing the usual values attributed to these actions. This strategy promotes factionalism by causing a breakdown in the laws of evaluative naming (virtuous acts are named treason, and vice versa), and in the process, naming an enemy Other against whom violence becomes a heroic act. Democracies today can better recognize the societal dangers of *stasis* that Sophocles' play reveals by abandoning a Hegelian interpretation of it.

Correspondences

Jean Anouilh's play *Antigone*, based on the ancient story, premiered in Paris at the Théâtre de l'Atelier on February 6, 1944, during the Nazi occupation. Played in contemporary dress, the present situation of *stasis* in the country bled into the play's performance, despite the playwright's avowedly apolitical intent. Among the audience, collaborators with the Vichy regime and sympathizers with the Resistance applauded the same lines, as both sides heard in the words spoken a justification for their own, opposing positions.[192] The historical moment of this performance brought the ambiguities of *Antigone* alive as a crisis of public evaluation. To read the drama's enactment as purely against foreign rule diminishes the Vichy situation.[193] The French Resistance to Vichy, with its factions and conflicting loyalties, was indeed a civil war, one that spilled over into the Algerian War, where many of those recently acclaimed for saving the French nation from the Germans allied themselves on opposing sides in the anticolonial war that followed. The ambiguities of *stasis* cannot be cleansed from this history's remembrance.[194] The filial line of descent takes a turn: from Sophocles/Thucydides to Josephus, and only then to Jean Anouilh. Without this historical detour, we will not save ourselves from entrapment in the post-Hegelian snare.

For a piece of the past to be touched by the present, there must be no continuity between them.

—WALTER BENJAMIN, *DAS PASSAGENWERK*[195]

Methodological relationship between the metaphysical investigation and the historical one: a stocking turned inside out.

—WALTER BENJAMIN, NOTES TO THE *TRAUERSPIEL* STUDY[196]

3 HISTORY AND METAPHYSICS: ON PHILO OF ALEXANDRIA

Septuagint

The historical object that bears the name Septuagint is a translation, the rendering into *koine* of Hebrew Scripture that was appropriated as the Old Testament of the Christian Bible. Its title ("Seventy"), referenced by scholars with the Roman numerals LXX, indicates the number of translators involved according to the legend that has come down to us in the *Letter of Aristeas* (ca. 200 BCE).[1] It names as initiator of the project the Ptolemaic king of Egypt Philadelphus II (285–246 BCE), who is said to have sought a translation of Judaic wisdom for his library at Alexandria, in which he wished to collect "all the books in the world."[2] Aristeas reports that at the king's request, the high priest in Jerusalem sent to him 72 translators fluent in Hebrew and Greek, who were lodged on the quiet island of Pharos outside of Alexandria, and in 72 days accomplished the task. Legend has it that miraculously, they were in complete agreement as to the appropriate Greek equivalences for the original Hebrew texts, a linguistic confluence that gave credence as to the divine legitimation of its contents.[3]

Although far from the only koinic Greek translation of note at a time and place that, as we have seen, was commonly bilingual, the Septuagint's longevity as the Christian biblical Old Testament gives it a unique significance.[4] Wasserstein calls it "surely the most momentous literary enterprise in the annals of western mankind."[5] Hadas-Lebel counts this translation among those "silent, anonymous, and undated events which have changed the face of the world."[6]

The heart of the Septuagint consists of the first five books of the Bible (Tanakh in Judaism, Pentateuch in Christianity) that contain the Torah, or "law" (*nomos*) in the extended meanings of this term.[7] These texts describe the creation of the world, of the first human beings and all of life within it, and relate the earliest stories of Judaic ancestry in its relationship to God, including the exemplary lives and actions of Noah, Abraham, Isaac, Jacob, and (centrally) Moses as lawgiver. Further books tell of the ruling kings, bridging time between mythic past and recorded legend of the Jewish people. Not all of the Septuagint books became canonical for the Christian Bible; the latter focused on those texts legible as prophetic of the coming of Christ (crucially, the books of Daniel and Isaiah).[8]

The issues raised by the transmission of the Septuagint are ripe for the kind of partisan disputes with which the discussion of Josephus has made us familiar.[9] This is not surprising, considering the facts of the case: The Hebrew sacred Scripture undergoes a "Greek" (*koine*) translation that is ordered, allegedly for his own enlightenment, by an Egyptian king and executed by bilingual (Hebrew-Greek-speaking) Jews. It is used in synagogues for several centuries as an aid to non-Hebrew-speaking Jewish worshipers throughout the Hellenic world. Yet this translation, "the greatest achievement of Hellenistic Jewry," left no lasting impression insofar as "nothing of the Septuagint is found in the tradition of historical Judaism."[10] And while for a short time the Septuagint version was the liturgical source simultaneously in synagogues and Christian churches (the first Christians had no other sacred scriptures than the Old Testament),[11] the Septuagint "as we have it, is a version that is contained in manuscripts written, without a single exception, by Christian scribes and without exception contaminated by Christian scribes or editors."[12] The fact that the Christian tradition of appropriation considers this motley legacy unproblematic attests to a prejudice that furrows deep through the history of Christendom, which views Judaism's refusal to recognize Jesus as Christ/Messiah as a forfeiture of its right to inherit the sacred scripture that Jewish writers themselves produced.[13]

Historians speak of the Septuagint being "snatched away" from Jews,[14] an act of "hijacking"[15] that counts as "one of the most remarkable take-over bids in history."[16] And yet Jews at the time seem to have given up LXX without a fight.[17] Rabbinical Judaism that emerges in the wake of the Judaean War is aware of the Septuagint and the role that it plays among Greek-speaking Jews, but has not left us commentaries on this text. The latter's exclusively Christian line of descent includes works by Clement, Ignatius, Justin Martyr, Tertullian, Augustine, Eusebius, and Jerome, to name a few. And yet, ironically, the first and foundational commentary on the Septuagint, upon which all of these theologians depended, was written by a practicing Jew who had no inkling of Christianity. This was Philo of Alexandria. It is his work that concerns us here.

Philo of Alexandria

Philo of Alexandria (ca. 20/10 BCE–41/50 CE) was a *koine*-speaking, Jewish-practicing, Hellenic-trained philosopher, who visited Jerusalem (during Jesus' lifetime),[18] was a friend and creditor of the Judaean king Agrippa II, was related by marriage to the king's sister (and Titus' mistress) Berenike, and headed a delegation of Alexandrian Jews to the emperor Gaius Caligula in Rome.[19] Such a span of identity contexts was unremarkable for a man of his family's wealth and influence. Philo's commitment to Judaism is considered beyond reproach.[20] His knowledge of philosophy was formidable, spanning Platonism, Stoicism, Pythagoreanism, Egyptian philosophy, and more. His lifework was an exegesis of the Septuagint translation. His commentary opens up a remarkably vivid image of the first-century intellectual world.

It is with Philo that the LXX translation leaves legendary status as described in the *Letter of Aristeas* and enters a space of verifiable historical connections. Flavius Josephus knew the writings of Philo, who was his senior by a generation.[21] But Josephus is the only Jew of his time whose extant work refers to Philo.[22] Despite attempts to produce a continuous tradition from Philo to the rabbinical tradition established after the fall of the Second Temple, that tradition seems to have ignored him as completely as it did the Septuagint translation.[23] Indeed, the fate of Philo's own work is inextricably bound to that of LXX.[24] When second-century Christians take over the Septuagint, when it "changes hands, moved like a residential property," Philo is taken along as a collateral possession.[25] From the second century CE, "the Christian writers adopted Philo almost as one of their own."[26]

In this strange inverse kinship strategy, where the (Christian) sons adopt their (Jewish) father (or Judaic mothers have a Christian daughter),[27] legitimating lineages are produced anachronistically, after the fact. It is commonly asserted that without Christian attention, we would not have Philo's work today. At the same time, Philo's work resists the established historical narratives, opening up Judaic thought to a far more universal historical perspective than that particularism with which it is branded today. Here it may be noted that the case for Christian appropriation is not the whole story. The tenth-century CE Karaite Jewish writer Jacob Qirqisani, and the Cairo Geniza fragments written by Jews, refer to an "Alexandrian" who may well be Philo, initiating speculation that Philo may have been known through a Syrian-Christian translation—or perhaps even one in Arabic.[28] If the latter is the case, Philo's work might provide a link to Islamic philosophy, and to the reception of ancient Greek philosophy/astronomy/music theory by the Basra-born ninth-century philosopher/scientist al-Kindi, as well as his student, Afghanistan-born Abu Ma'shar, and even the great Islamic Platonist al-Farabi (d. 951 CE in Damascus).[29]

Philonic exegesis of LXX in the first century CE produced a philosophical synthesis across cultures, articulating a cosmological integration of metaphysics and governance, science and aesthetics that marked a unity across different knowledge terrains. Yet today Philo is approached by pulling apart this synthesis into categories that for modern historians are easier to digest.[30] The point is that Philo recognized no such separations. His work is situated within a confluence of traditions, flowing freely among categories that modernity insists on isolating, not only those of conventional historical differentiation (Hellenic, Jewish, Christian, pagan), but also specific fields of philosophical inquiry that are maintained by modernity in quasi-monastic separation.

Exemplary here are the three separate critiques of Kant that set boundaries between transcendental reason (scientific truth), practical philosophy

philo christianus

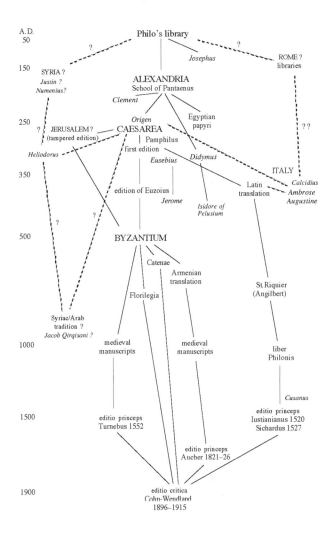

3.1

Schematic representation of the history of the transmission of the Philonic corpus.
Courtesy of David Runia and Brill Publishing House.

(ethical practice), and aesthetic judgment (value judgments of the sensible world). Kant felt it was necessary to disaggregate these aspects of philosophical reflection—an action for which philosophy, as he knew, paid a heavy price.[31] It is Kant who provides a modern foil for this chapter's discussion, because the stark differences that emerge illuminate fundamental limitations of the modern episteme—as Kant himself was quite consciously aware. For the sake of scientific certainty, he believed he had to sacrifice philosophy's enlightenment role regarding what he acknowledged were the most important questions of concern to human beings. Given the risks of dogmatism to the philosophical endeavor, he felt the sacrifice worthwhile—and dogmatism for him was the inevitable consequence of arguments based on religion, in the modern sense of this term. But if, as we shall argue, for Philo's project the very distinction between religion and science is a distorting descriptive category, the implications can be enlightening in themselves.

Consideration of the Philonic synthesis across the time gap of modernity challenges inherited patterns of knowledge. In contrast to the oppositional schema of Enlightenment/Romanticism, empiricism/theory, science/humanities, reason/aesthetics, Philo demands of us analogical skills. His is a method of parallels, doubling, pairing—specifically, the thinking together of Plato and Moses, and through them, theology and reason, theory and practice, beauty and law. Kant sustained the unity of reason across philosophical domains by bracketing experiential content when considering the forms of knowledge, so that reason's logical principles (*cognitio ex principiis*) could be reflected upon in a realm from which the historical particularities of knowledge (*cognitio ex datis*) had been excluded.[32] He relied upon this primal abstraction in order to provide results in keeping with the logic of transcendental subjectivity that attempts to square the circle between the individual thinking subject and thought's universal claims. Philo provides us with a different philosophical experience, if we allow ourselves to be open to it. For this purpose, we need to bracket not content, but historical appropriations that have imposed legitimating lines of philosophical descent. The thinking required to appreciate Philo is not about identity, or empathy with the Other, or subsuming difference under universalizing concepts. The premise is that philosophy as a human practice is inherently communistic, and translation is a requirement of its truth claims. To allot ownership of thought to any partial humanity is thus a contradiction in terms.

Law's Levels: Philo's Contribution

As we saw in the previous chapter, "law" (νόμος) in Hellenic antiquity refers to multiple aspects of social life, from ancestral law and custom, to written law, to the naming laws of language. Antigone's right to bury her brother is based on an appeal to unwritten law of divine origin that conflicts with the current legal decree of the king. Thucydides (like Herodotus) recognizes the diversity of valid laws on local levels, which do not claim universal status. The ancients also refer to laws of nature—including human nature, which, being as it is (according to Thucydides),[33] can lead to chaotic disorder, including civil war. For the ancient Greeks, justice, not nature, was the normative model for social life.[34]

Bringing the diverse understandings of law into harmony required philosophical intervention. This was achieved by Philo of Alexandria through his exegesis of various themes of the Septuagint. Philo's accomplishment in layering these meanings of law has been called "architectonic."[35] Kant used the same term to describe his own philosophical endeavor.[36] Philo constructed philosophy indirectly through allegorical readings of sacred texts, whereas Kant's building blocks were principles of reason derived through direct reflection on the thinking process. And yet neither was intent on building philosophy as a completed ontological structure. In Kant's understanding, the architectonics of this dwelling would be sturdy and of lasting value precisely because the project was limited in its aims. By explicating what reason can*not* do, it is in large part a negative instruction, focusing on what is *not* possible for philosopher-builders to achieve.[37] In the Philonic synthesis, the significance of the negative, while positioned radically differently, is no less crucial. Wisdom is the recognition of the limits of human understanding. Unity among levels of philosophical truth is achieved as consonance rather than identity, producing resonances among differences rather than a self-standing philosophical edifice. Philo's is a "*disconcerting* architecture," given the indirect method that exegesis necessarily entails.[38]

Philo's philosophy cannot be named "religious" in the modern sense of the term because his reasoning is based on science: knowledge through observation of the natural world. Scientific study of the regular motions of that world—the seasons, life cycles, the interrelatedness of nature, and the movements of the heavenly bodies—revealed, through careful observation, the structuring laws of the cosmos. Eternal and universal, these "laws of nature," not cultural convention, were his standard of truth.[39] Philo shared with the Stoics of his time an understanding of the distinction between appearances—accidental and irregular—and their underlying order, insight into which was a demonstration of "right reason" (*orthos logos*/ὀρθὸς λόγος). The laws discovered by astronomers, geometricians, mathematicians, and others manifested the rational order which underlay the world of appearances. The wise man ordered his life in accord with it, whereas the multiple forms of law found in human communities, based on local customs and conventions, did not have the same status. For the Stoics, this gap between laws of nature (*physis*/φύσις) and civic law (*nomos*/νόμος) remained unbridged.[40] The moral practice to which the Stoic aspired was to bring his own conduct in accord with the "common law" (*koinos nomos*/κοινὸς νόμος)[41] of reason that governed an imagined cosmo*polis*, an ideal cosmic city, one that remained at a distance from earthly forms.

The phrase "law of nature" (*nomos physeos*/νόμος φύσεως) was not used by the early Stoics, but it appears in Cicero (106 BCE–46 BCE) and frequently in Seneca (4 BCE–65 CE), Roman philosophers whose lifespans bracketed Philo's. In their works it signifies not only the regularity and inevitability of nature's course, but also its prescriptiveness, as the divine ordering of the world.[42] This understanding, then, was not original with Philo. What the latter initiated, on the basis of the Septuagint text, was a theological comprehension that brought together nature and right conduct with the specific laws that Judaic scripture contained, thus asserting that the laws given by God to Moses and described by the latter as author of the Torah/Pentateuch were in accord with the laws of nature created by God, hence "stamped with the seal of nature."[43] Martens writes: "The law of

Moses, divinely given, could in no way contradict the law of nature, divinely implanted in the world at creation. Philo is thus able to claim more than any Greek or Roman author could or would."[44] When Philo writes that it was "the good fortune of the Jews" to have as their law, preserved in written text, a "true copy of the law of nature," he is claiming that Judaic law, and only this among the various *nomoi* (he mentions Lycurgus and Solon by name), is universal.[45] "It is thus not an invention of the human mind, but a reflection of unchanging realities."[46] It cannot contradict nature, because it has its source in nature's creator; thus the law given to Moses "is a law for the whole world."[47]

Modern historians describe this argument; *as* moderns, they do not engage with it. Unlike Philonian exegesis that aims at truth, the exegesis of historians is a search for motive.[48] Commonly, Philo's motive is described as apologetic, justifying Jewish beliefs against the critics as evidence of defensiveness, even an inferiority complex vis-à-vis the Greek philosophers. Philo has been interpreted to fit the standard European story of Jew versus Greek, wherein his work appears as a "compromise between Jewish particularism and Hellenistic universalism."[49] In fact, of course, Philo was reversing this modernist shibboleth: it was Judaism whose laws were universal. The Hebrew-koinic linguistic harmonies of the Septuagint translation were evidence of this. As for Christianity, in his time it was a particularistic phenomenon that did not merit his attention.

Doxography—the tracing of citations of earlier literature made by authors themselves—is invaluable for interpretive accuracy, and Philo's texts show the influence of multiple others.[50] Yet the tracing of these elements to specific predecessors or contemporaries in order to discern who influenced whom should not obfuscate the larger point, that the intellectual milieu was shared among those who saw their task as an inquiry into truth.[51] While many recent historians recognize this common discourse, the search for motive continues. Niehoff writes: "there is indeed no sign that Philo was defensive" in his attempt to "inscribe Jewish customs into nature."[52] Niehoff describes Philo's "strategy" as aimed at a Jewish audience, hence the Greek context was less relevant. Rajak considers Philo's commentary—like the Septuagint translation itself—a matter of survival within this context.[53] For Martens, the motive for "Philo's mighty claims" to monopolize legitimacy for Jewish law as "the only one worth following," while indeed an apologia, was at the same time "the logical and necessary outcome of his philosophical thought."[54] But was this "mighty claim" not, after all, a form of cultural hubris? Just how could Philo make the universalistic claim that Mosaic law is in "harmony" with the world, and that "the man who observes the law . . . [is] regulating his doings by the purpose and will of Nature"?[55]

As in the case of Flavius Josephus, we will refrain from the two explanatory models, identity and motive, that are preferred by historians. An evaluation of Philo's project positioned at the intersection of history and philosophy will need to proceed differently. Rather than a genealogy of identities for which origins and influences are sought, and rather than a hermeneutics of authorial intent, we will deal with the very salient issues that Philo addresses—because the questions are of serious philosophical concern. Kant takes a different orientation to these issues, which he pursues with equivalent consequence. For Kant, it is the transcendental subject, not a transcendent God, who is lawgiver to nature; the abstract unity of rational law replaces Philo's analogic levels. The juxtaposition of their projects has merit beyond the comparative categories of similarity and difference. It provides a *historical* image, a three-dimensional focus that, precisely by resisting the impulse to purify philosophical questions through conceptual abstraction, is able to sharpen them, demonstrating that they are accessible only through the historical concreteness of their appearance. As Alex Kagamé observes, "these questions have a way of becoming in some way clarified once they are posed simultaneously" in two different "philosophical languages." When Kagamé observes that Descartes' "famous formula, I think, therefore I am has absolutely no meaning in Bantu languages," he acknowledges that the place of philosophizing enters into the language of its expression and that this, moreover, signals a necessary philosophical practice: "the theory of truth as correspondence between a statement and reality" must "be put to the test of translation."[56]

Historical translation, we have argued, is a two-way street. This premise puts out of commission the presumption in the history of metaphysics that later philosophies are more advanced—a teleology of the concept that is enshrined in Hegelian idealism. Common to all philosophizing is the enactment of desire for metaphysical understanding, the search for which is necessarily positioned within the contingencies of historical experience. Once we relinquish the modernist prejudice that the history of philosophy is a continuous progression in thought, once we level the playing field so that the consequences of these different approaches are followed with an equally critical eye, we can acknowledge that there are moments, to which any philosophy is vulnerable, when the inner coherence of the argument persists at the expense of its truth. However, the immanent logic of a philosophical argument is not its completion. Philosophical practice reflects on the world of appearances, the empirical world, of which history is the record. History thereby enters into truth, not as relativizing context, but as substantive validation. What is meant by this is not strategic, not what *effect* a philosophy has in its instrumental implementation, but rather, what, as concrete content, in its historical specificity, it *names*. We take as accurate the one constant that Theodor W. Adorno allowed to philosophy: "that there is no category, no valid concept that might not be rendered invalid at the moment when it is cut off from the concrete context to which it really belongs."[57]

Philo the Pythagorean

Where, then, to enter the architectonics of Philo's philosophy? Shall we begin at the beginning? Shall we retrace the ordering of the Septuagint, from the time before time, before the genesis of the cosmos, and follow Philo's commentaries that focus on the first five biblical books as they move from the cosmogony, the creation of nature and nature's laws, to the allegorical commentaries, to legends and deeds of the Jewish patriarchs that culminate in the life of Moses, the wisest among them—Moses, the embodiment of virtue and the unwritten, "living law" (*nomos empsychos/* νόμος ἔμψυχος) who leaves as "marvelous memorials to his wisdom" the written law itself?[58] Moses, of course, was not present at the beginning; he had no empirical knowledge of the creation of the world. Moses, alleged by Philo to have authored the Torah/Pentateuch, did not "write" these books.[59] Such difficulties are insurmountable if Philo is judged as a modern philosopher whose objective is to present what he as an individual thinker holds to be true. But Philo's philosophy is a commentary on a philosophical text that, he claims, expresses truth in the most "beautiful" way. Philo's exegesis is open, his rhythms diverse, as he moves across Septuagint contents, doubling back to earlier books, repeating themes in variation, elaborating them in different forms. His commentary moves among modes of expression, at one moment literal, then symbolic, and frequently and extensively allegorical. If there is a system here, it is not one that systematically unfolds.

An alternative passageway is suggested by the second-century Christian author Clement of Alexandria, who refers to Philo as "the Pythagorean."[60] His comment is productive, not as an identity (the term Pythagorean is far too broad),[61] but because this description, in contrast to his inheritance among Christians, places emphasis on the aspect of Philo's scientific understanding that is most foreign to our own, hence the task of translation, as more difficult, is philosophically more revealing. Pythagorean science provides Philo with the connection between the sensible, perceptible realm of nature and rational intellect as it governs and orders the world, through the structural features of mathematical relationships and the analogous reasoning that like affects like.

Daryn Lehoux describes the science of the first century generally in these terms: "[S]ym-metry means 'co-measuring,' discovering relationships among diverse realms," so that "ways of explaining parts of it will also explain other parts . . . symmetrical[ly] across physical, ethical, theological, and psychological dimensions."[62] The "unity" that emerges from this principle is not one of identity but rather of harmony among analogical levels, composed of cross-connections and intercompatibilities: "Order that repeats in multiple directions, across very different kinds of explananda paints a picture of a universe that is not just vertically reflective, but multidirectionally symmetrical. It is this symmetry that not only allows one aspect of the universe to reflect another aspect—whether it is humans and the zodiac or the elements and the seasons—but that allows the known truths of one branch of knowledge to reveal hidden truths of another."[63]

By means of numerical relations, "like is known by like." This principle has been considered fundamental to Pythagorean teaching.[64] Mathematical truths underlie the harmonious elements of the cosmos. Numerology, the study of numbers, is not a supplement to the truth of the cosmos but its very condition of possibility. It is easy for the modern reader to discredit such a premise. However, as it permeates not only Philo's writing but philosophical thinking for the next millennium, we will do well to consider the rationality of the claim. Harmony for the Pythagorean is no mere metaphor. It is the acoustical expression of lawful numerical relations that mathematical ratios provide, and it is foundational to philosophy from the time of Plato in the fifth and fourth centuries BCE to the Hellenic astronomer Ptolemy in the second century CE, the Roman Christian Boethius in the sixth century CE, the tenth-century Islamic philosopher al-Farabi, the Islamic neo-Platonist Ibn Sina (Avicenna) in the eleventh century CE, the Italian Renaissance philosopher Marsilio Ficino, and the sixteenth-seventeenth-century English scientist Robert Fludd.

The *locus classicus* for this science is music, and its discoverers were not philosophers but the makers and players of instruments.[65] Barker explains on the basis of the monochord, a one-stringed instrument: "If you take a stretched string of even thickness and constitution, and pluck it, producing a pitched sound, and then divide it in half with a bridge and pluck one of the resulting sections, the second note sounded will be exactly an octave above the first. If instead you divide it two thirds of the way along, and pluck the longer section, the note sounded will be at the interval of a perfect fifth above the first pitch; and if you divide it three quarters of the way along and again pluck the longer section, the note will be at the interval of a perfect fourth above that sounded by the whole length. Hence the octave is associated with lengths in the ratio 2:1, the fifth with lengths in the ratio of 3:2, and the fourth with lengths in the ratio 4:3."[66] The ratios remain the same no matter how the notes are generated, and no matter what the pitch.[67]

So much for the physics of these mathematical relations. Now consider the sound: you can hear these ratios; they "strike the ear in a special way, characteristic of no other interval within that range"; they were named

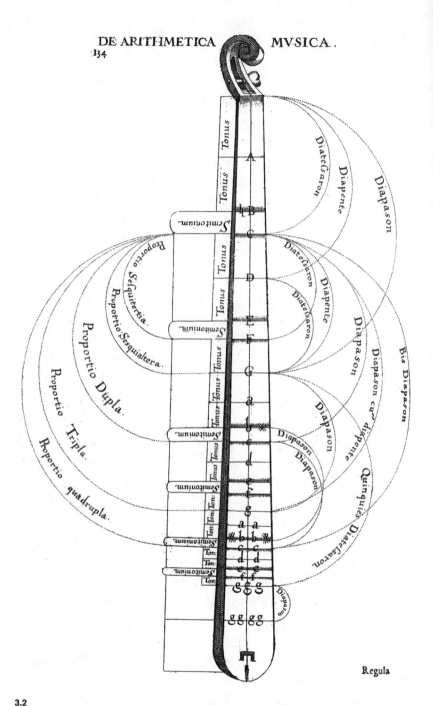

3.2

The monochord and its harmonic intervals. From Robert Fludd, *De arithmetica musica*, 1618.

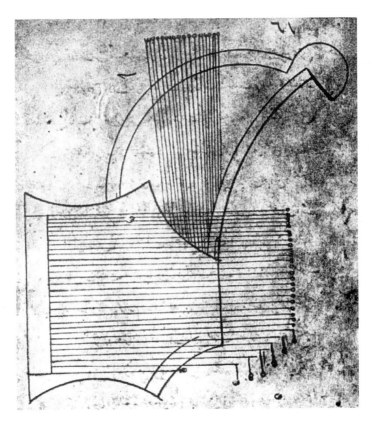

3.3
Illustration from al-Fārābī (about 870–950), *Kitāb al-Mūsīqī al Kabīr*, drawing of a musical instrument related to the lyre, called *šāh-rūd*.

"concords" (*symphoniae*/συμφωνίαι), heard together "as a single thing, its theoretically distinct elements fused into a unity."[68] Mathematical properties have sound—or, as the Pythagoreans expressed it, emphasizing the objective reality of this phenomenon: sound "has number."[69] And specific mathematical proportions have pleasing sounds. In other words, the relationality of numbers is audible; it enters into the sensible world. And we discover a further meaning of the word *nomos* as "law" that is often not recognized by modern commentators. In Pythagorean (and Platonic)[70] thought, *nomos* refers to a form of music, or speech that is song. Musical ratios, as an aesthetic and pleasurable sensory experience, are thus another level, a manifestation and meaning, of law.

But there is more. This convergence of intellect and aesthetically pleasing sensation is described as *kalos* (καλός), a word that means not only "beautiful" but "good," thereby tying the *nomoi* of harmonics to judgments of value.[71] The concords of music, among which the diapason (octave ratio of 2:1) as the simplest is the "most virtuous," are analogous to the ordering of the good society.[72] Harmony has an ethical dimension as virtuous practice in social life. Philo refers to those "excellent men" who honor as their father not the many gods but the one, "right reason" (ὄρθος λόγος), "admiring the well-arranged and all musical harmony of the virtues."[73]

By entering into these relationships through the realm of aesthetics, the numerical topology of which reveals the regularities behind the appearances of nature, we arrive at constant principles ordering the movement of nature, which can then be seen to accord with the ethical practice, "the good" (τό καλλόν) that produces social concord. It is the mathematical, metrical ordering perceived by the senses, aesthetics in the literal meaning of the term, that demonstrates the interconnectivity of the natural world as lawful, rational, and pleasing to human perception, hence the practical model for virtue. "It is not surprising, then, that speculations about the ways in which diverse items of any sort could be organized to form a coherent whole, one thing from many, commonly took the peculiar acoustic and mathematical properties of these musical intervals as their inspiration and starting point."[74]

The number system of relationality based on musical theory provides the medium through which the realm of the intellect makes contact with the sensible world in ways that affect fundamentally practical life. The good, the beautiful, and the scientifically true are analogically intertwined, so that knowledge of them is mutually reinforcing. This relationality is a powerful key to the Philonic method. Philo describes the interconnectivity of all of these domains of truth in his exegesis of the opening chapters of the book of Genesis. His interpretation of the Creation demonstrates via analogy (not identity) that the web of truth is equivalent to the "beauty-goodness" (κάλλος) of the breadth and breath of all that is.

But before we look more closely at Philo's commentary, let us keep the dialogue going, and allow Kant to enter the conversation once again.

In his lectures on the *History of Logic* (1800), Kant praised Pythagoras for taking the first step, via mathematics, to the kind of abstract reflection that characterizes philosophy, that is, without "the guiding thread of pictures."[75] Yet ultimately, Kant continues, Pythagoreans expected too much, a kind of "magic" of numbers, "casting pictures aside and putting numbers in their place."[76] The status of mathematics is particularly key for Kant. As an "organon of thought," it has "a fitness to solve a manifold of problems," allowing us "to extend our cognition in regard to a certain use of reason," as opposed to abstract logic, that "cannot expand our cognition, but only correct it."[77] Mathematics is "rules *in abstracto*."[78] Its universal, changeless laws are the "necessary laws of understanding."[79] But numbers for Kant have no reality independent of the human mind that thinks them—an issue, incidentally, that mathematicians continue to debate.[80]

Kant locates the laws of science in the reasoning subject, divorced from both moral implications and sensory content. In his innovation of what he calls a "transcendental aesthetic," the forms of space and time are conditions of the possibility of knowledge whereby the subject constructs the objects of sensory experience. The objects in their relationships are not themselves the entryway to truth. Mathematical ratios are laws imposed by reason on the world of appearances that the latter necessarily obeys. When Kant turns in his second critique to moral theory—what is the good?—he resigns himself to the most abstract of premises, *the good will wills the good will*, while the concrete content of morality remains undetermined by rational subjectivity itself. Only after this, as a third critique, does Kant turn to the realm of aesthetic judgments regarding beauty and the teleology of nature, in hopes of bridging the severed spheres of knowledge that his objective idealism has produced. During his time, opposition to this ordering came in the form of Romanticism, which recouped for itself the excluded domains of Kantian reason but retained his initial gesture of beginning with the subject, thereby consigning aesthetics to the space of the imagination, exemplified not by science but by art.[81] What is at stake here is the possibility of reawakening the skills of relationality that Pythagorean methods employ. For that, a non-Romantic relationship to nature's creation is mandatory. It demands a turn to the priority of the object, and indeed the necessity of a kind of magical thinking, in the sense of a mimetic moment in cognition that follows the object's lead, lest mathematics itself be reduced to an instrument of domination.[82]

For Philo, beauty is scientific insight into the mathematical ratios of the world that, objectively, all craftspeople must follow, whether artists, architects, or astronomers. That the cosmos is in itself mathematical is made acoustically evident in the properties of musical sound. Philo's commentary on the book of Genesis that contains an account of *cosmopoiesis* (cosmic creation) is predicated on this science. It is relevant that the most significant scientific tracts of his era were written as a form of poetry, considered mimetically appropriate to the knowledge they contain.[83] Manilius' *Astronomica* is an astrological "song" (Latin: *carmen*) that renders "mathematical sums in verse."[84] Lucretius' *De rerum naturae* is a philosophical poem describing the (Epicurean) atomistic structure of the universe.[85] The word *kosmos* means both order and ornament, hence beautiful order, and according to the first-century CE doxographer Aëtus, "Pythagoras was the first to call the sum of all things *kosmos*, on account of its inherent order."[86]

The biblical text of Genesis describing the creation of the cosmos, which for Philo is philosophically central, circulates within secular modernity as a narrative for children, religious teaching in an early, ingenuous form. Its fragments appear in Western discourse as familiar, yet tinged with the dismissive quality of cliché. A critical historical metaphysics cannot proceed in this fashion, as Philo's philosophical understanding of this text is anything but naïve. Here is a case of the effect of modern historicism that we discussed in the methodological introduction to chapter 2. There the example was Marx's description of mimetic thinking practiced by the ancient Greeks as "childish," a projection, we proposed, of Marx's own lack, an underdevelopment of his mimetic capacity that was the reason for his limited appreciation. The point here is similar: if the Bible is read by children, it will be understood on a childish level. Among adults, uncritical acceptance of the biblical text characterizes fundamentalist belief, and cannot do justice to the philosophical insights it contains. Western theorists understandably avoid the text, most especially the book of Genesis, lest they be accused of creationism. As every self-respecting modern thinker knows, this passageway into deep time has been closed ever since, as Nietzsche wrote, "a monkey stands at the entrance."[87] But fascinating is the possibility that this monkey, the evolutionary forebear of humans, may be more comprehensible to Pythagorean cosmology, based as it is on an ecology of interrelations manifested in the natural world, than to the law-giving, subject-centered, instrumental reason of Kant. Because of the shortcomings of the modern episteme in dealing with critical ecological issues faced by the planet as a consequence of modernity's practices, Pythagoreanism is experiencing a revival of interest among theorists. Philo, too, can be read in this light.

In the Beginning . . .

When Philo speaks of the author of the Tanakh/Pentateuch and therefore writer of the book of Genesis, it is Moses as philosopher whom he describes. He tells us that Moses had reached, at an early age, "the very summits of philosophy," learned across multiple regional traditions (Philo names Egyptian, Greek, Assyrian, and Chaldean)[88] and multiple sciences: "knowledge of the heavenly bodies" as well as "arithmetic, and geometry, and the whole science of rhythm and harmony and metre, and the whole of music, by means of the use of musical instruments."[89] In regard to cosmology, the most influential and respected philosophical account in Philo's time was Plato's *Timeaus*, and detailed scholarship has revealed the pervasive resonances with this work in Philo's commentary. While direct references are rare—Philo is after all commenting on Moses' text, not on the dialogues of Plato—the analogies are striking, as will be clear in what follows to readers familiar with Plato's work.[90] Plato, whom Philo considered the wisest of the Greeks and "sweetest of writers," is described as comparable to Moses in many ways.[91] While the constellation of elements in their philosophies is differently arranged, both Plato and Philo reflect the Pythagorean heritage that they shared.[92] But before getting caught in the problem of who influenced whom and how, it might be better to take the position that philosophical wisdom would be expected to sound in harmony, no matter what its source. This is in keeping with

Philo's own claim that every "man of virtue" and every "lover of wisdom" was related to each other "like musical instruments, skillfully tuned in all their tones," and would thus "sound in harmony" in all of their "explanations."[93]

Moses, then, wiser even than Plato, is "speaking philosophically" about "the creation [genesis/γένεσις] of the world" when he puts expressions "in God's mouth."[94] We are reminded from the start that the story of creation has a human author, whose account can be compared in its excellence to others. Philo writes that whereas some philosophers' accounts of the world's genesis were either "naked and unadorned," hence "unphilosophical," or "mendacious and full of trickery" in an attempt "to bewilder the people," Moses, on the contrary, "made the beginning of his laws entirely beautiful and admirable, neither at once declaring what ought to be done" nor inventing or relaying "fables" of others.[95] Genesis describes the making of the physical cosmos in terms of the laws that govern it, "under the idea that the law corresponds to the world and the world to the law, and that a man who is obedient to the law, being, by so doing, a citizen of the world, arranges his actions with reference to the intention of nature, in harmony with which the whole universal world is regulated."[96] And the key to this harmony is the Pythagorean ordering of number.[97] Philo's interpretation of the very first verses of Genesis depends on number, ascribing to Moses a philosophical sophistication that is crucial for all that follows.

"Day one" (ἡμέρα μία in Gen 1:5) is not *in* time but *before* time.[98] The beginning and most perfect of numbers that corresponds to God's singular Being is thus an exception.[99] The cardinal "one" of creation's beginning is separated from the ordinal numbers that follow ("second day," "third day," etc.), distinguishing between the idea of creation and its realization.[100] The distinction in wording resonates with the Hebrew original, confirming LXX as the correct translation.[101] (The English [King James] translation of ἡμέρα μία in Genesis 1:5 as "first day" obliterates the difference.) This linguistic detail is, writes Runia, the "trump card" of Philo's speculative philosophy.[102] God creates on day one not the world but its archetype, the intelligible world (κόσμος νοητός) as a model for the elements of the world of sense perception (κόσμος αἰσθητός).[103] These are the prototypes for all there is, which with "sufficient correctness" one can call "ideas" (ἰδέαι)."[104]

The consequence is that the entire cosmogony of Judaic scripture opens up to metaphysical speculation. For these ideas, these archetypes, function philosophically in the same manner as Platonic forms—to which Kant, still with Plato in mind, refers as "things-in-themselves" (*Dinge-an-sich*). Kant maintains that access to them by human intellect is definitively blocked. Significantly, in terms of this block, Philo does not presume otherwise. Our intellect, while modeled in God's image, has access through the sciences to nature's ordering laws, but not to the realm of Being in itself.[105] Philo writes that it would be "impious" to claim to know the "archetypal idea" of creation; we cannot "describe or even imagine" the "world which consists of ideas."[106] While Kant would have described the attempt to know things-in-themselves as philosophical hubris that transcends reason's secure terrain, their assertion of limits to human intellect is shared.

Now, were we to continue our Kant comparison at this point, it would lead us to a triangle of philosophical thinkers—Plato-Philo-Kant. Aristotle would need to enter as well, and Spinoza, Heidegger, and Derrida might be added to the mix, as we settled ourselves within the discipline of philosophy proper. But to do so would be to lose the historical ground we have gained thus far. Historical contextualization would be all that remained in this comparative approach, while philosophical insights would lose their transparency to history on their way to becoming concepts. So let us make a different move, and focus on the methodology of exegesis—lacking in Kant, but relevant to our own philosophico-historical practice. Entering a chain of texts, reaching back to grasp a surviving document of ancient philosophy—of which there are, relative to modern times, exceedingly few—the object recedes with every new attempt. To be specific: we have been commenting, through the lens of the best of scholarly commentators, on the handful of extant copies of the writings of Philo, which comment on the *koine* translation of sacred books that Philo claims are the writings of Moses, who in turn is "putting words in God's mouth"—a God whose world of ideas it would be "impious" to claim to know.

We are deliberately refusing to enter into the lineage of Christian appropriation of Philo's text that has been victorious in history, choosing instead a bastard line of descent, hoping thereby to redeem him from his orphaned status, not by rejecting his Jewish self-consciousness, but precisely by affirming its most daring and controversial claim, that is, the illumination of universality that Philo's interpretation revealed in Mosaic "law," reflected in the Jewish practices of his time. Exegesis is not what distances us from Philo's world. Indeed, it is the most modern of methods, the only one left standing after the death of God and the rise of single authors. What has changed is the status of the text. Philonian exegesis reveres the scripture and strains to salvage, through philosophical expertise, its most problematic philosophical claims. In contrast, modern exegesis privileges the new. Authors gloss their predecessors, relegated to apprentice status until some Copernican-like turn (linguistic turn, aesthetic turn, cosmological turn) launches their name in the marketplace of ideas, to be taken up for any one of a number of reasons, none of them limited to authorial intent.

Our philosophico-historical approach is in search of an alternative to both exegetical strategies. Translation across extreme distances is affirmed as validation, not in the Septuagint sense of exactness, but because the strenuous effort to traverse the arc between past and present provides training in boundary-crossing. It wants to prohibit the construction of the Other. Rather than establishing binaries of difference, each element of philosophical thinking is allowed an autonomy of interrelations, so that, not unlike individual arithmetical numbers, the elements are drawn into a multiplicity, indeed an infinity, of potential connections.

In the context of globalization, interpretive glosses of the few texts (now online)[107] that survive from antiquity, a period that was largely nonliterate, have undergone a fertility-enhancing procedure. Exegesis is generative. And that is a good thing. One will never reach the limits of interpretations, but only expand them as the desire for knowledge proliferates. Philosophy is a specific structuring of this desire, this wanting-to-know of science. *Philo-sophia* names the love of wisdom. In Greek it bears a woman's name, Sophia, who, as we shall see, enters Philo's presentation at a crucial point. Where Kant, toeing the narrow path of reason, avoids desire as digression (*Abschweifung* in German), we will insist on it—as did the young Walter Benjamin who, in his unaccepted/unacceptable *Habilitationsschrift* (required for university teaching), announced: "Method is detour" (*Methode ist Umweg*).[108] We continue.

Logos, Music, and the Law

And God said: let there be light; and there was light [Καὶ εἶπεν ὁ θεός[:] Γενηθήτω φῶς. Καὶ ἐγένετο φῶς]. (Gen 1:3)

Moses describes creation as a linguistic act, prompting Philo's speculation on the double significance of *logos*.[109] *Logos* is the spoken word, and also logic as human understanding. Philo uses *logos* consistently to represent the ideal forms that are brought into visibility in the cosmogenerative act of God's speaking, so that God as Being and the world as appearance, while not identical, are inseparable. The intelligible world fashioned on day one "is nothing else than the Word of God when he was already engaged in the act of creation."[110] Moreover, God's "exceedingly great gift" is that the human intellect is formed on the "archetypal model" of God's own *logos* and bears its stamp.[111] Runia comments: "The Logos thus bridges the gulf between transcendent and physical reality."[112] Yet even this formulation implies too great a differentiation. The creative word that brings the invisible archetype into being *closes* that gap. The word as *cosmo-logos*, the rational ordering of the world, is at the same time the practice of creation. The word as generative activity, *bio-logos*, is the creative force of life itself.[113]

Philo describes the *logos* as God's "instrument" (*organon*). We will do well to consider this term not in the limited sense that was adopted by Aristotle's students to define his several treatises on logic but, rather, with an explicitly Pythagorean understanding.[114] *Organon* is the word for musical instrument, and Philo makes the metaphorical connection clear: "God is the invisible musician perceptible by the intellect."[115] Pythagorean number has long been appreciated as important to Philo's exegesis. However, in the silent inheritance of written texts, the specifically musical understanding of number has gone strikingly unnoticed.[116]

This omission calls for commentary. It needs to be kept in mind that the cultural practices of societies of antiquity were oral. Vergil sang the *Aeneid* to the emperor Augustus. Writing was meant to be performed. Even the production of texts was oral: authors read their works in progress to literary circles; small groups of copyists worked together to record the oral dictation of a reader. As a historical object, then, the text had a different status. A book, a "bible" (βιβλίος), gave permanence to living speech. Its lasting presence was a requirement for philosophical interpretation. Exegetical practice looked for hidden meanings that enhanced the spoken word, opening it up to multiple levels of meaning. The Mosaic texts enabled both. Their "beautiful" wording could be read aloud; their depth of meaning could be plumbed philosophically. Similarly, music that was performed provided the audible experience of beauty, whereas the universal theory of number was needed to explain its harmonic creation. In this sense, arithmetic was a mode of exegesis that never left the sensory world behind.

Modern exegesis has lost this physicality that connects both language and number with sound. Among interpreters of Philo, the notable exception to this lack is Louis Feldman, whose attention to audibility in Philo's texts demonstrates, clearly, that "Philo was steeped in music."[117] He writes: "All Greek literature originally, we must remember, was in poetic form, and was never recited but rather sung."[118] Feldman's own exegesis enumerates the multiple ways that musical analogies are central to the philosophical insights that Philo finds in written scripture. "Indeed, the universe itself is to be viewed . . . as a most harmonious symphony between things on earth and in the heavens, in accordance with the laws of musical proportion."[119] Philo is explicit: the principle of division that governs the act of creation is related to musical harmonies, beginning with the first division of heaven and earth, from one into two, the model for the "double diapason" (double octave, the most beautiful of Pythagorean ratios) "from which sounds the most perfect system of harmony is produced."[120] This harmony continues with the parting of day and night, evening and morning, light and darkness, sun and moon, and, "very beautifully," male and female.[121] The divisions created by God's word separate and unite simultaneously: "Out of the same thing opposite things are produced, having the ratio of parts to the whole."[122] Philo refers to the creation of every living thing as exhibiting interdependencies like "notes of a lyre."[123]

The one God is the beginning of number (there is no zero).[124] The "sharpened edge" of God's "all-cutting word," writes Philo, creates a "perfect equality of differences," not unlike "the just balance of the two parts of a scale"; "and when one thing is bisected, then the opposite parts are easily known."[125] Divisions are into wholes, integers rather than fractions, collections of ones, written in ancient Greek by alphabetical letters: $\alpha = 1$, $\beta = 2$, $\gamma = 3$, $\delta = 4$ . . . .[126] In the creation, every number plays an ordering role: the parting of the cosmos into four regions—earth, heavens, seas, air[127]—the five perfect geometrical solids, the six days of creation[128]—and the most "marvelous," most "beautiful beyond words" is seven.[129]

The Number Seven

Philo elaborates: "Nature delights in the number 7."[130] While all of the numbers have multiple appearances in the world, seven is supreme: the seven planets,[131] the hebdomadal periods of women and the moon, the seven stars of the Big Dipper by which sailors set their course. Evidence of the seven in creation extends to the number of human senses, human orifices, stages in life, and vowels in language, whereas the seven strings on a lyre are mimetic of the "assemblage of the seven planets," which in their proportional relations are "most musical."[132] Seven has received the "highest honors" among mathematicians, comprising all the "harmonic proportions" arithmetical and geometrical, containing the four of the square and the three of the triangle; the seven is also "the source of that most beautiful diagram which describes all the harmonies, that of fourths, and that of fifths, and the diapason."[133] Pythagoreans "compare it to the Ruler of all things."[134] For Philo, writes Niehoff, "seven is the numerical value which informs the structure of the whole universe"—not because of scriptural description (the seventh day as God's rest from his labors), but because of "simple observation."[135] The point is that the number seven structures the story of creation as a reflection of the structure of the world—not the other way round.

3.4

Coin, ca. 40 BCE, depicting minorah with seven branches, issued by Antigonus II (d. 37 BCE), last of the Hasmonean kings of Judaea. Philo writes: "[W]e must remind our readers . . . that the sacred candlestick and the seven lights upon it are an imitation of the wandering of the seven planets through the heaven . . . and brilliant beyond them all is he who is the centre one of the seven, the sun" (*Quis rerum divinarum heres sit* 221). The British Museum, 1888,0512.29. © The Trustees of the British Museum. All rights reserved.

The periodic return of the constellations, the repetitive motion of the heavens, the regularities of the seasons, these temporalities of nature set the rhythm not only for individual well-being (the soul unites the sensory and intellect in harmony)[136] but for collective life as well. The contours of Jewish law emulate the natural order. The "sharpened edge" of God's "all-cutting Word" finds its mimetic counterpart in the priest's sacrificial knife.[137] The tunic of the priests with a "fringe of pomegranates round the ankles, and flowers, and bells" holds emblems of spring and flowing water, while "the bells are the emblem of the concord and harmony that exists between these things."[138] The Sabbath, celebrating "the birthday of the world," punctuates collective life as a mimetic reenactment of the creation itself.[139] The "special sanctity" in Passover rests on the first and seventh days, singled out because God "wished to create a harmony as on a musical instrument between the intermediate and the extremes."[140] Jewish collective life, in which the seven reigns supreme in accord with the harmonies of nature, justifies Philo's claim for the universality of Jewish practices. The sacrifices are offered jointly "on behalf of the whole nation, and indeed, if one should tell the real truth, in behalf of all mankind."[141] Jewish rites and rituals, based on the lunar-solar calendar, are mimetically tied to the ordered cosmos, representing the welfare of humanity as a whole.

In all of this, music is Philo's constant analogy.[142] The study of music is necessary for virtue; the life of a sage is a "lyre which avoids excesses"; the acts of a virtuous man are "attuned to the harmony of his words."[143] And Moses' soul was "in such perfect attunement with the virtues that he produced the most beautiful of symphonies when he plucked its strings, to such a degree were his actions harmonious with his virtues."[144] Mathematics is a "harmony of proportion," as are the choirs of men and women who sing God's praise.[145] The practices of Jewish worship are thus the enactment of musical laws (*nomoi*). "And a man would not be far wrong who should say that in all these things there might be discovered that archetypal and real model music . . . the art that is the most necessary and the most advantageous to human life."[146]

Reading the musical in Philo's exegesis brings sound into the sacred text, the elaboration of which disrupts the silence of modern scholarship. Philo's focus on music keeps exegesis bound to the material world that, as God's creation, remains the source of metaphysical inquiry. The sensory cosmos is in his words a "gate" to the intelligible cosmos.[147] Musical theory is no mere accessory to thought. Philosophical reason, never fully abstract, is tied to the transcendent by nature itself.

The Aesthetics of Truth

The case for the preeminence of aesthetics in philosophy has its own heritage. Several centuries after Pythagoras, the musical theorist and mathematician Ptolemais of Cyrene—a woman—criticized as methodologically inconsistent those Pythagoreans who strayed too far in the direction of abstraction. Her argument bears repeating here:

Pythagoras and his followers wished to treat sense-perception (*aesthesis*) as a guide for reason (*logos*) at the beginning, to provide it as it were with an initial spark, and after setting off from these starting-points to work with reason by itself, divorced from perception. Hence if the system discovered by reason in the course of their work no longer accords with perception, they do not turn back, but accuse sense-perception of having gone astray, and say that reason by itself has discovered what is correct and refutes perception. . . . But these people are altogether refuted by the fact that they accept something perceived at the beginning, and then forget about it.[148]

We will continue our focus on this choice of initiating philosophy by entering into its problematic via aesthetics and thereafter never abandoning its mandate to connect philosophical truth with material life and theoretical knowledge with ethical practice, deploying reason substantively rather than formally in the pursuit of truth. This direction matters, because although science has developed exponentially since Philo's time, although mathematics has become incomparably more sophisticated than the numerological schemata that operate in Philo's understanding, it would be wrong to presume that humankind has resolved the cosmological issues that, for our species, remain of vital existential concern. Pythagorean metaphysics is performative. It makes sound.

Musical expressions are not invented. They are discovered. In German the word for the practices of both discovery and invention is the same: *entdecken*. The word means to uncover, to disclose. The monochord contains all differentials of sound, and their arrangement in increasingly complex harmonies can be woven into a Pythagorean understanding as the potentialities of musical sound that intensifies the metaphysical claim. For musicians who push the boundaries of their craft as a form of knowledge, it remains a spiritual practice. John Coltrane saw music as "'a reflection of the universe.'"[149]

This mimetic principle of discovery/invention is the experience not only of musicians. Visionaries too perceive images as coming from outside themselves. Thompson, scholar of John of Patmos' book of Revelation, writes of the perceptibility of revealed truth (in visions, music, science, and words):

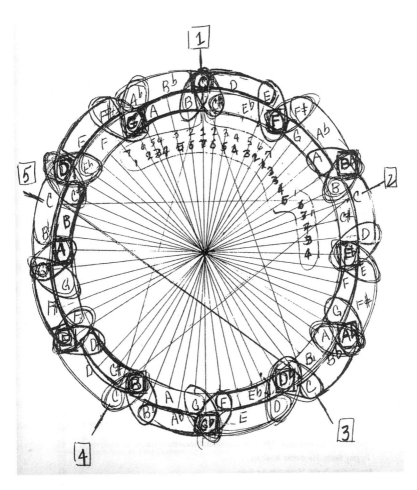

3.5

Circular diagram of harmonies, by John Coltrane, presented as a gift to Yusef A. Lateef, as it appears in Lateef's *Repository of Scales and Melodic Patterns*. With the permission of the Estate of Yusef Lateef. All rights reserved.

First of all, John [of Patmos] says the words are not his; they were given to him. . . . That is not bizarre. In fact, artists and theorists often have had the same experience. Homer and Virgil named a Muse as the source of their words. Einstein dreamed parts of his theories and felt that his ideas came from outside him. The pianist, Keith Jarrett, explains that he does not make music; he only allows the music to be played. Dizzy Gillespie said, "All the music is out there in the first place, all of it. From the beginning of time the music was there. All you have to do is try to get a little piece of it. I don't care how great you are, you only get a little piece of it."[150]

Chora

In the closing decades of the twentieth century, Western metaphysics came under attack from multiple directions both within and without. Plato loomed large in these debates, as the founding (phallocentric) father of the hegemonic (Western-centric) tradition. These debates are now so entangled within the contemporary reception of ancient philosophy that it becomes difficult to loosen the knot of historical appropriation sufficiently to inscribe Philo's thinking within them. A simple insertion distorts both philosophical moments beyond their capacity to be fruitful. As we have seen, an interpretation of Philo that proceeds with the tools of post-Kantian philosophy leads to the conclusion that his usefulness has been definitively superseded. But another form of inheritance is possible, one that does not ventriloquize the past in present debates but aims at expanding our capacity of thought through mutual respect of both temporal moments. What follows is a test case in the practice of historico-philosophical exegesis that aims to open up the past in a rearrangement of the conceptual residues. If we exit the story of continuous development that structures the modern project of the history of philosophy, and consider as a point of entry the constellation of meanings that circle around one word central to contemporary debates, we discover that Philo has already placed it together with Platonic elements in a different configuration, one that does not reinscribe the limitations of Western modernity's epistemological credo. That word is *chora*.

Chora (χώρα), meaning place/space, is a common Greek word that takes on multiple roles in Plato's *Timaeus*. It locates a space of a "third kind" (τρίτον γένος)[151] between the world of forms—eternal and unchanging—and the transitory world of nature as manifest to the senses, that produces a logic of oppositions privileging Being (τὸ ὄν)[152] over becoming, idea over matter, essence over appearance. Contemporary theorists have argued that these dyadic hierarchies are mirrored in patterns of social domination.[153] *Chora* as a third element is foreign to these oppositions, and yet it cannot be kept out of the Platonic system. It intrudes in the *Timaeus* in multiple guises—as receptacle, mother, and nurse.[154] Kristeva proposes that this third element is precisely the unassimilable feminine that disrupts the hegemonic order.[155] Irigaray names the *chora*: woman as such.[156] Derrida's very different strategy is to seize upon the required addition of a third kind as a fundamental indeterminacy in Platonic metaphysics, unsettling the binaries that subtend the Western philosophical tradition that is always, already undermined from within.[157] Derrida has criticized Kristeva's reading as an attempt to ontologize the disruptive feminine, the maternal body, that which cannot be incorporated within the system, and thereby incorporate it, an exegetical strategy that Kristeva criticized because it eliminates (in Miller's words) "any possibility of a real beyond, of a real revolution, of real resistance."[158]

With Philo, we appear to be on very different philosophical terrain, far removed from these French theoretical debates. In Philo's writings, the word *chora* (χώρα) appears frequently in its everyday sense as a synonym for place (τόπος), and it is translated characteristically as "country."[159] It is not used in the extended metaphorical sense that strikes these theorists as productive.[160] Yet the multiple meanings of the Platonic *chora*—receptacle, mother, nurse—do appear in his discourse, where their radically destabilizing function persists, as we shall see.

Philo does not problematize the ontological boundary between Being and beings, essence and appearance, with which contemporary phenomenology is so concerned—or perhaps more accurately, he refuses to allow it. He states explicitly that a third space between the forms and visible matter does not exist; indeed, it *could* not. The gap between Being and becoming is crossed by the power of God's *Logos* in the act of creation itself. Philo denies (or at least defers) this problem, so close in his reading of Genesis is the active, creative Word to perceptible life. The "world which existed in ideas [cannot] have had any other local position [τόπος] except the divine reason [λόγος] that made them; for what other place [τόπος] could there be for his powers which should be able to receive and contain . . . any single one of them . . . ?"[161]

The centrality of Pythagorean aesthetics, the connectedness of the visible and invisible world as the starting point of philosophical understanding, is in play here. Ontological proof of God has to do less with his status as Being than with his creative power, as manifest in the beings of the visible world. The dynamic attribute of God's Word provides *practical* proof of his existence. The ordering of the cosmos in Pythagorean terms— proportion, harmony, and number—ties together the visible cosmos with the forms. Nature *is*, it has being in this ontic sense, and humans, while capable through their intellect of gaining knowledge about it, are not themselves the creators—indeed, they are the last to come on the scene, the table of creation being already laid out for them by a generous God.[162]

The Pythagorean starting point in the sensory-aesthetic realm is the first sign of God's existence. All science of the empirical world then follows as evidence. Of the created world and its lawful order we have every sensory assurance; we rely on its ordering laws of number, motion, and structuring forms, harmonizing our actions with them when we model buildings by geometric forms, navigate the seas with the aid of the stars, cultivate land according to the seasons, practice medicine with biology and botany, and produce musical harmonies. The freedom that we possess to practice virtue in accord with these harmonies is proof as well. The ease with which Philo moves from sensory metaphor to intelligible form, from likeness to the ineffable is made possible by his absolute confidence that the created world that we sense and see has a first cause that we cannot see by the (faint) images that we use to describe it.[163] Science is practical proof that God exists. But this does not extend to knowledge regarding his essence. In short, we know the god of nature, but this does not mean that we can ever know the nature of God.[164]

Now, the modern philosophical position is that the idea of the transcendent is immanent within the human subject, and the thought of God's

Being does not amount to ontological proof of his existence. It is revealing that Kant himself, in accepting this argument, incorporates the language of Plato when he posits the necessity of a "third kind," a mediating aspect between the sensory appearances of phenomena and the categories of rational understanding. This "third kind" he names the *schemata*. Lodged in the human intellect, the *schemata* refer to our capacity to structure empirical objects according to laws of reason. Kant attributes this human capacity to "an art concealed in the depths of the human soul, whose true modes of activity nature is hardly ever likely to allow us to discover and have open to our gaze."[165] For Kant then, as well as Philo, knowledge of the visible world rests on a principle of unknowability. But in Philo's case the consequences are more extreme. For Kant, God cannot be known *by reason*, hence his existence is not certain. For Philo, God's existence is certain, yet he cannot be known at all.

The literalness with which God seems to exist in the language of Moses and of Philo's commentary, despite Philo's frequent warnings against anthropomorphic illusions, gives a concretion to his philosophical expression that encourages this anthropomorphizing tendency, whereby the whole issue of a gap between Being and beings (that required the third space of the *chora*) disappears from view.[166] Philo never wavers from his insistence on the limits of knowledge of the intelligible realm, so that a dual reading is exegetically required. But at the moment of Moses' own experience of God, the gap is exposed as glaring, and the very coherence of Philo's philosophical cosmogony appears to unravel.

To on / ho ōn (τὸ ὄν / ὁ ὤν)

For Plato, Being (τὸ ὄν) is itself the world of forms, the ideas after which the visible world is modeled.[167] Philo never uses the Greek term in this way, reserving τὸ ὄν exclusively for reference to God—who, however, according to Jewish practice, cannot be named. At this point we must confess to an anachronism that has been imposed throughout this discussion. We have followed the Christian practice (and that of Philo's translators) of using the word God (with a capital G), which is foreign to Philo's discourse.[168] When the Greek word "god" (*theos*) appears in Philo's texts, it is in the general sense used in antiquity for deity, or as an ethnic distinction (e.g., the Egyptian god, the god [*theos*] of Abraham).[169] The Septuagint's employment of the Tetragram, YHWH (which appears on the earliest of surviving papyrus fragments, and is the conventional Jewish handling of the ban on images), does *not* appear in Philo.[170] Instead, writing as a philosopher, Philo refers to the one god, *ho ōn* (ὅ ὤν), among a panoply of gods (*theoi* in this more general sense), as the *only* god, and equates this term with *to on* (τὸ ὄν), Being itself.[171] McDonough has pursued this issue of naming, tracing the first practice of equating *to on* and *ho ōn* (τὸ ὄν and ὅ ὤν) to the first century BCE (by Seneca and Plutarch); hence this non-Platonic equivalence was available to Philo.[172] McDonough claims: "It is difficult to overestimate the importance of this *pre-existing convergence* of God, τὸ ὄν, and ὅ ὤν for the development of Philo's thought."[173] The interplay of the terms "serves as a microcosm of Philo's entire intellectual enterprise."[174] Specifically, this equation provides the exegetical key to the very moment of Mosaic revelation.

Paralleling Plato's allegory of the cave that describes the process of leaving the shadow realm of mere appearances, Moses ascends to the top of Mount Sinai to be in direct communion with Being.[175] Philo's wording of this meeting strips away the literal narrative of an accessible God. At the climactic scene of Moses' revelation on Mount Sinai, the consequence of which is the written law of ten commandments (*deka-logos*), the theological description turns deeply negative. Philo's interpretation of Moses' account is striking in its exposure of this process, dissolving the cloud of anthropomorphic metaphor that has surrounded God from the beginning of creation. Moses, "the greatest of all, a God [*theos*] to men" (*De vita Mosis I* 158), is denied experience of the ineffable.[176] The "light" from Being remains for Moses darkness.[177] And when Moses asks for a name, this unspeaking, unseen god is given to say:

I am that I am [ἐγώ εἰμι ὅ ὤν].

This is the wording of Exodus 3:14 in the Septuagint translation; it equates the verb form of Being with the One who is.[178] Philo readily glosses this passage on several occasions within the philosophical tradition described above, making it clear that even this name is "an abuse of terms; for the living God [τὸ ὄν] is not of a nature to be described, but only to be [ἀλλὰ μόνον εἶναι]."[179] The very act of God speaking is not to be taken literally.[180] The sound of God's voice is compared to a musical instrument, "like a breath passing through a trumpet"; and even this is mere metaphor, describing "an invisible sound to be created in the air, more marvelous than all the instruments that ever existed, attuned to perfect harmonies."[181] The divine Logos is an *organon* of unalloyed speech, too subtle for hearing to catch it—indeed, not audible at all, but only "visible" to the soul.[182] The Word of God as described in the Septuagint is now clearly only the words of a human; God's own nature is "unspeakable."[183] Moses, so perfect in his virtue as to embody the law (νόμος ἔμψυχος)—so close to God as to be exemplary, indeed, a "partner" (κοινωνός) of God[184]—remains ignorant of God's name, is denied the vision of God's face, cannot hear the divine Logos, can only see with his soul.[185]

This philosophical tipping point changes the metaphorical framing of the scene. For it is at this moment that the multiple meanings of *chora* appear. The divine figure shifts to wisdom, Sophia. She is granted godlike attributes.[186] In this gender inversion, a woman plays the inseminating role.[187] It is the philosopher himself who becomes the receptacle who opens the "womb" [μήτρα] of his mind to receive the "invisible, spermatic, technical, and divine word" of her wisdom.[188] Sophia is "mother" [μήτηρ], while the "father of the universe" remains unseen. Creation subsides into its human counterpart. If in Genesis from the One come two, now, on earth, from two comes one. Biology inverts and recapitulates cosmology. The created world is proven with each new birth. It is Sophia as mother who brings life into the world, as the seed (σπέρμα) of all things and source of fresh beginnings.[189] And Sophia is called "nurse" [τιθήνη], who guides and trains Moses, as mothers train their children.[190]

When in Philonian exegesis the gap between God and even the most virtuous of humans becomes absolute and no anthropomorphic respite is allowed, Philonian philosophy becomes negative theology. The apophatic understanding of the divine—evident with the appearance of descriptive terms using negating prefixes (in-visible [ἀ-ειδῆ], shape-less [ἀ-όρατον], in-corporeal [ἀ-σώματον], in-effable ἄρ-ρητος)—affirms transcendence only through negation, beyond the limits of human language. The oracular phrase "I am that I am"—an answer that is not an answer—demands of human beings unrelenting humility. In comparison, Descartes' variant of the statement, "I think, therefore I am," appears commonplace. And Derrida's negation of presence seems timid. Derrida's anarchic concept of *différance* is immanent to human logos, in contrast to negative theology's appeal to an ultimate, higher reality, which remains external to human language that—with fluidity of meanings and plasticity of symbols—describes it.[191] The difference is the degree of risk. Philo's reading of Moses produces the effect of a theological construct that is binding on ethical action even after its scaffolding is taken away. True wisdom leads to this parardox: absolute commitment in one's practice to an unknowable transcendence is the highest level that humans can attain.[192]

Unlike the mystical tradition of negative theology that came later, encouraging solitary communion with the divine, for Philo a return to the community is required. It might be said that whereas modern philosophers derive practical philosophy from ontological arguments, Philo's Pythagorean metaphysics is itself a philosophy of practice, and the entire Jewish scripture is legible as a handbook of virtue.

The "Law" on all of its levels is a guide to action. But this guide, too, is expressed in the negative. When Moses, divinely inspired by the "Father of the universe," brings back to his people the written law, we are absolutely forbidden to believe these are God's words.[193] The very thought of this makes Philo exclaim: "Away! Let not such an idea ever enter your mind; for God is not like a man, in need of a mouth, and of a tongue, and of a windpipe."[194] Negation does not stop there. These laws themselves are striking in their formulation. The affirmative commandments are a paradox: "to think that there is but one God, the most highest, and to honor him alone"[195]—the One who cannot be named or known, and of whom it is thus forbidden to make images—and to keep the Sabbath, which "in effect says: Always imitate [this invisible, unknowable] God."[196] The fifth, "the honor to be paid to parents," pivots from the first tablet that lists the sacred duties to God, to the second tablet that "comprehends the obligations towards our fellow creatures."[197] Yet codes of positive law consisting of historically embedded mandates, particular customs and specific punishments, find no anchorage here.[198] The five laws of action inscribed on the second tablet tell us what must *not* be done. These negative commandments—not to murder, not to steal, not to lie, not to violate public oaths, not to covet others—are addressed to the individual.[199] At the same time, they are the necessary mandates of social harmony, and they apply equally, hence democratically to all.[200] It is precisely the lack of ethnic specificity of this negative mode of legislation that for Philo justifies their universal claim, not merely for Jews but for all people, confirming "that each separate individual by himself when he is an observer of the law and obedient to God, is of equal estimation with a whole nation, be it ever so populous, or I might rather say, with all the nations upon earth. And if I were to think fit I might proceed further and say, with all the world."[201]

Allegory

We must therefore have recourse to allegory . . .[202]

Jewish practitioners of the mystical *Kabbalah* have appealed to Philo.[203] Within Christianity, neo-Platonic mystics have adopted forms of negative theology.[204] Islamic gnosis, a rich source of neo-Platonic mysticism, can be considered negative theology as well.[205] Striking in Philo, however, is his lack of mysticism, his persistent adherence to a discourse of reason, necessitating a critique of irrational superstition and unwarranted belief. God's words in the Septuagint were only ever the inspired words of Moses, a human philosopher. The divine Logos is inscribed in *his* books (*logoi*).[206] The bulk of Philonic exegesis is bent on demonstrating the reasonableness of the Jewish scripture. The whole text must be scrutinized by reason, and where it is lacking in a literal interpretation, an allegorical reading must be deployed.[207]

Allegory is analogy, extended metaphor, that allows for correspondences across differences, mapping a rationally difficult semantic terrain.

Allegory marks the gap between Being and beings. Biblical language can be read—indeed, must be read—in multiple registers. The gender shift to Sophia, indicative of fluidity of meanings, signals the openness of the sacred text to a chain of allegorical translations. Ancient philosophers understood allegory as an antidote to myth, a form of disenchantment.[208] In Philo's work it operates in this way. One could say that allegorical exegesis *performs* the gap that the *chora* names. Philo goes full out in its practice when he "unfurls the full sails of his brilliance to the blowing winds and, leaving dry land behind, makes for the open seas." This is Jerome's description of Origen as allegorist; Kasemar writes that it might have been said about Philonian exegesis.[209] Philo compares Noah's ark in the shapes of its parts to the structures of the human body, with its "holes like nests" and "indivisible joints."[210] He tracks the multiple metaphorical appearances of trees: "trees of life, trees of immortality, trees of knowledge, of comprehension, of understanding; trees of the knowledge of good and evil . . . must indisputably have been plants of a rational soil, which was a road to travel along, leading to virtue."[211] He describes the creation of woman from Adam's rib as an allegory for the relation of flesh to the mind, body to soul, pleasure to virtue. Indeed, women are largely symbolic in Philo's readings: "Hagar and Sara are not women, but 'minds,' the one which engages in the preliminary studies or liberal arts without moving beyond them, the other the mind which strives for virtue."[212] The tower of Babel, whereby God removed "sameness of language," was not punishment but, rather, the necessary alienation that prevents humans from copying the wrong examples, or merely being swayed by words.[213] This reading of the story of Babel goes against convention, and it would not be difficult to discover an analogy to Philo's lived situation of Roman imperial hegemony that was a force for sociocultural uniformity, which he believed should not be equated with universality as philosophical truth. The dispersal of peoples, like the proliferation of meaning, is interpreted allegorically as a good thing, "to dissolve the company of wickedness, to put an end to their confederacy, to destroy their community of action," allowing the virtuous, banished by tyrants, to return.[214]

Philo seems to suggest that *diaspora* (διασπορά), which means scattering, is the condition of possibility of universal law. He describes the act of scattering as "sometimes done with a view to production, and growth, and increase of other things," in the way that "God, the planter of the world, wishes to sow in everyone excellence."[215] Philo (like contemporary historians)[216] reads the Mosaic exile as allegory rather than historical record. To the question "why the lawgiver gave his laws not in cities but in the deep desert," he answers that it was to "purify" the souls of those who received it.[217] Moses "wished to lead the race of mankind, hitherto wandering about in trackless deserts, into a road from which they should not stray, that so by following nature it might find the best end of all things."[218] He observes that only in the desert by night can one see the brilliance and beautiful arrangement of the stars.[219] Lest one settle in a "region of wickedness" mistaking a physical place for "the region of virtue," Philo praises the allegory of homelessness: to be "led out" of the deceit of the cities is at the same time to be "led into" a place of wisdom.[220] This is "speaking not with reference to the motions of the body, but to those of the soul."[221]

Philo cites Moses: "I am a stranger and sojourner among you."[222] Abraham is "an "emigrant" who "had no city to inhabit."[223] Indeed, "all the wise men mentioned in the books of Moses are represented as sojourners, for their souls are sent down from heaven upon earth as to a colony," where "they dwell for a while" in the earthly abode "as in a foreign land."[224] Their Jewish identity is not privileged in Philo's account; virtue is not an ethnicity's exclusionary possession.

Moses is a "citizen of the world . . . on which account he is not spoken of as to be enrolled as a citizen of any particular city in the habitable world."[225] Correspondingly, God gave to Moses "the whole world as a possession suitable for his heir."[226] Philo cites the proverb: "That all the property of friends is common [κοινὰ τὰ φίλον]," giving to this proverb no attribution.[227] Diogenes Laertius (third century CE) tells us that a Pythagorean considers nothing private: "for friends everything is κοινόν (common)"—suggesting that this is Philo's unnamed source.[228]

While lives of the Jewish patriarchs occupy a central role in the Septuagint, Philo "has very little interest in these narratives as historical record. . . . Rather, in his eyes, the historical part of the Pentateuch constitutes an allegorical portrayal of the ethical and spiritual progress of the individual."[229] The narratives provide "a more practical kind of ethical instruction," as "exempla that have prescriptive moral force."[230] Philo sees the patriarchs themselves as "laws endowed with life and reason."[231] They are exemplary sage-kings, a Pythagorean conception that Martens believes was a source for Philo.[232] Again, the focus is on practice. Mimetic emulation ("forming oneself in the image of the original")[233] is pious practice that brings harmony to the community as a whole.

The actions of the patriarchs are the visibility of virtue in the world.[234] There is philosophical significance to this claim that needs to be understood in connection with the Platonic forms. What Plato calls "ideas"— including justice, temperance, courage—*come to life* in the actions of wise men.[235] They are the instruments through which the forms of virtue appear as perceptible in the world. As Kamesar writes: "The virtue of an individual man was important not so much in its own right, but in so far as it revealed a universal form of virtue."[236] Each virtuous act in a specific situation adds to our understanding of this universal form. The acts are transient, as are the lives of the individuals who perform them.[237] But through these actions, "every virtue is erected like a pillar in imperishable solidarity"—just as, "when some musician or grammarian is dead . . . their ideas survive, and in a manner live as long as the world itself endures."[238]

Not through inner feeling or belief, but in the form of a quality of actions viewed by others, is virtue attained. The process is very different from the Protestant interiority of moral conscience that is incorporated into the German philosophical notion of the subject. A passage in Kant's first critique (spoken of by Adorno as "the finest pages ever written about Plato")[239] gives expression to the moral dilemma that confronts the modern subject as a consequence of the disenchantment of nature and the privatization of belief: "For when we consider nature, experience provides us with the rule and is the source of truth; but in regard to moral laws, experience is (alas!) the mother of illusion, and to obtain the laws about what I *ought to do* from what is *done*, or to seek to limit them thereby, is extremely reprehensible."[240] "[O]ur reason naturally soars to cognitions . . . far beyond the point where any object capable of being given by experience could ever be congruent with them."[241] This "intellectual soaring" justifies retaining, from the Platonic theory of the forms, those "ideas" of virtue as "archetypes of things themselves" that are vital, "primarily in whatever is practical, i.e., whatever rests on freedom."[242] Ideas are internal to the subject: we have a "model of virtue" as a "true original in our own mind."[243] The will to act in accord with this idea is the manifestation of our freedom.[244] And the fact that "no human being will ever act in a manner adequate to what is contained in the pure idea of virtue, in no way proves that there is in this thought anything chimerical: For it is still only by means of this idea that any judgment about moral value or lack of value is possible."[245] Just how far humanity can progress toward the telos of realizing virtue remains a question open to future time.

There is telos in Philo, but it is like Plato's, a teleology of the good, not a goal of historical time. The negative theological motif among modern thinkers provides a description of the false world in the name of a utopian future (here Adorno and Ernst Bloch are exemplary).[246] In the Philonian texts there is no history in the modern sense, no messianic promise, and no afterlife. Time is rhythm and order, manifested in the predictable motions of the heavens.[247] Our immortality lies in the actions and wisdom of our lives. As for extant theories of an end to the world, Philo considers them unreasonable. Given the perfection of this creation, modeled on the divine archetype, how could God destroy it for another one?[248]

For Philo, evil is not an ontological category but a false practice—when a true one is possible.[249] "[F]or every man has at the beginning simultaneously with his birth, a soul which is pregnant with twins, namely good and evil, bearing the impression of both of them."[250] And we come here to the final meaning of the *chora*, as "shaking." In Plato's *Timaeus*, the shaking movement of the χώρα, as the "nurse of generation," is ambivalent: she causes ordering motion like a sieve, "separating farthest from one another the dissimilar, and pushing most closely together the similar," while "in no part of herself is she equally balanced, but always unevenly in every part, and is herself shaken [σείεσθαι]."[251] For Philo, however, balance is the harmonious ordering of the soul, while the wicked, "tuned in an inharmonious symphony," are in a constant state of shaking.[252] This is a rare occasion when Philo appeals to the Hebrew name: Shinar: "[A]ll those who have quitted the region of virtue and have set forth to go over to folly, have found a most appropriate place in which they dwell, which is called in the Hebrew language Shinar. And Shinar in Greek, is called 'shaking' [ἐκτιναγμός]; for the whole life of the wicked is shaken, and agitated."[253] Evil, then, is the antithesis of order: "confusion is a name most appropriate to wickedness."[254] It follows that the steadiness of the Mosaic law is its valorization: "[T]he enactments of this lawgiver are firm, not shaken by commotions, not liable to alteration, but stamped as it were with the seal of nature herself, and they remain firm and lasting from the day on which they were first promulgated to the present one, and there may well be a hope that they will remain to all future time, as being immortal, as long as the sun and the moon, and the whole heaven and the whole world shall endure."[255]

Meta-Allegory

Modern histories of philosophy have tended to describe the relation between Plato and Philo as a story of decline: Philo is seen as subject to oriental influences that allegedly typified Hellenism; as a Middle Platonist, he was susceptible to a more religious way of thinking, and a more dogmatic reading of Plato, preparing the way for a theological takeover of philosophy by Christianity, whereas Plato himself produced a purer philosophy of reason, hence its capacity to connect directly to modern thinking over the heads of the theo-philosophical others in between. We have tried to interfere with this story, as have other recent scholars. Some of these have asked whether there is a system within Philo's allegorical texts when considered as a whole. Kamesar makes a minimalist case: "What one can say with certainty is that the systematic nature of the allegorical interpretation in the Philonic corpus distinguishes it from other ancient Jewish allegorical exegesis."[256] Sandmel goes much further. "Philo employs recurring allegorical equivalencies to put together a more or less systematic elucidation of the Pentateuch as a whole, and not just of individual episodes"; Philonic allegory, then, is indeed architectonic: "the roof, and floor and their component parts have been brought together into a unified structure."[257] This structure according to Sandmel amounts to a "grand allegory of the soul"; the Pythagorean inspiration is recognized here, specifically the meaning of number.[258]

Viewing the multiple levels of meaning in Philo's commentary as comprising a meta-allegory reminds us that written texts in the first century differed as historical objects from their modern counterparts. Their rarity within a predominantly oral society encouraged the thought that an additional layer of philosophical meaning could be transmitted by the way the text was formed.[259] Considering the text *as* text suggests a connection between Plato and Philo overlooked by the standard interpretive story of decline. Socrates was an oral philosopher, but Plato was a philosopher of writing. We are encouraged to read not simply the arguments of the dialogues, but the interrelated design of the whole. A written text holds the words in place, while readers can move backward and forward from various perspectives. Derrida criticizes moderns for missing the distinction between written and spoken word; but this difference was not lost on the ancients. When practice and ritual, when singing and recitation were the rule, the written word had a different status as the structuring form of thought, meaningful in itself and worthy of philosophical contemplation.

The belief that Pythagorean doctrines are hidden within Plato's work was held generally by Middle Platonists. Kennedy gives evidence that they were right to think so, going so far as to argue that, around the oral teachings of Socrates as a whole, Plato has constructed in writing a numerically persistent Pythagorean shell.[260] He has used the method of stichology—counting lines of individual dialogues as they survive on papyrus documents—to propose that the rhythm of the argument as it unfolds in the oral speeches (of Socrates, Timaeus, and Diotima) harmonizes with the ancient musical scales.[261] Kennedy's line counts are produced by the word program of computers that divides text into columns, mimetic of the line counts on papyri that had uniform columns with uniform numbers of lines, and the finding is: "Plato, adhering to a Pythagorean aesthetic, built a similar, musical structure into his dialogues."[262]

This method has been widely criticized because it involves guesswork and pseudo-precision, making multiple assumptions about meanings of the text's visual arrangement that simply cannot be determined today.[263] But Kennedy's musical Platonism is not invented out of thin air. The surviving text of Theon of Smyrna, a neo-Platonist of the late first century CE cited by Kennedy, is entitled *On Mathematics Useful for the Understanding of Plato*. Rather than a commentary on Plato specifically, it is a Pythagorean text on numbers, the second part of which is devoted to music theory, including the harmonies, intervals, and consonances, and the cosmological significance of such relationships in understanding the heavens and created world.

Music is the sensory experience of time. And interpretation of a *written* text, across time, is a skill that demands knowledge of the way silent numbers can be made audible again. Theon wrote: "By transmitting what has been handed down by those who came before us, we have composed an essential compendium for those intending to understand the works of Plato."[264] His approach to music provides a summary of the neo-Pythagorean knowledge that characterizes Philo's time:

> Music is not merely an arrangement of rhythms and melodies, but simply a system of the whole. Its *telos* is unification and harmonization. Indeed, God is the harmonizer of discords, and God's greatest work is using music and medicine to make enemies friends. In music, they say, is the unanimity of things, and moreover the rule of the best over all. And music by nature arises as harmony in the cosmos, good law in the city, and temperance in households. Music is an arrangement and unity of the many.[265]

Aesthetics and Knowledge

Within the modern era, mathematics as the measure of magnitude has replaced Pythagorean harmonics as the expression of relationships between things. This process is fundamentally connected to the disenchantment of the world whereby nature submits to knowledge based on mastery and control. Mechanics becomes the measure of the physical world. As metaphor, it extends across social phenomena, from the artifice of Hobbesian sovereignty, to the deist view of the cosmos as itself a vast machine, to the Marxian critique of the human body-as-machine from which labor is extracted for a profit.

Charting the historical course of Enlightenment reason, Adorno and Horkheimer demonstrate the paradoxical consequences of the world's disenchantment, whereby reason in mimicking this machine *organon* comes to resemble its experimental mode. Instrumental reason they name it, and they describe its dialectical transformation into unreason, as mythical as any pre-Enlightenment thinking that it opposed. When reason is reduced to a formal method, applicable to any content whatsoever, when it ceases to be the criterion for critical evaluation of substantive effects, it harmonizes its practice with the development of weapony for the destruction of every living thing.

Nostalgia for an enchanted nature is not the point of this critique. Rather, the catachrestic use of mechanistic terms to conceptualize lived experience is under criticism. In the twenty-first century, biology is replacing mechanical physics as the field of the expansion of knowledge. The new *organon* is neither the musical instrument nor the mechanical one, but micro-optical imaging technologies that are disclosing before our eyes the processes of life's creation. Theorists in recent years have added to the critique of Enlightenment reason a critique of politics as it affects the *bios*, physical life. They have protested against the reduction of human existence to bare life. They have brought ecological awareness in considering the situatedness of living beings, their codependencies and mutual determinations. The epistemological implications of biosciences are still in their infancy.

Philo's allegorical understanding of creation provides a historical image when placed alongside the metaphors that scientists themselves are discovering as the fitting names for what they are observing. Whereas the patriarchal expression of procreation had focused on the act of impregnation, molecular biologists speak of the division of cells, from one to two (there is no zero), and they name these replicating/replicated wholes "mother" and "daughter." The DNA is a paired string; elements of the genome are letters—g a t c—that in their marvelous combinations have an analogue to Pythagorean numerology where whole integers are written as letters:

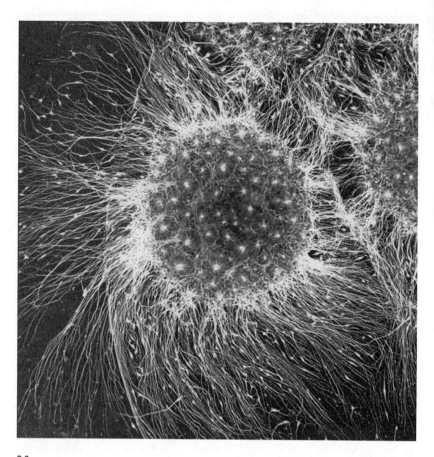

3.6
Micro-optic image of human neural rosette primordial brain cells, differentiated from embryonic stem cells in the culture dish (used to study brain development and Huntington's disease). Drs. Gist F. Croft, Lauren Pietila, Stephanie Tse, Szilvia Galgoczi, Maria Fenner, and Ali H. Brivanlou. Image courtesy of Dr. Croft.

α β γ δ. The micro-optical images of cell division (blastos/βλαστός)[266] are stunningly beautiful; the life force they depict is utterly opposed to the inertness of the machine.[267] In the *koine* of the Septuagint, the *sperma* is the plant seed or embryo, which in its creative force mimics the allegorical creativity of the Logos. Today's biological sciences share vocabulary with this language. Medicine is knowledge as practice, its ancient oath is the negative commandment to "do no harm." In this period of historical transition that is moving away from the equation of scientific progress with progress itself, when the instrumental language of Bacon's *organon* is expressed as genetic manipulation and the Kantian division between science and morality is still the order of the day, we feel the pressure of environmental urgency. The capacity to control experiments on nature, given the complexity of interrelations of the gene regulatory network, remains unknown.[268] What emerges perhaps from this historical image is the recognition that the categorical divisions between nature and culture, human and animal, confidently held by the modern advocates of disenchantment, cannot be reasonably sustained.

4 HISTORY AND IDENTITY: ON JOHN OF PATMOS

Whose Book?

This chapter concerns the last book of the Bible, "Revelation"—in *koine*: *Apocalypsis* (Ἀποκάλυψις). As a historical object, the book of Revelation, or Apocalypse, emerges within an expansive field of interpretations in no way dominated by biblical scholars. The history of its reception is legible as a history of the West in its entirety, including secular modernity.[1] Readings of Revelation are as various as Eusebius' commentary on Constantine's Christianization of the Roman Empire,[2] Christopher Columbus' record of his voyages of discovery,[3] Martin Luther's biblical translation,[4] Isaac Newton's metaphysical speculations,[5] and reflections on revolution by political radicals from Friedrich Engels[6] to Leon Trotsky[7] to Ernst Bloch.[8]

The book's account of natural and human catastrophes, leading to a judgment of the damned and the saved in the context of the destruction and renewal of creation, continues to convince readers of its clear and present danger. The book's vivid imagery is embedded in popular culture. Apocalyptic eschatological sensibilities provide the backlight to contemporary debates regarding the meaning of Middle East violence, millennial reckonings of the year 2000, and speculations as to the Anthropocene's longevity. Amidst the many repossessions of this first-century work, the text is held responsible for a vision of the world's end in a literal sense, a falling off the edge of time, rather than the more limited possibility of the end of the episteme of Western modernity, with its shibboleths of progress which conflated eschatology and linear time, and in which an "end of history" was first conceived.

The book of Revelation names its author: "I, John . . ." and its place of writing, Patmos, an island off the coast of the Roman province of Asia, now western Turkey.[9] No longer mistaken as the writer of the Gospel of John, today the name John of Patmos is perhaps the only noncontroversial aspect of his account.[10] For much of the history of Christian Europe, his book was presumed to have been written shortly after Jesus' death, perhaps contemporaneous with the preaching of Paul, and anticipating the near future, specifically the destruction of the Jerusalem Temple in the Judaean War. However, scholars since the 1990s have recalibrated the book's appearance to a later date, after the events to which it is believed to refer.[11] This fact is critical for the book's interpretation: history is in the text. Apocalypse is not a prophetic *prediction* of the future, but a prophetic *accounting* of the recent past.[12] If John's visions are emptied of the historical realities of the time, they take on a hyperbolic dimension that rigidifies their meaning and robs them of their power as critique. Written, it is now presumed, as late as 96 CE, the text brackets the century that has been our concern, exposing the actualities of the world in which it was written.[13] This historically specific revelation opens out to directions that previous conceptualizations of history have closed off, no longer a story limited to the concerns of Western Christendom, but one that embraces those eastern others, moving us away from a clash of civilizations to a history of civilizational overlaps and a network of interconnections.

John's text provides an exemplary case of the categorical confusions that plague historians of this period, because later distinctions between Christian and Jew cannot be successfully imposed. His Revelation became the final prophecy of the Christian New Testament (joining the "Old" Testament based on the Septuagint), but its adoption into the Christian canon was gradual and not without controversy.[14] Jesus "the anointed one" (*christos*/χριστός) is mentioned several times, but the identification "Christian" does not appear. The anointed one is a figure visible in the heavens; he promises that he is coming. But Jesus' teachings as described in the four gospel books are not in evidence.[15] John makes no reference to Paul—not to his missionary work, his letters, his trial, or his death. He writes in *koine*, not Hebrew or Aramaic. He addresses "assemblies" (ἐκκλεσίας, retroactively translated as "churches")[16] in seven cities of the *koine*-speaking, Roman province of Asia, whose "trials and tribulations" he says that he shares, admonishing each in turn for specific failures of ethical practice, while praising their successes.[17] It is in this context that John makes a single statement concerning collective identities, a reference critical of "those who say they are Jews and are not."[18] Yet this negation is not followed by a determinate indication of who *is* a Jew, and why, for a Christian text, that matters.

John's Identity

The question of John's identity has been central to the book's interpretation. The very boundary of difference between Christianity and Judaism would appear to be at stake. And yet this boundary simply cannot be discerned.[19] The best of scholarship on the first century recognizes that "an uninformed application of the category 'Christian' can skew the scholarly enterprise irreparably."[20] The meaning of "Jewish" in the first century in no way excluded believers in Jesus as messiah. And of course, the whole message of Paul—Jewish-born and earlier an opponent of those believers—was that Gentiles, too, could be the chosen people of the Judaic God.

Scholars dig into these *in*determinations. David Aune, whose three-volume study set the modern standard of commentary on Revelation, favors the view that the book was written over several decades, during which time John became convinced that belief in Christ's appearance is crucial, so that from now on, being Jewish means believing in Christ, and can mean nothing different. Hence, those whom John claims are "not Jews" are actually Jews who have not become Christians.[21] Elaine Pagels, whose expertise in relevant texts is no less formidable, cautions against anachronistic use of the term Christian to describe the telos of John's evolution in belief, observing that such terminology "conveniently recapitulates what Christians typically have seen as a progression from Judaism to Christianity," thereby projecting onto first-century sources what later generations of Christians saw as "the course of salvation history."[22] But Aune is not denying the "Jewishness" of John when he describes him as Christian—quite the contrary: John, he announces, was "a card carrying Jewish apocalypti[ci]st."[23]

Pagels' solution for identifying those whom John disparages as "not Jews" is to shift the focus to Paul, whose missionary work was carried on in some of the same areas of the province of Asia as the churches John addresses, so that John would have been fully aware of Gentile converts to the Jesus movement; *they* are the people John condemns, hence distinguishing himself definitively from Paul.[24] Aune, however, observing that there is no polemic between Jews and Gentiles in this text, asserts that "the author, while certainly of Jewish origin, espoused a 'Pauline' type of inclusivism."[25] Pagels, well aware that John never mentions Paul and is apparently untouched by his mission, proposes that Paul's Gentile followers were not known by his name.[26]

Aune and Pagels are united, significantly, in their opposition to a long interpretive tradition that sees the work of Paul as marking a definitive "parting of the ways" between Judaism and Christianity. The claim of a Pauline rupture as the break that established Christianity was articulated in the second century by the bishop Ignatius of Antioch, who "set up a boundary against heretics," becoming "the first, so far as we know, to aggressively identify himself and his fellow believers as 'Christians' over against what he sees as the adherents of an inferior and obsolete 'Judaism.'"[27] The claim of a Pauline break was still being argued in the early twentieth century by the influential Lutheran theologian Adolf von Harnack (1879–1930), who credited Paul with delivering the "new people [*Volk*]" of Christ from a Judaism "sapped of all vitality."[28] And it was expressed in the late twentieth century by the secular, Marxist philosopher Alain Badiou, whose celebration of Paul's rupture (carried out in strictly atheistic terms and with no anti-Semitic intent) reinscribed a supersessionist logic by claiming for Paul's teachings a breakthrough that left behind Jewish particularism for a new philosophy of universality.[29] Against these Pauline imaginaries of an absolute distinctiveness of Christianity and a totally different tradition of Judaism, Daniel Boyarin, with much of recent historical scholarship on his side, has argued that Paul was himself a "radical Jew."[30]

Our focus is on John, not Paul. The descriptive adjective "apocalyptic" is deployed extensively in contemporary discourse in reference to his visions, which are alleged to predict the catastrophic destruction of the existing world.[31] And yet within religious scholarship proper, John of Patmos remains a marginal figure.[32] Theoretical discussions tend to dismiss his work, disparaging the intellectual significance of this writer and of those who cite him today. But the late dating of John's text brings a historico-empirical dimension to its content that challenges the predictive nature of the text, and demonstrates the critical importance of its temporal specificity. Paul, whose vision and conversion occurred shortly after the crucifixion, believed that Christ's reappearance—*parousia*—was immanent, that it would happen in his lifetime.[33] Thirty years after Paul's death (a whole generation), John writes with the knowledge of delay. In a world that seems reluctant to respond, into which imperial power continues to insinuate itself, the messianic moment dissipates; conviction threatens to disappear. The last words of his book are a promise: "'surely I am coming quickly,'" followed by a plea: "'Amen, come Lord Jesus'" (Rev 22:20).[34]

New Sources

Shortly after World War II the discovery of two new caches of primary documents—the Dead Sea Scrolls, and the papyri of Nag Hammadi—shook the field of first-century studies. This was a case where the unearthing of new texts did not resolve but, rather, complicated the hermeneutic project. The scholarship of Aune, Pagels, and Boyarin is deeply inflected by these discoveries, which have exposed the inadequacies of previous conceptual maps and caused the toppling of long-standing beliefs. Both discoveries—made accidentally by local inhabitants—occurred in highly politicized contexts that skewed their popular reception. The Dead Sea Scrolls were found (1947–1956) in 11 caves at Qumran, Jordanian land that was occupied by Israeli forces after the 1967 war, when the state of Israel pressured for their transfer of ownership.[35] The second discovery (1947) was of 50 papyrus codices near the town of Nag Hammadi on the Upper Nile north of Luxor. After harrowing attempts by the Egyptian government and others to rescue the papyri from the black market, they became the possession of the Coptic Museum in Cairo.[36] Despite national partisanship, capitalist designs for profit, scholarly rivalries, and sectarian suspicions, the slow, careful work of scholars in international collaboration has been impressive. Both discoveries bear on the historical actuality of John's book of Revelation and, specifically, the question of identity.

Dead Sea Scrolls

At the Dead Sea site, almost a thousand Hebrew scrolls have been unearthed, many in fragments.[37] Multiple copies have been found, sometimes in different versions, of those books that were shared with the Septuagint, and/ or would later become canonical in the Hebrew Bible.[38] The Pentateuch is most frequently represented, as well as the prophetic books Isaiah (22 copies), Jeremiah (6), Ezekiel (7), and Daniel (8) that were also referenced by John of Patmos in his Revelation. There are texts from the Second Temple era that never entered the Septuagint canon—the book of Jubilees, for example, that speaks of a seven-year obligation to cancel all debts.[39] A "manual of discipline," later called the Community Rule, provides rules for a sect presumed to be the Essenes, who were highly praised by both Josephus and Philo.[40] Philo connects them with Pythagoreans in their lifestyle. Pliny the Elder's *Natural History* locates the Essene sect in the vicinity of the Dead Sea, leading to the theory that the Qumran discoveries were a library of scrolls assembled by their community.[41] A collection of Thanksgiving Hymns (Hôdāyôt, 1QH) and Songs of Sabbath Sacrifice (4Q), as well as songs from the biblical Psalms, Ecclesiastes, and Lamentations, have also been found, indicating the importance of community singing of hymns to God. Fellowship with the angels is a frequent theme, an otherworldly focus that some have seen as a movement away from the temple cult and land-based territory of Judaea.[42] Messianic texts with eschatological themes of judgment, the end of time, and the establishment of a New Jerusalem resonate closely with John's Revelation.[43] Copies exist of the noncanonical 1 Enoch, 4 Ezra, and 2 Baruch, themselves "apocalypses" written very close to the date of John of Patmos' text; 4 Ezra and 2 Baruch are interpreted as explicit reactions to the destruction of the Second Temple in Jerusalem.[44] A document named the War Scroll (1QM) tells of an apocalyptic battle between the Sons of Light and the Sons of Darkness that has been connected with the "combat myth" in the book of Revelation.[45] The diversity of thought found here suggests that those who collected them, whether or not they had withdrawn from the city of Jerusalem and its Temple cult, were ecumenical in their interests and assemblage of texts. Despite their isolated location, the collection included the thinking of Jews throughout the diaspora, from Babylon to Jerusalem, from Alexandria and Antioch to Anatolia. The Dead Sea Scrolls' discovery allows us to recognize the multiple forms of sacred writings that comprised this library of Hebrew (and some Aramaic and Greek) texts, and thus the wide range of Jewish practices and belief. An important aspect of scholarly interest has centered on the relevance of the scrolls to the New Testament and their blurring of lines of difference between Christian and Jew.[46] The common origins and overlapping contents of these traditions make it impossible to extricate from the material remains any pure line of descent.

Nag Hammadi Papyri

The 13 papyrus codices discovered near Nag Hammadi (Naj 'Hammādī), a town close to the caves at Jabal al-Tārif mountain overlooking the Nile, are in Coptic, a written form of Egyptian with affinities to the Greek alphabet that was initiated after the arrival of Alexander the Great.[47] The find contains evidence of more that 53 documents, of which 41 were previously unknown. The documents are not original but date from 350–400 CE—that is, from the first decades after the Roman Empire's embrace of Christianity.[48] However, they are presumed to be translations from older texts in Greek/*koine*, a significant number of which contain sayings attributed to Jesus and his disciples.[49] There are hidden or "secret" (apocryphal) books by disciples—James and John—and "revelations" (apocalypses) of Peter, James, and Paul. A Gospel of Thomas, the name of the disciple credited with missionary work in India, begins: "These are the hidden sayings that the living Jesus spoke."[50] A "Gospel of Truth" sees the meaning of Christ as waking humans up from forgetfulness to "bring knowledge" and "rectify" a "cosmic error" in the world's creation, by establishing "a proper, harmonious relationship to their originator."[51] These texts never became part of the Christian canon, although they circulated among knowledge communities in search of truth. One such community is presumed to have collected and later hidden the codices at Nag Hammadi.[52]

The Nag Hammadi codices have been grouped together by scholars with previously known "Gnostic" texts, called that by the early Christian Church that considered them heretical. Of late, the term has come into question.[53] There was no Gnostic sect. There is no singular Gnostic teaching. The word *gnosis* means simply "knowledge," but for the early Church the name took on a function of differentiation, allowing the production of exclusionary boundaries against heretics, a practice allowing belief to be corralled into a particular orthodoxy that the Church hierarchy could successfully control.[54]

Within the Nag Hammadi find are "revelations, or apocalypses galore."[55] As alternatives to John's text, many of these visions do not elaborate scenarios of destruction, although the "shaking" of creation is described, when "[t]he thrones of the powers were disturbed because they were overturned, and their king was afraid."[56] Many are testimonials of ascent to a truth that is mystical, transcendent, and beyond comprehension. Their message, writes Pagels, is that revelation is an "ongoing process," available to all those who would seek truth, instructed in "dialogue with the risen Jesus," through an experience of gnosis, or "intuitive knowing."[57] Jesus's appearances in these texts are thus multiple and various—at times a transcendent figure, at times very human, at times appearing "in the tradition of Jewish teachers of wisdom."[58] Not all the texts concern Jesus. A group of "Platonizing Sethian treatises" connect directly to the texts of Philo.[59] One of the Sethian figures, Allogenes (*allo-genes*, literally, "another seed"), is described as "the stranger," recalling Philo's description of Moses as "a foreigner, not of this earth."[60] There is a strong mystical element, as Allogenes withdraws from the multitude and looks within himself for knowledge of God, ascending through levels (*aeons*/αιῶνας), aided by various mediating female figures: Sophia, wisdom herself, as divine mother; the higher figure Youel, literally "She-to-whom-all-the glories-pertain"; and Barbelo, "the Mother-Father, the first Human, the holy Spirit," "the androgynous one with three names."[61] Their revelations to Allogenes are delivered as a negative theology of the nameless Invisible Spirit, whose nature is described in contradictions: "immaterial matter, numberless number," "who can only be known by not knowing him."[62]

Striking is the fact that female voices are heard in these documents. They sing and are addressed in song. "The Prayer of Thanksgiving" is sung before a common meal:

Life of life,
we have known you.
Womb of every creature,
we have known you.
Womb pregnant with the Father's nature
we have known you.

. . .

One protection we desire:
that we not stumble in this life.[63]

In "Thunder, Perfect Mind," a female voice reveals: "For it is I [egō eimi/ἐγὼ εἰμι who am the first and the last":

I am the honored and the scorned.
I am the whore and the holy.
I am the wife and the virgin.
I am <the mother> and the daughter.
I am the limbs of my mother.
I am a barren woman who has many children.
I have had many weddings and have taken no husband.[64]

This voice speaks in binaries of *in*clusion: "I am the voice whose sounds are many . . . I am the utterance of my own name"; "I am hearing adequate for everyone / and speaking that cannot be repressed"; "I am uneducated / and people learn from me"; "loved everywhere" for bringing forth life, and "hated everywhere" for bringing death."[65]

Notable is the wide geographical range manifested in these documents—not only Egypt and the eastern Mediterranean but also India and Persia are in evidence, suggesting an entire network of philosophical exchange.[66] Contemporary scholars have discovered connections between the papyri and "themes that resonate with Indian traditions of spiritual union, both Hindus and Buddhists."[67] One text ends with a colophon referring to the Persian spiritual leader Zoroaster.[68] Manuscripts with reference to Jesus are abundantly diverse. Meyer writes: "Those that are marginally Christian or non-Christian may show Jewish, Greco-Roman, Platonic, or Hermetic characteristics, often in fascinating combinations."[69] Fowden describes the Egyptian connections, and we recognize themes found in Philo of Alexandria's exegesis on Jewish Scriptures as well. In the *Discourse of 8th and 9th* the ascent is to spheres that lie above (and superior to) the planetary seven that "constitute the Harmonia, the cosmic framework moved by fate."[70] This papyrus is related to the Corpus Hermeticum of the Egyptian wisdom teacher Hermes Trismegistus that was "widely read" in the first century CE.[71] Fowden writes that the Hermetic Corpus was a "central constituent of Graeco-Egyptian religious discourse"; he calls it a *koine* in the religious sense.[72]

Universalism as a Method of Exclusion

The Nag Hammadi texts "show an astonishing range of diversity."[73] Correspondingly, the Dead Sea Scrolls manifest the rich and diasporic extent of Hebrew-written wisdom.[74] In short, if the Dead Sea Scrolls display the existence of multiple Judaisms, the Nag Hammadi papyri provide evidence for multiple Christianities. Such multiplicity of thought runs counter to the needs of institutionalized power.[75] In the case of the early Christian church, the historical move to orthodoxy produced a category of outsiders, forcing a unity of belief that claimed universality for itself. Hence the inherent contradiction: there could only be one church, catholic and universal, but this entailed the drawing of boundaries in a series of acts that excluded others, defining an orthodoxy that was by definition *not* universal. The production of orthodoxy was a practice that demanded the prior act of exclusion, and this is what heresy was all about.[76]

Until the new document finds, our understandings of the nonorthodox views were muffled, strained through the language of those who condemned them. When historians replicate this narrative, they reinforce the idea that history belongs to exclusionary identities that can be traced to a (purified) source. There are two dividing lines here: the production of a discourse of heresy excludes the others whose time you share, whereas the claim of a fundamental break between Judaism and Christianity produces a historical division, a parting of the ways that plays into a supersessionist narrative of Christian universality as a historical success that leaves a particularistic Judaism behind.[77]

Lifting the Conceptual Grid

Contemporary scholars are working hard to reverse these patterns. Categories of religious identity are being abandoned as useless and, indeed, harmful for understanding.[78] The words "Christian" and "Jewish" are inextricably tangled, both with each other and within themselves. Any search for origins will discover at the source, not a purity of identity categories but the moment of these categories' disappearance.[79] It is exemplary of every conceptual difference that turns to historical origins for its legitimation that in the beginning there *was* no difference. Conceptual clarity, lacking at the source, is subsequently imposed. This complicity between the construction of a concept and the concept's retroactive appropriation of past history is seldom the conscious focus of philosophers or historians. The event is supposed to be the birth point of the concept, the eruption of the new that breaks with the old, but that itself is a theological idea, perhaps the fundamental idea of Christianity, but also of course of messianic Judaism as well.

Boyarin summarizes: "There was no Jewish orthodoxy in the first century out of which Christianity 'grew' and from which it diverged and then parted."[80] Smith, referring to the practice of Jewish circumcision, remarks that "even with respect to this most fundamental division, we cannot sustain the impossible construct of a normative Judaism. We must conceive of a variety of early Judaisms, clustered in varying configurations."[81] Rather than distinguishing between Christian and Jewish identities, historical material questions their existence. The creative richness of first-century thought is the consequence of mixing, multiplicity, diaspora. Blurred edges, not binaries, are the marking of this moment. King's work on Gnosticism refutes the fundamental orientation of theologians like Adolf von

Harnack, who "located the essence of Christianity in the earliest and purest form of the teaching of Jesus" uncontaminated by Hellenic influences, but also broken off from Judaism.[82] Harnack perpetuated the Lutheran doctrine of *sola scriptura*, a reading of the Gospels as closest to Jesus and hence to truth; but historical research, tracing the textual translations and institutional mediations through which we have inherited these scriptures, has demonstrated repeatedly that the idea of scriptural permanence is an illusion.[83]

We speak today of reality as constructed by the discourses used to describe it. But we are vague about the logic of that claim, which often dwindles into descriptions of narrativity or rhetorical framing. By what right do we proceed in that fashion, when the philosophical goal is not to produce narratives, but to rescue truth? The consequences are serious, given the fact that the later boundary-markings between religions play historically into divisive convictions of "us" versus "them" that so predictably lead to the logic of enemy others, toward whom every barbarism is allowed. Might it not be argued that the truth in this moment of birth is not rupture, but precisely an interconnected constellation of elements? How can our tidying up of the fragments of the past proceed in a way that allows them to be grasped by the mind, without the ordering of conceptual exclusions? The first century bears witness that porosity in thought, before concepts atrophy as empty categories of exclusion in the mind, is precisely the historical condition that needs to be acknowledged—and more, revered—as the transitory moment of truth's appearance in history.[84] Perhaps only in historical concreteness can an image of the universal come into being, one that is blurred, cluttered, disappearing, and (like χώρα) difficult to catch. But this procedure would entail a different understanding of universality, not uniformity that excludes difference, but diversity that embraces it.

How does John of Patmos' Revelation fit into these considerations? Not only does he avoid the word "Christian" and leave us in the dark as to who is a Jew. Unlike the early Christian patriarchs intent on institution-building, he never uses the word heretic: "this term never occurs in John's book, nor, so far as we can tell, in his vocabulary."[85] Yet John is clearly and decisively opposed to those whom he sees as God's enemies. It is not false doctrine that John deplores, but false practice. To discover John's positioning within this expansive field of investigation, we will need to take a different tack.

Koine

The need to remain conscious that the meaning of *koine* is "common," not "Greek," is emblematic of the difficulties we have faced in this study. We have found consistency of terminology impossible. To learn Greek in the first century was not an exclusionary act, but a way of entering into the extent of the imperial world. It was the language of translation that allowed imperial communication to take place. The word "Greek" was understood then as precisely *koine*, a *common* language overflowing the boundaries of territory, people, and belief. The written sources available to us as texts or inscriptions, meant to be shared across localities, are today called *koine* to emphasize this fact, and to distinguish language, as the common use of Greek words and letters, from *ethne* as Greek populations.

To absorb the fact that *koine* provided entry by imperial Romans into the civilized world that extended from the eastern Mediterranean to the Nile, from the Red Sea to the Indian Ocean, from the Euphrates to the Indus—its trade, its literature, its accumulated knowledge—takes conscious effort.[86] The task is made difficult by the fact that scholarly interest in the first century has long been skewed toward Europe and the West, which at the time were on the margins of this common literacy. Well-established centers where the *spoken* language was *koine*—Alexandria (now in Egypt), Antioch (now in Syria), the province of Asia (now in Turkey)—were focal points in this network. In those cities, multiple ethnicities—including large numbers of prominent Jews—spoke the shared Greek of *koine* as their first and perhaps only language.[87] In these cosmopolitan centers, bilingual knowledge was not required, as it was, for example, in Latin-speaking Rome.[88]

Koine as a language is not an "eastern" or "oriental" phenomenon, but the centripetal force of a common, Hellenic world.[89] The confusions that revolve around this linguistic sharing are a consequence of clashing contemporary interests in the first-century sources. Concepts lap over this material from incompatible directions, producing crosscurrents that muddy the interpretation of the limited sources that remain. Their clarification demands scholarship that begins with the material, rather than the conceptual schema of historical appropriation. The linguist Gregory Horseley provides that corrective in his introductory chapter to recently discovered documents of the era, insisting, against disciplinary segregations, that both temporally and spatially, *koine* needs to be treated as a single phenomenon:[90] "It was *the* Greek language of the Hellenistic and early Roman periods."[91] *Koine* was the language of documents in foreign policy and imperial diplomacy from the Red Sea to the Black Sea, including Armenia, the Caucasus, Judaea, Nabataea, Arabia, and the Parthian East.[92] *Koine* was the language of trade; a *koinonos* (κοινωνός) was a trade or business partner. The changes in written *koine* that developed gradually after Alexander's conquests of indigenous peoples were manifested transregionally. The Second Sophistic writers' self-conscious deployment of atticisms that began in the first century (Flavius Josephus was one such writer)[93] was a reaction to the use of *koine* across the region in the same temporal moment.[94] Focusing on this "atticising reaction," classicists have been led to claim that only biblical Greek is *koine* ("common" in the sense of simpler, cruder)[95] and the rest is their own, "Hellenic" domain[96]—while Protestants have affirmed the singularity of New Testament Greek for positive reasons, indicating the specialness of Christian scripture.[97] Both arguments, writes Horseley, are based on "too narrow distinctions" that "are better regarded as representing different levels of linguistic behavior."[98] For example, it is evident that different genres of writing had different vocabularies—that of written letters would be different from official documents, demanding a "shift in stylistic tone"; however, scholarship that attempts to establish biblical Greek as a distinct dialect of *koine* repeatedly fails.[99] Horseley notes a specific attempt to designate John of Patmos' language, unique among New Testament books, as "ungreek," an argument that he finds "disquieting," based on a presumption of "Semitic influence" that "forgets the situation of the ancient reader," including the probability that *koine* was the *primary* language of Jews in Palestine.[100] "Jewish Greek," he writes, "is a ghost language. And like all ghosts, it needs to be laid to rest."[101]

The Names of Power

There is another point of interest, however, that concerns not the linguistic structure or tone of the book of Revelation, but rather the specific wording of the text and its resonance with the contemporary world. And here one finds an anomaly. Whereas the New Testament in general is strong in its references to the Old Testament (Septuagint), John's Revelation is more so than any other book—not in terms of direct quotations, but rather images, literary allusion, echoes of prophecies, ideological elements, and parallel themes. Beale and Carson write: "No other book of the N[ew] T[estament] is as permeated by the O[ld] T[estament] as Revelation," providing for John's book a depth and breadth of resonances with traditional scripture that legitimates his own prophetic text.[102] However, while the New Testament is influenced by the Septuagint's literary references, the latter's "actual influence on the *vocabulary* of the N[ew] T[estament] is small . . . less than is normally supposed."[103] And again, the text of John is exemplary, departing from both LXX and Hebrew scripture.[104] But if his vocabulary was not deeply indebted to the Septuagint—and if the Gospels were not yet ready at hand for his use—where did the nonscriptural words of John's revelation circulate? In what contemporary discourses did they appear?

Again, the evidence speaks to the necessity of lifting disciplinary boundaries that modernity has imposed on first-century experience. While Revelation's (Old Testament) images resonate as a protest against Hellenic visual culture, the words that name authority, divinity, and justice are taken directly from the language of Roman imperial power.[105] Striking when one reads across the texts without their being conventionally segregated (pagan versus Christian, secular versus religious, historical versus theological) is how the descriptive terms of Roman imperial power are *re*appropriated and claimed for the One God and his "son" in the text of John. When scholarship traces intertextual influence solely within the traditions of sacred scripture, this aspect, crucial for understanding, is lost.

"Savior" (Σότερ) was the title of praise for emperors whose civic beneficence eased the hardships of life. Rome ruled the Asian cities by the "grace" (χαρῆς) of the emperor who, beginning with Augustus, was

4.1

Flavian statue of enthroned Jupiter/Zeus, first century. The State Hermitage Museum, St. Petersburg. Photo by Andrew Bossi (CC BY-SA 2.0).

4.2

Enthroned emperor Augustus as Jupiter/Zeus, first century. The State Hermitage Museum, St. Petersburg. Photo by Pavel Demidov, Alexander Lavrentyev. Photograph © The State Hermitage Museum.

called even in Rome the "son of god" (*divi filius*/υἱὸς θεοῦ). The emperor's arrival into a city and return to Rome were the cause of loud acclaim and celebration (*adventus* in Latin; *parousia*/παρουσία in *koine*; the term is used to describe Jesus's second coming). The emperor's death, like that of Jesus, initiated his ascension into the heavens (apotheosis/ἀποθέωσις), brought there by the winged figure of victory, marking his eternal being as a god.[106] A cluster of words—honorific titles shared with the vocabulary of imperial power—appear in the first of John's visions of the Throne: "Almighty" (Παντοκράτωρ), "the Lord God" (κύριος ὁ θεός), and "son of god" (ὁ υἱὸς τοῦ θεοῦ).[107] Designations describe the one who comes from heaven, sitting on a throne (ἐπὶ τὸν θρόνον καθήμενος), accompanied not by weapons of war but by a lamb, looking as if slain, who alone is "worthy" (ἄξιος) of opening the seven seals of creation, and to whom praises are sung in continuous song by worshiping elders prostrate before them.[108] The eternity of God (ὁ ὢν)[109] and not the emperors is averred repeatedly, and the rule of "our lord and his anointed one" is promised for this world in hymnic verse.[110]

Interpreters have surmised that this throne scene was an actual description of early Christian (or Jewish) liturgy. But in a seminal essay of 1983, Aune proposed an imagery of negation: "John's description of the heavenly ceremonial practiced in the throne room of God bears such a striking resemblance to the ceremonial of the imperial court and cult that the latter can only be a parody of the former."[111] Cultic honors given to the emperor, then, are envisioned as a mockery of divine power.[112] And if so, John's visions combat the irreverent claim of a merely human being to embody, by the fact of earthly domination, the ideals of justice and mercy, and the right to sovereignty over all of creation. The Revelation of John provides a counter-cosmology. The language of imperial power is turned against itself in defiance of the hegemonic order of the world.[113]

And I saw on the right hand of the one sitting on the throne a scroll . . . sealed with seven seals. . . . And I saw a Lamb looking as if it had been slain, standing in the center of the throne, encircled by the four living creatures and the elders. . . . And the saints sang a new song. (Rev 5:1–9)

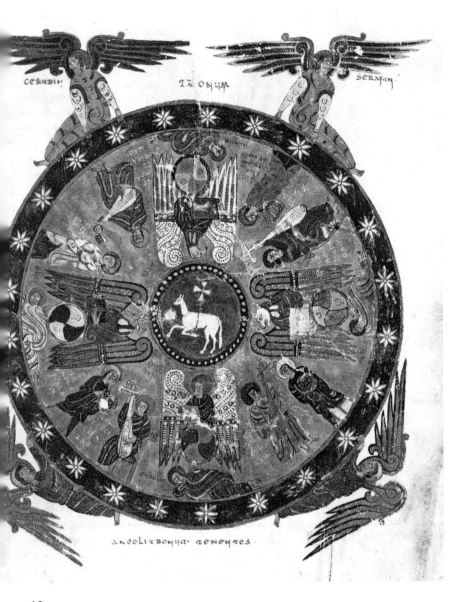

4.3
Worship of the Lamb within the harmonic ordering of the heavens. From the Morgan Beatus
(MS M.644), illustrated commentary on the book of Revelation, Andalus (Muslim Spain), ca.
945 CE. Vol. I, fol. 86v. Spain, San Salvador de Tábara. The Morgan Library & Museum.
The Morgan Beatus is one of 26 extant illustrated manuscripts of the *Commentary on the
Apocalypse* by the eighth-century Saint Beatus of Liébana, copied in Andalusan monasteries
over a period of several centuries.

4.4

Aureus of Augustus, 28 BCE. Gold coin, obverse: head of Octavian, showing the future emperor's head with the legend "imp. Caesar Divi f[ilus] cos. vi" (son of the deified Ceasar, 6th consulship); reverse: Octavian, seated on a throne and holding a scroll, and the legend "leges et iura R[es] P[ublica] restituit," signifying his restoration of public order. In contrast, the book of Revelation relates the moment of that order's destruction when "the sky receded like a scroll" and "the stars in the heaven fell to the earth," shaken [σειομένη] by the force of a cosmic wind (Rev 6:13). The British Museum, 1995,0401.1. © The Trustees of the British Museum. All rights reserved.

Emperor Cults

> I am tempted to describe apocalypticism as wisdom lacking a royal patron.
>
> —JONATHAN Z. SMITH[114]

We are back to the beginning, to our first chapter's discussion of the cult of the Roman emperors, and the fact that in the province of Asia the emperors were worshiped as gods during their lifetimes.[115] Emperor worship was practiced in the cities of all the "seven churches of Asia" to which John's letters were addressed.[116] Three of these had the status of *provincial* cults that required the permission of the emperor and the acceptance of other cities in the province for their establishment. Pergamon, as head of the province of Asia, was the first, initiating an imperial cult to Augustus and the goddess Roma in 29 BCE, the year that Octavian first took the name Augustus Caesar.[117] The Aegean port of Smyrna during the reign of Tiberius was the second, having successfully competed against Sardis for the honor.[118] Ephesus, increasingly the dominant seaport on the coast, established during the reign of Domitian a third provincial cult, dedicated to the *Sebastoi* (August Ones).[119] The other four cities addressed in John's letters, all of them inland, established local, municipal imperial cults on their own initiative.[120] The most important was Sardis, the ancient Lydian capital that had served as the western outpost of the Persian Empire, where a fragment of Augustus' *Res gestae* has recently been found.[121] The close-by city of Philadelphia that, with Sardis, was severely damaged by an earthquake in 17 CE, established an imperial cult in gratitude to Gaius Germanicus (Caligula) who aided in the rebuilding of both cities, motivating them temporarily to change their names to Caesareia and Neocaesareia.[122] Philadelphians claimed special kinship with the city of Ephesus and honored its cult to the *Sebastoi* established under Domitian.[123] Laodicea, at the intersection of north-south and east-west crossroads, was a wealthy commercial and banking city on the Lycus River thought to have been the city John addressed, but it was a second, "Phrygian" Laodicea further east that became a significant provincial cult to the emperor a century later.[124] Thyatira, a city of trade guilds on the road from Pergamon to Sardis, has

4.5

Cities in the province of Asia addressed by John in the book of Revelation

left us numismatic evidence of a municipal cult, indicating a priesthood and altar where sacrificial meals were prepared.[125]

These cults are now recognized as of central significance for the text of Revelation, although the mere fact of emperor worship was not unique to the cities John addressed.[126] By the end of the first century, municipal cults numbered close to one hundred in the province of Asia and more in neighboring Galatia, among them the temple to Augustus in Ancyra, inaugurated ca. 25 BCE, which (as we saw in chapter 1) inscribed on its wall after his death the entire text, in Latin and *koine*, of the *Res gestae divi Augusti*.[127]

Evidence of imperial cults has been found throughout the peninsula of Anatolia.[128] Municipal cults proliferated on the basis of local initiatives, while the provincial cults, reflecting the increased power of certain cities within the imperial context, were few in number, the cities acquiring the title *neo-koros*, literally, "temple protector," a word that originally referred to the officials from high-ranking families (women were among them) who supervised and financed the cult, but later was used as the prestigious name of the city itself.[129] Neokoros as title of an Asian city indicated the presence of a temple to the Roman emperor and his family that was recognized province-wide and linked, by grant of permission, directly to Rome.[130] Recent historians have provided evidence for the wide dispersal of emperor cults not only in the Hellenic world but in the western provinces and even Italy itself.[131] Their work is a challenge to the long-standing hermeneutic habit of western accounts that separate the west's own history from the taint of deifying human rulers: imperial worship in such accounts was seen as an "eastern" influence imposed on the inherently more rational mentality of the west.[132] Gradel protests: "this view, implicit in much of the scholarly literature, basically rests on the notion of such worship as an absurd blasphemy towards the one and true God," a Western-centric view that despite the professed secularism of modern scholarship is, writes Gradel, "patently Christianizing."[133]

What Were the Cults?

The book of Revelation clearly expresses opposition to Roman imperial power. And it just as clearly opposes the worship of false gods. The cults as a point of convergence would seem the obvious focus of condemnation. But understanding the nature of the book's protest requires distance. Emperor worship was not religion in the modern sense of the term. It was not supported by any metaphysical principle. It lacked the Protestant inflection of religion as a deeply held belief, relating to an inner realm separate from political life.[134] And it also lacked the subsequent, Christianized Roman Empire's form of politics as a theocratic imposition of power. The cults need to be understood, rather, as a practical discourse of life in the *polis*—in the words of Price, a "public cognitive system" that, through a multiplicity of communal practices, articulated relations between ruler and ruled.[135] As Friesen writes: "If we ask whether imperial cults envisioned a divine or human emperor, we have already framed the question inappropriately"; rather than "questions of ontological status," the "crucial issue was the role of imperial authority in creating the kind of society which pleased the gods."[136] Price, whose anthropological approach to the emperor cults has been determining for recent research, states clearly: "To follow the conventional distinction between religion and politics privileges the view of [a modern] observer over that of the Greeks and makes it impossible to understand the dynamics of the imperial cult."[137] Imperial critique, not theological speculation, was expressed in the book of Revelation, and if we impose upon the first century the modern dichotomy of concepts, religion versus politics, we will miss this fact completely.

Emperor worship was the idiom of public practices that affirmed local hierarchies of power. Unique in the province of Asia was not their existence but the degree to which these practices grew to dominate collective life in the *poleis*, so that refusing to participate in the imperial cults meant not just "religious" isolation, but exclusion from the practices of power and public recognition. Gallusz writes: "The influence of the imperial cults was all-permeating. Nothing was left untouched, because they were deeply connected with public religion, entertainment, commerce, governance, architecture, household worship and other aspects of everyday public and private life."[138] The cults provided the occasion for the performance of civic practices, including sacrifices, hymnic singing, processions, and athletic games, engaging all of the city's inhabitants.[139] And they connected local communities to a whole calendar of festivals that were celebrated province-wide.[140] The temporal rhythms of civic life were regulated by these festivals, superimposed on celebrations of a city's patron goddess whose worship accompanied that of the imperial family, the "August Ones" (*Sebastoi*). The calendar of festivals marked the measurement of time as *chronos* (χρόνος)—"chronic" in the sense of the predictable repetition of monthly and annual events, expressing the imperial acclaim of attunement with the divine order of the constellations, equinoxes, signs of the zodiac, and seasonal cycles from planting to harvests. Participation in the cultic practices was not required. No coercion was involved. But one could not be part of civic life without it.

Imperial Cosmology

In the province of Asia, ca. 9 BCE Augustus was celebrated for founding a new world order, a temporal event with cosmological significance.[141] The provincial council in Pergamon offered a crown as prize to whoever could propose the highest honors for the emperor, son of God (*divi filius*). The winning proposal, by the Roman proconsul Paullus Fabius Maximus, was that the entire province honor "the birthday of the most divine Caesar," giving these reasons:

> We could justly consider that day to be equal to the beginning of all things [τῶν πάντων ἀρχῆι ἴσην]. He restored the form of all things to usefulness, if not to their natural state, since it had deteriorated and suffered misfortune. He gave a new appearance [σχῆμα] to the whole world, which would gladly have accepted its own destruction had Caesar not been born for the common good fortune of all. Thus a person could justly consider this to be the beginning of life and of existence [αρήν τοῦ βίον και τῆς ζωῆς], and the end of regrets about having been born.[142]

The timing of the proposal coincided with the implementation of Augustus' refined solar calendar, developed by his adoptive father Julius Caesar (based on an Egyptian prototype), that insured unprecedented accuracy in connecting events between heaven and earth.[143] The fact that Augustus' birth date, September 23—"the ninth day before the Kalends of October"[144]—coincided with the fall equinox (when day and night times are in harmonious balance) was a convergence in time considered not by chance, but "clearly . . . according to some divine counsel."[145] The date was to be celebrated as the start of a new era of peace and prosperity, conflating two meanings of *arche*: beginning and rule. If the local calendars of the *poleis* differed in their schedules of other festival celebrations, the equinox provided the organizing principle on which all municipal officeholders would begin their terms.[146] Augustus' birth date would then be "the one, uniform New Year's day for all the polities"; the new decree in honor of Augustus, "encompassing all his virtues," was to be inscribed on a stele and set up in Pergamon's temple to Augustus and the goddess Roma, "so that the action devised by us for the honor of Augustus should endure forever [μείνη αἰώνιον]."[147]

Emperors never visited the Asian cities in the first century as living rulers.[148] Yet as divine figure, the emperor was inserted within cosmological systems and interlaced within preexisting structures of power. This province had a unique characteristic. Unlike neighboring Galatia which had been settled by invading Celts, and unlike other, conquered *ethne* that were depicted in local art, the cities of Asia drew on Greek mythology to claim common ancestry not only with each other, but with Rome as well.[149] Within the imperial context, the Asian cities appealed to the narrative of the Trojan War to established a special relationship with the Roman emperors. For it was Aeneas, son of the goddess Aphrodite and kin to Trojan royalty, who was said to have fled from the Asian city of Troy (near Pergamon) to settle on the Italian peninsula and become the ancestor of Remus and Romulus, mythic founders of Rome. The advantages of this narrative were reciprocal: Augustus used this Hellenic heritage as a means for his own imperial legitimation.[150]

Koinon

A shared ancestry had already produced a unique governing form in the cities of the province of Asia. They were associated with one another as a league, a relationship that, both before and after the coming of the Romans, had the name *koinon* (κοινόν)—a word the root of which, of course, was shared with the "common" language spoken. Through this word, local history entered the book of Revelation.

Some historical background is necessary. While the Trojan War, if it indeed took place, is dated ca. 1200 BCE, the Asian cities traced their settlement to Greek colonists after the Persian wars (fifth century BCE), who came from Athens perhaps, and/or islands of the Aegean.[151] The settlers were named in the ancient sources the Ionians.[152] Recent archaeology provides evidence of trade as the activity that connected these cities.[153]

4.6

Relief from the Sebasteion at Aphrodisias, first century CE, depicting Aeneas' flight with his son from the sack of Troy (now Hisarlik, Turkey), carrying his father Anchises of the royal Trojan family, who holds a box containing images of Troy's ancestral gods. The legendary Aeneas and his group of immigrants from the area, refugees of the Trojan war, resettled in Italy to become the progenitors of Rome, as described in Vergil's poem the *Aeneid* (29–19 BCE) that elaborates Homer's original mytho-historical account in the *Iliad*. The female figure floating behind and helping them escape is Aphrodite, Aeneas' mother and patron goddess of the city of Aphrodisias (now Geyre, Turkey). This relief is a panel from the Sebasteion discovered in that city. Missing in this depiction of three generations of men is Aeneas' wife, who is described by Vergil as perishing during the escape. See *Aphrodisias Sebasteion* [*Sevgi Gönül Hall*], ed. Mesut Ilgim (Ankara: Yari Kredi Yayınları, 2008). New York University Excavations at Aphrodisias (G. Petruccioli).

Peace was a prerequisite for the safety of traders—protection from piracy in the Mediterranean and from land troops invading from the east. The Ionian *koinon* evolved as an alliance of cities that preserved the "common peace," not only against outside threats but among the cities themselves. This form of federation entailed acquiescing to rule by a larger power or king, a practice of submission that paradoxically guaranteed the cities' "autonomy" and "freedom," due to the protection of a vastly superior power.[154] Figures of Olympian gods and mythic heroes were shared in the settlements' foundational narratives, providing a common Hellenic culture that was reconfigured according to the requirements of contemporary imperial rule.[155]

Burrell writes of this *koinon* at the time of its imperial incorporation: "Though the name translates as 'league' or 'commonality' [or even 'commonwealth'], it was not a subset of official imperial administration, nor did its geographic lines have to correspond exactly to the borders of a Roman province."[156] However, because of the way the cities were bequeathed to Rome, the names *koinon* and province were interchangeable. The territorial continuity between pre- and postimperial Asia was a consequence of the fact that the Attalid king of Pergamon (Attalos III) willed his status as ruler to Rome in 133 BCE when he died without heirs, as a way of keeping the *koinon* from falling into civil war. This bequeathal was in a sense a return, as it was the Romans who first granted the lands to the then-reigning Attalid king, Eumenes II, by the treaty of Apemea (188 BCE), marking the Roman Republic's defeat of the Selucid Empire.[157] Eumenes II ruled this greatly enlarged territory of cities as their "common benefactor" (*koinos euergetes*) relying on local elites, to whom he passed on the agriculturally rich royal lands, while financing building projects (including a library of ca. 200,000 volumes)[158] and dispensing grain in times of famine.[159] Eumenes II earned with these practices the title of "savior" and even "god."[160] It was he who built the famous altar of Zeus in Pergamon that, along with the later temple to the goddess Roma and god Augustus, earned from John a very different title for this city: the place where the "throne of Satan" dwells.[161]

In the Asian *koinon*, imperial iconography saturated public space. "Everywhere he looked, John would have found inscriptions, statues, temples depicting the triumphs of the Roman gods," i.e., the military victories of living emperors.[162] The emperor cults were insinuated fully within the local vernacular of power and its legitimacy. The paradoxical outcome was that incorporation into the larger imperial power of Rome, which continued the Attalid precedent of light taxation, did not weaken local elites but strengthened their dominance. Divine honors bestowed upon the absent emperor provided validity for existing social hierarchies, while incorporation into imperial trade increased opportunities for accumulation of private wealth. The emperors' portraits were stamped on coins, communicating the connections of imperial power with every act of monetary exchange. Over 300 *poleis* of Anatolia issued their own coins, many picturing particular emperors and the local temples in their honor.[163] In the iconography of the coinage, there was a merging of living emperors and the pantheon of gods, temples and crowns, history and myth.

Aphrodisias

Archaeological evidence is brilliantly revealing. A remarkable find in 1979 of the ruins of Aphrodisias has been excavated to reveal an entire first-century city developed by Roman veterans of war, located southwest of Laodicea at Lycus in the province of Asia.[164] Among the constructions unearthed is an almost intact complex of temple and agora, framed by a three-story-high portico structure that is covered with sculpted reliefs. Known as the Sebasteion, it was the site of a municipal imperial cult where sacrifices to the reigning emperor were carried out, oaths of loyalty to the emperor were made annually, and ceremonies honored the emperor with songs of praise. The Sebasteion, constructed by local elites and making use of local marble and skilled craftsmen, makes visible not only the physical space of a municipal cult—merging marketplace (agora) and divine worship (temple)—but also its cosmology of imperial legitimation. We can presume affinities between our seven cities and Aphrodisias, which in addition to its municipal cult contributed directly to the *neokoros* cult of Ephesus as well.[165]

The sculpted reliefs on the architectural façades of the Sebasteion depict the Julio-Claudian imperial family (Augustus to Nero) juxtaposed

4.7

The Sebasteion at Aphrodisias before reconstruction. Unlike the imperial forum in Rome, in many ways its prototype, the structure had commercial shops rather than administrative offices on the bottom level. The plaza was narrower, the flanking porticoes three (rather than the usual two) stories high. Photo by Mesut Ilgum.

with the gods, taking advantage of the parallel Greek and Roman pantheons in order to articulate local religious traditions and myths within the new political situation.[166] In surviving reliefs, emperors appear visually indistinguishable from the gods. They are nude and monumental in size, "treated in strikingly elevated, Hellenic manner, designed to present them as part of a new enlarged Olympian pantheon."[167] The figures include Apollo, Demeter, Bellerophon and Pegasus, Heracles, Centaurs and Lapeths, the Muses—as Smith writes, "an international *koinē* of myth, with accompanying images in the arts, that was part of the basic cultural minimum for educated Greeks and Romans under the empire . . . to invoke, through

4.8
Sebasteion, Aphrodisias. Photo by Carlos Delgado (Wikimedia Commons, CC BY 3.0).

a series of its familiar and authorized images, the world of Greek culture and religion, into which the Roman emperors are to be incorporated in the upper storey."[168] The parallels in iconography are unmistakable (images 4.9 and 4.10). The relief of the god Okeanos, ruler over oceans, is visually linked to a relief of the emperor who as active agent claims mastery over land and sea.[169]

This, then, was the world as experienced in the cities that John addressed. Through the integration of emperors and myth, the permanence of empire was etched in stone, and the difference between historically specific events and the eternal realm of myth was obliterated. Divine permanence was bestowed upon the imperial order at the same time as local power was enhanced and loyalty to the system ensured. That the Roman emperor, like the kings before him, ruled a *koinon* of provincial cities by protecting their "freedom" (*eleutheria*) not only from outside forces but from each other,

4.9
Sebasteion relief sculpture of the god Okeanos (Ocean), North Building, inv. 1980-93, 1980-120. The relief would have been paired with Earth, and together they represent worldwide empire without end. New York University Excavations at Aphrodisias (G. Petruccioli).

that the ceremonial practices of submission to imperial power secured each city's "self-rule" (*autonomia*), while binding them together province-wide through emperor worship which worked to strengthen, not weaken, the power of local elites[170]—these descriptions provide further caution against anachronistic appropriations, reminding us that to misread these terms through their modern political meanings is as obfuscating as naming the emperor cults a religion that worshiped humans, literally, as divine.

But it also draws our attention to the appearance of a word in the book of Revelation that otherwise is easily overlooked. In John's final vision of the divine city, the new Jerusalem promised to the worshipers of both the Lamb and "the one who sits on the throne," the command is given clearly: "nothing *koinon* will ever enter it."[171] The English rendering of this word hides its root meaning. The standard translation of *koinon* in Revelation 21:27 is "impure" or "sinful," which can only be based on inference. There are words in the book of Revelation that merit translation as "sin."[172] However, *koinon* is not one of them.[173] The inference of interpretation would appear to be based on the text's immediate reference to those who do "shameful or deceitful" things. But by eliding the specific meaning of *koinon*, the translation identifies sinners as an abstract category, obscuring the local realities to which such judgments applied. Revelation states specifically: "the dead were judged according to what they had done"—their works (ἔργα), that is, the way they lived their lives, not their identity.[174] Nonetheless, identities are brought into interpretations of *koinon*. The inference "impure" is preferred by those who connect John's text to Judaic law, under the assumption that Jews deemed not "halakhically pure enough" are forbidden to enter John's new Jerusalem.[175] This connection would seem plausible if the practices of purity implied in this case were taken to mean "Jewish identity markers as we know them from elsewhere": *Shabbat* (maintaining the Sabbath), *kashrut* (dietary laws), and circumcision; however, none of these are mentioned explicitly in Revelation.[176] The alternate translation, "sinful," loads the word *koinon* with a millennium of later meanings that became possible only after earthly power adopted Christian discourse as its own, allotting entry into the heavenly city to those who, out of fear of eternal damnation, were required to obey Christian

4.10
Sebasteion relief of Claudius, who strides over land and sea. On the right, a female figure with fish scale skirt hands him a co-steering oar. The left figure reaches to him a cornucopia with the fruits of the earth. South Building, inv. 1979-108. New York University Excavations at Aphrodisias (G. Petruccioli).

authority and adhere to Church orthodoxy, which promised salvational happiness after death so that John's Revelation became synonymous with Judgment Day and resurrection from the dead as prophecy's last and final word.[177]

With the Protestant rejection of Papal authority in the sixteenth century, "sinfulness" came to refer to the corrupt practices of the priests of Christianity itself. Martin Luther read his own times, in which Islamic Turks threatened Europe, as a sign of the last days. He wrote in *Table Talk*: "Antichrist is the pope and the Turk together; a beast full of life must have a body and soul; the spirit or soul of antichrist is the pope, his flesh or body the Turk."[178] The Protestant Reformation's reading of one of Revelation's most powerful images, the whore of Babylon who rides the seven-headed beast of Rome and basks in the sensuality and luxury of worldly wealth and excess, is a mnemonic device that encapsulates the Protestant conception of evilness and sin.

But if we read the term in a *wordly* way, that is, if we pay attention to the first-century historical object that it names, then *koinon* describes the entirety of civic life as it was lived in the cities that John addresses. By rejecting the structural arrangement of power's legitimation in the province, John's revelation challenges profoundly the legitimation of earthly rule. There appears in his text a different image, with striking analogies to the imperial ones we have considered above, that becomes legible as a radical critique of the legitimating function of the imperial cults of the first century:

> Then I saw another mighty angel coming down from heaven. He was robed in a cloud, with a rainbow above his head; his face was like the sun and his legs were like fiery pillars. He was holding a little scroll that lay open in his hand. He planted his right foot on the sea and his left foot on the land, and he gave a loud shout like the roar of a lion. When he shouted, the voices of the seven thunders spoke. . . . Then the angel I had seen standing on the sea and on the land raised his right hand to heaven. And he swore [ὤμοσεν] by the one living for ever and ever [τοὺς αἰῶνας τῶν αἰώνων], who created the heavens and all that is in them, and the earth and all that is in it, and the sea and all that is in it, that there shall be time [*chronos*/χρόνος] no longer.[179]

Not the mere fact of the emperor worship was blasphemous. Paul had, after all, acquiesced to living alongside the Roman order—as had both Josephus and Philo.[180] Rather, the all-embracing function of imperial practices in the *koinon* of Asia was the impetus for John's counter-cosmology. The staging and performance of imperial power defined the whole of public space and daily life, collapsing any meaningful distinction between sacred and profane and with that the very idea of critical differentiation.[181] The philosophical radicality of John's counter-cosmological revelation is its rejection of the imperial order's rituals of time (*chronos*) as the calendar of civic life. It rejects the hymns in praise of the emperor and sings a "new song" (Rev 5:9). It envisions a new place—a realm of transcendence that cannot be appropriated by earthly rulers. To "swear by the one living for ever and ever," as the angel does in Revelation 10:6, is to echo the loyalty oath owed to the emperor while diverting its addressee.[182] John's visions attest to the idea that the world we see is not all there is, that appearance and reality are not identical. Such a line of demarcation is drawn not between religion and politics, or between Christian and Jew. It is a line between the existing world and truth. Today we would call John's message a political protest—and of course, in the *wordly* meaning of the term *polis*, it was. But this was not simply a partisan polemic against other "religions" in order to favor *his* god over others. Rather it was a sustained critique, tied tightly to the historical specifics of his world, envisioning that world in a radically altered way—without the sheltering protection of patronage by power.

The Traps of Translation

This chapter has followed several ways that religion has functioned to divide human beings: Jew versus Christian, heretic versus true believer, and finally sinner versus saved. We have persistently argued that the wordliness of the text provides a salutary countereffect when it draws us into the past and away from our own presuppositions, thereby demanding of us a different register of hermeneutic responsibility. Philological scrupulousness is not a mere ornament. It resists the current of later appropriations, not in the name of a purer meaning (*sola scriptura*), but in the name of the nonidentity with the continuum of history to which transcendent discourse has repeatedly given voice. We have viewed words that appear in the texts as philological passageways into the past, providing insights fruitful to philosophers who turn to history for inspiration, and who approach the transcendent fully aware of the dangers of falling victim to the exclusionary identities to which religious readings are vulnerable. We will close this chapter with one more example of the traps of translation that attentiveness to the wordliness of John's text reveals.

Doulos

"Slave of God," John calls himself in the opening verses of the book of Revelation. He belongs to no earthly master. The word in *koine* for slave is *doulos*/δοῦλος. It is repeated multiple times in John's text (and is a common word also in Paul's discourse).[183] In early modern Europe, in vernacular translations of the Bible, the word *doulos* received a whitewashing. The word "slave" was rejected by translators, and "servant" was substituted instead. In the canonical King James version of the Bible (1604–1611 CE) *doulos* was translated as "servant" in all cases of its appearance (e.g., Paul: "servants, obey your earthly masters . . .").[184] The word "servant," never "slave," appears not only when John (or Paul) names himself in particular, or Christians in general, but also when *doulos* is contrasted with "free man" (*eleutheros*). Martin Luther's German vernacular translation (1522 CE) has a similar substitution: every time *doulos* appears, whether in the Old Testament or New, the word *Knecht* (servant) rather than *Sklav* (slave) appears. Slaves, of course, were very much present in the discourse and reality of early modern Europe, so that the avoidance of this term had the effect of excluding actually existing slaves from biblical address. This is despite the fact that in Hebrew scripture (*'ebed*), Septuagint Greek (*doulos*), and Vulgate Latin (*servus*), this exegetical differentiation does not exist.[185] All of these words mean slave. When nineteenth-century German philological expertise made it clear that *doulos* was indeed the ancient word for slavery, the finding caused embarrassment for Protestants uncomfortable with acknowledging the Gospels' acquiescence to slavery. Those who claimed the benefit of this philological correction were the slaveholders of the American South, who were keen to read the biblical passages of Paul as saying "slaves, be obedient to your masters."[186]

Modernity produced another exclusion in biblical meaning, precisely by its reading of *doulos* in a positive light as "servants." The book of the Jewish prophet Isaiah in the Septuagint uses the term *doulos* to speak of Jews as the chosen people of God who receives their loyalty and obedience despite the trials and tribulations they endure. This Old Testament text becomes crucial for the argument of Protestants that they have taken over this role. For them, Isaiah's prophecy refers to the later coming of Christ; it is he who was "despised and rejected" (Isaiah 53:3), not the Jews who, with anti-Semitic impact, are read as having *done* the despising when they crucified the Messiah allegedly prophesied by Isaiah.[187] The anachronistic distortions of Protestantism were made possible by the claim that the clear and correct interpretation of Scripture evolved progressively through time, from Jews to Roman Catholics to Protestants, and was predictive of present-day events. By reading Isaiah as historically prophetic, Protestants—specifically in the new Dutch Republic[188]—could speak of their nation as Zion, and the country of Holland as the "new Jerusalem."[189] A double exclusion was thereby codified in vernacular translations: one explicitly against Jews (and Muslims)[190] insofar as Protestants, historically most recent, claimed a monopoly of the status as God's privileged, and the other an indirect implication that discussions of African slaves referred to a distinctly different phenomenon.[191] In the early days of European nationalism, then, just as in the early of the institutional Church that, as we have seen, produced a discourse of heretical outsiders, the universality of Christianity was articulated through exclusionary acts of identification.[192]

Translation and Transcendence

John's text contains the transitory historical reality that surrounds him. In maintaining its temporal authority despite the ephemeral times and places in which the text has been deployed, acquired meanings have twisted its interpretation into the contradiction that exclusion is the path to universality. Indeed, any text that claims to speak of transcendence is vulnerable to such distortions over time. Hence the philosophical problem: when speaking of transcendent and eternal things, words must struggle to remain true against the grain of the changing realities they name. And history writing, rather than appropriating truth as history's own unfolding, must acknowledge its inherent and inevitable limitations in this light. But if we insist on translating in a *wordly* way, exposing the history that has been absorbed within the text, if we resist the temptation to impose specifically "Jewish" or "Christian" standards of evaluation, or to allow vernacular translation strategies of early modern Europe to exploit its transitory meanings, the philosophical effect can be one of epistemological liberation from the exclusionary identities that claim us.

5 CONSTELLATIONS

This last chapter avoids a conventional conclusion. The book's whole purpose has been to speak across communities and discourses of understanding by opening up connections that have not previously been recognized, rather than to replace one schematic understanding with another. To those in the habit of discovering at the close of a book a quick way to comprehend the contents as a whole, I apologize for the inconvenience. But it is the mimetic experience of reading itself that has been emphasized, and disorientation is not the least of its salutary effects.

The construction of constellations, a method already at work in the previous chapters, is continued in this final chapter. It consists of four sections containing arrangements of material that shift the center of gravity toward the present. Again, John's text provides a focus. Compared with the works of Philo and Josephus, the book of Revelation presents the most difficult challenge for a philosophical reading. Its superabundance of images, monstrous forms, shifting geographies, and dreamlike juxtapositions creates a visual landscape that resists the logic of words. Yet this is the text that seems to matter. Strands of organized religion within all of the three Abrahamic monotheisms believe in the prophetic power of sacred texts. The book of Revelation continues to be read by millions as eschatological signs operating in our time. Within the secular public sphere, the word "apocalypse" circulates with a persistence the intensity of which seems to increase in inverse relation to an actual belief in religious prophecy. The present global pandemic has been drawn into its discursive frame. Contemporary culture is replete with visions of physical annihilation. The discourse of the Anthropocene as a historical era of limited duration due to global warming and environmental degradation is pervasive within scientific as well as religious anticipations. These concerns are justified, the dangers are real, but dwelling on their catastrophic potential, whether religiously or scientifically defined, can be paralyzing if the historical trajectory is granted all-powerful agency above the heads of us, merely human beings whose actions have played a seminal role in bringing these conditions about.

This chapter elaborates connections between past and present moments that a history freed of conventional ordering allows. The word "constellation" is to be taken literally. It is a method that draws lines of connection among disparate historical fragments so that an image becomes visible that can be recognized as our own concern. As trial arrangements, constellations do not start by knowing the epistemological frames or categories that are needed to construct them. They are open to the movement of their parts, overlapping connections and additions from elsewhere. The particularities of John's visions are fragments that already float, unanchored, in cultures of modernity that have been affected by Christianity and/or the West. Metaphorical staples to some, they are vaguely familiar to others. These "some" and these "others," speaking on different platforms of enunciation, have often lost trust with one another. The lines of connection that are drawn here aim for legibility across perspectival divides.

As historical images constructed out of the particulars of past and present, constellations have the goal of making visible a different angle of vision from which to approach philosophical questions raised by them. The philosophical reflections they contain are not theology. But they do go beyond empirical description and, as reorientations of thought, aim to shift the axis slightly, perhaps just enough to alter present consciousness by means of energy generated across the expanse of time between then and now.

I. HISTORICAL PARTICULARITY AND PHILOSOPHICAL UNIVERSALITY

Particularity of Time

Translating from our own, arbitrary and abstract sign for the time when the book of Revelation was composed, 96 CE, historians consider it more remarkable for what was *not* occurring than for what was: "Under Domitian, the provinces flourished."[1] There is no record of religious persecution in the province of Asia or elsewhere at the time.[2]

Although it is now clear that executions of Domitian's personal, political enemies increased late in his reign that ended with his assassination in 96 CE, "there is no support for a systematic campaign against Christians in Rome or elsewhere."[3] Moreover, there is no need to distinguish between "Christians" and "Jews" in this regard—any more than does John's text that (as we have noted) sets up no binary schema based on these categories. If the former were not persecuted during Domitian's reign, the latter were not excluded from civic life.[4] Defeat of the rebels in the Judaean War did not change the situation for Jews elsewhere.[5] Important synagogues existed in the Asian cities specifically, and the rights of Jews to their religious practices were protected as part of the imperial definition of freedom. Religious identity does not explain the fact that John's condemnation of the worldly order of imperial Rome was categorical.[6]

Here again is a case where the superimposition of modern conceptualizations has obfuscated our understanding. In nineteenth-century Europe, the phrase, "the Jewish Question," described an existing incompatibility between "religious" and "political" identities, as a consequence of which practicing Jews were socially segregated and without equal political rights. But in the first century CE, such civic structuring does not seem to have been the case. It is now considered most likely that throughout the eastern Mediterranean, Jews were citizens of *poleis* in which many had resided for generations, with equal rights *as well as* imperial protections of their separate communal practices. Their status was protected before the coming of the Romans, and was not altered by it.[7]

Just as in the case of Nero's persecution of Christians in the city of Rome in 64 CE, the recorded cases of violence against Jews within "Greek" cities have received great attention.[8] There is no doubt that multiple, serious instances occurred.[9] The case of Flaccus, the Roman official who interfered with the rights of Jews in Alexandria in 38 CE, and recorded in Philo's brief *In Flaccum*, is a famous instance, an event that included mob violence against Jews.[10] Significantly, however, this event is described in the extant sources as *stasis*, that is, *civil war*, which, as we have seen throughout our discussion of Josephus' *Judaean War*, presumes the unity of a population that is temporarily undermined by conflict *among* citizens, rather than by an alien presence within it.[11]

Jewish identity in the first century remains a focus of controversy among historians.[12] We have skirted its centrality with the same care that has led us to mute the most vociferous voices claiming ownership of the whole conception of Year 1, based on the life and teachings of Jesus as the Anointed One (Greek: *Xristos*/Hebrew: *Mashiah*), that is: Christians of today. Instead, the whole thrust of our analysis has been to resist preoccupations with present identitarian concerns, in order to listen to the texts otherwise. We have insisted that only an anachronistic reading would judge this choice as perverse, and that such anachronisms do violence not only to the material remains of the past, but also to the potential for understanding in and of our own time. So much of the most recent research has worked diligently to liberate us from the constraints of exclusionary ownership of history that it would seem not only ungrateful but unconscionable to refuse the new freedom that such scholarship now allows.

Recently scholars have proposed that it was the relative privileging of Jews that caused resentment among fellow-citizens, leading to protests and even violence against them.[13] While Jews were not required to worship the gods or join the cults, the latter were expensive to maintain so that, as Ritter writes regarding the province of Asia, given the centrality of the emperor cults within the shared life of the *polis* and, moreover, given the considerable costs involved in the festivals to the local gods that included the divinized emperors, it is not surprising that others complained that since they were "kin" (συγγενεῖς), at the very least Jews should "offer financial support for the public service of their gods."[14] Surely, the inducement to join in public cults would have been enormous, as it was the medium for any expression of civic pride, power, and generosity. Ritter leaves the question open as to "how those prominent enough to hold public office could balance their citizenship status with the Jews' need to refrain from the sacrifices (whether taking part or offering them) and priestly offices, which were a staple of the life of a citizen."[15] But if we reject ordering John's message under the category of religious identity, and if assimilation, not segregation, was the problem, then the unique radicality of John's text reflects how his experience at the end of the century contrasted generationally with other earlier figures we have considered.

Universality of Address

He who has an ear, let him hear . . . ['Ο ἔχων οὖς ἀκουσάτω . . .][16]
He who has an ear, let him hear, what the Spirit says to the assemblies [ἐκκλησίας]. (Rev 2:7)
He who has an ear, let him hear what the Spirit says to the assemblies; To the one who overcomes [νικῶντι] I will give to eat from the tree of life, which is in the paradise of God. (Rev 2:7)
He who has an ear, let him hear what the Spirit says to the assemblies. (Rev 2:29)
Behold, I stand at the door, and knock: if anyone hears my voice, and opens the door, I will go in to him, and will eat with them, and he with me. (Rev 3:20)
He who has an ear, let him hear what the Spirit says to the assemblies. (Rev 3:22)
He who has an ear, let him hear. (Rev 13:9)

There is a tendency among modern interpreters of Revelation to reduce John's message to a very local scale in which he is seen as competing with other prophets in the area.[17] Pagels is specific: "John knew that he was competing with *other* prophets, and was angry that some of his hearers were also listening to them and heeding their messages";[18] they were "probably" like him, "travelling prophets," which, she has argued, likely included followers of Paul.[19]

Interpreting John as a provincial figure diminishes his theological significance, which would be a welcome outcome for many readers of the text who find its themes of divine punishment, earthly suffering, and violent death distasteful. But if it leads us to impose upon the first century a neoliberal eternity of competition within a marketplace of ideas, then the frame of competing prophets is clearly anachronistic. Again, attention is required to the gap between past meanings and our own. The surviving sources do reveal, precisely in the province of Asia, an extended discourse about competitive practices, but it was commonly concerned with rivalry among cities rather than between individuals whose victories brought glory to them.[20] Burrell provides critical clarity: "the terms of discussion in documents and speeches of the Roman East in the first three centuries C.E. do not translate happily into modern English terms; Western culture has a much more ambivalent attitude toward competition. Where the documents speak of *philotimia*, 'love of honor,' we often translate 'rivalry.'"[21] Instead, honorable practices, rather than the mere fact of winning, were deemed as deserving the title "first."[22] Competition was for recognition that translated into status and prestige.[23] Cities accumulated multiple titles and minted coins of recognition, establishing a hierarchic "web" within the *koinon*.[24]

Here we may note the special role of the hymnodes, male choruses dedicated to the praise of the emperor that evolved in the first century as an institution of provincial power. Music has been a focus of our study, and emperor worship was deeply engaged in its performance. The hymnodes were of cultic importance as a regular practice of worship, honoring the emperor in song.[25] Friesen explains that they "began as a network of choirs from all Asia that gathered to sing the praises of Augustus at the provincial temple in Pergamon. Their duties apparently expanded as new emperors took the throne, new festivals arose, and more travel was necessary."[26] These choruses made regular trips to the provincial capital of Pergamon timed in accordance with the festival calendar to participate in the imperial cult rituals, establishing relationships with each other that enhanced their function as a province-wide network of elites.[27] Writes Friesen, the word "hymnode" should not mislead us: "[T]he men were involved in other activities as well. . . . The inclusion of sons and grandsons also gave the group a trans-generational character and a socialization function, frequent meetings no doubt encouraging business and economic collaboration."[28] The evidence indicates that the choruses increasingly funded themselves, paying membership fees, hosting banquets, and making municipal donations that enhanced their public status. "The hymnodes of the god Augustus and the goddess Rome were a wealthy, elite group of 35–40 men who engaged in religious practices together. Their regulations show no signs of direct control by the city or the koinon."[29] The honors they received from the cities included loaves of bread, wine, and crowns as "probably part of the choir's costume."[30] The cult music has not survived, but musical harmonies, as we have seen, celebrated the unity of the cosmos.[31] The ritual practices themselves participated in the ordering of the world. If indeed pecuniary advantages accrued to leading cities, the primary motive of competition was honor.[32]

John's visions speak to this koinic world and shift its ground. The repeated hymns in the book of Revelation honor the one God who is patron deity of a "holy city," the new Jerusalem that is seen "coming down out of heaven from God."[33] Its beauty outshines all others; no earthly city can compete. The construction is not marble or granite but precious stones.[34] Hymnic song provides continuous praise to the invisible "one" who sits on the throne, and only the vulnerable lamb who joins him there is judged "worthy" (ἄξιος) to open the seven seals of God's creation.[35] Musical instruments—kitharas (κιθάραι), stringed instruments resembling lyres but commonly translated as "harp"[36]—play in accompaniment.[37] And the elders who sing as God's hymnodes bow down before the throne and cast their golden crowns before it.[38] In a loud voice they sing:[39]

"Holy, holy, holy
is the Lord God Almighty,
who was, and is, and is to come." (Rev 4:8)

"For you created all things
and by your will they existed and were created." (Rev 4:11)

"Worthy is the Lamb, who was slain,
to receive power and wealth and wisdom and strength
and honor and glory and praise!" (Rev 5:12)

5.1

Illustration from Beatus of Liébana, commentary on John's book of Revelation, Andalus (Spain), tenth century CE. (Biblioteca de Serafín Estébanez Calderón y de San Millán de la Cogolla.) Depicted are "those who had been victorious over the beast and his image and over the number of his name": "They held harps [κιθάραι] given them by God and sang the song of Moses, the servant [δοῦλος] of God, and the song of the Lamb. . . . 'For you alone are holy. All nations will come and worship before you'" (Rev 15: 2-4).

The hymns continue until the worshipers comprise "a great multitude that no one could count"; "wearing white robes and . . . holding palm branches in their hands," the symbol of victory, they stand before the throne and the lamb "from every nation and tribe and people and language."[40] And the heavens respond to their songs with thunder, flashes of lightning, earthquakes, and the shaking of the cosmos.

John tells us multiple times that he is speaking to anyone who can hear him. This is the Pauline inclusiveness to which Aune refers.[41] His last message is an open invitation: all are invited to enter the city and drink from the fountain of the water of life.[42] Its gates of pearl are never shut: "the glory and honor of nations will be brought into it."[43] And in the center of the "great street of the city" stands a "tree of life" with fruits for each of the months, and the leaves of the tree "will be for the healing of nations."[44] His closing message repeats: "And let him who hears say, 'Come!' Whoever is thirsty, let him come; and whoever wishes, let him take freely of the gift of the water of life"[45] (Rev 22:17). This audience transcends ethnic, linguistic, and tribal divisions. Such a reading goes beyond the limits of the model of local competition, at the same time that it reveals John's visionary transformation of the visual and auditory environment of his time.

A Community of Hearers
And I saw . . . [Καὶ εἶθον . . .][46]

Striking in this context is the second-person address of the book of Revelation. This is not a philosophical treatise, not onto-theology in Philo's sense or even the form of a Platonic dialogue. Prophetic address is usually direct. It predicts, it warns, it speaks in riddles.[47] But John's book describes to others what he sees. This is relational discourse, a practical structuring of truth. The book depends on this form of address that asks the hearers of his words to see what in empirical reality cannot be seen. John conveys, to all of the senses, visions that defy ordinary sense. It has been proposed that John as testimonial writer may not even have existed. Philosophically, that is not determining if what is important is the community of hearers addressed as a protest against the imperial appropriation of sensory life. Revelation does not set up a binary opposition between the present and a future time or place. Rather, its words denaturalize present existence. The world looks back at John in a way other than its everydayness—not *another* world, but *this* world differently perceived.[48] He revisions the experiences of his hearers— their *poleis*, their song, their assemblies, their worship, their crowns, their living trees and waters. The visible and invisible interpenetrate; transcendence is experienced within the immanence of daily life. In the context of cities that are saturated with images of gods and emperors, the life-in-common of the *polis* appears transformed, and an unrepresentable God seems more real than imperial figures of worship whose stone-cut images surround his hearers in human form.

Scholars commonly approach John's writing as rhetoric, intended to sway his audience to his position. Whitaker is exemplary, arguing that John uses vivid description, or *ekphrasis*, a technique that can be found in ancient textbooks of rhetoric, in order to manipulate the emotions and engender fear in his audience: John's visions are "not an end in themselves but function as ocular proof with precise persuasive goals."[49] This understanding fits with the idea of competing prophets wherein John assumes the polemic position of a partisan.[50] But the repetitions, restartings, and multiple perspectives that he provides, the ambiguity of the symbols, the nonidentical return of themes, as well as the universal inclusion of the community of address, are not partisan characteristics.[51] If we view philosophically the situation of second-person address, then a different analysis is possible.

One cannot see the world differently alone. To doubt the veracity of the everyday, actually to see the existing order as *dis*order, is an isolating experience that John's words invite us to overcome. What distinguishes a hallucination from a community of believers is the collective that receives it. Enlightenment rationality is intolerant of those who propose counterfactual perceptions, particularly when they draw others to their cause, and indeed such skepticism is appropriate. Yet the capacity, collectively, to imagine otherwise is fundamental to what it means for humans to conceive of a better world, and Enlightenment thinking shares in this belief. Hoff, interpreting the fifteenth-century writings of the mystic Nicholas of Cusa, describes the community-constructing nature of second-person address, which rests its conviction on the trust of others.[52] The inability of any one of us to perceive a new reality alone requires this community, as a necessity not of rhetoric but of faith.

Nicholas of Cusa intrigues philosophers today because, as a Renaissance figure, he is a contemporary of those considered the founding figures of that modernizing rupture which initiates our own times. Cusa shares with his era an interest in freedom from church authority, but from the perspective of collective monastic practice rather than that of the self-reflecting individual.[53] Hoff observes a "paradoxical outcome" of the diminished significance of liturgical response—active, communal participation in performance of the sacred—that followed the Protestant Reformation with its silent practice of biblical reading: the more accessible the word of God becomes, the more available to a literate reading audience, the less the liturgical ability to *see* what is *heard* in common. Hoff explains: "Thanks to Gutenberg and the Reformation, 'the Bible' became available to every literate individual; but its significance appeared now, more than ever, to be a hidden secret, since the practice of listening to the word of God was no longer based on its identical repetition in the variable contexts of liturgical performances. . . . The liturgical focus on the habit of listening became replaced by the ideological focus on rhetoricians, preachers, theologians, and catechists who relied on their natural or trained capacity to *make themselves heard*. This was the hour of charismatic reformers who enjoyed their ability to hear themselves preaching."[54] But there is more to the atrophy of collective sensibility.

Modern subjectivity is the perspectival vision of the individual. Much has been written of the Renaissance invention of perspective, whereby the mathematical construction in two dimensions of a three-dimensional space sets up a singular position for the viewer. Leon Battista Alberti's text *On Painting* (1435 CE) is the reference for this artistic achievement.[55] Perspectival vision proposes truth as objective because mathematically fixed, and defines universality as the identity of subjects who, occupying the same viewing position, see the same image: "The vanishing lines reflect the invisible eye point of the viewer, putting the latter in the position of a sovereign observer who can control the space of his perception as if it were nothing but a mirror image of his subjective position."[56] The sovereign power of the individual subject produced by this "oculocentrism" is implied in modernity's concept of universality.[57] This "eye point" becomes the "thinking I" (*cogito*) of Descartes.[58] Self-centered in the extreme, it is also monovalent. Hoff sees it as responsible for a reduced understanding of monotheism, no longer allowing or, indeed, *requiring* multiple and disparate human witnesses. He opposes to this "the poly-unity of created 'ones' that transcend the difference between identity and difference."[59] The infinite is not visible but only audible.[60] Hence the necessity of a community of trust in which to hear others tell of their experiences, which remain invisible to us.

Behold he comes with clouds; and every eye shall see him. (Rev 1:7)

If every vision needs concurrent sightings ("every eye shall see him"), perhaps not in the same way. In our differences we need each other. Such an approach to universality as a philosophical idea is not partisan but partial, not identical but in-common. "To believe in what others say is what gives access to the thought of the one."[61] The opacity produced by our partiality cannot be abolished, and therefore trust is the prerequisite: "I have learned to *believe* what other people have revealed to me in *words*."[62] Granted, trust is vulnerable to deception—by the anti-Christ, the demagogue, the rhetorician, the powerful, all those who deliberately deceive. But demagogues insist on unison, and Nicolas of Cusa's point is a very different one. Hoff explains the philosophical experience: "If I am looking at someone who reveals to me that she is seeing something that I cannot see from my own perspective (e.g., myself), I am starting to *perceive* that there is something *invisible* to me. . . . I am familiar with the reality of the invisible since I have learned to listen to other people. I do not only *know* that the viewpoint of other people is inaccessible to me; I can *see* the invisible, whenever I look at a face that is able to look at me."[63] The idea of universality that can be rescued from John's relational mode of address is, then, a plurality of views under conditions of opacity which oblige mutual trust, as well as training in the ability to hear what others see. One might not better describe the *telos* of any community of writers and readers.

Timing Is Everything

Time as *chronos* (χρόνος) is measurable time. It describes the cycles of the seasons and other regularities of nature. *Chronos* can be predicted, and the practices that correspond to it are ritualistic and repetitive.[64] But *kairos* (καιρός), as a *quality* of time, is unpredictable, a "passing instant" that calls for spontaneous judgment and decisiveness of action.[65] As a category of knowledge, *kairos* refers to "[t]he uniquely timely, the spontaneous, the radically particular."[66] The experience of *kairos* is a heightened awareness of the moment. No matter how greatly anticipated, its coming surprises us. It alters perception. It is not the same as messianic time, although the latter is surely kairotic in its appearance. In the messianic moment the world is seen in a radically different light, when definitions of judgment and right action may reverse themselves because the very ground of judgment is transformed.

Kairotic time runs alongside chronic time and touches it as a possibility and hope. The figure of Paul looms large here. His approach to messianic time has been misunderstood by modern philosophers who presume Paul's "Christian" temporality as a radical break.[67] In fact, Paul uses *chronos* and *kairos* interchangeably: with the coming of the Messiah (anointed one, *Christos*), these two times have become one. Paul sees himself and all of his generation as living in the *now* of messianic time. He speaks of Christ's "arrival," *parousia*, the word used to celebrate the coming into a city of a conquering general or imperial emissary but, above all, the arrival of the emperor himself. This use of the language of imperial practice as metaphor marks Paul's assurance of already living in messianic time and in God's grace (χάρις) that is supreme over human law. Absolute faith in God supersedes absolute loyalty to the emperor. Paul states in his letter to the Romans that imperial law must be obeyed because "there is no authority except that which God has established."[68] That is to say, Paul's superimposition of *kairos* onto *chronos* alters fundamentally the perception of obedience to earthly power, which now is to be obeyed because it no longer matters. Paul is not calling for rebellion against the law. After the coming of the Messiah, Roman law is irrelevant. Earthly law remains in place but its power is deactivated.[69]

Messianic time, then, is the instance when *chronos* and *kairos* converge. This moment of synchrony is pregnant with possibility. But it is also precarious, because sources of earthly power are now capable of appropriating its potency. This happened with the institutionalization of the early church, which assumed the prerogative to proclaim heresies and monopolize orthodoxy of belief. But even more determining was 324 CE, when Constantine's conquest of the East led to the Christianization of the

Roman Empire itself. It initiated a double reading of *chronos* and *kairos* as the defense of imperial power. Its articulation was the achievement of bishop Eusebius of Caesarea, church apologist for the emperor Constantine, who produced chronological tables of parallel histories wherein all of time—from Abraham to Constantine—became legible as God's plan.[70] Eusebius' chronological tables noted moments of synchrony between events such as the birth of Augustus and that of Christ, leading to the eventual convergence of Christian Church and Roman Empire and providing a massive hagiography of Constantine, whose present rule appears as a culminating moment in time.[71] Constantine converted to Christianity because under the banner of its God, he won a battle at the Milvian Bridge against a rival to the Roman imperial throne. From this moment on, Christian history could be read in terms of its victories in battle, and battles as victories against the devil.[72] The times of conquest and salvation, understood as permanently synchronized, allowed one to be read off against the other. With this merging of temporal readings, messianic time loses its critical capacity to oppose earthly rule. It is a dangerously obfuscating moment.

The Obfuscations of Empire

Consider what happens to Paul's teachings, specifically, when the momentary convergence of *kairos* and *chronos* rigidifies. Any nominally Christian government must then be obeyed, whoever rules, and however that rule is implemented. The mandate to submit to the victors in history violates the deepest meaning of *kairos* as messianic time. To this day, Paul's letter to the Romans is read selectively to justify submission to power.[73] Not only empire has been defended in this way, but the institutions of American slavery and South African apartheid, and any unjust law.[74]

At the end of the first century, John was far from the cusp of a Christianized Roman Empire, and much too close to Paul not to be troubled by the clear indications of a growing gap between the coming of Christ envisioned by Paul and the status of power of imperial Rome. In 96 CE, the delay of the *parousia* was evident, at the same time as the imperial order was toppling once again. Domitian, at age 44 and without heirs, was assassinated by his enemies in Rome.[75] Contemporaries described the last

5.2
Victory of Constantine at the Milvian Bridge, detail: Constantine charging into battle on a white horse under the sign of the cross; below him, his mother Helena, crowned empress, on a lyre-back throne. The lower scene is identified by inscription as the "finding of the true cross" (EYPECIC TOY TIMIOY CTAYPOY). Miniature, ca. 885 CE. Bibliothèque Nationale, Paris (Ms. Grec 510).

years of his reign as chaotic, disordered, filled with tyrannical actions of imperial paranoia when, to cite Tacitus, "no longer intermittently and with occasional rest periods but in a single, unbroken convulsion he drained his country's blood."[76] This was the ignominious end of the Flavian line. Domitian, whose grandiose building projects had included a new imperial cult center in Ephesus dedicated to the *Sebastoi* and a colossal statue of the emperor himself, was not only denied the customary posthumous

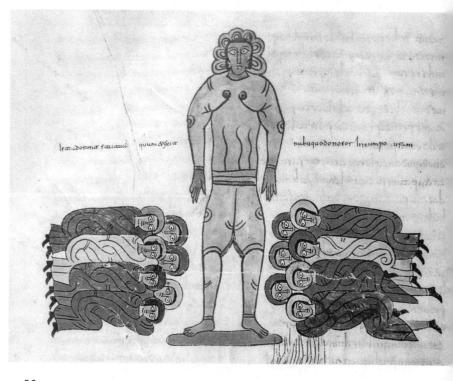

5.3

Illustration from the Morgan Beatus showing the huge statue described in the dream of Nebuchadnezzar, interpreted in Daniel 2:24 as referring to the transiency of the four kingdoms of earthly power. The book of Daniel, included in the Septuagint translation, was written at the time of the Maccabee revolt (second century BCE), concerning the earlier time of the Babylon captivity (sixth century BCE). In John of Patmos' book of Revelation, Daniel is a multiple reference point. Hence its inclusion in the illustrated manuscripts of Beatus of Liébana's commentary on Revelation, of which the Morgan Beatus is exemplary. The Morgan Library & Museum. Detail: MS M.644., fol. 248v. Photo by Joseph Zehavi.

apotheosis.[77] The Roman Senate went further, issuing a damnation of his memory (*damnatio memoriae*).[78] With this act, the very antithesis of deification, his image and name were stricken from public memory.

Delay

One can, and Philo of Alexandria does, accept the world as God created it without messianic anticipation.[79] Writing in the early decades of the first century, Philo was sanguine about Augustus' rule.[80] Even the appropriation of the title *theos* did not seem to him undeserved for an emperor whose superior virtue was demonstrated.[81] Hadas-Lebel asks: "Did Philo believe in a collective salvation? Did he share the Messianic expectation which, since the end of Herod's reign, had gripped many minds in Judaea? Nothing suggests that this is so."[82]

Josephus, too, accepted the cyclical ordering in time (*chronos*) of historical events, including the repetitive rise and fall of empires, to which the book of Daniel refers. Roman rule was in accord with God's will, at least for his time.[83] He knows of the messianic texts and warns against them: "Josephus relates how the Jewish rebels had interpreted a prophecy promising a coming savior for their own purposes, bringing needless destruction upon themselves when it was obvious to him that the oracle spoke of Vespasian."[84]

Paul's embrace of *kairos* as messianic time rendered cyclical time inoperative. He died under Nero as a martyr; exactly when and where are unknown. A generation after Paul's good news, John too believed in the *parousia*, the immanence of which had disappeared. It does not matter whether John was a refugee from the Judaean War, the messianic hopes of which were shattered.[85] It does not matter whether he was a follower (or rival) of Paul, whose messianic assurance was not realized. Loss of the Jerusalem Temple, the delayed *parousia*, the present-day complacency of Jews in the context of prosperity and pressures for cultural assimilation, along with the eclipse of the Flavians and *damnatio memoriae* of their last emperor, lent in John's time a sense of urgency to the task of taking back the language of divinity, eternity, and harmony that had been falsely and deceptively usurped by imperial Rome.

Writing at the end of the century and perhaps at the end of his life, John experienced a gap between messianic time and the time of imperial rule, hence the fleetingness of convergence between *kairos* and *chronos*. His text chronicles a waxing and waning of distances between these temporal dimensions—a half hour, a month, a thousand years—but with no over-arching order, no coherent sequence.[86] It begins with hope, "for the time is at hand [ὅ γὰρ καιρὸς ἐγγύς]" (Rev 1:3), and ends with a promise, "Yes, I am coming quickly [Ναί, ἔργομαι ταχύ]" (Rev 22:20).[87] Within the text, time expands and contracts, is delayed and comes quickly. But for now, messianic time is in abeyance. John writes (Rev 8:1):

> And when he opened the seventh seal, there was silence in the heavens . . . for about half an hour.*

---

* We noted in chapter 1 that the explicit temporal duration of "about half an hour" (in Rev 8:1 ὡς ἡμίωρον) was not identical to ours. Time was measured with sundials, and each "day" had 12 hours, the length of which changed in constant correspondence with the movement of the sun; the length of a 12-hour day was thus shorter in winter than in summer, and hours and half-hours varied accordingly. The placing of this moment of silence at the opening of the seventh seal is therefore meaningful, as the seventh hour, exactly in the middle of the twelve hours of day, always and at all times of year would begin precisely at noon.[88]

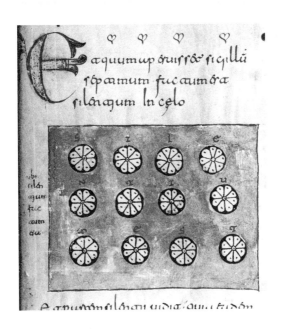

5.4

Illustration from Beatus of Liébana's commentary on Revelation 8:1, "… there was silence in the heavens," from the Morgan Beatus, Andalus, tenth century CE. The Morgan Library & Museum. Detail: MS M.644., fol. 133r. Photo by Joseph Zehavi.

5. 5

Heavens depicted on the painted ceiling of the rock-hewn church of Bet Maryam, Lalibela, Ethiopia (twelfth century). Photo: Adam Jones (Wikimedia Commons. CC BY 2.0). Both these depictions of the heavens, across the expanse of geography from Christian Andalus to Christian Lalibela, give as image of a star the 8-point rosette.

II. APOCALYPSE IS NOT OUR PRESENT

In the beginning[89] God created heaven and earth ['Εν ἀρχῇ ἐποίησεν ὁ θεὸς τὸν οὐρανὸν καὶ τὴν γῆν]. (Gen 1:1)

You are worthy, our Lord and God, to receive glory and honor and power, for you created all things . . . [ἄιξος εἶ, ὁ κύριος καὶ ὁ θεὸς ἡμῶν, λαβεῖν τὴν δόξαν καὶ τὴν τιμὴν καὶ τὴν δύναμιν, ὅτι σὺ ἔκτισας τὰ πάντα . . .] (Rev 4:11)

Arche/ἀρχῇ is the word for rule. But it has another meaning—beginning as origin, first cause. It opens the biblical book of Genesis recounting the Creator's initiating power ('Εν ἀρχῇ . . .).[90] Philo of Alexandria accepts the metaphor, common among philosophers, that compares the creation of earth with the construction of a city.[91] John of Patmos envisions a new world, correspondingly, as a new Jerusalem. The analogy has always been approximate, as the *archi*-tect works with material already created, already at hand, and infused by the *dynamis* of human labor.[92] The builder uses mathematical rules of measure and structure that are manifestations of God's *logos*, laws that are "stamped with the seal [*sphragis*/σφραγίς] of nature" and that rule in God's "house" (*oikos*, cf. *oiko-logia*, eco-logy), laws valid throughout the world.[93] Philo speaks of the seals impressed on nature as the manifestation of God's ideas.[94]

Emperors fashioned themselves as consummate builders; Rome was the prototype of the heavenly city.[95] Each emperor left his mark in marble, and sealed his authority in stone. Each initiated the founding of provincial cities, where local elites accrued power as patrons of construction. The mimetic relationship between imperial rule and divine creation was persistent, even as lived experience exposed its limits. The emperors as "saviors" provided funds by their "grace" for restoring buildings destroyed by earthquakes. They doled out grain to the public in times of famine. And yet they could neither cause the earthquake nor prevent the famine. As the other side of creation, nature's destructiveness was divine terrain. Earthquakes, plagues, famines, floods, and volcanic eruptions were signs of transcendent power not only for Christians and Jews but for pagan Romans as well. The book

5.6

Angel of the Abyss and the Locusts, Escorial Beatus, illustrated manuscript of Beatus of Liébana's commentary on Revelation, Bibl. Del Monast., &II.5, f. 96v. Real Biblioteca de San Lorenzo. "The locusts looked like horses prepared for battle. On their heads they wore something like crowns of gold, and their faces resembled human faces. Their hair was like women's hair, and their teeth were like lions' teeth. They had breastplates of iron, and the sound of their wings was like the thundering of many horses and chariots rushing into battle. They had tails and stings like scorpions" (Rev 9:7–10).

of Revelation is full of such events as a series of woes unleashed upon the earth. Instead of harmony in the heavens, the counterpoint to the worshipers' hymns is a cacophony of sound. The creator God speaks with thunder; he displays his power with the shaking of the earth.

Undoing the Seals of Creation

The One who placed the seal of his word on all created beings could empower the breaking of that seal, and in the book of Revelation it is the enthroned Lamb who is judged "worthy" to initiate this task.[96] The seven seals that corresponded to the seven days of creation are opened, and the scrolls of heaven roll up, releasing visions of this world's last days. The first four seals broken unleash four horsemen that bring war and death, a fifth lets loose locusts shaped like horses for battle, with faces like humans, hair like women, teeth like lions, and the tails of scorpions.[97] The beast from the sea is like a leopard, with the feet of a bear and mouth of a liar, and "with ten horns and seven heads, with ten crowns on his horns"[98]— prodigious signs for pagans as well in the first century of creation gone awry.[99]

The opening of the sixth seal initiates a tremendous earthquake: "The sun turned black like sackcloth made of goat hair, the whole moon turned blood-red, and the stars in the sky fell to earth, as late figs drop from a fig tree when shaken by a strong wind. The sky receded like a scroll, rolling up, and every mountain and island were removed from their place."[100] John's vision evokes the words of the prophet Isaiah.[101] But intertextual allusions between John's texts and the Septuagint book of Isaiah, while significant, are not sufficient for interpretation. The "shaking" of creation was a lived experience of those who heard his words. Bauckham writes: "The Greco-Roman world took earthquakes seriously as signs of divine displeasure, and the first-century world, Asia Minor in particular, experienced devastating earthquakes in which great cities, including some of the seven of Revelation," suffered "catastrophically" and "called forth imperial aid":[102] Philadelphia and Sardis in 17 CE; Sardis again in 26 CE; Laodicea in 60 CE.

The Italian peninsula, too, was vulnerable. The Latin philosopher Seneca described a major earthquake near Mount Vesuvius (62 CE) that inflicted "great devastation on Campania. . . . Sheep died and statues split. Some people have lost their minds and wander about in their madness."[103] He comments on the terrors felt: "What hiding-place do we look to, what help, if the earth itself is causing the ruin, if what protects us, upholds us, on which cities are built, which some speak of as a kind of foundation of the universe, separates and reels?"[104] Seneca's affective wording accords with John's: "Then the kings of the earth, the princes, the generals, the rich, the mighty, and every slave and every free man hid in caves and among the rocks of the mountains. They called to the mountains and the rocks, 'Fall on us and hide us from the face of him who sits on the throne and from the wrath of the Lamb! For the great day of their wrath has come, and who can stand?'"[105]

The 62 CE earthquake was followed that same day by a tidal wave at Ostia, the port city for Rome. Two hundred ships in the harbor were waiting to unload, those that arrived from Alexandria and Carthage once a year carrying vital grain supplies for Rome. All of them were engulfed by the tsunami and the cargoes lost.[106] An earthquake in 68 CE signaled the end of Nero's reign.[107] The natural historian Pliny the Elder considered the quake a fitting portent of the subsequent year of civil war.[108] But it was the eruption of the volcano Vesuvius in 79 CE that provided the most extreme and violent manifestation of nature's power.

Vesuvius

Mount Vesuvius, near the Bay of Naples that was a hub of Mediterranean trade, erupted on (our dating) 17 October 79 CE.[109] The rumblings of an earthquake began the event. A column of gases and ash shot up from the mountain in several branches of fire, releasing a strong sulfurous smell. Scientists tell us the pyroclastic cloud of volcanic particles and gas ascended 32 kilometers (20 miles) high, enveloping the site in darkness, and debris of pumice stone and black pieces of burning rock fell not only into the waters of the bay but as far as 70 kilometers from the site. Within a radius of 10–15 kilometers, there was complete destruction of human settlements. Nearly instantly, the port cities of Pompeii and Herculaneum were buried beneath a thick layer of volcanic stone and ash. Their entire populations succumbed.

Pliny the Elder was present as commander of the Roman fleet. The volcano claimed his life. His nephew Pliny the Younger witnessed the explosion from close by. Years later, when the historian Tacitus asked that he describe the event,[110] he wrote that the earth trembled, buildings tottered, and the sea was "sucked away" so suddenly "that great quantities of sea creatures were left stranded on dry sand." From the mountaintop "a fearful black cloud was rent by forked and quivering bursts of flame, and parted to reveal great tongues of fire." Among the "panic-stricken crowd" attempting to flee, some "prayed for death in their terror of dying. Many besought the aid of the gods, but still more imagined there were no gods left, and that the universe was plunged into eternal darkness for evermore." A "poor consolation," he wrote, was "the belief that the whole world was dying with me and I with it."[111]

Dio Cassius, writing more than a century later, reported that the darkness had reached not only Rome, "filling the air overhead and darkening the sun," but also Africa, Syria, and Egypt. In Rome the experience caused "no little fear . . . since the people did not know and could not imagine what had happened, but, like those close at hand, believed that the whole world was being turned upside down, that the sun was disappearing into the earth and that the earth was being lifted to the sky."[112] The disaster, compounded by a major fire that destroyed many temples to the gods in Rome, "seemed to be not of human but of divine origin."[113] This massive destruction occurred in Titus' first year of rule. He responded in the appropriate imperial manner, traveling in person to Campania and appointing officials to organize relief and reconstruction. We are told that "Titus provided the necessary funds from his own resources and from the property of the many people who had died in the eruption without heirs"; he "gave special privileges to the [neighboring] towns that had offered assistance to these refugees" from the "devastated areas around Vesuvius [who] fled."[114] This admirable behavior earned the emperor praise. But when the earthquake was followed by a great plague, Titus himself was afflicted. He died after a reign lasting just over two years. This confluence of events tested the legitimacy of imperial rule.

Sensory effects analogous to those described by Pliny the Younger are scattered throughout the text of Revelation: "fire and smoke and sulfur" (Rev 9:7, again 9:8); "fiery lake of burning sulfur" (Rev 19:20, again 21:8); "the sun and the sky were darkened" (Rev 9:2, cf. 8:9 and 8:12); "flashes of lightning and an earthquake" (Rev 8:5); "a third of the living creatures in the sea died" (Rev 8:9); and, most explicitly, "something like a great mountain burning with fire was cast into the sea" (Rev 8:8). Scholars are conscious of the relevance of Vesuvius to John's text.[115] Revelation's later dating makes these comparisons unavoidable. It may seem surprising then, given the fame of this eruption, that little interpretive meaning is made of it.[116] Yet the tendency of scholars to cluster this thematic in John's text together with the other (pagan) sources and other (Mediterranean) catastrophes is justified. There is nothing unique, or uniquely Christian, about John's reading of natural disasters.[117] Whereas for us such a catastrophe would have been read into linear time as its culmination, for John the destruction of Pompeii is neither the climax of his book nor the climax of his historical moment. The scattered elements in Revelation that resonate with the Vesuvius eruption, as well as with various local earthquakes, are not held in place by an overarching narrative line. Rather, catastrophic events erupt into his text with the randomness of the weather, and this is totally in keeping with the meaning of the word *kairos* as both revealed time and meteorological conditions. In Revelation, the frightening aberrations of nature are an unpredictable yet incessant testing of the claim of divine approval of the Roman imperial order.

True to his age, in which linear time was not recognized, there is no chronological progression etched within John's prophecy. To read time in this way is to distort historical understanding by superimposing on the text the centuries-later idea that the book of Revelation traces through linear time the eschatological progression of events of history as a whole, leading to a final and total catastrophe. How can this have been the meaning, when time then was not reckoned in our way?[118] It is worth taking the time to question how the modern interpretation came to be, as the effects of this understanding produce significant tremors in public discourse today, distorting our understanding of both history and the philosophical questions that such catastrophes of nature reveal.

Last Days in Our Time

Pompeii as the scene of destruction was not a permanent historical image.[119] The city truly disappeared, and the rich volcanic soil of Campania nurtured a return of the wine production that figured as a leading export in long-distance trade. The destroyed city's discovery ca. 1600 brought no call for its unearthing. It was in the 1740s, at both Herculaneum and Pompeii, that archaeological excavators worked to restore the sites, attracting tourists from Europe's educated elite. Within the human-centered context of the Enlightenment, the ruins of Pompeii were figured as a testament to the fleetingness of life's sensual pleasures and the irrevocable loss that history entails.[120] The resurrection of Pompeii in the wider public imagination had to wait until 1834, with the appearance of Edward Bulwer-Lytton's historical novel *The Last Days of Pompeii*. He reanimated the city with characters legible as contemporaries, producing an enduring image of Vesuvius at the moment of its catastrophic end. The book gave birth to an entire genre of disaster narratives that, as mass entertainment, have had a remarkably successful run.[121]

The novel's archaeological detail was carefully researched.[122] Its message, however, was pure Victorian moralism: the pagan populace, debauched and spoiled by luxury and wealth, brings deserved punishment upon itself.[123] The story separates vice from virtue, while providing voyeuristic descriptions of the sinfulness of the flesh. Amid this depravity of sexual license and sinful greed, the "Nazarene" hero and Hellenic heroine are saved by a poor blind slave girl, who alone can lead them through the volcanic darkness to the port. They flee by sea to Athens, convert to Christianity, and live there among others of the faith. In fact they were already proto-Christians. Vesuvius' eruption brings divine rescue to him from a lion that kneels and turns away, and to her from being raped by an evil Egyptian priest. A merciful "God above them" restores order after their frightful ordeal.[124] The book of Revelation is referenced directly: "Woe! woe! ye strong and mighty! . . . Woe to the idolater and the worshipper of the beast!"[125]

There is no evidence of any Christian presence in the excavations of Pompeii.[126] The novel's anachronistic rendition resurrects first-century history as a Christian allegory for nineteenth-century Europeans.[127] And in this retroactive construction, the dichotomy of virtue and sin provides a schizophrenic reading of the British Empire: Britain brings Christian values to its empire, while risking depravity at home from imperial excess. Slavery is presented in terms of the "property rights" of slave owners.[128] The villain, an (African) Egyptian, "spins dark oriental spells."[129] The slave girl saves the grateful hero and heroine while losing her own life.[130] The heroic couple's destination is the Greece to which British Romantics went in the 1820s to defend the Greek *poleis'* ancient freedom, and where the poet Lord Byron lost his life fighting against the Ottoman (Muslim) Turks.

Popular Apocalypse

The Last Days of Pompeii was a bestseller among the better classes. But it was as a visual spectacle that the book's story became paradigmatic within mass culture.[131] A theater adaptation came quickly. The catastrophe of Vesuvius was a favorite theme for nineteenth-century oil painters, a prototype of what became known as the "apocalyptic sublime."[132] London's Crystal Palace included in 1854 a simulacrum of Pompeian rooms. Photographs and stereoscopy of the site followed. But it was as a pyrotechnic sensation, with lifelike volcanic flows and the smell of burning sulfur, that the masses of the public were drawn into the simulated event and the longevity of the *Last Days of Pompeii* was ensured.[133] Fascination with destruction as a form of entertainment provided the thrill of danger from a safe distance. These productions made use of new industrial techniques to create a scenario of history in its entirety, a theme that underwent multiple iterations once Hollywood took over the pyrotechnical tasks.

Marcel Proust's novel *À la recherche du temps perdu* (*In Search of Lost Time*), set in Paris at the turn of the twentieth century, figures Vesuvius as a metaphor for the first aerial bombing in World War I. Proust describes the shelling that sent citizens to shelters as lava pouring down from above. Paris is Pompeii in its last days of "mindless frivolity"; this "degenerate and obsolescent society" is at the brink of catastrophe, as its whole way of life threatens to disappear as lost in time.[134] The twentieth century of

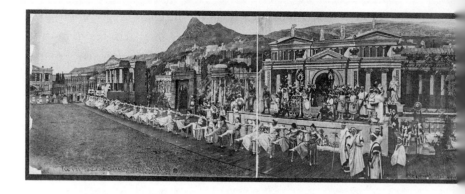

5.7
Scene from a pyrodrama of the *Last Days of Pompeii*, produced by British fireworks entrepreneur Henry J. Pain, shown here at Coney Island, New York, where productions occurred
regularly from 1879 to 1914, combining music and dance with the Vesuvian narrative. Library
of Congress Prints and Photographs Division, Washington, D.C.

world wars brought a proliferation of cities that died in the flames of aerial
attacks: Guernica, Warsaw, Stalingrad, Coventry, Dresden, Hiroshima,
Nagasaki. Now humans, not nature, were the source of the destruction, and
not even the skeletons of the victims survived.[135] The essential irrationality
of modernity is located here: scientific progress becomes the disaster that
it purports to prevent. The inventions of human reason are turned against
their creators. Modern apocalypticism thus has a structure nonconcordant
with the book of Revelation. The contested issue is a Faustian one, whether
to bargain away one's soul to the devil to satisfy a limitless desire for the
controlling power of knowledge promised by Enlightenment reason. In the
industrial era's version of this dilemma, morality, understood as obedience
to the repressive dictates of religious and state authority, is set against
desire—but also against knowledge—as good combatting evil. Drawn into
this either/or dichotomy, philosophy suffers.

In 1841 (contemporary with *The Last Days of Pompeii*), the left-
Hegelian philosopher Bruno Bauer published anonymously a parody of
John's Revelation, ventriloquizing through the voice of a Christian pastor
a mock condemnation of Hegelian philosophy for attempting to put
Reason on the throne. The book, *The Trumpet of the Last Judgment: Against
Hegel, the Atheist and Antichrist*, is "an ultimatum," as Bauer puts words

5.8

Caird M. Vandersloot's two-step march composed in 1904, inspired by Bulwer-Lytton's novel
The Last Days of Pompeii. A decade earlier, the American composer John Philip Sousa, also
inspired by the book, created a suite that he considered his finest work. In 1971, the English
rock band Pink Floyd performed in the amphitheater of Pompeii, recording an album and a film.
Courtesy of Kenneth Lapatin.

into the progress-denying pastor's mouth, who professes to be scandalized by the Hegelian claim that Reason, as the sum total of human intellect, is itself God. This apotheosis of the human mind claims that human reason "progressively advances" in a constant, developmental state.[136] The claim is blasphemy, Bauer has his Christian pastor lament. When the book of Revelation speaks of the Beast, it "has Hegel the antichrist in mind"; indeed, Hegel has "more horns than the Beast of the Apocalypse."[137] In "heathen drunkenness," Hegel "revels with the Greeks," preferring their libertine practices to Christian morality, a choice that poses a mortal danger to both Church and State.[138] Germany is "nothing to him"; instead, Hegel imbibes from the "cup of the harlot," which is identified as French philosophy.[139] As the worst of his abominations, Hegel supports the French Revolution. "Vive la liberté! Do you hear the revolutionary cry? Vive l'égalité! Hear it! All are one! All are equal! God and Man the same! Horrible! Abominable!"[140] In the pastor's attack, copious citations from Hegel's work are the surreptitious messages that make Bauer's case for him: "We now finally show how Hegel has dissolved Christianity."[141] This is the apocalypse: "We are at an end!"[142]

One hundred years after Bauer's viciously optimistic attack on religious authority, Adorno and Horkheimer traced a dialectic of Enlightenment that, by the mid-twentieth century, turned Hegelian optimism on its head: reason, triumphant, collapses back into myth, the modern myth that human-created technology has taken us beyond nature so that we are in control, when in fact we have submitted to instrumentalized reason as a new and deadly form of domination over all of nature, including that very vulnerable nature which is ourselves.[143] Today the very success of industrial progress even in peace times—especially in peace times—has intensified this concern. Industrial society imposes a human imprint on the natural world that, it is feared, has already sown the seeds of our demise. Our very being on earth in this way threatens the human species in its entirety.

The Anthropocene

Awareness that the Anthropocene is a period of natural history, in which human practice has transformed nature to the point of its destruction, is the revelation of our time. Reason itself exposes as myth an uncritical faith in reason. It can be argued that those who refuse to accept this truth, or those who plan personal planetary escape—by science or by rapture—lack both wisdom and humility.[144] And nature does not suffer human hubris kindly. Nature's forms of destruction can be regenerative. The rich sedimentation, left by repeated eruptions of Vesuvius, continues to support abundant vegetation. The tectonic plates that thunderously explode, causing earthquakes, volcanoes, and subsequent tsunamis, are cooling mechanisms vital for life on any imaginable planet, as they allow the escape of heat otherwise intolerable for living organisms. Not so the global warming caused by human practices. Still, species extinction does not change the fact that life itself is extraordinarily resilient—only, perhaps, not for ourselves.[145]

Natural History Today

Pliny the Elder's first-century *Natural History* has been revisited as a source of inspiration for contemporary scientific research. An international collective of vulcanologists, geologists, archaeo-biologists, soil scientists, and others collaborated for almost half a century to produce *The Natural History of Pompeii* (2002), a study that shifts the focus from exclusive concern for

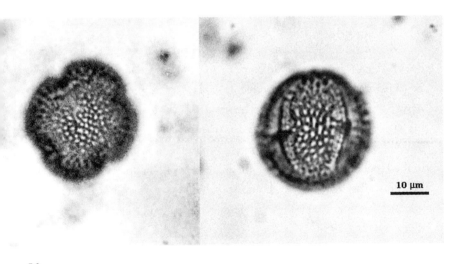

5.9

Citrus limon pollen from the Casa delle Nozze di Ercole e Ebe in Pompeii, Italy. From Marta Mariotti Lippi, "Ancient Floras, Vegetational Reconstruction and Man-Plant Relationships," *Bocconea* 24 (2012): 105–113. Courtesy of Marta Mariotti Lippi.

human victims at the site.[146] Their painstaking research has unearthed and catalogued the evidential residues of plant life and pollen, and a striking number of species that can be found in the fertile, "fossil soils" (paleosols) that contain an astonishing array of life: 184 plants, and the pollen of 95 others, multiple species of fish, marine and freshwater invertebrates, insects, amphibians, land and sea shells, reptiles, birds, and mammals, as well as living organisms identified as depicted on mosaics, sculptures, and the wall paintings of gardens. Catalogued are types of wood as both trees and furniture, local and imported (beech, ash, ebony, maple, citrus, laurel, grapevine, chestnut, hazelnut, walnut, elm, poplar, oak, cyprus, hawthorn, olive, fir, pine), fodder plants (grasses and clover), flowering plants (peonies, crocus, violets, acanthus), fruit-bearing plants (plums, dates, mulberry, strawberry, fig trees, pomegranates), plants used for medicine (aloe, oleander, opium, and others). Modeled after the cataloguing work of Pliny the Elder who lost his life at Pompeii, this collection shifts away from a merely human focus to a world that modern humans have only self-centeredly understood, connecting sensibilities across millennia and manifesting a respect for creation that approaches the biblical.

And the earth helped the woman . . . (Rev 12:16)

We recall the biblical commentary of Philo of Alexandria, who rejected the idea that the world would come to an end. Perfect at creation, there was no cause for God as himself perfect to replace it. Despite "the indescribable power of fire and water," Philo believed the world itself was indestructible.[147] Modern science has robbed us of this faith. But it is interesting to follow Philo's reasoning in deciphering the allegorical meaning of the story of the Flood, told by the "sacred historian" Moses, that destroys evil but not life. Noah, he writes, is chosen not because he is perfect, but because he is grateful. It is mankind's ingratitude that caused God to let loose the Flood that destroys.[148] Philo speaks out against those who "oppressed the land . . . continually in their covetousness pursing unrighteous gains," by violating the law that it shall rest fallow and "recover breath," just as men are to rest in "recurring periods of seven days":

5.10
Pompeii mural, garden wall, depicting laurel, roses, a warbler, and Solomon's seal. Photo: Stefano Bolognini.

5.11
Large fish mosaic with 24 identified kinds. Roman mosaic from house VIII.2.16 in Pompeii. Naples National Archaeological Museum, 120177, triclinium of house VIII, 2, 16.

For instead of granting to men who are in the truest point of view their brothers, as having one common mother, namely, nature, instead, I say, of giving them the appointed holiday after each period of six days, and instead of giving the land a respite after each space of six years without oppressing it either with sowing of seed or planting of trees, in order that it may not be exhausted by incessant labours: instead of acting thus, these men, neglecting all these admirable commandments, have oppressed both the bodies and souls of all men over whom they have had any power, with incessant severities, and have torn to pieces the strength of the deep-soiled earth, exacting revenues from it in an insatiable spirit beyond its power to contribute, and crushing it out altogether and in every part with exactions not only yearly, but even daily.[149]

The earth's shaking that destabilizes the "perfect and complete" harmony of creation is only a temporary manifestation, caused not by sin but by evil—precisely the evil of human beings who fail to appreciate the "free gift" of nature's plenty—providing a lesson in endurance—John's word is hope (*hypomone*/ὑπομονῇ)[150]—until the original harmonies are reestablished.

A striking image in Revelation precedes the eschatological horrors of war and judgment: "a great wonder in heaven; a woman, clothed with the sun, and the moon under her feet, and upon her head a crown of twelve stars." Pregnant, about to give birth, she is chased by a red dragon whose tail draws "the third part of the stars of heaven," casting them to earth: "that ancient serpent called the devil or satan, who leads the whole world astray." The woman is "given two wings of a great eagle, that she might fly into the wilderness, to her place [τόπον] prepared by God," and where she is nourished [τρέφεται] "for a time [καιρὸν], and times [καὶ καιροὺς], and half a time [καὶ ἥμισυ καιροῦ]. . . . And the serpent spewed from his mouth water like a river" that caused a flood to "sweep the woman away. . . . And the earth helped the woman, and the earth opened her mouth, and swallowed up the flood which the dragon cast out of his mouth."[151] Attempts to identify this woman clothed with the sun have been multiple:[152] she is Mary, mother of Christ, or the newly founded Church as His bride. She is the nation of Israel. Or she is African, burnt by the sun. Today, with awareness of the Anthropocene, what stands out most vividly in this image is not her identity but her life-giving power, birth as the other side of death, aided by a nature that welcomes and protects.

Don't Blame John

I [am] the alpha and the omega, the first and the last, the beginning [*arche*] and the end [*telos*] [ἐγὼ τὸ ἄφα καὶ τὸ ὦ, ὁ πρῶτος καὶ ὁ ἔσχατος, ἡ ἀρχὴ καὶ τὸ τέλος]. (Rev 22:12)

5.12

William Blake, *The Great Red Dragon and Woman Clothed with the Sun* (c. 1805). Rosenwald Collection, National Gallery of Art, Washington DC, 1943.3.8999. Courtesy of the National Gallery of Art, Washington D.C.

Literature on the Anthropocene that conflates the meaning of apocalypse with the final catastrophe—a literal end of the world—mistranslates not only *apocalypsis*—revealed knowledge—but also end, *telos*, which means not termination but fulfillment, goal.[153] The modern reading of the coming Messiah is as a one-time historical event; but John's is an orientation within time that affirms the multiple irruptions of *kairos* into *chronos* and sees each morning as the visible sign of hope. No blind faith in God is called for, but also no blind faith in progress, the fantasy that we moderns are beyond catastrophe.[154] Thompson insists that for John "[t]he hope implied in 'enduring steadfastly' [*hypomone*] has nothing essentially to do with predicting the future," but is, rather, "an orientation toward the present."[155]

We are wrong to blame John's prophecy for the pending disasters of our own making. The message of his text is not catastrophe but hope. Martin Luther King understood the book of Revelation in this way when, less than a week before he was assassinated, he spoke at the National Cathedral in Washington:

> Thank God for John, who centuries ago out on a lonely obscure island called Patmos caught vision of a new Jerusalem descending out of heaven from God, who heard a voice saying, "Behold, I make all things new; former things are passed away." God grant that we will be participants in this newness and this magnificent development. If we will but do it, we will bring about a new day of justice and brotherhood and peace. And that day the morning stars will sing together and the sons of God will shout for joy.
>
> —Reverend Martin Luther King, Jr., March 31, 1968[156]

III. WOMAN ON THE MARGINS

Luxury for Whom? Peace for Whom?

> Woe! Woe, O great city, O Babylon, city of power! In one hour your
> doom has come! The merchants of the earth will weep and mourn over
> her because no one buys their cargoes any more—cargoes of gold, silver,
> precious stones, and pearls, fine linen, purple, silk and scarlet cloth; every
> sort of citron [scented] wood, and articles of every kind made of ivory,
> costly wood, bronze, iron and marble; cargoes of cinnamon and spice,
> of incense, myrrh and frankincense, of wine and olive oil, of fine flour
> and wheat; cattle and sheep; horses and chariots; and bodies and souls of
> human beings. (Rev 18:10–13)

The book of Revelation envisions the destruction of a great shipping empo-
rium that John names the biblical Babylon but intends as imperial Rome,
enumerating a cargo of goods lost in the mercantile disaster. Bauckham
has thought to examine this cargo list not as frequently done, in terms
of intertextual concordance with Old Testament parallels, but rather as a
record of the "concrete political and economic realities of the empire in his
time."[157] Frankincense and myrrh;[158] cinnamon and spices; gold, precious
stones and deep-sea pearls;[159] ivory and citron wood, fashioned into "every
kind" of form;[160] fine linens and silk in purple and scarlet hues.[161] This list
reads like a manual of Roman long-distance trade.[162] John disparages the
self-appropriation of these earthly delights. But in his final vision of the
Holy City, the God who created nature provides its beauties in abundance
to adorn the heavenly new Jerusalem.[163] In contrast, Rome's imperial elite
squander their privately accumulated wealth for exclusionary ownership of
the items of luxury goods acquired in this eastern trade. Writes Bauckham,
"Rome lives well at her subjects' expense."[164]

Imperial Violence

> [T]o steal, butcher, rape, they call by the lying name "empire," and when
> they make desolation they call it "peace."
>
> —TACITUS, *AGRICOLA* 30.3–4, DESCRIBING THE ROMAN CONQUERORS BY
> CALGACUS, LEADER OF THE BRITONS

John's cargo list includes the "bodies and souls of human beings" (σωμάτων καὶ ψυχὰς ἀνθρώπων), presumed to be slaves.[165] Roman imperial slavery is not easily subsumed under modern categories of slavery[166]—partly because, as we saw in chapter 4, the word "slave" (*doulos*) was differently understood; partly because the society as a whole was extremely brutal.[167] Physical violence was deeply entrenched in imperial life, and forced labor was the reality of its material production from mining and construction to military and domestic service.[168] Rape of women was the standard practice of victorious armies. Their bodily submission became the visual representation of defeat.

5.13 and 5.14
Two life-size reliefs of the Sebasteion, Aphrodisias, that celebrated Roman victories of conquered peoples. The young and naked female body stands in for the entire *ethnos* of a defeated enemy. Left: Nero defeats Armenia, South Building. Right: Claudius defeats Britannia, South Building. New York University Excavations at Aphrodisias (G. Petruccioli).

The Judaean War entailed an occupying Roman army that destroyed towns and villages and devastated the countryside for four years, culminating in the siege of the city of Jerusalem in 70 CE that brought famine and massive slaughter to its inhabitants.[169] Roman solders were not allowed to marry. Exploitation of local resources included that of women.[170] The violation of women by victorious armies was so predictable that, according to Josephus, when in 73 CE the last holdout of Jewish rebel families at the fortress of Masada was faced with certain defeat by the Roman soldiers, the men slaughtered their wives to save them from rape and their children from slavery before turning their weapons on themselves.[171] The case in the Roman province of Britannia is no less notorious. Britannia's queen Boudica was punished for her rebellion against Rome by being "stripped and lashed like a common criminal," and her daughters were raped "as spoils of war," demonstrating that royalty and class position were not a protection against bodily violation.[172] Patriarchy is too general a concept to capture the deeply disturbing logic of these practices, which speak as well to the peacetime handling of women in the Roman imperial world.[173]

The Trade in Women

Women are the focus of this constellation. The very brutality of their treatment in the first century provides a chilling reminder that, for millennia of human history, women's bodies have not been acknowledged as their own. Their procreative function has been appropriated and exchanged by the men who determined their value. This history resonates with particular poignancy among African American women who are the descendants of those brutalized within the modern slave trade. As scholars, they have precipitated a radical, "womanist" reading of the Bible, as part of the extraordinary transvaluations involved in interpreting biblical texts against the grain of their historical complicity with racial oppression. It is they whose work becomes exemplary here, because it keeps our focus on the critical effects of John's discourse within the context of Roman imperial power. The exposure of injustice in its specific historical manifestations forms the core of truth's translation over time.

Women in the Roman empire have been described as "breeding machines," no matter what their social status.[174] "The purpose of marriage was the birth of legitimate children. . . . The high death rate among infants and small children required the average Roman woman to give birth to between five and six live babies merely to leave behind at her death replacements for herself and her husband."[175] Excavated at the site of Pompeii, the skeleton of a pregnant woman of around 16 years of age shows physical harm due to early pregnancy: "Unfortunately, since they were usually married at such a young age, many women in this society became pregnant before they reached physical maturity . . . as soon as was physiologically possible. Many of these girls died trying to give birth with immature pelves."[176]

Women's social position was derivative of their fathers and husbands.[177] Their rights to property were mediated through male relations, and adultery, which meant confiscation of property, was punishable by death. Girls were traded up socially in marriage alliances arranged by fathers across networks of power. Prepubescence was desirable as a condition of the trade. Emperors and kings cemented friendships and neutralized competitors by this traffic in marriageable women.[178] Families living in foreign cities were disposed to exchange daughters within their own ethnic communities, in the physical space of which women's movement was tightly constrained. Among Jews, many (Philo included)[179] supported this practice. Note that the cosmopolitan tendencies of long-distance trade relied on familial connections and, at the same time, placed pressure on the intramarriage practices that were considered vital for controlling the conditions of pregnancy and sustaining cohesion of the ethnic group.[180] Hardly unique, but particularly well documented, was the diaspora of Jewish communities from Babylonia and Syria to Alexandria and Rome, and its relationship to the marriage strategies of ruling families in Judaea.

Judaean Kings

The kingdom of Judaea was not the modern state of Israel in embryonic form.[181] Nor was it a historical continuum of the biblical mythical past.[182] Throughout the first century it was a battleground of intersecting interests and conflicting claims, multiple economies, and demographic distinctions. Its ruling families were rivals; they fought each other and married strategically. Their alliances—with Nabateans, Parthians, Romans—were chosen for reasons other than collective identifications.[183] The Hasmonean dynasty ruled in Judaea in the first part of the first century BCE, dominating the principal land trade routes connecting Mesopotamia, Aetolia, Egypt, and Arabia.[184] Split loyalties within the Judaean royal household led the Roman Republic to intervene and establish by Roman Senatorial decree a new Judaean dynasty, declaring Herod the Great as "King of the Jews" (40/39 BCE)—meaning, in this case, the ruler of a Judaean territory under Roman control. Builder of the Masada fortress and enhancements to the Jerusalem Temple, Herod constructed from scratch a new port city, Caesarea Maritima, that inserted Judaea into the eastern and Mediterranean trade.[185] Herod's ethnic identity is complicated.[186] As a Jew, his Nabatean mother, an "unconverted" Arab woman, is ignored. Herod executed his Hasmonean Jewish wife Mariamne along with other family members, including his own sons. But he never wavered in his commitment to Rome.[187] Roman support was reciprocated to the Herodians over generations, despite the royal family's continued struggles against internal rivals.[188] In addition and dovetailing with Roman imperial interests, the Herodian rulers were connected with the Egyptian/Alexandrian elites through both trade and personal relations.

Berenike

Elite circles were small and overlapped. The women born into them were privileged objects of marital trade. Philo of Alexandria was the brother of "Alexander the Alabarch," in charge of highly lucrative Roman customs taxes collected from the Red Sea trade.[189] This man's two sons, Philo's nephews, were prominent figures in the region. The eldest, Tiberius Julius Alexander, was tightly connected with the Roman military and the governance of both Egypt and Judaea, and in these capacities, Josephus tells us, he "did not persevere in his ancestral practices."[190] His positions involved the violent suppression of a rebellion of Jews in Alexandria in 66 CE as well as in Judaea, where he was present under Titus' military command at the siege of Jerusalem and destruction of the Temple.[191] It was the second son, Marcus Julius Alexander, who became kin with Herodian royalty when Berenike, daughter of King Agrippa 1 (Herod the Great's grandson) was provided to him for marriage. She was just pubescent.[192] He was engaged in a private import-export business connected with the Red Sea port of Berenike, the name of which his young bride shared.[193] He died suddenly (43/44 CE), and his child-widow was married to her uncle, ruler of the Roman-controlled kingdom of Chalcis, strategically located militarily and commercially in today's north Jordan and south Syria. He also died (49 CE) and Berenike went to Caesarea Maritima to live with her brother Agrippa II, now King of Judaea by Roman decree.[194] This brother-sister rule (reminiscent of Cleopatra's co-rule and marriage to her younger brother)[195] was interrupted by Berenike's third marriage to Polemo of Cilicia on the southeast coast of Anatolia that was undertaken, Josephus suggests, to silence rumors that she and Agrippa had an incestuous relationship, which Jewish (and Roman) practices strictly forbade.[196] Polemo underwent circumcision, agreeing to lead the lifestyle of Jews.[197] Yet Berenike left him several years later and returned to her brother's palace. According to Josephus, she was present when riots broke out against Florus, the Roman procurator (64–66 CE) who had seized the Temple treasury in Jerusalem by claiming the money was owed to Rome, and who suppressed the rioters against him, butchering thousands.[198] She was present with her brother in the "extraordinary scene" described by Josephus, of Agrippa II as king and Berenike as queen, on the temple rooftop trying to convince Jerusalem of the hopelessness of any attempt to rebel against the Romans, given the extent of imperial power to which God had seen fit to grant such success.[199] Attempts at mediation that included Berenike's personal plea to Florus failed and citizens were massacred in her presence, leading ultimately to the outbreak of the Judaean War.[200] In none of Josephus' accounts of these appearances is Berenike herself given voice in speech. This last point is important. Berenike's is a story told by others.

When Vespasian was sent by Nero with two legions to quell the rebellion, his son Titus came as military support. He met Berenike, and she became his consort in this, the most lucrative trafficking of her person.

The alliance with Judaea's rulers sealed Vespasian's victory not only over Judaea but also over his rivals in the Roman civil war. The Herodians sided with the Flavians, using their wealth and influence to support Vespasian on his campaign to become emperor. Josephus after his capture claimed that "an ambiguous oracle" found in Jewish scriptures of a coming messiah "in reality signified the sovereignty of Vespasian."[201] It was Tiberius Julius, Berenike's brother-in-law by her first marriage, who proclaimed Vespasian emperor in Alexandria in 69 CE, and he was second in command under Titus the next year when Jerusalem was captured and the Temple razed.

Imperial Victory

Vespasian returned to Rome to secure his imperial title with an *adventus* of military glory. Josephus reports that while Titus was still in the east (at Caesarea), he had 2,500 Jewish prisoners killed in the arena to celebrate his younger brother Domitian's 19th birthday.[202] He toured the eastern empire, presumably with Berenike at his side, holding triumphal processions and victory celebrations. In some Syrian spectacles, Titus made Jewish captives serve to display their own destruction.[203] These spectacles could not have shown more clearly the brutality of military victory, the appalling consequences of *stasis* in the Judaean war, as well as the nonidentity between the Jews in rebellion and the Judaean royal family, hence the ambiguity of what, indeed, it meant to be a Jew. Berenike appears to have been compliant in these events. A pawn in the game of trading sex for power, she belonged to the winning side.

In 71 CE, after the destruction of the Temple, Titus came to Rome to unite with Vespasian and his younger brother Domitian and to celebrate the triumph that marked their ascendency, laying claim to dynastic permanence for the Flavian imperial line.[204] Josephus in *Bellum Judaicum* provides a vivid account of the event. Vespasian and Titus appeared clad in purple robes to recite the customary and legitimating prayers. Floats three stories high joined in the parade, on which prisoners enacted the Judaean battles in which they were defeated. The triumphal procession, led by gold and ivory images of Nike, winged goddess of victory, was followed by the three Flavian men—Vespasian in full triumphal regalia,

Titus in a triumphal chariot, and Domitian on a magnificent horse.[205] In this spectacle of divinely ordained victory, the spoils of war were paraded past the crowds.[206] Included in the procession were, specifically, the holy items taken from the Jewish Temple: the golden table of shewbread and cup, together with silver trumpets, and "the seven-branched lampstand, the Menorah, and finally, the tablet of the Jewish Law."[207] Four years later, in 75 CE, Berenike traveled with her brother Agrippa to Rome. During this visit, she lived openly with Titus as man and wife.[208]

What was the plan? That Alexandria would become the capital of a newly conceived empire? That Titus would rule the east in concert with (or even opposed to) Vespasian?[209] That he would marry Berenike, the "Jewish" queen, securing thereby loyalty—and trade advantages—among Jews throughout the diaspora, from Anatolia and Antioch to Alexandria and Parthian Babylonia?[210] Did the Flavians propose for the Judaean god to find

5.15
Relief from the Arch of Titus, built under the emperor Domitian, ca. 81 CE: triumphal procession carrying the menorah and shewbread table from the Second Temple to Rome; close-up of the golden shewbread table and cup and silver trumpets. Wikimedia Commons. CC BY 3.0.

a new abode in Rome now that Jerusalem's temple had been destroyed?[211] In Europe's early modern period, when wars of royal succession were being challenged by nationalist sentiments, the figure of Berenike, the "second Cleopatra," became popular. Racine's tragedy *Bérénice* (1670 CE) depicts anachronistically Titus and Berenike as lovers who placed duty to their respective nations above their personal affections.[212] Sources tell us that the couple had real affection for each other. And yet to narrate this relationship as a love story cannot begin to expose the multiple lines of imperial and economic power that traversed this woman's body, not to speak of its Jewish identifications.

When Vespasian died in 79 CE—the same year Josephus' *Bellum Judaicum* was published—Titus acceded as emperor, and Berenike returned to Rome. Resistance to her presence caused her quick dismissal.[213] We know that in Titus' first year as emperor, the disastrous volcanic eruption at Pompeii occurred as the major event of his reign, and soon thereafter a plague took his life. The sources are silent on the ultimate fate of Berenike.

Domitian as the new emperor built an arch to honor Titus that celebrated, centrally, his victorious return from the Judaean War. It was completed in Rome in 81 CE, with Titus' apotheosis depicted at the top of the arch, ascending to heaven carried by an eagle that was the symbol of Jupiter. In 96 CE, Domitian had begun the construction at Ephesus of a temple to himself that housed a giant imperial statue when he was assassinated and the Roman Senate condemned his memory. That same year, John of Patmos completed the book of Revelation.

The Whore of Babylon

The great harlot . . . [τῆς πόρνης τῆς μεγάλης . . .] (Rev 17:1)

The luxury trade of women as wives was described as a kind of prostitution, trading sexual partners for wealth and influence.[214] Sexual prudery was not the issue. Rather, it was control of women's bodies that were lost to the group in such actions of exchange. The attractions of wealth encouraged disloyalty to these social patterns. Indeed, adultery was viewed as treason. It is in this sense that scholars today approach the disgraced figure, the "whore

5.16
Titus rising to the heavens on the back of an eagle. Interior ceiling, Arch of Titus, ca. 81 CE.
Photo: Anthony M. from Rome, Italy. Wikimedia Commons. CC BY 2.0.

of Babylon" (Rev 17:5), who figures prominently in the book of Revelation. Bauckham writes: "The primary meaning of the harlot image in Revelation 17–18 is economic."[215] Luxury trade makes Rome the harlot city, the locus of accumulated wealth and its ostentatious display—and Rome, built on seven hills (Rev 17:9), is the city of Babylon in Revelation.[216]

Important here is the treasonous implication of the harlot image. It connects to the metaphorical use of the phrase found in the Old Testament, "whoring after false gods," which could refer to actions of both sexes.[217] Gaca writes: "The metaphor of spiritual fornication informs what it means to identify women as 'harlots' or 'whores' (pornai/ποόρναι) in the Septuagint. . . . The label pornē/πόρνη serves to vilify women for worshipping in a manner alien to the way of the Lord, and hence the community."[218] "[T]ainted with bastardy" was the phrase Philo used to refer to nonpriests eating sacred things, hence taking privileges of a priest.[219]

5.17

Dea Roma coin of Vespasian, minted in 71 CE in the Roman province of Asia. Obverse: head of Vespasian, laureate with aegis. Reverse: the goddess Roma reclines on the city's seven hills; to left, wolf and twins; to right, River Tiber. This image has been compared to Revelation's description of the whore of Babylon: "The seven heads [of the beast] are the seven hills on which the woman sits. They are also seven kings." The British Museum, 1872,0709.477. © The Trustees of the British Museum. All rights reserved.

Frankfurter contributes that in Jewish texts of this period, *zenut*, the Hebrew equivalent of *porneía* (πορνεία), "often refers to intermarriage" seen as an act of sexual impurity.[220]

> And I saw a woman sitting on a scarlet beast that was covered with blasphemous names, having seven heads and ten horns. And the woman had been clothed in purple and scarlet, and was glittering with gold, precious stones and pearls. She held a golden cup in her hand, filled with abominations and the filth of her adulteries (πορνείας). This title was written on her forehead: A MYSTERY, BABYLON THE GREAT, THE MOTHER OF PROSTITUTES [ΠΟΡΝΩΝ] AND OF THE ABOMINATIONS OF THE EARTH. (Rev 17:4–5)

Scholars connect the image of the whore of Babylon with John's condemnation of a local prophetess of Thyatira whom he names Jezebel, after an Old Testament queen who seduced Israel into idolatry.[221] Aune argues that John's metaphors need not have been meant to be merely locally applied. If indeed he was a "Palestinian Jew" and refugee from the Judaean War, "it is reasonable to suppose that he shares the hostility that any Jews from Palestine had toward the Romans and the various rulers of Judea that the Romans manipulated."[222] This does not prove that Berenike was literally meant by the text, as opposed to any number of women whose person was exchanged in the empire for earthly gain. As Thompson reminds us, "Logical stories are not necessarily true stories"; questions such as "what might be reasonable to believe" can be "deceptive, however seductive, because lacking warrant, they always go beyond our evidence."[223] Just as there was no clear identity of a Palestinian Jew in the first century, so identifying the whore of Babylon—a local priestess? the Judaean queen?—is not a possible or even a very meaningful task. What does matter for a critical reading of the text today is identifying the practices that, then as now, violate the ethics of communal life: private amassing of extremes of wealth, patriarchal exchange of wives and daughters for power and profit, and physical brutalities carried out with impunity by those with power over others, whatever the identity of the perpetrators.

5.18

Whore of Babylon, color illustration from the Martin Luther translation of the Bible published in 1534. Workshop of Lucas Cranach.

Translation from the Margins

Contemporary theoretical approaches dealing with issues of power and exploitation have been used fruitfully in interpreting the book of Revelation, which can be read on many levels as a document of liberation. Easily related to the text are class critiques of economic inequalities and postcolonial critiques of Roman imperial policy.[224] Feminist commentators have had a more difficult time. Schüssler Fiorenza concurs with the historical conclusion that the figure of the whore needs to be understood metaphorically as the city of Rome and not individual women.[225] Yet the vituperative language of this metaphor in the text remains problematic: the harlot woman is made to personify disloyalty to the group by that very trafficking of her being which makes her the object, not the subject of exchange.[226] In the text she is "abused and horribly destroyed," a scapegoat figure who may evoke sympathy rather than condemnation.[227] It is not easy to redeem what Pippin considers the deeply misogynist view of women expressed in the book: "Political, economic and religious structures are subverted in the Apocalypse, but women's roles and functions remain the same."[228] The problem would then rest with what Pippin calls the Western and male-centered readings of this figure that have continued into the present.[229] In short, it is the mode of inheritance of the book of Revelation that keeps the misogyny of the text in play.

"Signifying on"–Inside the Meaning of Words

The African American, "womanist" strategy of reading allows us to cut through the heritage of ungodly biblical claims. The novelist Zora Neale Hurston observes that some people are able to "get inside the meaning of words," allowing them to *signify on the meaning of texts* in a critical way.[230] Her own work demonstrates this expertise. Martin writes: "Hurston convincingly signifies upon all forms of authority in the biblical narratives, including the portrayal of a deity who resembled (in the tradition of pro-slavery apologists) a 'White, Old, Massa-like God.' Hurston rewrites and revitalizes the biblical traditions in a restorative act of 'cultural translation,' giving God a 'remodeling job' by signifying on the Bible—or at least on the White version of the Bible."[231]

This method separates the transcendent truth of the text from its linguistic limitations, allowing Martin to redeem, specifically, the book of Revelation. Martin begins where we began this constellation, with the mention in Revelation of the trade in slaves, the "bodies and souls of human beings" (18:11). She recognizes herself in the mirror of this image due to the heritage of slave trade that unites them, and is able thereby to "tilt the hermeneutical mirror" so that it aligns, not with isolated figures in John's text but rather with the marginal beings on his cargo list, whom he himself mentions only briefly. She does not attempt to redeem what is unredeemable in John's text—a problem that is not new for African American biblical scholars. But she can and does affirm this prophet without a patron as a "marginalized author" who has mastered the art of "signifying on" the "mighty Empire of Rome" by providing a structural critique of power that, like the womanist critique, uses the master's language against itself.[232] The nimbleness of her hermeneutic shift in the alignment of biblical interpretation keeps constant focus on the liberating power the text contains.

Until the lions have their historians, tales of the hunting will always glorify the hunter.

—KENYAN PROVERB[233]

To whom does a messianic text belong? The answer can only be: the dispossessed. The philosopher and civil rights leader Howard Thurman knew this when he entitled his book *Jesus and the Disinherited* (1949). Thurman shared with his contemporary and friend Gandhi a commitment to nonviolent resistance with the goal of social justice, and strongly influenced Dr. Martin Luther King, Jr. Thurman relates the strategy of his maternal grandmother Nancy Ambrose who, kept illiterate by the slavery into which she was born, was read *to* from the Bible, but now she would not hear of Paul. She told Thurman: "Always the white minister used as his text something from Paul. At least three or four times a year he used as a text: 'Slaves, be obedient to them that are your master . . . , as unto Christ.' Then he would go on to show how it was God's will that we were slaves and how, if we were good and happy slaves, God would bless us."[234] She insisted that the meaning of the text must adhere to her criterion of describing a "God worth believing in."[235] A text the interpretation of which diminishes the humanity of its hearers cannot speak truth concerning justice or any other transcendent idea.

Every Generation Reads Anew

Every age must strive anew to wrest tradition away from the conformism that is working to overpower it. The Messiah comes not only as the redeemer; he comes as the victor over the Antichrist.

—WALTER BENJAMIN[236]

Hermeneutic practice needs to pass through the experience of the living if it is not to fall victim to the tradition of oppression. There is a philosophical connection between Thurman's grandmother's criterion of reading and the approach of Thurman's contemporary, Walter Benjamin, who spoke of the cultural treasures of the past as the spoils carried forward in history by the victors. Hurston's method of "getting inside the meaning of words" suggests an analogy with Benjamin's metaphor of the dwarf of theology who gets inside a chess-playing puppet called "historical materialism" and, through a system of mirrors, guides its hands so that the puppet wins every time. The historical context of Stalinism in which Benjamin was writing required of theology that it infiltrate the secular texts of Marx so that their truth would not be lost. Like Thurman, Benjamin argued for the necessity of rescuing the texts from their deceptive bequeathal by and to the powerful. He wrote that only for a redeemed mankind would the past be citable in all of its moments. The first awareness must be how miniscule is the record that we examine, and hence, "The historical construction is dedicated to the memory of the anonymous."[237] How much suffering have humans inflicted against others *as* the Other? How many women raped? How many bastard children disowned? How many botched abortions?[238] How many wives kicked downstairs?[239] How many children left as found-lings to become slaves?[240]

Kairos as messianic time is not a linear progression. Martin knows this when she writes: "Here [in the 'signifying' practice] the uniform function of early Jewish and apocalyptic literature becomes most evident, for it represents the mixture of protest and hope on the part of oppressed believers against unjust or imperial powers."[241] Translation as a space of philosophical critique passes through the reality in which the text is read. Its concern is not cultural difference, but the persistence of structures of injustice despite these differences. The eternal recurrence of domination is not natural, not ordained, not inevitable, but discovered anew by every generation that possesses a weak messianic power to overcome its oppressive forms. "To grasp the eternity of historical events is really to appreciate the eternity of their transience," wrote Benjamin.[242] He envisioned the messianic age (a classless society) not as "the final goal of historical progress" but as its "so often failed but finally [*endlich*] achieved interruption."[243] The task given to every generation would then be to break the cycle of repetition, not to mistake human-caused suffering for God's plan.

IV. HISTORY AND TRUTH

The Philosophical Task

The double interest of this book, history and philosophy, has required the rejection of speculations concerning history as a whole. Rather, philosophical questions have been viewed through the prism of historical particulars, because only through them can truth find the concrete content that substantiates its claims. Both history and philosophy have an investment in truth. This is what ties them together. And yet the practice of discovery in each provides only a temporary convergence, because the truth that guides them thrives on different centers. In our reading of first-century texts, this momentary alignment has been the goal.

For historians, truth is an empirical matter—of a special sort. A close parallel, and one that connects the historical emergence of a new literary genre to the elevation of history writing as a form of knowledge, is the detective story.[244] Forensic inquiry is the task of collecting evidence about past events by reading material remains. For the historian, archaeology plays this role, but if textual evidence has been preserved, then witness reports take center stage. The goal is a true image of an event that by its very nature is transitory. The event has disappeared. Only the traces remain.

The method of historians developed out of the practice of biblical exegesis.[245] And yet it inverted the focus, privileging the temporary as opposed to the eternal, and truth as humanly contingent rather than as the realization of a providential plan. The historian acknowledges that the preservation of evidence is aleatory—a matter of chance. But it would be wrong to translate this insecurity of ground to mean the absence of any claim to truth. Rather, truth matters, and yet the goal of the historian is inherently problematic because every actual increase of knowledge reveals the scope of ignorance that remains. The deeper the historian digs into the past, the more unknown terrain is exposed. Burrell, cited frequently above, describes in her 400-page monograph the experience of working with the "varied and intermittent sources" available to her: "Writing about [*neokoroi* cities], then, is like surveying at night; there is a general darkness, though occasional moonlight allows some understanding of the terrain, and once in a while a fortunate flash of lightning illuminates some crucial detail fully."[246] What compels historians to strive for this partial revelation of the past? Their motive is other than a desire for completeness. A historian is not a collector. Not completion but "illumination" is the goal—that is, a kind of revelation, one that bears on the questions of philosophy and recognizes, with humility, that, in the practices of inquiry that matter, mastery is not possible.

For philosophers, truth is the lodestar always out of reach. To love wisdom is to rescind possession of it. (Pythagoras is said to have described his way of life as *philosophia* rather than *sophia* for this reason, as mere humans can only strive after wisdom.)[247] But when philosophy, in seeking to move beyond the immanence of lived time, touches the past, when it makes the work of historians its point of ignition, it needs to resist the temptation to claim philosophical truth as one with the course of history—a hermeneutic crime, one might say, that turns the texts of history into a new mythology, marshaled to justify our present order as history's rationally ordained culmination.

Philology—the study of the meaning of words not reducible to the psychology of the author—is the science that binds history to philosophy. When philology is put to use by the historian, words disavow the claim of the present to read the past as immediately its own. They become, rather, a point of entry into an unknown place; here the philosopher takes over as guide. The knots into which words become entangled in the history of their appropriation limit their philosophical power. Words are sewn into the fabric of tradition in a warped way that from a critical distance can be discerned as a pattern of covering history's tracks. Philological critique frees the historical objects named to speak another way, telling us something new. It is here that philosophy parts company with patrimonial readings that revere those ancestral lines of descent (based on sheer survival!) to which tradition bears witness. Hence, this book's central question—how to read history philosophically—requires a task of translation that does not cover the past with the language of the present, but reads the fragments that remain against the grain of their appropriation by history's winners.

Ambiguity/Polysemy

Truth is not simplistic. Precisely because words are labile in that to which they refer, truth plays cat-and-mouse with literal meaning. John's language in the book of Revelation shows this. Philosophically, that can be seen as its strength. If historians acquiesce and submit to what Foucault called the long baking process of history that hardens the meaning of texts, John's reading of past oracles and prophecies celebrates/contemplates ambiguity.[248] Words that reference earlier prophecies abound in the book of Revelation, yet meanings morph confusingly.[249] Symbols crash into their opposite. The lion turns into a lamb.[250] The lamb reverses its role and shepherds people.[251] The number seven, sacred in the book of Genesis, slides across a field of possibilities: the "mystery of the seven stars that you saw in my right hand" are the angels of the seven churches, and the seven lampstands are the seven churches, the "seven golden candlesticks" of the menorah.[252] The Lamb, too, has "seven horns, and seven eyes, which are the seven Spirits of God."[253] But the number seven also identifies the seven heads of the bestial hydra and the seven hills of adulterous Rome. Seven angels bring seven plagues; as emissaries of God, they bring both woes and salvation;[254] divine wrath terrifies;[255] and the divine promise is to "wipe away every tear from their eyes."[256] The antichrist moves into celestial view, in close proximity to the redeemer.[257] An angel "cast out of heaven" becomes a dragon, a serpent, and "deceives the whole world."[258] A beast with "two horns like a lamb" speaks as a dragon and "deceives the inhabitants of the earth."[259] Indeed, deception is a continuous threat.[260] The "unblemished" (ἄμωμοί) are those who do not lie.[261] But given the polysemy of images and words, how is lying to be known? John has been charged with bringing satan into play. The world appears divided between the damned and the saved. And yet the polarities of good and evil cannot be clearly sustained because in this text binaries coexist.[262] Words, like swords, are double-edged: sweet on the tongue, they turn the belly bitter.[263] The mark of the beast and the mark of the redeemer are not easily distinguished. The unspeakable, unknowable name of God is on the forehead of the redeemer, written in the book of life "from the beginning."[264] Yet who, merely human, can read divine language to tell the difference?[265]

Whitaker comments: "Deception is the crucial characteristic of evil for the author of Revelation."[266] Those who have sinned have made errors of judgment: Revelation 1:5 uses the word ἁμαρτιῶν, from the root α-μαρτ, that means to fail, err, miss the mark, in contrast to the martyr (μαρτ-ήρ) who witnesses truthfully. Erring, missing the path, is the literal meaning of a word that is translated as "sin"—crucially, in describing the acts of the whore of Babylon, whose "sins (ἁμαρτίαι) are piled up to heaven."[267] A repeated insistence on the ambiguity of the referent requires listeners to exercise their interpretive judgment—not to "sin" by erring and missing the mark; not to tolerate or be deceived by the liar. John calls this practical capacity "wisdom" (σοφία).[268] The positioning of this word in John's text is at the hinge between past prophecy and current events. "Here is wisdom: the number of the beast is the number of a man. His number is 666."[269] Numbers are letters, and these numbers—600, 60, and 6—spell out the name of Nero, last of the Julio-Claudian emperors, who was rumored to have survived his forced suicide and fled to the Parthians in the east, threatening (promising) repeatedly to return in John's time. With this reference to Nero, we would appear to be on solid historical ground. But still a decipherment is required: "The seven heads are seven hills on which the woman sits. They are also seven kings. Five have fallen, one is, the other has not yet come; but when he does come he must remain a little while. The beast who once was, and now is not, is an eighth king. He belongs to the seven and is going to his destruction."[270] The riddle-like reference leads historians to count the Roman emperors, although with differing results, as even here the meaning is obscure: "While this text seems relatively clear, scholars have interpreted it in a bewildering number of ways."[271]

John's text is a confounding composite of past prophecy and present history. The narrative structure doubles back and moves sideways, repeats and breaks apart.[272] Its meaning is the ambiguity of meaning. Allegory is only partially operative as a literary form that would tie it to symbolic certainty—the name of Babylon for Rome, for example, that layers the lived catastrophe of the Judaean War onto the earlier destruction of Jerusalem by a Babylonian king.[273] The book of Revelation has no coherence as an allegorical whole. Instead, there is an additive sequence, linked together by the repetition of "and . . . and" (*kai . . . kai*). Strikingly, this connecting word begins the vast majority of its sentences, unlike any other New Testament book.[274] The effect is to loosen the textual fabric. The surrounding world enters into it, palpable not only through visible images but by means of all of the senses: the smell of sulfur, tastes bitter and sweet, the touch of linen, the covering warmth of the sun—a world of multivalent signs, where to miss the mark is a real and present danger. Within this profusion of worldly things, the book's overriding concern is judgment, both human and divine. Human judgment evaluates the ambiguities of the situation in exercising the freedom to act. Divine judgment makes its evaluations according to what each person has done.[275] The word for judgment in *koine* is *krisis* (κρίσις),[276] from which our word "crisis" is derived.

Time and the Text

Hermeneutics—John's and our own—attends to the power of the text to illuminate a transitory world. Whereas John draws on the wisdom of past prophecy to decipher an ambiguous present, for the historian the process is reversed: the task is to decipher an uncertain past. The original scene of historical events is the "effaced" but still "organizing force," writes Michel de Certeau.[277] He insists: "Even by returning endlessly to the oldest primary sources, by scrutinizing the experience that linguistic and historical systems mask as they develop themselves, historians never apprehend origins, but only the successive stages of their loss."[278]

With John's text as a source, the hermeneutic problems mount. If inner-textual evidence ties the book of Revelation to a specific place (province of Asia) and time (late first century) and a certain constellation of events (the Judaean war, the destruction of Pompeii, Domitian's reign), it must be kept in mind that no first-century copy of this text exists. The earliest remains are second-century fragments. The earliest New Testament manuscripts do not include John's final prophecy.[279] The earliest approximation of a full text of Revelation dates to the third century. All variants—papyri, uncials, minuscules, translations, and the second-century patristic citations—are vulnerable to scribal tamperings. If this primary source still claims the historian's attention, it is not because its reading provides textual certainty. Rather, it is because John's words materialize a world beyond the limits of our temporal horizon. This making visible of the invisible, the disappeared, is the power of the historian's work. Body returns in thought as re-membering, the resuscitation not of a soul, but of a life.

Philosophical questions emerge from this inverted resurrection. It is not possible merely to flesh out the text of another time, another place, with present meanings, as if the skeleton, the schema remained intact and, once reanimated, could fit the framing structures of our time. In the case of the first century, secular modernity has imposed categories of separation— religion/politics; Christian/Jew; aesthetics/reason—that, as we have seen, did not then exist, so that the presentist construction of the historical object already disqualifies the historian's task. De Certeau writes: "history does not resuscitate anything."[280]

A fundamental philosophical issue is raised by time's infiltration into linguistic expression, which is to say, texts have a temporal index. Words survive the historical disappearance of what they name. This is the source of anachronistic naming. The *pax Romana* and its namesakes, *pax Britannica* and *pax Americana*, are separated by two millennia. These modern forms echo the past rhetorically in effect to justify themselves. Alternatively, historians use the brutal reality of the Roman peace—Tacitus noted famously that the Romans made a desolation and called it peace—as a critical wedge to undermine modern empire's self-justification. But both critics and supporters proceed as if the concept of empire were timeless, bestowing upon it a determining significance regardless of the historical particulars of its appearance. Quentin Skinner protests against the method of "abstracting particular arguments from the context of their occurrence in order to relocate them as 'contributions to allegedly perennial debates.'"[281] Anachronistic reading of past texts through the fantasized stability of key concepts leads to results that "may be classified not as histories but more appropriately as mythologies."[282] One can go further: the birth of history in the modern sense is also the beginning of modernity's construction of its own mythic origins *as* history. De Certeau acknowledges: "History is probably our myth. It combines what can be thought, the 'thinkable,'" with stories of origin "in conformity with the way in which a society can understand its own working."[283]

In the double vision of history suggested here—not only as critique of history-become-myth, but also as philosophical rescue of the material traces it provides—the first task is to translate words in a way that lets the past escape the impositions that have been placed upon it, allowing historical details to slip out of the conceptual frames that have carried them forward. The evidence (*stasis, nomos, koine, doulos*) recedes from the horizon of modern understanding because the past and present do not align. The part that vanishes from modern optics is its most valuable aspect because it challenges the inherited traditions of power. Rather than attempting a full recuperation, we enter into the text in order to decipher the transitory history encoded in the words. This experience de-reifies, de-ossifies, de-bakes the hardening of the past into concepts, making legible something that cannot otherwise be read. How to "tilt the hermeneutic mirror" so that it does not reflect an immediate image of ourselves? How to extend the conditions of possibility that condense in our own moment in time, rather than using the past to naturalize the present along with the concepts and categories used to describe it?

A reader's relationship to the past is mediated by the account provided of it. It might seem to make sense, then, that as a historical object the book of Revelation is one with the history of its reception. The relativism that is implied philosophically would need to be accepted and embraced. Factual accuracy would exhaust the meaning of truth. Problems regarding the authenticity of the text disappear when meaning is reduced to its readings by others.[284] However, before modern historians could make this claim, something happened precisely with the historical reception of *this* book, *this* text that marked a restructuring of time itself. It took place, Reinhart Koselleck tells us, when a transformation of the reading of the book of Revelation converged with a transformation in the world order, ushering in a specifically modern meaning of history.[285] *Krisis* (κρίσις), the repeated word for "judgment" in John's text, was inscribed as *crisis* onto historical time in its entirety.[286] "From the second half of the eighteenth century on, a religious connotation enters into the way the term [crisis/*krisis*] is used. It does so, however, in a post-theological mode, namely as philosophy of history."[287]

Judgment of the World

The poet Friedrich Schiller wrote in 1784/5, "Die Weltgeschichte ist das Weltgericht": "The history of the world is the judgment of the world." In German, *Weltgericht* has the specific theological meaning of Last Judgment.[288] The modern understanding of this eighteenth-century definition referred to an actualized future, immanent within history as the endpoint of a linear chronology.[289] Koselleck writes that the impact of Schiller's dictum within this secularizing environment "cannot be overestimated": "The final judgment will not be pronounced from without, either by God or by historians in ex post facto pronouncements about history. Rather, it will be executed through all the actions and omissions of mankind. What was left undone in one minute, eternity will not retrieve. The concept of crisis has become the fundamental mode of interpreting historical time."[290] The temporality of crisis that characterizes modernity becomes fixed, stable, if you will, across discourses, from the politics of revolution to the science of economics, and Marx's theory of the crisis is an extension of it.[291] Perpetual crisis that leaves the future in doubt cannot be avoided, but only celebrated by true believers as progress. The alternative is a conservative lament. According to Koselleck, only now can all political concepts become secularized theological concepts. Only now is the ground prepared for the French Revolutionary reading of time. The eschatological concept of "crisis" becomes in radical theorists like Rousseau a philosophy of history that is both a secularization (*Verweltlichung*)[292] and an instantiation of the book of Revelation—its promise of a new world becomes a utopian future, the rupturing crisis that makes all things new.[293]

Koselleck's sweeping claims for the concept of crisis as key to the concept of modernity is open to the Skinnerian critique of concepts, isolated from their contexts, that take on a life of their own. But one thing is certain. The modern temporality that he is describing is not functioning in John's text. This modern trajectory of Apocalypse as immanent to the meaning of history as a whole is not in the book of Revelation. When John uses what scholars have named the "three times formula" (*Dreizeitenformel*), "the one who is and who was, and who is to come," it refers to the power of eternal being despite change, and messianic anticipation despite disappointment, rather than attributing power to change itself.[294] For John, futurity in the modern sense does not exist. Just as *chronos* is regular, measurable time but not linear chronological sequence, so *kairos*, John's contrasting term for time, is the evanescent and momentarily propitious synchrony of signs, not revolutionary rupture that signals no possibility of return.[295]

Kairos is not a calculatable moment; it cannot be placed on the calendar. Instead, it is a recurrent possibility, one that for John or any prophet without a patron is a historically specific expression of hope. The situated truth that kairotic time entails is lost in the fourth century CE, when, within a Christianized Roman Empire, earthly power and divine justice are no longer at odds but imagined as one and the same. The task of the Christian ruler (the *katechon*)[296] is to *hold back* time until the "end" (*telos/* τέλος), meaning the fulfillment or completion of time, which requires the reception of the Gospel message all over the world, and it is not by accident that Christopher Columbus cited Revelation in his journal of voyages to the "New" World.

The process of modernizing time, writes Koselleck, begins with the Protestant Reformation—but only as recognized *retroactively*, by the Enlightenment philosophers who came afterward: "Until well into the sixteenth century, the history of Christianity is a history of expectations, or more exactly, the constant anticipation of the End of the World on the one hand and the continual deferment of the End on the other."[297] Koselleck describes how progress is later read into successive historical interpretations of the book of Revelation itself, thus privileging *ex post facto* the Protestant reading. "Each earlier exegesis was conceived as an act of obscurity foreseen by God, whose successive illumination was the task of later interpreters. From the collective misinterpretations and their correction, there finally emerged the ultimate true insight."[298]

The ingenuity of the Protestant reading of Revelation was to take the text literally. Rome for the reformers was not Babylon, but Rome itself, the present, papal Rome of the sixteenth century, revealed at this time as the antichrist. But when history in the secular Enlightenment takes on the weight of theological truth, then Revelation must be read in relation to history as a whole. Modern historians have praised the Protestant privileging of the text in vernacular translation for its democratic implications. "According to Protestant expositions, the command to John in [Rev] 10:8–11 to take the 'little open book; read it, and prophesy again' was a divinely ordained prophetic image of the Protestant Reformation, which opened the Bible to all."[299] But when universal accessibility is tied to the need to comprehend history in its entirety, the inherent ambiguity of the text splinters into a multiplicity of sectarian readings (as does the Protestant faith), making its partisan politicization unavoidable. The reading of God's word as a decipherment of events, past and current, identifies enemies on earth. Partisans appropriate the eternity of the word in the face of the transitoriness of the world, so that all that is required is to identify: Who is the antichrist? Who is the redeemer? The imposition of prejudices and partial perceptions claims the entire patriarchal power of names. Is the antichrist the emperor of pagan Rome, the Muslim enemies of the crusaders, the Catholic pope, the USSR, or revolutionary Iran? Does God will earthly power to Vespasian, or Constantine, or Lenin, or Putin, or Trump? All of these positions have been argued from a partisan reading of the book of Revelation, which may be potentially the least democratic of forms.

This weaponization of historical interpretation is not ended by secular modernity. Rather, it fosters a split between those who maintain that secularization itself is the realization of reason as the only truth, and those who insist that John's book contains revealed truth in its every word. As opposed as secular rationalists and religious fundamentalists may be, they prove perfectly capable of converging in their identification of the enemy. A literal reading of a "new" Jerusalem, which is key to the Christian Zionist position, converges with Israel's secular nationalism, when both demonize Palestinians as Muslims and/or Arabs. The point is that reason and faith are both vulnerable to enlistment for war—which cannot be the true meaning of justice revealed. Koselleck, like most Western historians, does not enter into a discussion of Islamic apocalypse.[300] Surely Islam, among the three monotheisms, has history on its side in any chronologically progressive interpretation of time. Moreover, it could, and did, make the claim to being the most rational of these religions. Islamic thought's capacity for critical insights has been a constant in history.[301] But when secular modernity takes over as narrator of history's course, concealed within Western modernity's linear time, what Taubes calls "the magic spell of Christianity's historical success" is refortified by the hegemonic imposition of modernity, and "BC" and "AD" dating becomes truth for the rest of the world.[302]

Koselleck steps back to observe the history of ideas themselves and, as concepts, to track their historical unfolding. Skinner protests against the tendency of what he calls the "mythology of prolepsis," whereby events are defined in terms that later evolve: concepts develop, while an event has to wait for the future to learn its meaning, and the historian of ideas goes down the "scholastic path" of "resolving antinomies," while authors are blamed or praised according to whether they anticipate ourselves.[303] For Skinner, the tendency to read one's own reality and its prejudices into the past is countered by the search for authorial intent within the context of the writer's own time. *Pace* Skinner, we have insisted that the discovery of intent, whether of past author or present commentator, is not a possible or even desirable goal. Not the text within history but history within the text is, for the philosopher, the critical point. Because authorial intent is not knowable, Skinner's historicist contextualization can only be half the task, the first prerequisite. Its salutary distancing effect creates obstacles to immediate understanding and delineates the philosopher's concern.

Both Koselleck and Skinner emphasize the transient meaning of concepts in historical context, hence both oppose the ahistorical presumptions of normative philosophy. But the historicizing of concepts is not yet the philosophical rescue of the historical past. If Koselleck's weak Hegelianism and Skinner's robust historicism are both to be avoided, does philosophy have a way out?

Against the Concept

Modernity's distaste for transcendence privileges history over truth. In contrast, philosophy as historical translation entertains transcendence, while remaining apophatic (able only to determine what is *not* transcendent truth). Within modernity, the philosophical term *concept* takes over the role of the Platonic idea, tying this ideal realm to earth. The concept mediates between thought and world, constraining modern metaphysics to immanence. History is then both concept and content, both epistemological method and phenomenological truth, as if, at the level of abstraction, history could overcome the material transience of which it is composed.[304] How are philosophers to avoid this propensity of the concept to obliterate transitory, material history and turn history as a concept into an empty abstraction—if not Hegel's *Geist* (spirit/mind), then historicity, historicality, historicism—from which the particularities are allowed to disappear?

The concept emptied out of particulars insulates itself from the world in order to preserve itself. Blumenberg reminds us that Descartes believed this was, as a philosophical utopia, "eminently attainable": "This 'end state' of philosophy" (an apocalyptic finality of meaning!) would "correspond to the perfection of a terminology designed to capture the presence and precision of the matter at hand in well-defined concepts. In its terminal state, philosophical language would be purely and strictly 'conceptual': everything *can* be defined, therefore everything *must* be defined."[305] "Having arrived at its final conceptual state," writes Blumenberg, "philosophy would also have to relinquish any justifiable interest in researching the *history* of its concepts."[306] A concept, in this context, is an idea that absorbs its history, inspiring Nietzsche to say that no definition of a concept is possible, so long as this connection to history remains.[307] In contrast, the "wordliness" of the name proliferates content, moving by analogy across the particulars as they enter one and then another historical constellation.

Hegel developed the idea that the evolution of concepts was history writ large, unfolding in an eschatological-historical trajectory toward its own fulfillment. Concepts, while containing the past, supersede it, becoming careless of the transitory historical particulars in which they have been actualized. Hegel speaks disparagingly of "lazy existence" (*faule Existenz*), referring to the material substrate of history that ultimately does not interest the philosopher.[308] Only the rational is real. Only the history of philosophical thought is conserved as the ground that nourishes the present.[309] Once this sedimentation of history occurs, concepts are defined, not by the details of their past, but by a logic of binary oppositions—a structuring of thought that resembles the abstraction of myth. Grasped as a concept, the historical object excludes its "other" and takes on meaning by producing its conceptual twin: "religion" is opposed to politics; "history" separates itself from myth; "reason" leaves a residue of madness. And, most relevant to our topic: Jewish is not-Christian; Greek is not-Jewish. (For Hegel, according to Derrida, the Greek *is* the non-Jew—and Kantian philosophy is a form of Judaism.)[310]

When concepts lose their historical content they lose touch with truth. The forgetting of history leads to metahistorical fantasies: Ancient Greece is the origin of modernity. Reason is the possession of the West. Religion is a vestigial remnant of the past. If we work merely through negation to reverse the hegemonic poles of these logical binaries, we are still not free of their mythic spell. Without faith in historical supersession, therefore, dialectical thinking on its own is powerless to alter the epistemological field. The work of translation shifts the temporal direction: the past is not translated into the present but vice versa, the present into the past, in order to liberate us, not from religion, but from the binary distinction produced by the modern concept of it.

The concept is to the name as the corpse is to experience. The concept is the second death of material life. The critical philosophical task is historical displacement through an act of translation that animates the past in a language full of particulars that have not been stripped of their expressive capacity to name. "The philosophy of history merges with the writing of history."[311]

The concept is abstract, ahistorical, and can only be identified as a repetition of itself—class, patriarchy, empire—rather than the particular constellation in which crimes of history occur. And crimes there have been. The ground from which the present evolves is a war zone. (Benjamin condemned Hegel as "an intellectual man of violence, a mystic of violence, the worst sort that there is.")[312] What appear in such concepts and categories as eternal verities are deciphered instead as moments of missed opportunity to act against them.

The Task

Philosophical history is the undoing of the constraining order that keeps the past in place. The philosophical arc of historical exegesis is suspended (in open air) precisely here, touching a past in imperfect alignment with the present, demanding an animal's leap. A tiger's leap. The task is to liberate the past from the concepts that purport to contain it; to suspend the structuring schema of history as modernity's content.

To fall out of modernity itself.

Notes

INTRODUCTION

1. Theodor W. Adorno, letter to Walter Benjamin, cited in Susan Buck-Morss, *The Dialectics of Seeing: Walter Benjamin and the Arcades Project* (Cambridge, MA: MIT Press, 1989), p. 228.

2. A quotation from Walter Benjamin is fitting: "My thinking is related to theology as blotting pad is related to ink. It is saturated with it. Were one to go by the blotter, however, nothing of what is written would remain." Walter Benjamin, *The Arcades Project*, trans. Howard Eiland and Kevin McLaughlin, prepared on the basis of the German volume edited by Rolf Tiedemann (Cambridge, MA: Harvard University Press, 1999), p. 471 (N7a,7).

CHAPTER 1

1. *Anno Mundi* (Year of the World) was a reckoning of time based on the genealogies of the book of Genesis reaching back to the Creation, estimated by rabbinical as well as Christian chronologists, that was open to repeated revisions as the passing of time required.

2. The scanty evidence is conflicting, and with the turn to the year 2000 again became news, as it was not at all clear what this millennial date signified.

3. There are no scriptural indications of Jesus' birth year or day. The date December 25 was chosen in the early third century CE, close to the winter solstice (already a pagan festival of Saturnalia), while his conception nine months earlier corresponded to the spring equinox.

4. Emperors were not kings. They ruled by acclaim of the military and consent of the Senate. In our reckoning of time, Augustus' reign was from 16 January 27 BCE to 19 August 14 CE. For readers attempting to compute the years of his rule (why 40, and not 41 or 42 years?), note that in chronological time there is no Year Zero, so that 1 CE follows immediately after 1 BCE (the span from 27 BCE to 14 CE is thus 27 + 14 − 1 years), while the 8 months of the last year of Augustus' life are not counted as a year of rule.

5. Before Augustus, Roman coins depicted the heads of gods and goddesses with no date at all. After his death, coins by later Julio-Claudian emperors sometimes continued to be dedicated—without date—to *Divus* Augustus Caesar.

6. Caius died in 2 CE, Lucius in 4 CE. After their untimely deaths, Augustus adopted Tiberius, who, in 3 CE was joint consul with Augustus and became emperor with Augustus' death in 14 CE.

7. Reading dates on the coins is also complicated by the fact that legends in the West were in Latin, using letters for Roman numerals, while in the East, coins used Greek lettering for names and numbers (Greek numbers were written in single alphabetic letters). There is a special wiki devoted to dating coins: http://www.forumancientcoins.com/numiswiki/view.asp.

   For a treatment in hard copy, see *Roman Imperial Coinage*, abbreviated RIC, covering coins from the time of the Battle of Actium to late antiquity (31 BCE–491 CE). This catalogue was published over several decades, from 1923 (beginning under Harold Mattingly, numismatist at the British Museum) to 1994, and was a successor to the eight-volume catalogue compiled by the numismatist Henry Cohen in the nineteenth century. (See "Roman Imperial Coinage," Wikipedia.) For images, see http://www.ancientcoins.ca/RIC/.

8. Reading the abbreviated titles, names, and dates of Roman imperial coins necessitates reference to our own chronological time's standardized tables. See Zander H. Klawans, *Reading and Dating Roman Imperial Coins*, 4th ed. (Racine, WI: Western Publishing, 1977). First consul years accorded with the length of years of the (pre-Julian) Varronian calendar, and Varro's (erroneous) chronological list of magistrates.

9. "Due to the brevity of their rule, it is possible to date their coins with only a few days' uncertainty": Charles L. Murison, *Galba, Otho, and Vitellius: Careers and Controversies* (New York: G. Olms Verlag, 1993), pp. 93–94. See also the PhD dissertation of Jon Mark Holtgrefe, "The Characterization of Civil War: Literary, Numismatic, and Epigraphical Presentations of the 'Year of the Four Emperors'" (University of Oregon, 2011).

10. As Feeney observes: "We 'know' what a date is, or a year, or a calendar; it is all the more important to keep reminding ourselves of how often our understanding of such apparently obvious concepts will completely misrepresent the Roman equivalent—if indeed there is an equivalent. Studying Roman time becomes an exercise in trying better to understand our own." Denis Feeney, *Caesar's Calendar: Ancient Time and the Beginnings of History* (Berkeley: University of California Press, 2007), p. 4. In fact, ours is the Gregorian calendar, based on the Julian calendar but adjusted by Pope Gregory XIII in 1582 and now the most used in the world. "The [Gregorian] calendar spaces leap years to make the average year 365.2425 days long, approximating the 365.2422-day tropical year that is determined by the earth's revolution around the sun" ("Gregorian Calendar," Wikipedia).

11. Feeney, *Caesar's Calendar*, p. 12.

12. Months themselves, although already "our" lengths (as our Gregorian Calendar is close to the Julian one), cannot be counted our way: "We start at the beginning of the month and count forward: January 1, 2, 3 and so on. The Romans did not do this forward counting. They had three fixed points in each month, and they counted down, 'backwards,' to

whichever of these points was coming up next. Each month is split in half by the Ides (*Idus*)," which was the 15th day in long months and the 13th day in short February: "The only catch here is that the Romans counted inclusively, counting both pegs at the end of a sequence instead of only one as we do, so that nine days before the Ides for them is eight days before the Ides for us" (Feeney, *Caesar's Calendar*, p. 152).

13. Feeney, *Caesar's Calendar*, p. 185. "[O]nly with Caesar and his new calendar do the *fasti* themselves become part of the honorific 'language of power'" (ibid., p. 188). The forced nature of this attempt at harmonization was recognized at the time by Tacitus, who complained about what Feeney calls "the radical incommensurability between the imperial monarchy and the fundamental rhythms of Roman time" (ibid., p. 191).

14. Feeney, *Caesar's Calendar*, p. 16.

15. Feeney, *Caesar's Calendar*, pp. 53–55.

16. The Romans "are not connecting numbers; they are connecting significant events and people. In so doing they are not placing events within a preexisting time frame; they are constructing a time frame within which the events have meaning" (Feeney, *Caesar's Calendar*, p. 15).

17. "[I]t remains an imaginative challenge of the first order to attempt to intuit how the Romans and Greeks were able to move around in past time without numerical coordinates" (Feeney, *Caesar's Calendar*, p. 15).

18. Some attention was given to chronology in ancient Rome. In the first century BCE, Marcus Varro attempted to produce an exact timeline of Roman history, based on the sequence of the consuls of the Roman Republic, and Augustus inscribed this schema on the arch of Augustus in Rome. This was in line with the lists that existed not only of the earlier Etruscan kings in Italy but also of kings in the East, where the procedure, by year of rule of a sequential dynastic reign, amounted to a historical chronology. In contrast, the Roman Republic's dating by consulship was like American presidential terms, i.e., not immediately legible as historical time.

19. It was not uncommon for cities to issue coinage, often with dates of their founding (in Latin written "A.U.C.," *Ab Urbe Condita*). In the *fasti* under Augustus, "every ten years a numeral stands for the number of years that have elapsed since a foundation date" of the city of Rome, years that, however, start on a different date—in April, not January (Feeney, *Caesar's Calendar*, p. 174). But messianic significance is qualitatively different.

20. Robert Deutsch, "Coinage of the First Jewish Revolt against Rome: Iconography, Minting Authority, Metallurgy," in *The Jewish Revolt against Rome: Interdisciplinary Perspectives*, ed. Mladen Popović (Leiden: Brill, 2011), p. 361.

21. In opposition to the earlier identification of this image as a stem with three pomegranates, Ariel writes: "A priestly staff or even *the* staff of the high priest is intended." Donald T. Ariel, "Identifying the Mints, Minters and Meanings of the First Jewish Revolt Coins," in Popović, *The Jewish Revolt against Rome*, p. 387.

22. France's revolutionary gesture impressed the victors of the Haitian Revolution. Dessalines decreed that citizens of the new nation of Haiti were to "live the new life, starting with 'Year 1'" in place of the AD calendar year 1804. Neil Roberts, *Freedom as Marronage* (Chicago: University of Chicago Press, 2007), p. 123. Year Zero was applied to the takeover of Cambodia by the Khmer Rouge (April 1975), intended as a communist radicalization of French Revolutionary time.

23. Martin Goodman, "Coinage and Identity: The Jewish Evidence," in *Coinage and Identity in the Roman Provinces*, ed. Christopher Howgego, Volker Heuchert, and Andrew Burnett (Oxford: Oxford University Press, 2005), p. 165. In fact, dating coins was an indication of a city era as "autonomous" (albeit under the protection of a king or emperor), a commonplace in the area of Palestine, "an expression of local pride at being a unique entity governed by its own laws": "Thirty-eight Palestinian cities minted coins at various times during the Hellenistic and Roman periods. The vast majority of these coins bear dates, with the bulk of the dates involving individual city eras." Alla Kushnir-Stein, "City Eras on Palestinian Coinage," in Howgego, Heuchert, and Burnett, *Coinage and Identity in the Roman Provinces*, pp. 157–160. Interestingly, in AD 67/69, at the start of the Judaean conflict, two other Judaean cities, Caesarea Maritima (main base of Vespasian's military operations) and Sepphoris, "issued series of coins dated by the year 14 of Nero" (ibid., p. 161).

24. Feeney, *Caesar's Calendar*, p. 3.

25. This is Ya'akov Meshorer's conclusion (1982), cited in agreement by Deutsch, "Coinage of the First Jewish Revolt against Rome," p. 365.

26. Uriel Rappaport, "Who Were the Sicarii?," in Popović, *The Jewish Revolt against Rome*, p. 338.

27. The change in slogans "suits" Simon and his supporters, and "may inform our understanding of Simon bar Giora's propaganda strategy" (Ariel, "Identifying the Mints, Minters and Meanings of the First Jewish Revolt Coins," pp. 389 and 397). Ariel surmises that the slogan "freedom of Zion" on the bronze second and third year coins might be assumed as "struck by the Zealots with John of Gischala at their helm" (ibid., p. 396). Ariel's identification of the "Zealots" with the followers of John of Gischala is in tension with the observations of Rajak and Mason that the name "zealot" was descriptive of a practice rather than identifying a specific group (see below, chapter 2).

28. This leads Ariel (following J. S. McLaren) to propose that it was the high priests themselves who minted the silver coins, in or near the Temple, using the Temple treasury's high-quality silver: "The internal stability of the silver coins suggests that the military leaders of the revolt intentionally did not interfere, although they could have, with the priestly administration of that mint" (Ariel, "Identifying the Mints, Minters and Meanings of the First Jewish Revolt Coins," p. 396). Deutsch concurs: "The overwhelming majority of Great Revolt coins must have been minted by the authority of the Jerusalem temple priesthood" (Deutsch, "Coinage of the First Jewish Revolt against Rome," p. 368).

29. Ariel, "Identifying the Mints, Minters and Meanings of the First Jewish Revolt Coins," p. 375.

30. Robinson writes: "Obscurities envelop virtually every question we might wish to ask about early Islamic minting, not least of all because there was a great deal of regional variation, as Byzantine and Sasanian models were very closely followed. But it is precisely this—regional variation, fidelity to pre-Islamic traditions and the absence of centralized control that these imply—that changes so dramatically and quickly upon [the Marwanid leader] 'Abd al-Malik's defeat of [his rival] Ibn al-Zubayr [thus establishing the Umayyad Dynasty]." Chase F. Robinson, *'Abd al-Malik* (Oxford: Oneworld Academic, 2005), pp. 72–73.

31. The proposal was made by the Scythian monk Dionysius Exiguus at Rome in 525 CE; it was proposed again in the Latin world by Bede c. 731 CE and adopted with uneven success. See Georges Declercq, *Anno Domini: The Origins of the Christian Era* (Turnhout, Belgium: Brepols, 2001), for the story from a European, Latin perspective.

32. Garth Fowden, *Before and after Muḥammad: The First Millennium Refocused* (Princeton: Princeton University Press, 2014), pp. 80n and 85. Whereas Declercq (see note above) ignores possible Islamic influence, and does not deal with the fact that in the Christian East dates of acceptance varied widely (in Syria not until the nineteenth century), Fowden not only corrects this bias but has recently made the radical proposal that we reperiodize the history of all three monotheisms into two millennia separated by the Hijra; hence the title of his book.

33. Feeney notes: "If users of the B.C.E./C.E. grid were in the habit of making systematic synchronistic comparisons with the Islamic or Jewish calendars [of today], we would know what it was like for the Greeks and Romans; but not many people in the West habitually do that. That is something *they* [Muslims and Jews] have to do. The time [of] imperialism works in the favor of the users of the Christian time grid" (Feeney, *Caesar's Calendar*, p. 11). Western years are solar, Muslim years are lunar, and Jewish years are lunar-solar.

34. "Given that the Islamic New Year does not begin January 1 and that a Hijri [lunar] year is 11 days shorter than a Common Era year, there is no direct correspondence between years of the two eras. A given Hijri year will usually fall in two successive Western years. A Western year will always fall in two or occasionally three successive Hijri years." An approximate formula is: AH = 1.030684 × (CE − 621.5643); CE = 0.970229 × AH + 621.5643 ("Hijri Year," Wikipedia).

35. "Muslims still cannot narrate with any precision what happened before the hijra except by using BC/AD dates" (Fowden, *Before and after Muḥammad*, p. 78). The reason is that the pre-Islamic world is undifferentiated and named simply *jāhilīyah*, which means "ignorance," "barbarism," "lawlessness" (ibid.).

36. See "Ancient Dating Systems," Wikipedia, for an idea of the multiplicity of dating systems besides our own.

37. In her detailed commentary on the *Res gestae* Cooley writes: "The fact of his being first is repeated often enough"; "The idea of Augustus breaking new ground justifies the implicit

claim that his birth marked a new era in Roman history"; "Similarly, he can speak of 'my era'" and "I was the first and only one to have done this . . . as far as people living in my era recall.'" Alison E. Cooley, *Res gestae divi Augusti: Text, Translation, and Commentary* (Cambridge: Cambridge University Press, 2009), pp. 37–38.

38. Cooley refers repeatedly to this absence of temporal order; it "makes the task of chrono-logical political narrative of the age of Augustus incredibly tricky" (Cooley, *Res gestae divi Augusti*, p. 2).

39. The text is available in English online at: http://classics.mit.edu/Augustus/deeds.html. The *Res gestae divi Augusti* was read to the Senate in 14 CE, at their first meeting after the emperor's death and alleged *apotheosis* (elevation to the heavens, the realm of the celestial gods); Augustus himself adhered to constitutional propriety by not himself claiming divine status. Imperial deification is discussed in detail in chapter 4.

40. The fact that Hitler was shown a part of it during his visit in May 1938, "even before the reconstruction of the altar had been completed, illustrates the importance of the altar to the image of Mussolini's new Empire" (Cooley, *Res gestae divi Augusti*, p. 52). Parts of the Ara Pacis had been known since 1568, but excavation had to wait for mid-twentieth-century technology and political interest (ibid., p. 51).

41. A video of the newsreel of Mussolini's visit at its opening has been archived. See https://www.youtube.com/watch?v=CILr3dV3hxI.

42. The art critic Vittorio Sgarbi defined it as "a Texas gas station in the very earth of one of the most important urban centres in the world" (cited in "Museum of the Ara Pacis," Wikipedia). In December 2009 protesters, decrying the eco-unfriendly concrete of the museum, colored its fountain green, affixing a banner: "Earth First! Act Now" (ibid.)

43. Meier said of his building's becoming a "political football": "You just do your work. You do what you think you should do" (cited in Steve Rose, "When in Rome . . . ," *Guardian*, May 1, 2006, http://www.theguardian.com/travel/2006/may/01/travelnews.museums).

44. The Turkish Historical Society, founded in 1931, supervised the excavation of the *Res gestae*. Its work "benefitted from the personal interest of the first president" (Cooley, *Res gestae divi Augusti*, p. 46). Atatürk planned his own mausoleum in Ankara in 1930s imperial style. Mussolini made a photograph of himself with a replica of the Ankara one. For the close ideological ties of Turkey and Nazi ideology, see Stefan Ihrig, *Atatürk in the Nazi Imagination* (Cambridge, MA: Belknap Press of Harvard University Press, 2014).

45. Cooley, *Res gestae divi Augusti*, pp. 13–18.

46. Peter Thonemann, "A Copy of Augustus' Res Gestae at Sardis," *Historia: Journal of Ancient History* 61, no. 3 (2012), from academia.edu. Thonemann has demonstrated that a tiny and otherwise insignificant fragment of Greek text published in 1932 in a volume of the inscriptions of the town of Sardis (Buckler and Robinson, 1932) was actually (as Buckler in an unpublished letter had already suspected) a small fragment of the *Res gestae*.

47. Cooley writes: "[I]t is not safe to assume that the R[es] G[estae] D[ivi] A[ugusti] was universally published" (Cooley, *Res gestae divi Augusti*, p. 22), a conclusion not changed by the fact that her publication (2009) is too early to take cognizance of the Sardis fragment announced in 2012.

48. "If it was Augustus' intention to appeal for deification through the RGDA, he would have been well satisfied with the locations of the copies set up in Galatia in monumental complexes concerned with emperor worship" (Cooley, *Res gestae divi Augusti*, p. 41) The emperor cults of the Roman province of Asia (today Asia Minor) are discussed below in chapter 4.

49. Cooley tells us that various specific, skillful changes in the *koine* wording "adapted Augustus' words for an audience far from Rome" (Cooley, *Res gestae divi Augusti*, p. 19). These changes mitigated "the imperialist effects of the claims of conquest" (ibid., p. 16). The Greek translation also adds towns receiving financial help from Augustus on several occasions following earthquakes (ibid., p. 19). An attempt to glorify Rome in the Latin version contrasts with the same passage in the Greek translation that speaks of Augustus's accomplishments as a "gift" to the provincial populations. "Other changes in the Greek version reflect a willingness to acknowledge the monarchical nature of Augustus' position at Rome, which would perhaps be less openly acceptable at Rome itself" (ibid., p. 29). Local translators, therefore, "took care of tweaking the text" for provincial audiences (ibid., p. 39).

50. Cooley describes a variety of proclamations similar to the *Res gestae* that could have served as prototypes: not only Hellenic but also Persian, Egyptian, Babylonian, Elamite. She illustrates her commentary with maps, photographs, coins, and inscriptions that enhance a visual balance between East and West. Cooley, *Res gestae divi Augusti*, pp. 31, 33, and passim.

51. Hellenophiles have frequently made this claim. It privileges the source, disparages borrowing, and shores up the idea of cultural property.

52. For debates as to the significance of the limited intelligence from maps in determining Roman imperial policy of annexations, see Geoffrey Greatrex, "Roman Frontiers and Foreign Policy in the East," in *Aspects of the Roman East: Papers in Honour of Professor Fergus Millar FBA*, ed. Richard Alston and Samuel N. C. Lieu (Turnhout, Belgium: Brepols, 2007), pp. 102–173.

53. Phasis, a port city on the southeastern extreme of the Black Sea (in the kingdom of Colchis, today Georgia) was described in 100 BCE as the place where "people from sixty nations meet, all speaking different languages, including foreigners from India and Bactria" (cited in Raoul McLaughlin, *The Roman Empire and the Silk Routes: The Ancient World Economy and the Empires of Parthia, Central Asia and Han China* [Barnsley, UK: Pen & Sword Books, 2016], p. 118). McLaughlin has produced a series of books on the eastern trade, including *The Distant East* (2010), *The Roman Empire and the Indian Ocean* (2014), and *The Roman Empire and the Silk Routes* (2016). His general overviews are enhanced by the fact that he has consulted Chinese sources, including, significantly, the *Hou Hanshu* (compiled in the fifth century CE) that covers the history of the Han dynasty from 6 to 189 CE.

54. Scythians described by Herodotus (book 4) as a nomadic people merged with Indians in the Indus valley (McLaughlin, *The Roman Empire and the Silk Routes*, p. 70). In the first century, a Kushan dynasty (described in the *Periplus* as well as the *Hou Hanshu*) ruled this area. These rulers adopted as their title *devaputra*, the equivalent of the Latin *divi filius* that Augustus called himself. Originally of Afghanistan (on the silk route), the Kushan rulers had diplomatic contacts with the Roman Empire, Sassanian Persia, the Aksumite Empire (today's Ethiopia/Eritrea), and the Han Dynasty of China. The first Kushan emperor, Kujula Kadphises, reigned from 30 to 60 CE. Their most illustrious ruler Kanishka the Great (127–150 CE) promoted Mahayana Buddhism within his kingdom, and north and east to China; the expanse of his empire gave him control of the silk route.

55. Palmyra was a crossroads, and Palmyrene communities existed "along the Euphrates and the Persian Gulf, notably on the island of Bahrain" where they were involved in the pearl trade. Katia Schörle, "Pearls, Power, and Profit: Mercantile Networks and Economic Considerations of the Pearl Trade in the Roman Empire," in *Across the Ocean: Nine Essays on Indo-Mediterranean Trade*, ed. Federico De Romanis and Marco Maiuro (Leiden: Brill, 2015), p. 44.

56. The *Periplus* mentions the ports of Sarapion (today's Mogadishu) and Opone (today's Somalia) where Mycenean pottery, sixteenth to eleventh centuries BCE, has been discovered. On the Axumite (Ethiopian) and the Hadramawt (south Arabian) kingdoms that stood on opposite shores at the mouth of the Red Sea, see George Hourani, "Did Roman Commercial Competition Ruin South Arabia?," *Journal of Near Eastern Studies* 11, no. 4 (October 1952): 291–295. Hourani's answer to this question is no: the Arabian ports of Muza and Cane flourished in the mid-first century, as did Adulis, their wealth spurred by the greatly increased demand in trade because of Roman imperial presence. Insofar as Rome did not deal militarily with this trade network (unlike the later European imperial expansion into the area), this could be seen as a win-win situation.

57. In the late Republic, the Roman army invaded Parthia directly from Syria, rather than through the Armenian pass, leading to a humiliating defeat at Carrhae (53 BCE). Marc Antony then attempted to reverse this outcome (40–33 BCE), with severe losses. "To maintain discipline Antony ordered an immediate 'decimation' [Latin *decem* = 10] where one in ten of the soldiers in the disgraced units were selected for summary execution by their colleagues" (McLaughlin, *The Roman Empire and the Silk Routes*, p. 165). McLaughlin's version of these military efforts emphasizes the significance of eastern trade as a motivation for Roman foreign policy.

58. "From Armenia steppe invaders could ride directly into Roman Asia Minor or enter the Parthian Empire through its vulnerable northern frontiers" (McLaughlin, *The Roman Empire and the Silk Routes*, p. 121). After Nero's military victory over Armenia proved transitory, Rome continued to spar with Parthia for influence over Armenia's ruling family. Nero's Roman legions fought Parthian-backed forces for control of Armenia in a War of the Armenian Succession (58–63 CE)

59. The Han text *Hou Hanshu*, cited in McLaughlin, *The Roman Empire and the Silk Routes*, p. 66. Parthians first sent ambassadors to the Han government in the first century BCE. From 9 CE to 23 CE, the Han temporarily lost power, and took several more decades to reestablish control over the silk route of the western Tarim territories (historical Uyghur, east of Kyrgyzstan, in today's China); this desert land is traversed east-west by rivers. Roman contact with the Han imperial court was not made until the Maes expedition in 100 CE, and even then the entrepreneur who accomplished this personal reception traveled with an escort of Parthian traders. This expedition spoke *koine*, and the account of this trip was circulated throughout the Roman Empire: "The group was carrying lightweight silks that had been rewoven in Syrian workshops and had some imperial gold coins that bore the image of the Roman Emperor"; "For the first time Roman subjects in Syria and Egypt knew for certain that there was an oriental superpower in the Far East which manufactured large quantities of silk and steel" (*Hou Hanshu*, cited in ibid., p. 191). In contrast to the sustained remoteness of China, in the *Res gestae* Augustus prided himself on having been the first to receive ambassadors from India.

60. It is important to note that the taxes levied from the imperial provinces went directly to the *fiscus* (Lat. "purse" or "basket"), not beholden to Rome but controlled by the emperor as his private purse, from which he paid for the army loyal to his person. McLaughin states that military costs, over 330 million sesterces per annum, were "the single largest expense in Roman government spending," and proposes that in the first century the Red Sea customs tax alone covered most of that expense, as "the Roman Empire was receiving more than 250 million sesterces from the quarter-rate custom tax it imposed on its Red Sea frontiers"—hence the interconnections between the emperor's military power and the increase of long-distance, luxury trade (McLaughlin, *The Roman Empire and the Silk Routes*, pp. xix–xx).

61. "Octavian seized the accumulated wealth of the Ptolemaic Kingdom, and distributed the funds amongst the citizen population of Rome. The resultant commercial boom occurred at the same time as the Empire gained direct control over the Red Sea shipping lanes that led into the Indian Ocean" (McLaughlin, *The Roman Empire and the Silk Routes*, p. xix).

62. In 2001 Belgian speleologists found nearly 250 texts and drawings inscribed in a cave on Socotra (an island between Somalia and Yemen, named Discoursi by the *Periplus*) that date from the first century BCE to the sixth century CE, written in multiple languages, including Indian Brāhmī, South Arabian, Ethiopic, Greek, Palmyrene, and Bactrian scripts and languages. They were left there by sailors engaged in this trade.

63. Import revenues, presumably the same throughout the empire, were set at the high rate of 25% (the quarter tax). New information as to how this trade functioned is provided by recent archaeological work on the caravan routes from the Red Sea to the Nile, which has revealed a chain of *hydreumata*, deep-dug wells maintained by the emperor, providing traders and pack animals with water necessary for the journey across the eastern Egyptian desert to and from the major Red Sea ports of Myos Hormos and Berenike. The positioning of

the *hydreumata* indicates that the longer route from Berenike was preferred to a preexisting road at Edfu, and scholars have suggested the reason. The convergence of port roads on the Nile at the same fortified city of Coptos allowed customs officials to monitor the caravans of middlemen that transferred the goods to bonded warehouses at this site, before their conveyance down the Nile under seal to imperial warehouses at Alexandria: "[T]he shift from Edfu to Coptos as the Nile terminus of the route from Berenice [Berenike] enabled the concentration of State resources in forts and a single customs control point on the Nile at Coptos—which of course also served the Myos Hormos road." Andrew Wilson, "Red Sea Trade and the State," in De Romanis and Maiuro, *Across the Ocean*, p. 27.

64. A loan contract discovered in Egypt, known as the Muziris papyrus, provides insight into how the trade functioned. This contract (written in *koine*) lays out the terms of an agreement between an Alexandrian importer and a financier for a loan backed by the value of the 220-ton cargo on the *Hermapollon*, a ship returning from the Tamil trade port of Muziris (mentioned also in the *Periplus*; its exact location remains unknown). The Muziris papyrus is "exceptional" because of its "reliable assessment of the qualitative and, more importantly, quantitative dimension of the maritime trade that tied the Roman Empire to the Indian subcontinent" at a time (second century CE) of "the peak of this transnational trade, after a century and a half of quantitative growth." Elio Lo Cascio, "Afterword," in De Romanis and Maiuro, *Across the Ocean*, p. 165. Scholarship on this papyrus began in earnest in the 1980s; for an on-line translation (1990) by L. Casson, see http://www.uni-koeln.de/phil-fak/ifa/zpe/downloads/1990/084pdf/084195.pdf.

65. Federico De Romanis and Marco Maiuro, "Introduction," in De Romanis and Maiuro, *Across the Ocean*, p. 6.

66. John Sallis, *Chorology: On Beginning in Plato's Timaeus* (Bloomington: Indiana University Press, 1999), p. 110. *Chora* is discussed below, chapter 3.

67. I am grateful for knowledge of this book to the experimental scholar of images Shulamit Bruckstein Çoruh, who found it in Herbert Stein's bookstore in Jerusalem. She placed its image in what she called the "epistemic architecture" of an exhibition, "House of Taswir," that she curated at the Martin-Gropius-Bau, Berlin (2010–2011). She explains: "The house of Taswir is an imaginary institute for artistic and diasporic thinking that creates concepts from constellations yet unknown" (see http://www.taswir.org).

68. This is Bruckstein Çoruh's translation: Shulamit Bruckstein Çoruh, *House of Taswir: Doing and Undoing Things: Notes on Epistemic Architecture(s) = Zur Umordnung der Dinge: Notizen zu einer epistemischen Architektur* (Paderborn: Wilhelm Fink, 2014), p. 197. She continues: "On the right hand side of the page, there is the first sura of the Qur'an, opening the book / consisting of 7 verses according to Meccan tradition / in the name of Allah, the All-Merciful, the Most Merciful," etc. She comments: "A Jewish seal from within Islamic time, published in Prussian Protestant Berlin, in 1916 of the common era, in the midst of Europe, at the very moment it (was) turned into a slaughterhouse of war and bloodshed, 1916 years after the becoming flesh. . . . It seems to me, however, that GOLDSCHMIDT, the translator of the Babylonian Talmud into German, was writing his translation of the Qur'an from

'inside' Islamic history 'out' on to the Common Era thereby reversing periphery and center, remaining himself levitating in his own time/out of time" (ibid., pp. 198–199). The word "becoming flesh" is the biblical phrase for Christ's appearance (John 1:14).

CHAPTER 2

1. From Burckhardt's 1868–1872 manuscript (never intended for publication) in Jacob Burckhardt, *Über das Studium der Geschichte*, trans. in Thomas Albert Howard, *Religion and the Rise of Historicism: W. M. L. de Wette, Jacob Burckhardt, and the Theological Origins of Nineteenth-Century Historical Consciousness* (Cambridge: Cambridge University Press, 2000), p. 161. Howard describes Burckhardt's "youthful contempt for Hegelian historical optimism"; it was in the context of Hegel's "conflation of historical and philosophical ways of knowing" that Burckhardt, a historian of Italian Renaissance art, made the centaur analogy (ibid., pp. 160–161).

2. Walter Benjamin, "The Task of the Translator," trans. Harry Zohn, in *Selected Writings*, vol. 1: 1913–1926, ed. Marcus Bullock and Michael W. Jennings (Cambridge, MA: Belknap Press of Harvard University Press, 1996), p. 260. In the original German: "Denn der Satz ist die Mauer vor der Sprache des Originals, Wörtlichkeit die Arkade" (translation modified, as explained above); Walter Benjamin, "Die Aufgabe des Übersetzers," in Benjamin, *Gesammelte Schriften*, vol. 4: 1, ed. Tillman Rexroth (Frankfurt am Main: Suhrkamp Verlag, 1972), p. 18.

3. Benjamin, "The Task of the Translator," p. 260.

4. Benjamin, "The Task of the Translator," p. 260.

5. Samuel Weber, *Benjamin's -abilities* (Cambridge, MA: Harvard University Press, 2010).

6. This capacity of the object, its impart-ability (*Mitteil-barkeit*) in language, *is* an idea in Benjamin's writing, language's capacity to carry the name across the barriers of linguistic separation, pointing to a divine Word inaccessible to humans, yet demonstrated by the translat-ability (*Übersetz-barkeit*) of one language into another. It determines the "innermost kinship of languages," a "special kinship [that] holds because languages are not strangers to one another but are, a priori and apart from all historical relationships, interrelated in what they want to express" (Benjamin, "The Task of the Translator," p. 255).

7. In the Paralipomena to "On the Concept of History," Benjamin criticizes historians who "project the past into the present": "The false aliveness of the past-made-present, the elimination of every echo of a 'lament' from history, marks history's final subjection to the modern concept of science. In other words, the project of discovering 'laws' for the course of historical events is not the only means—and hardly the most subtle—of assimilating historiography to natural science. The notion that the historian's task is to make the past 'present' . . . is guilty of the same fraudulence, and is far less transparent." Walter Benjamin, "Paralipomena to 'On the Concept of History,'" in *Selected Writings*, vol. 4: 1938–1940, ed. Marcus Bullock et al. (Cambridge, MA: Harvard University Press, 2003), p. 401. In German: "Die Vorstellung, es sei die Aufgabe des Historikers das Vergangne

zu 'vergegenwärtigen' macht sich der gleichen Erschleichung schuldig und ist doch viel weniger leicht durchschaubar"; Benjamin, *Gesammelte Schriften* 1:3, p. 1231.

8. Let me clarify that I am proposing here a very different Copernican Revolution in the philosophy of history than Benjamin himself intended. My reception of Benjamin has been marked by working through the historical details of the Arcades Project that, as famously "failed," does not seem to be of present academic interest, at least not for philosophers. My goal, then as now, is not to be faithful to what Benjamin did, or would have done, had he been writing instead of me. Rather, Benjamin's work is good to think with.

9. For Michel Foucault on governmentality, see "Governmentality," and on genealogy see "Theatrum Politicum: The Genealogy of Capital—Police and the State of Prosperity," both in *The Foucault Effect: Studies in Governmentality*, ed. Graham Burchell, Colin Gordon, and Peter Miller (Chicago: University of Chicago Press, 1991). For Giorgio Agamben on bare life, see *Homo Sacer: Sovereign Power and Bare Life*, trans. Daniel Heller-Roazen (Stanford: Stanford University Press, 1998), and on states of exception, see Giorgio Agamben, *States of Exception*, trans. Kevin Attell (Chicago: University of Chicago Press, 2005).

10. Fergus Millar, *Rome, the Greek World, and the East*, vol. 2: *Government, Society, and Culture in the Roman Empire*, ed. Hannah M. Cotton and Guy M. Rogers (Chapel Hill: University of North Carolina Press, 2004), p. xi; again ("The World of the Golden Ass"), p. 313.

11. First published in France as Barbara Cassin, ed., *Vocabulaire européen des philosophies: Dictionnaire des intraduisibles* (Paris: Éditions du Seuil, 2004); in English as *Dictionary of Untranslatables: A Philosophical Lexicon*, ed. Emily Apter, Jacques Lezra, and Michael Wood, trans. Steven Rendall, Christian Hubert, Jeffrey Mehlman, Nathanael Stein, and Michael Syrotinski (Princeton: Princeton University Press, 2014).

12. Souleymane Bachir Diagne, in discussion, Cornell University, 2015. While the idea of philosophy as itself translation as articulated by him is significantly different from the task considered here, I am indebted in what follows to his lecture and seminar on this topic at the School of Criticism and Theory, Cornell University, summer 2015.

13. Already in 1998, Cassin described the "untranslatable" as not an end to the task of the translator, but "the interminability of translating: the idea that one can never have done with translation" (cited in Apter, preface to *Dictionary of Untranslatables*, p. vii). In contrast, Benjamin sees the "translatability" (*Übersetzbarkeit*) of languages as the condition of possibility of a universal language. We will have to consider: how might moving laterally across distances in time affirm a historical idea of universality, rescued from Cassin's conclusion that rigorous attention to "untranslatables" requires a philosophical positioning of "consistent relativism," when relativism is precisely the obstacle to a *rapprochement* between philosophy and history?

14. Diagne, seminar at the School of Criticism and Theory, summer 2015.

15. Diagne, seminar at the School of Criticism and Theory, summer, 2015.

16. Jean-Pierre Lefebvre's description, cited in Souleymane Bachir Diagne, *The Ink of the Scholars: Reflections on Philosophy in Africa* (Dakar: CODESRIA, 2016), p. 25.

17. Agata Bielik-Robson, "Marrano Universalism: Benjamin, Derrida, and Buck-Morss on the Condition of Universal Exile," *Teloscope* (Telos: Critical Theory of the Contemporary, June 8, 2015, https://www.telospress.com/marrano-universalism-benjamin-derrida-and -buckmorss-on-the-condition-of-universal-exile/). Bielik-Robson clarifies: "A 'Marrano philosopher' struggles to convince his readers that the Jewish mode of thinking is *not* alien to the spirit of universalism, just negotiates it differently: not as a ready-made declaration of a universal essence, but as an ongoing practice, something Walter Benjamin called 'the task of the translation'"; and on Benjamin: "for him the true universality emerges only through the clashes—or marriages—of two or more separate idioms."

18. Karl Marx, Introduction to the *Grundrisse*, trans. Martin Nicolaus, https://www.marxists .org/archive/marx/works/1857/grundrisse/

19. The translators into English of this essay—both Rodney Livingstone (in *Reflections*) and Edmund Jephcott (in *Selected Works*)—have chosen "faculty" rather than "capacity" for the German word *Vermögen*, a move that provides in English an unwarranted connection to Kant, whose text "The Contest of the Faculties" (famous for its reference to the French Revolution) bears the German title "Der Streit der Fakultäten." This accords with the contemporary wisdom, which puts great stock in the testimony of Scholem that Benjamin in his early years concerned himself deeply with Kant. True enough, but Benjamin's reception was deeply revisionist of the Kantian tradition. This emphasis is symptomatic of the remarkable assimilation of Benjamin's work into the academy that rejected him—the appropriating of his work within the European philosophical tradition of not only Kant but also the German Romantics as well as Nietzsche, even Heidegger. See as exemplary the entry by Peter Osborne and Matthew Charles, "Walter Benjamin," in *The Stanford Encyclopedia of Philosophy* (Fall 2015 Edition), ed. Edward N. Zalta, http://plato.stanford .edu/archives/fall2015/entries/benjamin/.

    While this entry expertly describes excellent academic work, it documents the absorption of Walter Benjamin into the history of ideas, drawing his work into present intellectual discussions very far from the historical emergencies of Benjamin's time. The latter, in my opinion, provides the angle of vision from which a historical materialist interpretation ought not to stray.

20. Walter Benjamin, "On the Mimetic Faculty," in *Selected Writings*, vol. 2: 1927–1934, ed. Michael W. Jennings et al., trans. Edmund Jephcott (Cambridge, MA: Harvard University Press, 1999), pp. 720–721. I have altered the translation of "*Tanzen*" from "dances" (a word that suggests an art form) to "dancing," because I believe Benjamin was connecting his discussion to the revolution in dancing as a form of popular culture that marks the 1920s and 30s, and that can be seen as a rebirth of the mimetic capacity that Benjamin has in mind.

21. Despite his continued enjoyment of Greek and Roman classical texts, in keeping with nineteenth-century European understandings Marx saw as "childlike" the mythic elements of ancient cultures that were preserved in classical forms of epic and drama, and were found in his own time in societies that he considered less historically developed than those of the

modern West. The critique of the West's celebration of scientific reason as itself a form of myth would come later (see, e.g., Theodor W. Adorno and Max Horkheimer, *Dialektik der Aufklärung*, 1947).

22. This approach to aesthetic forms as preconceptual and therefore primitive manifests Marx's debt to Hegel. In exposing Europe's "Hellenomania," Martin Bernal provides the relevant passage from Hegel that describes this appropriation of earlier periods by those cultures that come later, which Hegel saw as totally unproblematic: "The name of Greece strikes home to the hearts of men of education in Europe, and more particularly is this so with us Germans. . . . [The Greeks] certainly received the substantial beginnings of their religion, culture . . . from Asia, Syria and Egypt; but they have so greatly obliterated the foreign nature of this origin, and it is so much changed, worked on, turned round and altogether made so different, that what they—as we—prize, know and love in it is essentially their own." G. W. F. Hegel, *Lectures on the Philosophy of History*, cited in Martin Bernal, *Black Athena: The Afroasiatic Roots of Classical Civilization*, vol. 1: *The Fabrication of Ancient Greece 1785–1985* (New Brunswick: Rutgers University Press, 1987), p. 295.

23. Benjamin's critique of history as progress was not simply a reaction to the political events of the 1930s; it was deeply embedded in his materialist approach to history, one that did not exclude serious consideration of theology. Benjamin's rejection of the childhood metaphor saves his thinking from the then-dominant view that non-Western peoples, as historically undeveloped, were childlike, hence behind the West.

24. Walter Benjamin, "New theses C," "Paralipomena to "On the Concept of History" (1940), in *Selected Writings*, vol. 4, p. 403.

25. Historical experience mattered to Benjamin's philosophy of history as much as it did to Hegel. But he eschewed metahistorical levels of conceptualization. The literal shattering of the bourgeois world of his childhood—the consequence of areal bombings of World War I, the destructiveness to the human body that industrialized warfare facilitated—was embedded in collective consciousness and expressed in artistic forms (Surrealism, montage). The destructiveness of these historical transformations needed to be utilized rather than simply deplored. For Benjamin, the inventive piecing of the world back together was a moment in human creativity with revolutionary implications.

26. Benjamin, "On the Mimetic Faculty," p. 721.

27. See Alain Badiou, *St. Paul: The Foundation of Universalism*, trans. Ray Brassier (Stanford: Stanford University Press, 2003); Slavoj Žižek, *The Puppet and the Dwarf: The Perverse Core of Christianity* (Cambridge, MA: MIT Press, 2003).

28. Jones makes a similar point concerning Hellenic identity: "Hellenic patriotism, sometimes assumed to be equivalent to Hellenism, is a chimera." Christopher P. Jones, "Multiple Identities in the Age of the Second Sophistic," in *Paideia: The World of the Second Sophistic*, ed. Barbara E. Borg (Berlin: Walter de Gruyter, 2004), p. 14.

29. Just how you name Josephus will press a certain interpretation of this controversial figure. Yosef ben Matityahu names the Judaean Josephus who sided with the Galilean rebels at

the beginning of the conflict; Titus (prename) Flavius (family name) Josephus (cognomen) names the man who, captured by the Romans as a prisoner of war, prophesied that Vespasian and Titus would become emperors, joined the Flavian cause as a free man in 69 CE, and as a *peregrinus* (foreigner) was granted Roman citizenship by Titus, acquiring with the Flavian name a stipend to live in Rome, where he wrote his multiple works. See Werner Eck, "Flavius Iosephus, nicht Iosephus Flavius," *Scripta Classica Israelica* 19 (2000): 381–383.

30. Jacques Derrida, "The Eyes of Language: The Abyss and the Volcano," in Derrida, *Acts of Religion*, ed. Gil Anidjar (New York: Routledge, 2002), p. 205. The essay itself is a beautiful presentation of the relations of sacred and profane within language.

31. Whether or not it was a dividing point at all remains unresolved. See the anthology *Was 70 CE a Watershed in Jewish History? On Jews and Judaism before and after the Destruction of the Second Temple*, ed. Daniel R. Schwartz, with collaboration of Zeev Weis and Ruth A. Clemens (Leiden: Brill, 2012).

32. Mary Beard, "The Triumph of Flavius Josephus," in *Flavian Rome: Culture, Image, Text*, ed. A. J. Boyle and W. J. Dominik (Leiden: Brill, 2003), p. 545. Beard describes what she calls the "snubbing" of Josephus: "Just as earlier no 'classicist' would count the Acts of the Apostles as a 'classical' source, and for a long time managed to cordon off the history of Egypt as if it were a preserve of 'Egyptologists' alone, so they have allowed Josephus to be claimed by (or cavalierly left to, depending on your point of view) students of Jewish history, religion, literature and culture" (ibid.).

33. Beard, "The Triumph of Flavius Josephus," pp. 544–545. Mason concurs: "Jews have traditionally viewed him as a traitor to the Jewish people"; he notes that Josephus' name "does not appear in either version of the voluminous Talmud, which was finally edited in the fifth and sixth centuries, or any other early Jewish writing"—the first reference to him in Judaic texts is in the sixteenth century. Although a Hebrew version of a selection of his texts (known as the *Josippon*) was used extensively by Jewish commentators in the Middle Ages, his "perceived cowardice" has prevented him from being embraced by Zionist historians. Steve Mason, *Josephus and the New Testament*, 2nd ed. (Peabody, MA: Hendrickson Publishers, 2005), pp. 25–26. This has been true despite the value of Josephus' own version of Jewish history (*Antiquitates Judaicae*), a 20-volume history of the Jews from biblical times to the first-century present, and despite the fact that one of Josephus' texts, *Against Apion* (*Contra Apionem*), defended Judaic monotheistic faith, arguing in tandem with Philo of Alexandria for the superiority of the ethics and philosophy contained within the Torah. For Josephus' influence on Byzantine Christian culture, see the article by Steven Bowman, "Josephus in Byzantium," in *Josephus, Judaism, and Christianity*, ed. Louis H. Feldman and Gohei Hata (Detroit: Wayne State University Press, 1987), pp. 362–385.

34. It should be noted, however, that twentieth-century Hebrew scholarship, while conscious of its positioning within the politics of the Israeli national project, has been neither predictable nor simplistically partisan. For a perceptive discussion see Daniel Schwartz,

"From Masada to Jotapata," in *A Companion to Josephus*, ed. Honora Howell Chapman and Zuleika Rodgers (Malden, MA: John Wiley & Sons, 2016), pp. 419–435.

35. In 1992 an international conference in San Miniato, Italy brought together some 50 scholars of Josephus, initiating new interest and a proliferation of anthologies, dissertations, and debates. Since then, multiple colloquia have taken place. The Münster Josephus project held the first of a series of Josephus Colloquia in 1997. Particularly helpful for what follows have been the proceedings of a 2003 conference in Rome, *Josephus and Jewish History in Flavian Rome and Beyond*, ed. Joseph Sievers and Gaia Lembi (Boston: Brill, 2005).

36. The Brill Josephus Project, directed by Steve Mason and funded by the Canadian government: http://ancientworldonline.blogspot.com/2010/10/pace-project-on-ancient-cultural .html. For a helpful review of one volume of this major undertaking, which will include new translations and extensive commentary of all of Josephus' work, see http://www.josephus .org/FlJosephus2/brillReview2.htm.

   The past decades have seen translations into French, German, Hebrew, and Italian, as well as English. One needs to credit the global religious communities for their participation in translations of Josephus that have appeared, for example, in Korean and Japanese (countries with few Jews and many Christians), and aim to correct the traditional Christian association of Jews with killers of Christ. For critical bibliographies discussing the varieties of manuscripts and translations as well as secondary literature (stopping short of the most recent scholarship), the standard texts are Louis Feldman, *Josephus and Modern Scholarship, 1937–1980* (Berlin: Walter de Gruyter, 1984), and Heinz Schreckenberg, *Bibliographie zu Flavius Josephus* (Leiden: Brill, 1979).

37. Flavius Josephus, *The Jewish War*, vols. 2 and 3 of *Josephus*, Greek text with English translation by H. St. J. Thackeray, 8 vols. (London: William Heinemann, 1927). This bilingual text (for the Loeb Classical Library) is cited below as *Bellum Judaicum*, with book numbers and Greek line numbers corresponding to those in Thackeray's text. Thackeray tells us (introduction, vol. 2, pp. vii–viii) that a comprehensive collation of all good manuscripts was first made in the late nineteenth century by Benedictus Niese (6 vols., Berlin, 1887–1894). He comments on his own text: "The Greek text here printed is based on that of Niese, but is the outcome of a careful and independent investigation of the MS evidence collected in his great edition" (ibid., p. xxvii).

38. "The title by which we know Josephus' book is *The Jewish War*. This name is assumed to be the original one. . . . However, the evidence indicates rather that the work possessed no title at all." Tessa Rajak, *Josephus: The Historian and His Society*, 2nd ed. (London: Duckworth, 2002), p. 201. Thackeray tells us that Josephus himself in his later autobiographical text (*Vita*, 412) refers to the text as "Concerning the Judaean War" (περὶ τοῦ Ιουδαϊκοῦ πόλεμου). Extant texts that have relied on the Christian West for their survival are entitled *Bellum Judaicum*, whether they introduce a Greek version or a Latin translation. Niese's principal MS P has the expanded title: "Concerning the Judaean War against the Romans"; but the "majority" of the manuscripts employ another title: "Concerning the capture [Περὶ ἁλώσεως] of Jerusalem" and add "Judaean Histories," as do all extant mss. of the Russian

version. "Concerning the capture of Jerusalem" is found in Origen and Jerome (see Thackeray's introduction to his translation of the *Bellum Judaicum*, vol. 2, pp. vii–viii).

Titles matter: against whom was the war fought? (Jews? Jerusalem? Judaea? Rebel groups?) As editor of a new translation of *Bellum Judaicum*, Steve Mason considers "Judaean War" the more accurate translation of the title. On the website *Marginalia* (August 26, 2014), he describes the response: "In 2006, when the first volumes of Brill's *Flavius Josephus: Translation and Commentary* had appeared, an anonymous user of the PACE [Project on Ancient Cultural Engagement] website, which hosted the online version, was irate enough about our nomenclature to leave an anonymous complaint: 'Josephus wrote the *Jewish War*, not the *Judean War*!' How could I respond? The problem, of course, is that Josephus did not write in English. He called his work *The War (O Polemos)*, *The War of the Ioudaioi against the Romans*, *The Ioudaikos War*, or simply *The Ioudaikē*. How to render the un-translated terms? Josephus did not leave a will conveying his wishes to English-speakers. It is entirely up to us, if we are willing to face the perils of translating ancient texts, to figure out some principles and criteria." (https://marginalia.lareviewofbooks.org/ancient-jews-judeans-different-questions-different-answers-steve-mason.)

39. This position, which appears in the mid-second-century writings of Melito of Sardis, set the tone for Origen and other Christian theologians, including Augustine, Eusebius, and John Chrysostom. See Mason, *Josephus and the New Testament*, p. 13.

40. Hata writes: "Josephus interpreted the fall of Jerusalem and the loss of the Temple theologically not because the Jewish people did not accept Jesus as Christ but because, in his opinion, those who instigated the war against the Romans were not faithful to the Law and thus unworthy of *eleutheria* (freedom)" ("Editor's Preface," in Feldman and Hata, *Josephus, Judaism, and Christianity*, p. 17). This anthology commemorates the completion of the publication of the Japanese translation (by Gohei Hata) of the works of Josephus in 16 volumes (1975–1984).

41. For a complete (and complex) report of the extant mss., including multiple translations and extant online access, see Tommaso Leoni, "The Text of Josephus Corpus," in Chapman and Rodgers, *A Companion to Josephus*, pp. 307–310.

42. This has been recognized since the 1980s by Jewish historians who have worked against simplistic nationalist evaluations of the text. "Inasmuch as scholarship has blurred the distinctions between Palestine and the Diaspora and has noted a bewildering variety of Judaisms for this period, the question becomes much more complex: which variety of Judaism does Josephus represent?" Louis H. Feldman, "Hellenizations in Josephus' *Jewish Antiquities*: The Portrait of Abraham," in Feldman and Hata, *Josephus, Judaism, and Christianity*, p. 150.

43. See "Chronological Problems in BJ," Appendix 4, in Jonathan J. Price, *Jerusalem under Seige: The Collapse of the Jewish State, 66–70 C.E.* (Leiden: Brill, 1992), pp. 210–230.

44. Critics of Josephus point out that he does not mention his sources; however, this is equally true of Suetonius and Tacitus, hence not a unique phenomenon, but one that "follows

the convention of antiquity" (Doron Mendels, "The Formation of an Historical Canon," in Sievers and Lembi, *Josephus and Jewish History*, pp. 18–19).

45. An earlier confusion between Aramaic (spoken widely in the Parthian Empire) and Hebrew is a consequence of Christian traditions of inheritance that wrongly equated Jews as an *ethne* with Hebrew as a language. The extended use of *koine* and various Greek dialects by some Jews as a first (or only) language was not well understood until recently. On Josephus' priestly connections see Rajak, *Josephus*, pp. 29–31.

46. More precisely, Josephus describes the audience for this first version as "barbarians in the interior" (*Bellum Judaicum* 1.3): "Parthians and Babylonians and the most remote tribes of Arabia," along "with our countrymen [*omophilon*/ὁμόφιλον, literally, race, stock] beyond the Euphrates and the inhabitants of Adiabene [upper Tigris region]" (*Bellum Judaicum* 1.6). Of the latter, Josephus writes that the Judaeans hoped they "would join them in revolt" (*Bellum Judaicum* 1.5–6).

47. Mason, *Josephus and the New Testament,* pp. 64–65.

48. See Steve Mason, "Jews, Judaeans, Judaizing, Judaism: Problems of Categorization in Ancient History," *Journal for the Study of Judaism* 38 (2007): 457–512.

49. Mason, *Josephus and the New Testament*, p. 9.

50. *Bellum Judaicum* 1.3.

51. Hata pointed out this discrepancy between the Greek word and Thackeray's simple translation in a 1975 article: "In the Greek and Hellenistic literature, the verb μεταβάλλω [sic] in the active voice or μεταβάλλομαι in the middle or passive voice is frequently used in various senses," but the common words for "translate" are other terms, such as "μεθερμηνύω, μεταγράφω, μεταφέρω, μεταφράζω." "The use of the verb μεταβάλλω as meaning to 'translate' is very rare. . . . Similarly, we cannot cite any example in the LXX [Septuagint] and the other Greek versions of the Old Testament." Gohei Hata, "Is the Greek Version of Josephus' 'Jewish War' a Translation or a Rewriting of the First Version?," *Jewish Quarterly Review*, n.s. 66, no. 2 (October 1975): 90–91. It is interesting that Herodotus uses *metabole* to refer to the adaptation of Phoenician letters to accommodate the Greek alphabet (*Histories* 5.58.1). Thanks to Kathryn H. Stutz, the Johns Hopkins University, for that information.

52. Beard, "The Triumph of Flavius Josephus," pp. 546–547. She continues: "How far you take at face value his claims of inadequacy in Greek depends not only on your judgment of the style of the books (give or take those 'assistants'), but also on how far you suppose that Josephus himself had internalised the rhetorical culture of the Graeco-Roman world, which was honed on such protestations. What you think the 'assistants' (συνεργοί) did is anyone's guess; and hunches vary from a fully ghostwritten project (on this model, it would have been the assistants rather than Josephus who cast the whole work in a Thucydidean frame) to some minor repair work on the author's spelling and grammar" (p. 547).

53. As Josephus makes reference to the Temple of Peace (*Bellum Judaicum* 7.158) which opened that year, the *terminus post quem* (earliest possible dating) is 75 CE.

54. Simon Swain, *Hellenism and Empire: Language, Classicism, and Power in the Greek World AD 50–250* (Oxford: Clarendon Press, 1996), p. 7.

55. Note that "ethnical non-Greeks could appropriate the Greek past or even suggest that modern Greeks had no real connection with it" (Swain, *Hellenism and Empire*, p. 7). Africans and Egyptians were not excluded: Josephus had a patron in his later years (under Domitian), a dark-skinned bibliophile, lover of learning, and man of wealth named Epaphroditus (Rajak, *Josephus*, pp. 223–234).

56. See below, chapter 4, for reasons to resist the translation in the first century of *koine* as "Greek," regardless of whether "Greek" refers to the Second Sophistic's Atticized refinements.

57. An iteration of this class distinction in linguistic style and grammar occurred in modern Greece, so that scholarship emerging from eighteenth- and nineteenth-century philhellenism became entangled with twentieth-century political struggles over what should be the official national language. Swain explains that on one side were the supporters of "the *dhimotiki* (demotic) form, i.e. some sort of standardized version of the Greek that had developed naturally from *koine* (and in itself representing a diverse linguistic situation). On the other side were those who championed the *katharevousa* or 'purified' form, an atticizing version of Greek starting from demotic but improved by the addition of much classical vocabulary and grammar . . . [that] arose during the struggle for Greek independence among the followers of the great nationalist and classical scholar, Adamantios Korais." After independence, Korais' idea was "hijacked" as a "means of entrenching the power of the conservative ruling class," centered on the returning Greek noble families from Constantinople. The "battle between the language camps" remained as a class distinction after Greek independence until the defeat of the colonels in 1974, when democracy was restored and *dhimotiki* was officially recognized. "The leaders of the last non-democratic regime, that of the colonels, were particularly arch-classicizers" (Swain, *Hellenism and Empire*, pp. 35–36).

58. Swain, *Hellenism and Empire*, p. 39.

59. Swain, *Hellenism and Empire*, p. 3.

60. "The fact that poetic references permeate Josephus' Bellum is indisputable. . . . [Thackeray provides] specific examples of borrowing in the *Bellum* from Thucydides, Herodotus, Xenophon, Demosthenes, Homer, Sophocles, Vergil, and Sallust." Honora Howell Chapman, "'By the Waters of Babylon': Josephus and Greek Poetry," in Sievers and Lembi, *Josephus and Jewish History*, pp. 126–127.

61. The most thorough textual analysis of the parallels between Josephus' *Bellum* and Thucydides' *Peloponnesian War* is also the most vehemently critical of Josephus as a traitor to the national cause who manipulated the ancient parallels for purely propagandistic purposes: Gottfried Mader, *Josephus and the Politics of Historiography: Apologetic and Impression Management in the Bellum Judaicum* (Leiden: Brill, 2000). For a more balanced account of Josephus' intent, see Louis H. Feldman, "The Influence of the Greek Tragedians on Josephus," *The Howard Gilman International Conferences I: Hellenic and Jewish Arts*, ed. A.

Ovadiah (Tel Aviv: RAMOT Publishing House, 1998). Feldman's position generally is that there are both "Jewish" and "Hellenized" elements to Josephus's makeup. The question is whether such hybrid definitions are a sufficient solution to the difficulties that arise from utilizing identity categories in the first place.

62. Chapman, "'By the Waters of Babylon,'" p. 132. "Historical prose and poetry were not considered as far apart in antiquity as one might first think" (ibid., p. 126). Swain calls the "still common division in classical civilization studies" between history and literature "unhelpful" (*Hellenism and Empire*, p. 7n). I would add that the division between history and philosophy is unhelpful as well.

63. Chapman, "'By the Waters of Babylon,'" p. 124. Chapman does not put pressure on philosophical truth claims. Her texts are literary; Thucydides is only mentioned. Her point is a different one, concerning aesthetics and ultimately motive: "Josephus's use of Homer, Pindar, Sophocles, and Euripides grants his history a certain grace and grandeur, and was presumably done to please and impress his audience with his attempts at literary artistry and ultimately to move and to convince them of his point of view concerning the war" (ibid., p. 145).

64. Swain, *Hellenism and Empire*, p. 8.

65. Rajak (whose monograph on Josephus, first published in 1983, is still the critical standard) notes that even when the word is not used, it is implied in his account. Consistently, the "fomenters of civil strife" are "within the Jewish state, for it is there that the rebels are, in the first instance, creating innovation and revolution, rather than in the Roman empire as a whole" (Rajak, *Josephus*, p. 86). On the different model of Roman imperial civil wars, see Paula Botteri, "*Stasis*: le mot grec, la chose romaine," *Metis. Anthropologie des mondes grecs anciens* 4, no. 1 (1989): 87–100.

66. Rajak, *Josephus*, p. 91. In the Preface to *Bellum Judaicum* Josephus states: "For, that it ['my country'] owed its ruin to civil strife [στάσις οἰκεία] and that it was the Jewish tyrants who drew down upon the holy temple the unwilling hands of the Romans and the conflagration, is attested by Titus Caesar himself, who sacked the city" (*Bellum Judaicum* 1.10).

67. *Flavius Josephus, Translation and Commentary*, ed. Steve Mason, vol. 1B: *Judean War 2*, trans. and commentary Steve Mason (Leiden: Brill, 2008), p. 185 (editor's comment, no. 1398).

68. Of three volumes, we have now only fragments, but another text by Dionysius, *On Thucydides*, begins with reference to "my treatise *On Imitiation*, already published" (*Dionysius of Halicarnassus: On Thucydides*, trans. and commentary W. Kendrick Pritchett [Berkeley: University of California Press, 1975], 1.325, here p. 1). Here he builds on his view of Thucydides as worthy of emulation, albeit not without faults and failings. Note that his interest is in rhetoric as style, not content, and its effects on the reason and aesthetic tastes of the audience. On the all-important chapters in book III of Thucydides' *Peloponnesian War* (discussed below), Dionysius prefers the more straightforward, early chapters' description of the civil war in Corcyra that say "everything clearly, concisely, and effectively" (ibid. 28.372,

here p. 22). Chapters 82 and 83 receive his strongest criticisms: "The passages that follow these are contorted, hard to follow, and contain figures so curiously constituted as to look like solecisms [i.e., barbarisms]" (ibid. 29.373, here p. 23). He finds the "circumlocutions" and "embellishments" to be "annoying" and "tortuous," "obscure"; he opposes the tendency "to indulge in poetical substitution" and suggests changes into "plain words," rewriting sentences throughout these chapters in order to specify his criticisms (here pp. 24–26).

69. Jonathan J. Price, "Josephus' Reading of Thucydides: A Test Case in the Bellum Iudaicum," in *Thucydides, a Violent Teacher? History and Its Representations*, ed. Georg Rechenauer and Vassiliki Pothou (Göttingen: Vandenhoeck and Ruprecht, 2011), p. 79.

70. Jesus in *this* book by Josephus is not mentioned (cf. his later *Jewish Antiquities*). Yet the fact that the Judaean War and destruction of the Temple play a role in the Gospel writings brings them into dialogue with Josephus' work. Mason proposes that Josephus influenced the Gospels, rather than the other way around—Luke may well have been familiar with Josephus' narrative when he wrote his own account, as there are a number of incidents reported in common (see ch. 6, "Josephus and Luke-Acts," in Mason, *Josephus and the New Testament*, pp. 251–295). For a discussion of the relationship between Josephus' texts and Christianity generally, see Helen K. Bond, "Josephus and the New Testament," in Chapman and Rodgers, *A Companion to Josephus*, pp. 147–158.

71. Rajak, *Josephus*, pp. 90–91.

72. Rajak, *Josephus*, pp. 86–93. Similarly Josephus declares a prophet "false" not because of a set of beliefs, but because he acts falsely to assure 6,000 ordinary people, including women and children, who had taken refuge in the Jerusalem Temple that their God would make manifest the "the proofs of salvation" (cited in Rajak, *Josephus*, p. 90).

73. Rajak, *Josephus*, p. 93. His classification of different philosophical "schools" among Jews is not meant to be synonymous with political positions taken: First Philosophy = Pharisees; Second Philosophy = Sadducees; Third Philosophy = Essenes. What he calls "Fourth Philosophy" is connected to an earlier movement that opposed the Judaean census of 6 CE, which was committed to regard God alone as their Lord, necessarily implying resistance to Roman rule. Rajak believes this schema was not generally used, but was Josephus' own (ibid., p. 89).

74. "Thus we are left in the dark as to how the enemies of Rome aligned themselves within the Jewish religion" (Rajak, *Josephus*, p. 89). This issue, leaving open the question of just who the zealots were and what they have to do with Jewish nationalism—as well as Jesus' own position vis-à-vis Rome—is helpfully explained by Daniel R. Schwartz, *Studies in the Jewish Background of Christianity* (Tübingen: J. C. B. Mohr [Paul Siebeck], 1992), pp. 129–146.

75. Rajak, *Josephus*, p. 86.

76. Mader, *Josephus and the Politics of Historiography*, provides an extended account of parallel references as valuable scholarship, despite Mader's harsh and partisan critique of Josephus' motives. See especially Mader's chapter 3, "The Semantics of *Stasis*: Some Thucydidean Strands in *BJ* 4. 121–283," pp. 55–103.

77. Price, "Josephus' Reading of Thucydides," p. 86.

78. *Bellum Judaicum* 4.131–133, cited in Price, "Josephus' Reading of Thucydides," pp. 85–86. Compare Thucydides 3.81, on Corcyra. We use here as translation (due to its superior attention to linguistic detail) Thucydides, *The War of the Peloponnesians and the Athenians*, ed. and trans. Jeremy Mynott (Cambridge: Cambridge University Press, 2013).

79. "Plague and *stasis*, in the political pathology of Thucydides, are complementary paradigms of civic and social dissolution," leading "by different routes to the same state of desocialization and ἀνομία [lawlessness]," and they are found in Josephus as well (Mader, *Josephus and the Politics of Historiography*, pp. 56–57).

80. *Bellum Judaicum* 5.514. Sophocles' play *Antigone* (ca. 445 BCE), which thematizes the burial of the dead as a pious act, was roughly contemporaneous with the Peloponnesian War (431–404 BCE), as discussed below. On Titus' response to the unburied bodies, see *Bellum Judaicum* 5.519–520; also Chapman, "'By the Waters of Babylon,'" p. 139.

81. Mader, *Josephus and the Politics of Historiography*, p. 64.

82. Thucydides 3.82.4–7 (Mader, *Josephus and the Politics of Historiography*, pp. 61–64). As the radicals assume control in Corcyra, Thucydides notes a correlative radicalization in the language itself, a displacement of the conventional (or pre-*stasis*) connotations of political concepts and slogans to match the prevailing ideology.

83. *Bellum Judaicum* 4.124, 126, 279.

84. Thucydides 3.82.6–7; *Bellum Judaicum* 4.214–216.

85. *Bellum Judaicum* 5. 27–28.

86. Price contends that at this point it is difficult to translate *stasis* as "internal conflict," rather than rebellion or "uprising" against Rome, "for the word seems to refer to a violent rebellious action by one party which another party was trying to suppress" (Price, "Josephus' Reading of Thucydides," p. 91).

87. Josephus describes his initial role as protector of those engaged in the insurgency in Galilee as a military response to a perceived foreign invasion by Roman troops who had just subdued the Syrians, where Jews were massacred (*Bellum Judaicum* 2.560ff.) As a general, his actions were in line with the established rules of *polemos*. His imprisonment as a captive of war was ended by pardon. For details of his status as prisoner of war, see William den Hollander, *Josephus, the Emperors, and the City of Rome: From Hostage to Historian* (Leiden: Brill, 2014), pp. 69–91.

88. Price says that whereas in the Peloponnesian War, *stasis* began as a local event and became general, in the Judaean War, the dynamic was reversed: what began as an anti-Roman revolt became local. Yet he acknowledges the persistence of internal conflict: "Jewish society was riven from top to bottom during the years preceding the war—a real *stasis* which Josephus names correctly, and this many-sided societal split continued even after the war with Rome formally broke out." There was no unity among Jews even after the situation was complicated by Roman use of force. *Stasis* continued, "a complex series of clashes between

competing Jewish parties on the one hand and between Jewish forces and the Roman administration on the other" (Price, "Josephus' Reading of Thucydides," p. 96).

89. *Bellum Judaicum* 5.255. Josephus continues: "[T]he parties divided and fell to fighting once more, doing all that their besiegers could have desired. Certainly, they suffered nothing worse at the hands of the Romans than what they inflicted upon each other. . . . For I maintain that it was the sedition [*stasis*] that subdued the city, and the Romans the sedition [*stasis*], a foe far more stubborn than her walls; and that all the tragedy of it may properly be ascribed to her own people, all the justice to the Romans. But let everyone follow his own opinion whither the facts [*pragmasin*/πράγμασιν] may lead him" (*Bellum Judaicum* 5.255–257).

90. This is Mader's nomenclature in *Josephus and the Politics of Historiography*, p. 17.

91. Steve Mason, "Figured Speech and Irony in Josephus," in *Flavius Josephus and Flavian Rome*, ed. Jonathan Edmondson, Steve Mason, and James Rives (Oxford: Oxford University Press, 2005), p. 269.

92. Price parses the sentence: "For I say that the stasis overwhelmed the city, the Romans the stasis, which proved far more enduring than the walls themselves" (see above, note 85) and finds the word *stasis* misleading. He observes that the Latin translation of *both* internal war and rebellion is *seditio* (in English, sedition; see discussion of Hobbes below), and that this eliminates the problem "conveniently" (Price, "Josephus' Reading of Thucydides," pp. 90–92).

93. In Thucydides (3.39.2) the Corcyrans endured internal strife (*stasis*); but Mytelenians were engaged in a revolt (*apostasis*) against Athenian control. See Price, "Josephus' Reading of Thucydides," pp. 91–94.

94. By taking Thucydides out of context, "a partisan and subjective interpretation is given the appearance of 'scientific' analysis in the distinguished tradition of classical historiography. The reader who succumbs to this illusion becomes the polemicist's unwitting accomplice" (Mader, *Josephus and the Politics of Historiography*, p. 54).

95. Price, "Josephus' Reading of Thucydides," p. 97. Price finds Josephus' motive in the fact that "he belonged to the party which led the rebel state in 66 before being ousted from power in 67 by the extremists, whom he thus wanted to blame" (ibid.).

96. Mason, "Figured Speech and Irony in Josephus," p. 288.

97. *Bellum Judaicum* 1.30.

98. "[M]y work is written for lovers of truth" (τήν ἀλήθειαν ἀγαπῶσιν, *Bellum Judaicum* 1.30). Cf. Thucydides, who describes the main aim of his book as "the search for the truth" (ἡ ζήτησις τῆς ἀληθείας [1.20.3]). Price writes: "Yet as the reader continues beyond the grandiose first sentence, trouble arises," as he calls other accounts "partisan and distorting" and at the same time "adds that he shall not repress his own emotions but rather give them free rein and allow himself to 'lament the calamities which befell my country' (*BJ* 1.30)" (Price, "The Provincial Historian in Rome," in Sievers and Lembi, *Josephus and Jewish History*, p. 110).

99. See, for example, the revealing conversations of Benny Lévy with Jean-Paul Sartre, *Hope Now: The 1980 Interviews*, trans. Adrian van den Hoven, intro. Ronald Aronson (Chicago: University of Chicago Press, 1996), especially pp. 103–104: Lévy asks Sartre to comment on his statement in *Anti-Semite and Jew* that "there is no Jewish history," and Sartre admits he was "thinking of history in a certain well-defined sense," as "a sovereign political entity that has its own territory," which he recognized was basic to Hegel's philosophy of history, but which he now wished to reject. Thanks to Jonathan Boyarin for suggesting this example.

100. Daniel R. Schwartz, "Introduction: Was 70 CE a Watershed in Jewish History? Three Stages of Modern Scholarship, and a Renewed Effort," in Schwarz, *Was 70 CE a Watershed in Jewish History?*, p. 3.

101. Schwartz, "Introduction: Was 70 CE a Watershed in Jewish History?," p. 3. Gruen's work is seminal here: a fact "well known to specialists" is that "the dispersal of Jews had begun long before the Temple fell"; "To assume that the [diaspora Jews] repeatedly lamented their fate and pinned their hopes on recovery of the homeland is quite preposterous" (Erich S. Gruen, *Diaspora: Jews amidst Greeks and Romans* (Cambridge, MA: Harvard University Press, 2002), p. 234.

102. Schwartz, "Introduction: Was 70 CE a Watershed in Jewish History?," p. 3. Against descriptions of the revolt ending in 70 CE as leading "to the destruction of the last *independent Jewish state* in Palestine until the establishment of Israel," Sharon writes: "There is no doubt that these scholars knew very well that the Roman occupation of Judea began in 63 BCE, and that that is when the independent and sovereign Judean state [of the Hasmoneans] actually came to its end; but still, this is the picture reflected in various scholarly works." Nadav Sharon, "Setting the Stage: The Effects of the Roman Conquest and the Loss of Sovereignty," in Schwarz, *Was 70 CE a Watershed in Jewish History?*, p. 418.

103. Three revolts of Judaea within four centuries are often grouped together to produce a narrative of constant resistance to foreign domination: the revolt led by the Hasmonean Maccabees against the Selucids (Antiochus IV), 167–160 BCE, wherein (according to the book of Maccabees) *Judaismos* was defended against influences of *Hellenismos*; the Judaean revolt against Rome described by Josephus in the *Bellum Judaicum*, 66–73 CE; and Simon Bar Kochba's revolt against the Romans in 132–136 CE that led to the barring of Jews from Jerusalem. They were, however, very different events, and their conflation as anti-imperialist is a misleading simplification.

104. Michael Tuval, "Doing without the Temple: Paradigms in Judaic Literature of the Diaspora," in Schwarz, *Was 70 CE a Watershed in Jewish History?*, p. 236. In examining the diasporic literature of the first century CE, Tuval found "much less interest in the Temple and its cult, if any"; in its place this literature offers multiple "coherent Judaic worldviews and identities": "In some cases we saw the emerging ideal of Torah study as central, which in later rabbinic Judaism was to achieve its full supremacy as the focal act of divine worship" (ibid., p. 237). "Above all, we saw an overwhelming emphasis on ethics . . . always recognizably Jewish ethics, taught in the Torah of Moses" (ibid., p. 238). On the continuation

between the Pharisees and the later rabbis, see Schwartz, "Introduction: Was 70 CE a Watershed in Jewish History?," p. 9.

105. The translation was reissued in 1634 and 1648; Hobbes prepared a new edition in 1676. Two earlier vernacular translations existed, one in French, by Claud de Seyssel (1527), and, copied from this, one in English, by Thomas Nicolls in 1550. But Hobbes worked directly with Lorenzo Valla's version, known to him (as he tells us in his preface) through an edition by Aemilius Portus in 1594. Valla's translation, commissioned by the humanist Pope Nicholas V and completed in 1452, made use of several available Greek manuscript sources (presumed to have come from Constantinople after 1420), of which we have more than one copy, and still there are differences, indicating a possible missing text that preceded them. See Robin Sowerby, "Thomas Hobbes's Translation of Thucydides," *Translation and Literature* 7, no. 2 (1998): 147–169, esp. pp. 148–149.

106. The assumption that *polis* in the "true" sense is an urban center always possessing independent governmental institutions, hence "autonomous" (while the term used simply for urban center is *kome*), is not accurate—and the details of this inaccuracy are of fundamental significance. M. H. Hansen, as head of the Copenhagen Polis Center, has built up an inventory of the ancient use of this term, and writes against this scholarly "orthodoxy." Hansen cites Thucydides explicitly, who "uses *polis* both in the urban and the political sense of the word. The curious result of such a policy is the view that our sources often apply the term *polis* to a settlement that, according to modern orthodoxy, was not a *polis*. The contradiction has its root in the fact that modern historians who write about ancient Greece like to use the term *polis* synonymously with the term city-state. But city-state is a modern historical term which seems to have been coined in studies of the Roman concept of civitas, from which it was rapidly transferred not only to studies of the Greek *poleis* but also to investigations of Italian city-states from ca. 1100 onwards, of medieval German Reichsstädte, of Sumerian, Phoenician and Etruscan cities etc." Mogens Herman Hansen, "*Kome*. A Study in How the Greeks Designated and Classified Settlements Which Were Not *Poleis*," in *Studies in the Ancient Greek Polis*, ed. Mogens Herman Hansen and Kurt A. Raaflaub (Stuttgart: F. Steiner Verlag, 1995), pp. 45–46. Hansen further clarifies that the Greek *polis* was not, by definition, "autonomous": "This misconception is probably due to the tendency to think of the *polis* along modern notions of statehood: a state is by definition autonomous; the *polis* is the ancient equivalent to a state; thus the *polis* must be autonomous. If the term 'the autonomous *polis*' or 'city-state' is too deeply rooted to be eradicated, it must be kept in mind or rather explicitly stated that 'autonomy' has to be taken in only one of its modern meanings, i.e. in the minimal sense in which it comprises dependencies as well as independent communities and that it must not be mistaken for the ancient Greek concept of *autonomia* in the classical period." Mogens Herman Hansen, "The 'Autonomous City-State': Ancient Fact or Modern Fiction?," in *Studies in Ancient Greek Polis*, p. 40.

107. Rzepka questions the adequacy of this presumption: as a term, koinon *may* refer to a *polis* as part of a federation, but it may also refer to a part of the *polis*, the general assembly

as the "full citizen body" as opposed to a federal council. See Jacek Rzepka, "Ethnos, Koinon, Sympoliteia, and Greek Federal States," in *Euergesias Charin: Studies Presented to Ewa Wipszycka and Benedetto Bravo by Their Disciples*, ed. Tomasz Derda, Jakub Urbanik, and Marek Węcowski, *Journal of Juristic Papyrology*, supplement 1(Warsaw: Fundacaja im. Rafała Taubenschlaga, 2002), 225–247.

108. Regarding *stasis*: "Whereas other translators talk of party strife, civil disorder, or faction, Hobbes habitually translates the word as 'sedition'" (Sowerby, "Thomas Hobbes's Translation of Thucydides," p. 151). Here he is following Valla, who (like the ancient Romans) translates *stasis* in Latin as *seditio* (e.g., Thucydides 3.82.1). *Stasis* and *seditio* are not equivalents.

109. Athens had ca. 350,000 inhabitants over 1,000 square miles; most *poleis*, with ca. 10,000 residents, were large villages. On empire specifically see Ian Morris: "calling the political organization that the Athenians ruled in the fifth century an 'empire' is something of a misnomer. . . . Classicists have worried a lot about exactly what Thucydides meant when he used the word archē to describe the political organization that the Athenians led, but have worried far less about what they mean when they use the English word 'empire' as a translation for archē. I suggest that this has caused some confusion. . . . [B]y 404 neither Athens nor her rival states had succeeded in centralizing state power enough to become the capital of a durable, territorial Greek state." Ian Morris, "The Athenian Empire 478–404 BC," Princeton/Stanford working papers in classics, December 2005. See also Spahn's detailed examination of ancient Greek uses of the word *archē*, "difficult to reproduce" in modern languages. "The word 'rule' does only insufficiently capture its meaning in a strict sense. . . . Nor is the word synonymous with 'domination' in the modern sociological sense of Max Weber. Its most basic meaning alludes instead to *the first, the front position*, neither in a temporal nor in a spatial sense, but denoting power and authority." Peter Spahn, "Between Office and Tyranny, Internal and External Rulership: Archē in Herodotus and Thucydides," in *Thucydides and Political Order: Concepts of Order and the History of the Peloponnesian War*, ed. Christian R. Thauer and Christian Wendt (Houndmills, UK: Palgrave Macmillan, 2016), p. 59. Spahn notes specifically: "The German word 'Reich' and its equivalents in other Germanic and related languages . . . cover only a part of the semantics of *archē*, for they don't contain its basic meaning 'beginning, origin, cause'" (ibid., p. 81n). "Its significance for constitutional and international law remains vague and undefined, much in contrast to its Latin equivalent *imperium*" (ibid., p. 80).

110. In the nineteenth century and into the twentieth, at the height of the British Empire, "Thucydides was a necessary part of every young gentleman's reading in the public schools" (Sowerby, "Thomas Hobbes's Translation of Thucydides," p. 148). Spahn describes the discrepancy between modern readers' understanding and Thucydides' text. The latter cites speakers as equating *archē* with the tyrant metaphor for Athens' rule over the Delian League, and also in relation to domestic rule; the word *archē* "is the overarching term covering various meanings and functions: from regular office to informal, even tyrannical authority, within *and* outside of the polis. The lack of inherent distinction makes this term so very

useful for literature and rhetoric. Its significance for constitutional and international law remains vague and undefined, much in contrast to its Latin equivalent *imperium*" (Spahn, "Archē in Herodotus and Thucydides," in Thauer and Wendt, *Thucydides and Political Order*, pp. 75 and 80).

111. Schmitt has argued that in modern democracies there is a fundamental paradox of sovereign legitimacy, the fact that the sovereign can, legitimately, suspend the law in order to protect the nation-state from itself. Carl Schmitt, *Political Theology: Four Chapters on the Concept of Sovereignty*, trans. George Schwab (Chicago: University of Chicago Press, 2005). A transcendent role of nation-state sovereignty was not part of Lorenzo Valla's world. (It was Valla, after all, who proved that the Donation of Constantine, allegedly granting Western Christendom to the authority of the Roman Papacy, was in fact an eighth-century forgery.) The mediating figures between Valla and Hobbes on this point are Machiavelli (1469–1527), who read Thucydides probably in Valla's translation, and the French jurist Jean Boudin (1530–1596), theorist of state sovereignty who read Thucydides with enthusiasm.

112. For a description of how this happened, and of the complexities in interpreting Thucydides that had to be sacrificed in the process, see Josiah Ober, "Thucydides *Theōrētikos*/Thucydides *Histōr*: Realist Theory and the Challenge of History," in *Thucydides*, ed. Jeffrey S. Rusten (Oxford: Oxford University Press, 2009), pp. 434–478.

113. Ober, "Thucydides *Theōrētikos*/Thucydides *Histōr*," p. 437: "Thucydides reminds us that any proper theory of power must be grounded in a close analysis of human behavior in actual circumstances." Ober writes: "[P]erhaps his most cogent lesson is the necessity of intellectual humility in the face of the uncertainties, peculiarities, contingencies, and idiosyncracies which will continue to challenge theorists, historians, and policymakers alike" (ibid., p. 478).

114. Ober, "Thucydides *Theōrētikos*/Thucydides *Histōr*," p. 436.

115. Ober, "Thucydides *Theōrētikos*/Thucydides *Histōr*," p. 473. There are parts of Thucydides' account that support a realist interpretation, but his discussion of *stasis* is not one of them. In the bipolar Cold War worldview, seen through the lens of great-power (US/USSR) rivalry, domestic protests appeared as a consequence of foreign interference.

116. While Mader justifies his own "political" position with "religious" references, the opposite occurs in the case of those interpretations he condemns: "religious-eschatological specifics slide into psychological generalizations (themselves implicit value judgments) and dissolve within this secular matrix" (Mader, *Josephus*, p. 53).

117. Mader, *Josephus*, p. 52. For Mader, "nationalism" is synonymous with "religious beliefs."

118. Rajak, *Josephus*, p. 91 (cf. Mader, *Josephus*, p. 31). Rajak finds that the messianic motif is lacking, whereas the "moral motif," pursued by Josephus with "intensity," is not theologically based but "part of a continuous process throughout history, in which this is but one of many exemplifications of the same problem" (Rajak, *Josephus*, p. 92).

119. Paul S. Spilsbury, "Reading the Bible in Rome: Josephus and the Constraints of Empire," in Sievers and Lembi, *Josephus and Jewish History*. The "much-cited Book of Daniel" in the *Bellum Judaicum*, with its prophecy of four earthly empires that are followed by a fifth, the eternal kingdom of God, is part of Josephus' rhetoric in this process: "Thus the Roman Empire, like the empires of the Babylonians, Medo-Persians, and Greeks before it, is underwritten by God himself" (ibid., p. 225).

120. Price, "Josephus' Reading of Thucydides," p. 98.

121. Carl Schmitt, with reference to Jost Trier, *The Nomos of the Earth in the International Law of the Jus Publicum Europaeum*, trans. G. L. Ulman (New York: Telos Press, 2006), p. 74.

122. Daniel Boyarin, in Carlin A. Barton and Daniel Boyarin, *Imagine No Religion: How Modern Abstractions Hide Ancient Realities* (New York: Fordham University Press, 2016), p. 163.

123. Loraux (trans. Rusten) speaks of "political language," but my preference is language (or linguistic laws) "of the polis," in the sense of public language; as has been noted, "political" is a conceptual distinction with a specifically modern meaning. See Nicole Loraux, "Thucydides and Sedition among Words," in Rusten, *Thucydides*, p. 263.

124. June W. Allison, *Word and Concept in Thucydides* (Atlanta: Scholar's Press, 1997), p. 171.

125. "Civil strife ['Εστασίαζέ] therefore became a fact of life in the cities [τά τῶν πολειῶν], and those cities affected later rather than sooner, hearing what had happened elsewhere, went to ever greater extremes in inventing ingenious forms of attack and outlandish reprisals" (Thucydides 3.82.2). Poschenrieder writes that τά τῶν πόλεῶν (Thucydides 3.82.3) refers to "the parties in each city forcing the poleis into civil war. The parties are termed with a neutral expression thus stressing the fact that they are factors in the historical process" (Thomas Poschenrieder, "Material Constraints in Thucydides' Representation of History," in Rechenauer and Pothou, *Thucydides, a Violent Teacher*, p. 149). "In civil wars, the poleis are lacerated by the parties. The city *as a whole* does not act itself, is *no protagonist* of the events going on but *suffers* the clashes"; at other, peaceful times, the city is the protagonist, but that is when "the single citizens are absorbed into it" (ibid., p. 147). This distinction is criticized by Dionysius of Halicarnassus (instead of τά τῶν πόλεῶν, "it would have been better to say [more simply] 'the cities were rent by civil divisions'" (*Dionysius of Halicarnassus: On Thucydides*, ed. Pritchett, p. 23), but Poschenrieder says that it is a meaningful difference, and traces it through Thucydides' use of nouns in the genitive plural with τά throughout the text.

126. Dionysius' *On Thucydides*, as well as his history of Rome from its mythic past to the start of the first Punic War, were both available to Josephus. As we have noted, Dionysius was critical of the linguistic idiosyncrasies of the *Peloponnesian War*, considering them rhetorically unnecessary and obfuscating, an interpretation recently contested not only by Poschenrieder (see the previous note) but (less directly) by Allison and Loraux, three scholars on whose work I draw heavily in this section.

127. Thucydides 3.82.3–4. Poschenrieder writes that this is a problem of the "established value" (εἰωθυῖα ἀξίωσις), not meaning, so that "the positive and negative connotations must be

retained in order to justify or reprehend certain ways of behaviour by applying the old terms in a new way. Thucydides does not talk about the meaning of the words as such but about the application of these words on real facts" (Poschenrieder, "Material Constraints in Thucydides' Representation of History," p. 150).

128. Neither translators nor scholars appear to make this distinction between *onoma* and *logos*—curious, given the fact that in both ancient and modern Greek, the variants of *onoma* all connote name, whereas *logos* has meanings of a different sort: logic, reason.

129. Allison, *Word and Concept in Thucydides*, p. 169. "Thucydides says that the customary *axiosis* of the words (not the kind of action nor the meanings of the words) changed (was made to fit differently) in relation to the deeds, depending on people's *judgment of the situation* (*dikaiosis*). The focus is on *axiosis* and *dikaiosis*, not, it must be emphasized, *axiosis* and *erga* [act]" (ibid., pp. 169–170). In this context it is intriguing that the evaluative idea of *axiosis* returns in the book of Revelation to describe the lamb who alone is deemed "worthy" (ἄξιος) of highest praise (Rev 5:12; see below, chapter 4).

130. "Thucydides seems carefully to have avoided εἶναι [the verb 'is,' ontological being] here, except, of course, as it is implied in the manner of everyday speech" (Allison, *Word and Concept in Thucydides*, p. 175).

131. Allison, *Word and Concept in Thucydides*, p. 181. On *axiosis*: "to conceptualize is to be able to use words appropriately and to make the words fit actions or things depending on their 'value' as determined by society. Thus the same words can apply to different situations, depending on the speaker's conceptualization (a diachronic [i.e., historicized] perspective) or, as it is stated in 3.82, different words are made to fit same situations" (ibid., p. 181).

132. Loraux writes: "what *stasis* perverts is above all the assigning of *praise* and *blame*" (Loraux, "Thucydides and Sedition among Words," p. 271).

133. Thucydides 3.82.8. Alternatively: "so that neither one side nor the other practiced piety, only the speciousness of their language . . . enhanced their fame" (Loraux, "Thucydides and Sedition among Words," p. 275).

134. On the importance of this word for Josephus, see Boyarin's discussion of zealousness (*threskia*) versus piety (*eusebeia*) and how Josephus shows moments of respect for the zealots, despite his Thucydidean argument (Barton and Boyarin, *Imagine No Religion*, pp. 182–188).

135. Loraux is surprised by the appearance of ευσεβεια: "Piety? We find ourselves far from the 'secular' tone favoured by Thucydides" ("Thucydides and Sedition among Words," p. 275). Thucydides' aversion to "religious" themes is well known, although his text, while disavowing the role of religion in human affairs, gives evidence of its significance to the protagonists during the Peloponnesian War. See Simon Hornblower, "The Religious Dimension to the Peloponnesian War, or, What Thucydides Does Not Tell Us," *Harvard Studies in Classical Philology* 94 (1992): 169–197. Cf. Barton and Boyarin, *Imagine No Religion*, who insist that the modern understanding does not hold for this era.

136. Allison points out that this word indicates not intuitive intelligence, merely "thinking": "The dichotomy between a natural intuitive kind of thinking and one dependent on *nomos* is maintained in the text" (Allison, *Word and Concept in Thucydides*, p. 181). She notes, in contrast, the connection in ancient Greek texts between *nomizein* and *onomazein*, to evaluate and to name (ibid., p. 176).

137. Allison, *Word and Concept in Thucydides*, p. 181. "[I]t bestows upon the language user the responsibility for determining the worth of a fact and speaking about it" (ibid.).

138. Schmitt, *The Nomos of the Earth*, p. 77.

139. Thucydides 3.82.4; see Allison, *Word and Concept in Thucydides*, p. 175.

140. "[I]t is imperative to reemphasize the social and conventional view of language underscored by the use of *nomizein, axiosis,* and *diakaiosis.*" Allison, *Word and Concept in Thucydides*, p. 181.

141. Price notes the judgment "you speak well" (καλῶς λέγεις), a common phrase (in Sophocles, Euripides) of those who hear public debate: "learning from those who speak well is an honorable thing": Jonathan Price, *Thucydides and Internal War* (Cambridge: Cambridge University Press, 2001), pp. 48–49. Price (ibid., pp. 46–47) does not distinguish between *logos* and *onoma*, but only—following Dionysius—between *logos* and *ergon* (word and deed), which, according to Allison, does not capture what is at stake. Price is one of the few scholars to have written separate monographs on both Thucydides and Josephus. We have already discussed his claim of major differences between them. In regard to the collapse of the distinction between *stasis* and *polemos* discussed below, Price seems to suggest that Thucydides sees all of the Peloponnesian War as a civil war, hence Hellas as one ethnic and geographic identity.

142. Thucydides' "formulation of the issues seems to have been derived from observing the parallel phenomena of plague and *stasis*: as the plague perverted the social *nomoi, stasis* destroys the linguistic *nomoi*" (Allison, *Word and Concept in Thucydides*, p. 164). Cf. Loraux: "civil war simultaneously a *loimos* (plague) and also one of the evils attached to the human condition" ("Thucydides and Sedition among Words," p. 264). Poschenrieder points out the "echoes of medical language" in Thucydides 3.82.1–2 ("Material Constraints in Thucydides' Representation of History," p. 147n).

143. Allison, *Word and Concept in Thucydides*, p. 182.

144. "The neutral formulation also enables the historian to direct the reader's attention to the situations as such and allows him to view human factors and impersonal factors together" (Poschenrieder, "Material Constraints in Thucydides' Representation of History," pp. 156–157).

145. Poschenrieder, "Material Constraints in Thucydides' Representation of History," p. 156.

146. Poschenrieder, "Material Constraints in Thucydides' Representation of History," p. 153.

147. Poschenrieder, "Material Constraints in Thucydides' Representation of History," p. 153.

148. Allison, *Word and Concept in Thucydides*, p. 66.

149. "If *stasis*, like war, is conceived as *kinein* [motion; to move]—according to Thucydides, after the events of Corcyra it was 'virtually the whole of the Greek world that was moved (*ekinethe*)—we must not see in it merely a wordplay . . . but a very eloquent way of using the same designation for internal conflicts within cities as for the confrontation on the scale of the Greek world that gives the historian his topic" (Loraux, "Thucydides and Sedition among Words," p. 265).

150. M. I. Finley, "The Ancient Greeks and Their Nation," in *The Use and Abuse of History* (New York: Viking, 1975), p. 139.

151. "'Escalation of violence in reciprocal actions' in *stasis* turns out to be a good definition of *kinesis*" (Allison, *Word and Concept in Thucydides*, p. 166)

152. Loraux, "Thucydides and Sedition among Words," p. 264.

153. Loraux, "Thucydides and Sedition among Words," pp. 264 and 266.

154. Loraux, "Thucydides and Sedition among Words," p. 268.

155. Loraux, "Thucydides and Sedition among Words," p. 265. The citation is from Thucydides 3.82, where the word that appears in translation as "revolutionary change" is *stasis*.

156. This statement of Jost Trier, German linguist at Münster University and member of the Nazi Party, was cited by Carl Schmitt in *The Nomos of the Earth*, p. 74.

157. "It is evident that long ago what is now called 'Hellas' had no stable settlements, instead there were various migrations in these early times and each group readily abandoned their own territory whenever forced to do so by those with superior numbers. For there was no commerce and people were insecure about making contact with each other. . . . And the quality of land gave some groups more power than others, and that led to internal conflict [*stasis*], which destroyed them and at the same time encouraged outsiders to have designs on them" (Thucydides 1.1.2–3).

158. "Au début la stasis, donc. Mais aussi: au début, la guerre." Nicole Loraux, "Thucydide et la sédition dans les mots," *Quarderini di storia* 23 (1986): 99. I have modified Rusten's English translation of this text: "so it starts with stasis" (Loraux, "Thucydides and Sedition among Words," p. 265), to observe that both Loraux and Schmitt, in their choice of phrasing, seem (independently) to be making reference to the biblical verse of John 1:1: "In the beginning was the word" (*logos*). For more on *this* word, as used by Philo of Alexandria, see chapter 3.

159. Loraux, "Thucydides and Sedition among Words," p. 268.

160. Loraux, "Thucydides and Sedition among Words," p. 268. By a strange coincidence, Loraux uses a very *un*-Athenian term at this point. Civil war, she writes, was thus for the ancient Greeks "the abomination of desolation" (the term in the French original as well as the English translation), by which, apparently unwittingly, her French Judaeo-Christian context enters this text. This phrase is from the Old Testament book of Daniel (clearly

known to Josephus) that echoes also in the New Testament gospels of Matthew and Luke (not known to Josephus), who themselves describe the destruction of Jerusalem's Second Temple, alleged to have been predicted by Jesus, by citing Daniel's "abomination of desolation." Loraux thus unintentionally builds for us a bridge from Thucydides to Josephus.

161. Loraux, "Thucydides and Sedition among Words," p. 267. Respect for tradition holds Thucydides back from accepting a conflation of the two. For him, "the beautiful death is an absolute value, in opposition to the brutal violence of murder"; "the fact is clear: in The Peloponnesian War there is one place for the beautiful death and another for the eruption of *phonos*, and this arrangement is in strict accordance with orthodox civic ideals" (ibid.).

162. "So it was that every kind of wickedness [*kakotropia*, wicked intention, a neologism— see Allison, *Word and Concept in Thucydides*, p. 166] took root in Greece as a result of these civil conflicts. Simplicity of spirit [*ethos*], which is such an important part of true nobility, was laughed to scorn and vanished, while people were largely divided into opposite and mutually suspicious camps. No words were binding enough, no oath terrible enough, to reconcile them; all those who were sufficiently strong calculated that it was hopeless to expect any security and preferred to protect themselves against injury rather than rely on trust. And the less intelligent were the ones who most often came out on top. . . . Those, on the other hand, who disdainfully assumed that they would foresee things well in advance and that there was no need to secure by action what would come to them by power of intellect—they were instead taken off-guard and perished" (Thucydides 3.83.1–4).

163. Nicole Loraux, *The Divided City: On Memory and Forgetting in Ancient Athens*, trans. Corinne Pache with Jeff Fort (New York: Urzone/Zone Books, 2002), pp. 186ff.

164. The date of the first performance of this tragedy cannot be fixed, reminding us of the precariousness of chronological dating for ancient times. See R. G. Lewis, "An Alternative Date for Sophocles' *Antigone*," *Greek, Roman, and Byzantine Studies* 29 (1988): 35–50. Thucydides' account of the war, which is organized according to campaign years based on seasonal cycles rather than chronological dates (Mynott notes these divisions in his translation), covers the period 431–404 BCE.

165. Etman is "of the belief that Thucydides is Sophoclean in his historiography," hence conscious of the analogies to the drama in his account. Ahmed Etman, "A Light from Thucydides on the Problem of Sophocles' 'Antigone' and Its Tragic Meaning," *Antiquité classique* 70 (2001): 147. The dramatist Sophocles was also a public figure, elected to serve as general in the Athenian campaign against Samos in part due to the success of *Antigone*.

166. The standard Greek-English lexicon of Liddell and Scott gives for νεῖκος "quarrel, wrangle, strife, dispute before a judge"; Aeschylus uses the word πολύνεικής to mean "much wrangling." *An Intermediate Greek-English Lexicon Founded upon the Seventh Edition of Liddell and Scott's Greek-English Lexicon* (Oxford: Benediction Classics, 2010).

167. Antigone to Creon: "Nor did I deem that thou, a mortal man / Could'st by a breath annul and override / The immutable unwritten laws of Heaven. / They were not born today nor

yesterday; / They die not; and none knoweth whence they sprang" (Sophocles, *Antigone*, 450–457).

168. Suicide was a free act, the philosopher's noble death. But her *method* marks its feminization: "Hanging was a woman's death"; as an emblem of her sex, "Antigone strangled herself with her knotted [virgin's] veil." Nicole Loraux, *Tragic Ways of Killing a Woman*, trans. Anthony Forster (Cambridge, MA: Harvard University Press, 1987), p. 10. The throat (σφαγή) was the spot of slaughter in sacrificial victims.

169. This Hegelian understanding (which would have been unrecognizable to both Thucydides and Josephus) determines as well Agamben's reading of the "proper place" of *stasis* as a "zone of indifference" transgressing the "threshold" between the "unpolitical space of the family and the political space of the city." Giorgio Agamben, *Stasis: Civil War as a Political Paradigm* [*Homo Sacer II, 2*], trans. Nicholas Heron (Stanford: Stanford University Press, 2015), p. 16.

170. Family relations remain: men are the heads of the household (*oikos*), masters of women and slaves. This easy resolution has been challenged in recent receptions of Hegel: "The family is the 'basis' of the 'actuality of the nation,' a necessary matrix of sociality on which the state depends for the production of its citizens," and yet underneath this hierarchic relation, conflict remains: "The family ultimately remains a stumbling block to be overcome on the inexorable march towards the universal spirit." Miriam Leonard, *Athens in Paris: Ancient Greece and the Political in Post-War French Thought* (Oxford: Oxford University Press, 2005), p. 99.

171. See Brett de Bary's introductory remarks to her translation of Takahashi Yūji, "On Not Letting Death Die," in *Still Hear the Wound: Toward an Asia, Politics, and Art to Come*, ed. Lee Chonghwa, trans. Rebecca Jennison and Brett de Bary (Ithaca: Cornell University, Cornell East Asia Series, 2016), pp. lxv–vi. See also Nicole Loraux, *Mothers in Mourning*, with the essay "Of Amnesty and Its Opposite," trans. Corrine Pache (Ithaca: Cornell University Press, 1998). Loraux's psychoanalytic approach revolves around the figure of the mother (which Antigone was not).

172. The ambiguities exist on multiple levels: Antigone appeals to the ancient sanctities of the family which her own family in no way embodies: she is daughter of the parricide Oedipus who marries his (and thus her) mother. Creon as king and promulgator of law has the power to end *stasis*, so that to read him merely as a tyrant is a simplification.

173. It is the consensus of recent scholarship that women attended the theater as well as participating publicly in religious festivals; see Simon Goldhill, "Representing Democracy: Women at the Great Dionysia," in *Ritual, Finance, Politics: Athenian Democratic Accounts Presented to David Lewis*, ed. Robin Osborne and Simon Hornblower (Oxford: Oxford University Press, 1994), pp. 347–369. See also David Kawalko Roselli, *Theater of the People: Spectators and Society in Ancient Athens* (Austin: University of Texas Press, 2011).

174. She is affianced to Haemon, Creon's son, who finds her body and kills himself, as does his mother, Creon's wife.

175. Vernant writes that the citizen's "first duty" was "to regulate divine things that concerned the city"; indeed "[t]he gods were themselves political. There was religion in politics, and religion itself had a political dimension. In the end, the gods were citizens. They defended the interests of the city and were concerned with it." Jean-Pierre Vernant, "The Polis: Shared Power," in *Ancestor of the West: Writing, Reasoning and Religion in Mesopotamia, Elam, and Greece*, trans. Teresa Lavender Fagan (Chicago: University of Chicago Press, 2000), p. 174.

176. "For Hegel grounds his whole thesis of the relationship between ethical choice and sexual difference on Antigone's privileging of her sororal duty" (Leonard, *Athens in Paris*, p. 117). "'The loss of the brother is therefore irreparable to the sister and her duty toward him is the highest'" (Hegel, cited in ibid., p. 116). His discussion of *Antigone* in the *Phenomenology of Mind* displays a blindness to the problem of incest that seemed to some of Hegel's contemporaries more than problematic (ibid., pp. 117–118). On brother and sister: "They are the same blood which has, however, in them reached a state of rest and equilibrium. Therefore, they do not desire each other" (Hegel, *Phenomenology of Mind*, paragraph 457).

177. I am relying here on Leonard's account of the politics of the French reception of the classics after World War II: "Any study which ignores the ideological drive which shapes the reception of antiquity fails to do justice to the *relevance* of the classical past beyond the academy in debates about modern society" (Leonard, *Athens in Paris*, p. 16). Leonard's patience with post-World War II French intellectual debates that circled around Sophocles' *Antigone*, and her valiant attempt at mapping and synthesis, are to be commended.

178. For Lacan, Antigone's act of pure refusal represents the "heroic stance of psychoanalysis," an ethics positioned "beyond the limit." His defense of Antigone rejects a Hegelian reading completely, but at the cost of isolating her from the play, from history, from the *polis* (Leonard, *Athens in Paris*, pp. 111–112). Cf. the French feminist philosopher Luce Irigaray, who sees Antigone as a fully political subject: "for Irigaray, it is not Antigone but Lacan who rejects politics" (Leonard, *Athens in Paris*, pp. 100–101).

179. "'From our point of view, man is in the process of splitting apart . . .'" (Lacan, cited in Leonard, *Athens in Paris*, p. 101).

180. "Lacan's Antigone flees the state and its moral dictates to take refuge in an ethics of pure desire" (Leonard, *Athens in Paris*, p. 96). The works of Slavoj Žižek and Jacqueline Rose are able through psychoanalytic theory to engage the political again, but as a critique of contemporary society that does not challenge the Hegelian frame of appropriation of the ancients. See also Edward W. Said, *Freud and the Non-European*, intro. Christopher Bollas, response by Jacqueline Rose (London: Verso, 2003).

181. On the "Greek-Jew" opposition see Leonard, *Athens in Paris*, pp. 148–156 (especially p. 150).

182. Derrida, *Glas,* cited in Leonard, *Athens in Paris*, p. 136. Butler, too, reads *Antigone* against the grain of modernity's appropriation, reminding us that, as the daughter of Oedipus who killed his father and married his mother, the figure of Antigone was notoriously at

odds with familial conventions. She provides a brilliant dismantling of Hegelian prejudices of kin relations and the constraints of hetero-normativity that remains, nonetheless, a critique of *Hegel*, via Sophocles' original text (Judith Butler, *Antigone's Claim* [New York: Columbia University Press, 2000]). Feminist readings have gone very far in disrupting the post-Hegelian reading, while remaining within a modernist discourse. See especially Bonnie Honig, *Antigone, Interrupted* (Cambridge: Cambridge University Press, 2013).

183. Etman, "A Light from Thucydides on the Problem of Sophocles' 'Antigone,'" p. 151. Etman notes that Creon's claim to place the interests of the city before friends "is after all, only anticipating Pericles' Funeral Speech" in Thucydides' account (pp. 151–152).

184. *Antigone*, 733–734, cited in Etman, "A Light from Thucydides on the Problem of Sophocles' 'Antigone,'" p. 152.

185. Etman, "A Light from Thucydides on the Problem of Sophocles' 'Antigone,'" p. 152. Etman's argument is convincing on this point: "There is a fundamental sense in which Antigone is right. But among the antitheses of the play a simple contrast between villainy on the one hand (= Creon), and sweetness and light on the other (= Antigone), finds no place" (ibid., p. 153).

186. Analogies to the work of Heinrich Graetz on Jewish history, cited above, are evident.

187. Josiah Ober, "The 'Polis' as Society: Aristotle, John Rawls and the Athenian Social Contract," in *The Ancient Greek City-State: Symposium on the Occasion of the 250th Anniversary of the Royal Danish Academy of Sciences and Letters, July 1–4, 1992*, ed. Mogens Herman Hansen (Copenhagen: Munksgaard, 1993), p. 138. "Society" is Ober's translation of *koinonia*.

188. Ober, "The 'Polis' as Society," p. 137.

189. Ober, "The 'Polis' as Society," p. 139.

190. Ober, "The 'Polis' as Society," p. 138. In Aristotle's words, "If a *politeia* is going to be preserved, all the parts of the *polis* must wish it to exist and to continue on the same basis" (Aristotle, *Politics*, 1270b 21–22, cited in ibid., p. 137).

191. Vernant writes on the Homeric era that laws passed by the citizens within public space concerned "τα κοινα, the common affairs of the group. . . . [T]hey always began with the formula 'It pleased the Athenians that . . .' In this context, the city, the polis, was seen less as an institution than as the collection of those who made up the community. It was that community that would sovereignly decide. It was the law, then, that had the *basileia*; the law was king. There was no longer any personal, individual sovereignty; it was the community that was, in a certain sense, completely invested with the responsibility for sovereign decision" (Vernant, "The Polis: Shared Power," p. 173).

192. Sartre wrote: "Anouilh stirred up a storm of discussion with *Antigone*, being charged on the one hand with being a Nazi, on the other with being an anarchist." *Sartre on Theatre*, ed. Michel Contat and Michel Rybalka, trans. Frank Jellinek (New York: Pantheon Books, 1976), p. 40.

193. "Anouilh maintains the ambiguity, but personalizes the choice: a compromised life versus principled death—neither choice changes the circumstances: In this context, the tragic element itself becomes a private, individual affair" (Gary Chancellor, "Hölderlin, Brecht, Anouilh: Three Versions of Antigone," *Orbis litterarum* 34 [1979]: 80). In Bertolt Brecht's version of Antigone (1955), characters stand in for political positions, and partisan lines are clearly drawn: Creon is a Hitlerian figure, a "sly clown-tyrant"; Antigone is the embodiment of popular resistance. Polyneices deserts the front lines when he sees Eteocles fall; Creon would destroy all of Argos rather than surrender. When Anouilh's play was brought to New York City, the English translation purposely distorted the lines so that the play appeared unambiguously in accord with the Allied propaganda of its own moral superiority in the war.

194. For an overview of the complexities of loyalties and evaluative naming within Vichy France and in its aftermath, which spilled over into the Algerian War and is not fully resolved today, see Bertram M. Gordon, "The 'Vichy Syndrome' Problem in History," *French Historical Studies* 19, no. 2 (Fall 1995): 495–518.

195. Walter Benjamin, *The Arcades Project*, trans. Howard Eiland and Kevin McLaughlin, prepared on the basis of the German volume edited by Rolf Tiedemann (Cambridge, MA: Belknap/Harvard University Press 1999), p. 470 (N7,7). ("Damit ein Stück der Vergangenheit von der Aktualität betroffen werde, darf keine Kontinuität zwischen ihnen bestehen.")

196. Walter Benjamin, *Gesammelte Schriften*, vol. I:3, ed. Rolf Tiedemann and Herman Schweppenhäuser (Frankfurt am Main: Suhrkamp Verlag, 1991), p. 918 (trans. mine).

CHAPTER 3

1. "They were seventy-two in all" (*Letter of Aristeas*, addressed to his brother Philocrates [trans. in 1917 by H. St. J. Thackery], available online at https://archive.org/stream/theletterofarist00unknuoft/theletterofarist00unknuoft_djvu.txt. As was the case with Josephus' works, the title is Latin (*septuaginta* is the Latin word for "seventy"), while the text is koinic Greek.

2. See online text. Fowden tells us that Ptolemy II Philadelphus "is also said to have ordered Chaldaean, Egyptian and Roman (!) books into Greek." Garth Fowden, *The Egyptian Hermes: A Historical Approach to the Late Pagan Mind* (Princeton: Princeton University Press, 1993), p. 54. Such ecumenical collections prefigure the "House of Wisdom" institutions of Islamic rulers in Bagdhad, Fustat, and Cordoba.

3. Aristeas' letter is fictionalized in its construction in accordance with literary conventions; this does not mean it was a forgery. Giuseppe Veltri has made a detailed argument that the letter should be considered authentic: Veltri, *Eine Tora für den König Talmai. Untersuchungen zum Übersetzungsverständnis in der jüdisch-hellenistischen und rabbinischen Literatur* (Tübingen: Mohr Siebeck, 1994). For details concerning the status of this source, see ch. 1, "The Letter of Aristeas," in Abraham Wasserstein and David J. Wasserstein, *The Legend of the Septuagint: From Classical Antiquity to Today* (New York: Cambridge University Press, 2006).

4. Rajak notes the long-standing tradition of bilingual texts as a common feature in the Aramaic-speaking world as well as among speakers of Greek (*koine*). In her discussion of ancient translation precedents to the Septuagint, she observes: "In ancient Mesopotamia, lexical lists assisted a class of professional translators; they were called in Sumerian *eme-bal*, literally 'language-turners', a term startlingly similar to what would much later be the basic Greek term for translation [*meta-bal-on*]." Tessa Rajak, *Translation and Survival: The Greek Bible of the Ancient Jewish Diaspora* (Oxford: Oxford University Press, 2009), p. 24. See above, chapter 2, for a discussion of the Greek term μεταβάλων.

5. Wasserstein and Wasserstein, *The Legend of the Septuagint*, p. ix.

6. Mireille Hadas-Lebel, *Philo of Alexandria: A Thinker in the Jewish Diaspora*, trans. Robyn Frechet (Leiden: Brill, 2012), p. 59.

7. See the discussion of Boyarin on Josephus and the meaning of *nomos* in chapter 2. Interest in critical editions produced from extant copies remains strong, resulting in multiple centers of scholarship on different copies, especially the "Cambridge Septuagint" and "Göttingen Septuagint." See the website of the International Organization for Septuagint and Cognate Studies, which publishes a journal and holds yearly conferences (http://ccat .sas.upenn.edu/ioscs/editions.html), and the 13-volume Brill Commentary Series of the books of the Septuagint, concerned exclusively with the Greek text (https://www.logos .com/product/53612/septuagint-commentary-series). See also the French series, *La Bible d'Alexandrie*. The five books of the Tanakh/Pentateuch are Genesis, Exodus, Leviticus, Numbers, Deuteronomy, and these never vary in order. The Septuagint and Hebrew Bible have "important differences" (Rajak, *Translation and Survival*, p. 20), but the five books of the Torah (in Greek: *nomos*) are its core. For details concerning the variants in order and inclusion of the books, as well as a wealth of other philological details, see Jennifer M. Dines, *The Septuagint*, ed. Michael A. Knibb (London: T&T Clark, 2004). The Septuagint was replaced for Jews by the Masoretic Hebrew text: "The Masoretic Text (MT or 𝔐) is the authoritative Hebrew and Aramaic text of the 24 books of Tanakh for Rabbinic Judaism. It was primarily copied, edited and distributed by a group of Jews known as the Masoretes between the 7th and 10th centuries of the Common Era" ("Masoretic Text," Wikipedia).

8. The number and arrangement of books in both language editions is a complicated problem, given variations within the copies that have survived, indicating that there were multiple forms of Judaism during the Second Temple era: "Unfortunately, the study of this literary tradition is dominated by and neglected for the study of the various canonical anthologies made from it—i.e., the different Old and New Testaments. What we need is a history of the literature as a whole, a history based not only on what has been preserved, but on the evidence of what has been lost, and tracing not only the development of characteristic Israelite forms and themes, but also the various combinations and developments that resulted when this literary tradition came into contact with that of Greece." Morton Smith, "Terminological Boobytraps and Real Problems in Second-Temple Judaeo-Christian Studies," *Studies in the Cult of Yahweh*, vol. 1: *Studies in Historical Method, Ancient Israel, Ancient Judaism*, ed.

Shaye J. D. Cohen (Leiden: Brill, 1996), p. 102. For progress toward this goal, see above, note 7.

9. Emphasizing, in opposition to postmodern relativist historians, the significance of a distinction between historical fact and narrative fiction, Lester Grabbe takes us through recent debates on the heavily contested historical reliability of biblical accounts, informed by extensive archaeological evidence as well as extant Near Eastern texts, Assyrian and other. He describes the present consensus as throwing doubt on the patriarchal narratives, and also on stories of the conquests and the "united monarchy"; stories of Saul, David, and Solomon, often presumed to begin the "historical period," are unproven, at best folkloristic elaborations of what might have been a historical core (pp. 111–114). Grabbe writes on the exodus story: "Despite the efforts of some fundamentalist arguments, there is no way to salvage the biblical text as a description of a historical event" (p. 88). The Bible's "purpose was a theological and religious one" rather than "written as a record of the past"; hence none of the biblical books can be accepted as history without critical scrutiny, a test that is often failed (Grabbe mentions Daniel specifically), or at least inconclusive (pp. 223–224). See Lester L. Grabbe, *Ancient Israel: What Do We Know and How Do We Know It?*, rev. ed. (London: T&T Clark, 2007).

10. Wasserstein and Wasserstein, *The Legend of the Septuagint*, p. 16.

11. "It should not be forgotten that the earliest generations of the followers of the new religion had no other Bible than the Old Testament. In the first Christian centuries, the Greek Bible was used, even in the Western parts of the empire, both in Jewish synagogues and in Christian churches." Wasserstein and Wasserstein, *The Legend of the Septuagint*, p. 13.

12. Wasserstein and Wasserstein, *The Legend of the Septuagint*, p. 17. Even after the Bible was translated from *koine* into Latin (North Africa, second century CE, from which Jerome made the *Vetus Latina*), the Septuagint maintained its official position among Christians during much of the Roman Empire. Other translations used by early Christians included Coptic (Egyptian), Aramaic, and Armenian.

13. In Abrahamic religions, a messiah (Hebrew: מָשִׁיחַ, romanized: māšîaḥ; Greek: μεσσίας, romanized: messías, Arabic: مسيح, romanized: masîḥ) is a savior or liberator of a group of people. The concepts of messianism and a messianic age originated in Judaism, and in the Hebrew Bible; a moshiach (messiah) is a king or high priest traditionally anointed with holy anointing oil. Messiahs were not exclusively Jewish: the book of Isaiah refers to Cyrus the Great, king of the Achaemenid Empire, as a messiah for his decree to rebuild the Jerusalem Temple ("Messiah," Wikipedia).

14. Martin Hengel, cited in Rajak, *Translation and Survival*, p. 279n.

15. Williams describes the "steady encroachment by Christians upon the heritage of the Jews illustrated by, *inter alia*, that hijacking of the LXX for liturgical and hermeneutical purposes and their pillaging of it for personal names." Margaret H. Williams, *Jews in a Graeco-Roman Environment* (Tübingen: Mohr Siebeck, 2013), p. 381.

16. C. D. F. Moule, cited in Rajak, *Translation and Survival*, p. 279. Rajak comments: "Appropriation was indeed what transpired. But the simplicity of the statement may also be misleading, suggesting as it does a single act, a conclusive change of ownership accomplished at an early stage in that enormously complicated process of the 'parting of the ways'" (ibid., pp. 279–280).

17. Williams speculates that consequent Jewish uninterest in the Septuagint was a form of reaction, in that Jews "could assert their identity . . . by making more use of Hebrew, for this was an area where the Christians chose not to compete" (Williams, *Jews in a Graeco-Roman Environment*, p. 381).

18. Speculations that he may have been there during Passover 29 CE when Jesus was arrested, like theories that he may have met Peter in Rome, are not substantiated. On the life of Philo, see Daniel R. Schwartz, "Philo, His Family, and His Times," in *The Cambridge Companion to Philo*, ed. Adam Kamesar (Cambridge: Cambridge University Press, 2009), pp. 9–31.

19. This delegation presented to the emperor in Rome the case against the anti-Jewish rioters in Alexandria in 38 CE, averring Alexandrian Jews' loyalty to Rome that had long recognized privileges of Judaean self-government in the city. Philo's treatise on this event has been retranslated with extensive commentary by Pieter W. van der Horst, *Philo's Flaccus: The First Pogrom* (Leiden: Brill, 2003). Van der Horst describes Philo's text as "a mixture of historiography, pastoral theology, apologetics and theodicy" that describes events "in such a way that his Jewish readers are called upon not to doubt God's providence" (p. 12).

20. There is a debate as to whether Philo knew Hebrew; Winston writes: "although the evidence for Philo's ignorance of Hebrew is only cumulative, it is all but irresistible" (David Winston, "Philo and Rabbinic Literature," in Kamesar, *The Cambridge Companion to Philo*, p. 235).

21. Josephus mentions Philo in regard to his participation in the embassy to Rome. Feldman writes: "there is good reason to believe that Philo had direct or indirect influence on Josephus both in the 'Antiquities' and especially in 'Against Apion.'" Louis H. Feldman, *Josephus and Modern Scholarship, 1937–1980* (Berlin: de Gruyter, 1984), p. 14.

22. "The Rabbis do not mention him at all" (Kamesar, introduction to *The Cambridge Companion to Philo*, p. 4). The sixteenth-century scholar who "rediscovered for the Jewish world the virtually forgotten Philo" was Azariah dei Rossi (Winston, "Philo and Rabbinic Literature," p. 231).

23. On Philo's differences from the rabbinical halakhah (religious laws derived from the oral Torah), see Winston, "Philo and Rabbinic Literature," especially pp. 247–253. "The precise relationship of Philo's halakah to that of the Rabbis is complicated by the fact that Philo predates the earliest rabbinic compilations by about two centuries." While Talmudic sources "indicate close ties between the Alexandrian Jewish community and Palestinian Jewry, making it likely that the Oral Law was not limited to the borders of Palestine," and although there were parallel interpretive strategies between Philonian exegesis and rabbinical midrash, these "do not prove Philo's dependence on the latter" (ibid., pp. 248–250).

See also Martens' response to Naomi G. Cohen who "feels safe" in assuming they drew from a common storehouse of oral tradition, that such an understanding of the tradition is too general. John W. Martens, "Appendix 2: Philo and the Oral Law," in *One God, One Law: Philo of Alexandria on the Mosaic and Greco-Roman Law* (Boston: Brill, 2003), pp. 175–185. Martens argues: "Philo's references to the 'unwritten law' are better understood in the context of Greek legal and philosophical discussions than later, Rabbinic compilations of Jewish material, Halakhot, sometimes known as 'oral law'" (ibid., p. 175).

24. An earlier commentary by Aristobulus is dubious on multiple levels, in comparison (see Wasserstein and Wasserstein, *Legend of the Septuagint,* pp. 27–35).

25. Rajak, *Translation and Survival,* p. 280

26. Kamesar, introduction to *The Cambridge Companion to Philo,* p. 4. "Almost," but not quite: Philo's legitimacy remained an issue of Christian controversy (Arian, Gnostic, and otherwise).

27. "It is generally assumed that Christianity as a religion developed from Judaism in a kind of mother-daughter relationship." David T. Runia, "Philo and the Early Christian Fathers," in Kamesar, *The Cambridge Companion to Philo,* p. 210.

28. David T. Runia, *Philo in Early Christian Literature: A Survey* (Assen: Van Gorcum; Fortress Press, 1993), p. 15. "The question of the extent of knowledge about Philo and his writings by both Jews and Arabs in the early Islamic period is most intriguing, and it would be highly desirable if more research could be done in this area" (ibid., p. 16).

29. The Abbasid dynasty brought a translation movement to Baghdad's House of Wisdom that, like the Ptolemaic Library in Alexandria, was an attempt to gather books from the whole world. Plato and Aristotle were translated at this time; Ptolemy's (second-century CE) mathematical and astronomical treatise, *Almagest,* as well. No record exists of a translation into Arabic of Philo. However, according to Warburg Institute scholar Charles Burnett (specialist in later translations from Arabic to Latin, which provided for Europe the ancient Greek traditions that had disappeared there), much of this reception remains underresearched, so that no conclusion on this possibility can be drawn (private conversation, Cornell University, March 2017). I am in no position to speculate here. However, I note below (note 162) an interpretive detail of the story of creation that is the same in Philo and Abu Ma'shar.

30. The *Cambridge Companion to Philo,* cited frequently here, an anthology of excellent scholarship, demonstrates this modern preference for dismantling Philo's thought: separate chapters are delegated to ethics, theology, literary translation, Christian Fathers, Middle Judaism, and the later rabbinical tradition.

31. Cf. Kant's discussion of Platonic ideas in the *Critique of Pure Reason* (A312/B368–A 320/B377). We consider this section below.

32. Kant separated form and content for analytical purposes, not as a description of experience. Hence his clear statement of their necessary unity in understanding: "Thoughts without

content are empty; intuitions without concepts are blind." Immanuel Kant, *Critique of Pure Reason*, trans. Werner S. Pluhar and intro. Patricia Kitcher (Indianapolis: Hackett, 1996), A51/B75.

33. Thucydides, *The War of the Peloponnesians and the Athenians*, ed. and trans. Jeremy Mynott (Cambridge: Cambridge University Press, 2013), 3.82.2, p. 212: "Civil strife (στάσις) inflicted many a terrible blow on the cities, as always does and always will happen while human nature (φύσις ἀνθρώπον) remains what it is, though the degree and kind of the damage may vary in each case according to the particular circumstances."

34. See A. A. Long, "Law and Nature in Greek Thought," in *The Cambridge Companion to Ancient Greek Law*, ed. Michael Gagarin and David Cohen (London: Cambridge University Press, 2005), 412–430.

35. Runia speaks of "the cathedralic edifice of Philo's scriptural commentaries." David T. Runia, *Philo of Alexandria and the Timaeus of Plato* (Leiden: Brill, 1986), p. 526.

36. The term "architectonic" appears several times in Kant's *Critique of Pure Reason*. In the introduction: "Transcendental philosophy is here the idea of a science, for which the critique of pure reason is to outline the entire plan architectonically, i.e., from principles, with a full guarantee for the completeness and certainty of all the components that comprise this edifice" (Kant, *Critique of Pure Reason*, A13/B27 [Introduction B]).

37. Paula Manchester clarifies Kant's (often misunderstood) meaning in her article "Kant's Conception of Architectonic in Its Historical Context," *Journal of the History of Philosophy* 41, no. 2 (April 25, 2003): 187–207: "[F]or Kant the cosmopolitan meaning of architectonic requires that it not be based on an analogy to architecture and a project of construction, but instead on that of a 'teacher in the ideal' who attempts to further the essential ends of human reason by discovering systems that can interrogate doctrines for their truth and practical significance for the whole vocation of humanity" (p. 189).

38. In discussing Valentin Nikiprowetzky's "most important" work on Philo, Runia cites his description of Philo's indirect (exegetical) expression of the Septuagint as a "*disconcerting* architecture" (Runia, *Philo of Alexandria and the Timaeus of Plato*, p. 17).

39. Maren R. Niehoff, *Philo on Jewish Identity and Culture* (Tübingen: Mohr Siebeck, 2001), pp. 247–248.

40. While Cicero was partial to the laws of the Roman Republic which appeared threatened in his lifetime, he admitted: "'[T]he civil law is not necessarily also the universal law; but the universal law ought to be also the civil law. But we possess no substantial, life-like image of true Law and genuine Justice; a mere outline sketch is all that we enjoy'" (Cicero, cited in Martens, *One God, One Law*, p. 97).

41. Martens, *One God, One Law*, p. 10. Aristotle uses this term (*Rhetoric* 240) for unwritten law, common to all humankind.

42. Long, "Law and Nature in Greek Thought," p. 426. Long writes that this was in contrast to the Epicurean cosmos that had no divine plan; the Platonist Cicero, while not self-defined

as a Stoic, considered natural law to be the reason of the wise person that was marked by "complete indifference to time and place" (ibid., 429). Long cites the crucial passage from Cicero's *Republic*: "True law is right reason, in agreement with nature, diffused over everyone, consistent, everlasting, whose nature is to advocate duty by prescription and to deter wrongdoing by prohibition. . . . We cannot be absolved from this law by senate or people, nor need we look for any outside interpreter of it or commentator. There will not be a different law at Rome and at Athens, or a different law now and in the future, but one law, everlasting and immutable, will hold good for all peoples and at all times" (ibid., 429).

43. "[T]he enactments of this lawgiver are firm, not shaken by commotions, not liable to alteration, but stamped as it were with the seal of nature herself, and they remain firm and lasting from the day on which they were first promulgated to the present one, and there may well be a hope that they will remain to all future time, as being immortal, as long as the sun and the moon, and the whole heaven and the whole world shall endure." Philo, *De vita Mosis II* ("On the Life of Moses II") 14–15. The one-volume edition of Philo's works that we are using here is the C. D. Yonge translation (1854), newly updated (with changes based on Cohn-Wendland's superior critical text published between 1896 and 1914) under the supervision of David M. Scholer: *The Works of Philo: Complete and Unabridged* (Peabody, MA: Hendrickson Publishers, 1993). Titles of individual texts are given in Latin, followed by the paragraph number (not, as in Younge, with both section and paragraph numbers), in line with most contemporary scholarship.

44. Martens, *One God, One Law*, p. 97.

45. Martens, *One God, One* Law, p. 106.

46. Niehoff, *Philo on Jewish Identity and Culture*, p. 247.

47. Martens, *One God, One Law*, p. 98. Philo, crucially, translates the Hebrew word Torah as *nomos*, embracing its multiple meanings in this singular form (*Philo of Alexandria: On the Creation of the Cosmos According to Moses*, intro, trans., and commentary by David T. Runia [Leiden: Brill, 2001], p. 106).

48. For an overview of the variety of conclusions of twentieth-century Philo scholarship, see the introduction to Runia, *Philo of Alexandria and the Timaeus of Plato*, pp. 8–31. Runia's scholarship has centered on Philo. He has led the burgeoning field of Philo scholarship, and has been the editor of *The Studia Philonica Annual* (SBL Press) since 1989.

49. Niehoff, *Philo on Jewish Identity and Culture*, p. 247. Just where to draw the line between these categories has preoccupied scholars.

50. On doxography as it relates specifically to Philo of Alexandria, see Francesca Alesse, *Philo of Alexandria and Post-Aristotelian Philosophy* (Leiden: Brill, 2008).

51. Runia refers to this sharing as the "philosophical *koinē*" of his time (*Philo of Alexandria and the Timaeus of Plato*, p. 12).

52. "He is neither concerned to dispel prejudices of misanthropy nor to bridge oppositional cultures and integrate the Jews among the majority. He is, on the contrary, proud of the excellence of Mosaic legislation and praises its superiority over all other law codes. His statements were clearly meant for a Jewish audience who would identify with his self-confident position. They must therefore be understood in the context of constructing a distinctly Jewish discourse on culture." Niehoff, *Philo on Jewish Identity and Culture*, 248.

53. Rajak, *Translation and Survival*. Philo is a central figure in Rajak's study, which she describes as informed by a "post-colonial consciousness" regarding strategies of cultural survival, as well as by recent interest in the "social role of translation" as among the "weapons of the weak," and how its uses enabled Jews "to define their own hybrid identity" based on "their essential values in relation to the powers-that-be" (ibid., p. 7).

54. Martens, *One God, One Law*, pp. 97–99. Martens ascribes personal motive leading Philo to "indulge in apologetic on behalf of his people": "Who could blame Philo, given the precarious position of the Jews in Alexandria in his day?" (ibid., 98–99). Niehoff, on the contrary, warns against overemphasizing "the conflict between Gaius Caligula and the Jews which allegedly served as an overall context for Philo's apologetic discussion on natural law" (*Philo on Jewish Identity and Culture*, 248). On this historical incident, see above, note 19.

55. Philo, cited in Niehoff, *Philo on Jewish Identity and Culture*, p. 249.

56. Kagamé, cited in Souleymane Bachir Diagne, *The Ink of the Scholars: Reflections on Philosophy in Africa*, trans. Jonathan Adjemian (Dakar: CODESRIA, 2016), pp. 28–29.

57. Theodor W. Adorno, *History and Freedom: Lectures 1964–1965*, ed. Rolf Tiedemann, trans. Rodney Livingstone (Cambridge: Polity Press, 2006), p. 61.

58. *De vita Mosis I* 4. Philo's commentaries are overwhelmingly focused on the first five books (cited close to a thousand times), most especially Genesis and Exodus. Of the rest, Philo cites most frequently Psalms (19 times), then Samuel (9), Isaiah (5), Jeremiah (4), Proverbs (3), 1 Kings and Hosea (2 each), and Joshua, Judges, 1 Chronicles, Ezra, Job, and Zechariah (1 each).

59. For an attempt, informed by the latest archaeological findings, to parse the distinctions between myth and history during the era recorded in the Torah, see Mario Liverani, *Israel's History and the History of Israel* (London: Equinox, 2007). As for the translation process that produced the Septuagint, Rajak is surely correct in concluding that, *pace* Aristeas' letter, this scripture was the consequence of multiple authorships over multiple lifetimes in multiple cities: "the translations were a 'work in progress' for nearly four centuries, from perhaps the middle of the third century BCE to probably the mid-second century CE," engaging multiple dispersed translators, anonymous, over a broad stretch of time, at the end including "Christians" (Rajak, *Translation and Survival*, p. vi and passim). See also Emil Schürer, *History of the Jewish People in the Age of Jesus Christ (175 B.C.–A.D. 135)*, ed. and rev. Geza Vermes and Fergus Millar, 5 vols. (Edinburgh: T. & T. Clark, 1973), vol. 3.1, pp. 476–480.

60. "Clement is the first Christian author to make explicit mention of Philo, twice calling him a 'Pythagorean'" (Runia, *Philo in Early Christian Literature*, p. 132).

61. Recent scholarship on "Pythagoreanism" acknowledges that there are multiple versions of this philosophico-scientific tradition, emphasizing different areas of "politics, way of life, religion, mathematics and harmonics," and accounting for diversity and disagreement among historians (Carl A. Huffman, ed., *A History of Pythagoreanism* [Cambridge: Cambridge University Press, 2014], p. 7). Philo's direct references to Pythagoras are infrequent, but he is among those philosophers classified as "neo-Pythagoreans" who took a Platonic approach to philosophy. See Philo, *Quod omnis probus liber* ("Every Good Man Is Free") 2, and especially 19, where he considers "that line of Sophocles, which differs in no respect from the doctrines of the Pythagoreans—'God is my ruler, and no mortal man.'" (The play from which this line is taken is not known.)

62. Daryn Lehoux, *What Did the Romans Know? An Inquiry into Science and Worldmaking* (Chicago: University of Chicago Press, 2012), p. 178.

63. Lehoux, *What Did the Romans Know?*, p. 179.

64. See Andrew Hicks, "Pythagoras and Pythagoreanism in Late Antiquity and the Middle Ages," in *A History of Pythagoreanism*, ed. Carl A. Huffman (Cambridge: Cambridge University Press, 2014), p. 430; see also Andrew Hicks, *Composing the World: Harmony in the Medieval Platonic Cosmos* (Oxford: Oxford University Press, 2017), p. 200. Lehoux considers this principle fundamental to science generally during the Roman Empire. He cites the late second-century scientist Galen (130 CE–210 CE): "'In a word,' says Galen, 'like shakes hands with like,' ἑνὶ δὲ λόγῳ τὸ ὅμοιον τῷ ὁμίῳ γνώριμον. . . . It is telling that Galen's descriptions of the powers of all of the senses are couched in terms of their sharing an εἶδος [idea] with their objects: touch is earth-like (γεώδις), hearing air-like (ἀεροειδής), and smell is vapor-like (ἀτμοειδής)." Lehoux, *What Did the Romans Know?*, p. 124.

65. "Indeed, no Pythagorean *discovered* [the mathematical ratios]; they were already well known to instrument makers, as many sources record, especially to makers of wind instruments." Andrew Barker, "Pythagorean Harmonics," in *A History of Pythagoreanism*, ed. Carl A. Huffman (Cambridge: Cambridge University Press, 2014), p. 202.

66. Andrew Barker, "Ptolemy's Pythagoreans, Archytas, and Plato's Conception of Mathematics," *Phronesis* 39, no. 2 (1994): 114.

67. Barker, "Ptolemy's Pythagoreans," p. 116; Cf. Barker, "Pythagorean Harmonics," p. 186.

68. "[T]he attribute of concordance, as the ear perceives it, was regularly analysed . . . as a particularly intimate kind of 'blending' between two sounds. In these relations, it was said, and in no others, two sounds are heard not as two different things lying side by side, as other pairs of notes are, but as a single thing, its theoretically distinct elements fused into a unity." Barker, "Ptolemy's Pythagoreans," p. 114.

69. "And indeed all things that are known have number. For it is not possible that anything whatsoever be understood or known without this." Fifth-century BCE Pythagorean

Philolaus of Croton (fragment 4), cited in Daniel W. Graham, "Philolaus," in Huffman, *A History of Pythagoreanism*, p. 54.

70. Socrates calls the speech of the astronomer Timaeus a "*nomos*," in the sense of both law and song, in the Platonic dialogue that bears his name (Plato, *Timaeus* 29d).

71. The octave, the fifth, and the fourth as simple, whole-number ratios are not only "more beautiful" (κάλλιον); they are also "better" (Barker, "Ptolemy's Pythagoreans," pp. 117–118). Ptolemy, writing in the second century CE, elaborates this connection: "there are better and worse ratios, and one ratio [the duple/octave] is the best of all" (ibid., p. 135).

72. The perceptual feature of the octave (the duple ratio [2:1]) is the "finest" (καλλιστῆ) of the concords—most virtuous, most excellent, the best of its kind. Hence "mathematical truths are closely connected with truths about excellence and value" (Barker, "Pythagorean Harmonics," pp. 134–135). Barker is speaking of Plato's *Timaeus* here, but it holds as well for Philo that mathematics has "evaluative conceptions built into it"; Barker focuses as well on the seventh book of Plato's *Republic*, wherein "the mathematical disciplines . . . constitute stepping-stones to the dialectic through which philosophers may grasp the nature of the Good and the Beautiful" (ibid., p. 134).

73. Philo, *De confusione linguarum* ("On the Confusion of Tongues") 43.

74. Baker, "Ptolemy's Pythagoreans," p. 114.

75. Kant, cited in Daniel Heller-Roazen, *The Fifth Hammer: Pythagoras and the Disharmony of the World* (New York: Zone Books, 2011), p. 89. Kant's evaluation reflected a change in the nature of mathematics as a historical object, from the Pythagorean proportional relationship of numbers to mathematics as "measureless magnitude" (ibid., ch. 7).

76. Heller-Roazen, *The Fifth Hammer*, p. 91.

77. Immanuel Kant, "The Jäsche Logic" (first published 1800), in *Lectures on Logic*, trans. and ed. J. Michael Young (Cambridge: Cambridge University Press, 1992), pp. 528–529. This capacity to expand is characteristic of synthetic *a priori* knowledge, as opposed to *a priori* analytic thinking that is essentially tautological.

78. Kant, "The Vienna Logic" [supplemented by "The Hechsel Logic"], early 1780s, in *Lectures on Logic*, p. 261.

79. Kant, "The Jäsche Logic," p. 528.

80. Kant does not have the last word on this issue, which remains contested among scientists. See the sophisticated philosophico-mathematical account by Jeremy Gray, *Plato's Ghost: The Modernist Transformation of Mathematics* (Princeton: Princeton University Press, 2008). Gray cites the mathematician Alain Connes (1982), who considers numbers "real" in the nonsensory sense of Platonic forms: "There exists, independently of the human mind, a raw and immutable mathematical reality" (p. 440); Paul Bernays likewise considers mathematics as concerned with "mentally accessible but mind-independent objects" (ibid., p. 444); cf. the neurobiologist Jean-Pierre Changeux's more Kantian position that mathematics is

"a matter of syntax and semantics, of language, and of the workings of the human brain" (ibid., p. 440).

81. For German Romanticist (and Renaissance) interest in Pythagorean ratios, see Brad Prager, *Aesthetic Vision and German Romanticism: Writing Images* (Rochester, NY: Camden House, 2007), p. 47.

82. Adorno and Horkheimer described this danger as an inverted form of mimesis, and accused *it* of magical thinking: in the modern world, "mathematics made thought into a thing—a tool, to use its own term. Through this mimesis, however, in which thought makes the world resemble itself, the actual has become so much the only concern that even the denial of God falls under the same judgment as metaphysics. For positivism, which has assumed the judicial office of enlightened reason, to speculate about intelligible worlds is no longer merely forbidden but senseless prattle. Positivism—fortunately for it—does not need to be atheistic, since objectified thought cannot even pose the question of the existence of God. The positivist sensor turns a blind eye to official worship, as a special, knowledge-free zone of social activity, just as willingly as to art—but never to denial, even when it has a claim to be knowledge. For the scientific temper, any deviation of thought from the business of manipulating the actual, any stepping outside the jurisdiction of existence, is no less senseless and self-destructive than it would be for the magician to step outside the magic circle drawn for his incantation; and in both cases violation of the taboo carries a heavy price for the offender. The mastery of nature draws the circle in which the critique of pure reason holds thought spellbound." Theodor W. Adorno and Max Horkheimer, *Dialectic of Enlightenment: Philosophical Fragments*, ed. Gunzelin Schmid Noerr, trans. Edmund Jephcott (Stanford: Stanford University Press, 2002), p. 19.

83. Kant himself notes: "It is remarkable that the language of poets was the first one in which things that are objects of reason were expressed, so that philosophizing is greatly hindered by poetry" ("The Vienna Logic," *Lectures on Logic*, p. 261); and again: "The first philosophers were poets; it took time, namely, to discover words for abstract concepts" ("Dohna-Wundlacken Logic," ibid., p. 436). This modern development was not without cost, i.e., the ascendance of an ascetic reason that threatens to dominate nature both human and created, in short, the entire material world.

84. Manilius, first-century astronomer who took astrological skills seriously, presents the *kosmos* as "a realm of order and beauty that is governed by fate" as a nexus of cause and effect: "It is this underlying cosmology that enables the poet's claim that the stars are capable of causing events on earth and that humans are at all times affected by and, to some extent, able to affect their cosmic surroundings. . . . [T]he intimate interaction with the universe is one that engages human beings through all their senses." Katharina Volk, "Manilius' Cosmos of the Senses," in *Synaesthesia and the Ancient Senses*, ed. S. Butler and A. Purves (Durham: Aeumen, 2013), p. 103.

85. Lucretius considers the ongoing sequence of natural events random; appreciated by Henri Bergson and George Santayana, his theories of evolution in nature are considered by some as anticipatory of Charles Darwin. Kant, however, criticized Epicurus for "misology"

(hatred of reason) despite being "the best natural philosopher among all of the Greeks ("Vienna Logic," *Lectures on Logic*, 262).

86. Cited in Katharina Volk, *Manilius and His Intellectual Background* (Oxford: Oxford University Press, 2009), p. 19. The word κόσμος means ordered" in a good and beautiful way, as opposed to τάξις, order in a military sense.

87. Michel Foucault, "Nietzsche, Genealogy, History" (French publication, 1971; trans. Donald F. Bouchard and Sherry Simon, 1971), in *The Foucault Reader*, ed. Paul Rabinow (New York: Pantheon Books, 1984), p. 79.

88. Philo, *De opificio mundi* ("On the Creation of the World") 8.

89. *De vita Mosis I* 23–24. Training as a musician was, Philo believed, the best training for a philosopher.

90. There are only 10 specific mentions of Plato throughout Philo's commentaries, but these connections are nonetheless profound, and nowhere more so than in Philo's commentary on the creation of the world (*De opificio mundi*). David Runia has devoted an entire volume of careful scholarship to the influence of Plato on Philo's text by proceeding systematically through the works of each, making the connection in both directions, as a kind of cross reference. For a list of common themes in Philo and Plato, see Runia, *Philo of Alexandria and the Timaeus of Plato*, p. 490. Runia revisited this topic in a book that newly translates *De opificio mundi* and includes an extended commentary on each verse of Philo's commentary (*Philo of Alexandria: On the Creation of the Cosmos According to Moses*). Dillon represents the general understanding of Philo as a "fully-fledged Middle Platonist," although we lack documentary evidence concerning precisely of what that consists, as Philo is our major source; we otherwise do not know much about how Plato was read in first-century Alexandria (John Dillon, *The Middle Platonists: 80 B.C. to A.D. 220*, rev. [from 1977 ed.], with new afterword [Ithaca: Cornell University Press, 1996], p. 143, and on Philo generally, pp. 139–183).

91. Philo refers to Plato as "the sweetest of all writers" (*Quod omnis probus liber* 13), and refers to him again in "On the Creation" (*De opificio mundi* 119). Runia observes that Philo's "reflex" was "to avoid terms that are somehow peculiarly biblical and substitute the word that was commonly used in Greek literary contexts" (David T. Runia, "Philo's Reading of the Psalms," *Studia Philonica Annual* 13 [2001]: 113).

92. The astronomer Timaeus, after whom Plato's dialogue is named, speaks as a Pythagorean. If Plato was a follower of Pythagoras, "Pythagoras was a follower of Moses"; indeed, for Philo, "Moses was not only a philosopher, but the very father of philosophy, from whom all Greek thinkers take their best ideas" (Dillon, *The Middle Platonists*, p. 143). Dillon refers to specific texts of Philo that infer this lineage, adding that some earlier texts, with which Philo may have been familiar, had claimed that Pythagoras spent some time in Palestine (p. 143 and 143n). Fallahzadeh writes with direct reference to Pythagorean ratios and musical intervals: "the Greek influence on Arabic and Persian writing on music is obvious and well documented. It is probable that they inherited part of the Ancient Mesopotamian

tradition of writing on music theory" (Mehrdad Fallahzadeh, *Persian Writing on Music: A Study of Persian Musical Literature from 1000 to 1500 AD* [Uppsala: Uppsala Universitet, 2005], pp. 26 and 26n). Plutarch (45–120 CE) "states that Pythagoras based his precepts on secret teachings of the Egyptian priests" (Runia, *Philo of Alexandria and the Timaeus of Plato*, p. 532).

93. Philo is speaking of the "friends of Moses" who, similarly, "honor one as their father, namely right reason, admiring the well-arranged and all-musical harmony of the virtues" (*De confusione linguarum* 39, 43, 55). Runia is surely correct when he argues that Philo is not *reading* Platonic themes *into* the Torah, but genuinely finds them in Moses' texts (Runia, *Philo of Alexandria and the Timaeus of Plato*, p. 535). He points to a passage where Philo says Socrates was "taught by Moses, or perhaps moved by the phenomena themselves" (ibid., p. 530).

94. "After Moses had already put in God's mouth this expression, 'Let us make man,' as if speaking of several persons." Philo, *De fuga et inventione* ("On Flight and Finding") 71. The issue in this case concerning the expression in Genesis 1:26, "let us make man," is that it implies "a plurality of workers" in sensory communication with him. Philo maintains that God is "conversing with his own powers" (*De fuga et inventione* 69).

95. *De opificio mundi* 2. The reference points to Timaeus' account of the creation that needs to begin three times over.

96. *De opificio mundi* 3. This fusion of natural law and Jewish practice is the temporal schema of seven, as discussed below. Hence, Moses' description of the seven days of creation "lays a foundation for how humankind should live" (Runia in *Philo of Alexandria: On the Creation of the Cosmos*, p. 124).

97. Philo speaks of the Pythagoreans' "excellent doctrines" (*Quod omnis probus liber* 2) and specifically of their use of number on several occasions. Runia emphasizes that for Philo, the act of creation, involving as it does the measuring out of God's goodness and beneficence, "cannot take place without the use of number" whereby corporeal being is brought "to the greatest possible order"; "God uses every number and every form tending toward perfection when generating and perfecting each thing"; Runia compares this with Plato *Timaeus* 30a and 53a-b, "when the demiurge undertook to give [the primal chaos] form, by means of shapes and numbers" (Runia, *Philo of Alexandria and the Timaeus of Plato*, p. 291). But Philo's numerology "places Pythagoras before Plato," making use of the symbolism of the "special right-angled triangle to which the Pythagoreans attributed universal significance" (ibid., p. 292). Philo refers to his own treatise on arithmetic (since lost). Cf. Aristotle's statement of the Pythagoreans' manifesto: "the elements of numbers as the elements of all things, and the whole heaven is harmonia and number" (Aristotle, *Metaphysics* 986a1–3, cited in Barker, "Pythagorean Harmonics," p. 190).

98. "'In the beginning god created the heaven and the earth:' taking the beginning to be, not as some men think, that which is according to time; for before the world time had no existence, but was created either simultaneously with it, or after it; for since time is the

interval of the motion of the heavens, there could not have been any such thing as motion before there was anything which could be moved." *De opificio mundi* 26.

99. Philo comments: "And he allotted each of the six days to one of the portions of the whole, taking out the first day, which he does not even call the first day, that it may not be numbered with the others, but entitling it one, he names it rightly, perceiving in it, and ascribing to it the nature and appellation of the limit" (*De opificio mundi* 15).

100. "[T]he beginning spoken of by Moses is not to be looked upon as spoken of according to time"; rather, "it is the beginning according to number that is indicated" (*De opificio mundi* 27).

101. "This [ἡμέρα μία = day one] is a literal translation of the Hebrew original [*yôm 'eḥāḏ*], which uses the cardinal and not the ordinal number which is used for the remaining six days. In Greek the expression is striking, and Philo takes it as an indication that he must look for a deeper meaning. As it happens, it also fits in perfectly with an important doctrine of Greek arithmology. Philo thus now turns to a consideration of the arithmological features of the unit or monad. It should not be reckoned on a par with other numbers. It is the starting-point or principle (ἀρχή) of numbers and so is separate from them" (Runia in *Philo of Alexandria: On the Creation of the Cosmos*, p. 128). "For this reason the monad [μόνος = single, alone] is often associated with God" (ibid., pp. 128–129). Rabbinic commentators on "day one" (Genesis 1:5: *yôm 'eḥāḏ*) have claimed "that the expression 'one day' is to be understood as a *oneness beyond measure*; otherwise, they argue, the text would have surely rendered the 'beginning' as 'the first day' of creation. . . . This is the influential argument of [the eleventh-century exegete in France, known by the acronym] Rashi . . . [who relates] this one day of creation—to the future 'day of judgment' on which justice and peace will be established": Shulamit Bruckstein Çoruh, *House of Taswir: Doing and Undoing Things: Notes on Epistemic Architecture(s) = Zur Umordnung der Dinge: Notizen zu einer epistemischen Architektur* (Paderborn: Wilhelm Fink, 2014), p. 197.

102. "Philo is keen to show that the radical interpretation which he suggests and which gives the Mosaic account such philosophical depth can be persuasively derived from the Biblical text. His chief trump-card is the Hebraism ἡμέρα μία." Runia, *Philo and the Timaeus of Plato*, p. 169.

103. Runia writes: "both worlds form a totality (as cosmos) and both are 'beautiful' (καλόν)" (in *Philo of Alexandria: On the Creation of the Cosmos*, p. 138). He notes that Philo is the first to speak of the intelligible world in this way.

104. Philo, *De specialibus legibus I* ("The Special Laws I") 48. Runia emphasizes how "surprising" this is: "Who would have thought, when reading 'In the beginning God made the heaven and the earth,' that this refers to the creation of the *ideas* of heaven and earth?" (in *Philo of Alexandria: On the Creation of the Cosmos*, p. 124). Philo insists: "And we must understand in the case of every thing else which is decided on by the external senses, there were elder forms and motions previously existing, according to which the things which were created were fashioned and measured out" (*De opificio mundi* 130).

105. For Plato, the forms themselves remain invisible, but that which the philosopher sees with his mind is an exact imitation of them.

106. *De opificio mundi* 17.

107. Largely due to the generosity of theological organizations, searchable websites exist for the work of Philo of Alexandria in Yonge's English translation (used here): http://www .earlychristianwritings.com/yonge/ as well as his texts in Greek, on this Russian website: http://khazarzar.skeptik.net/books/philo/

108. Walter Benjamin, *Ursprung des deutschen Trauerspiels*, in *Gesammelte Schriften I*, vol. 1, ed. Rolf Tiedemann and Hermann Schweppenhäuser (Frankfurt am Main: Suhrkamp Verlag, 1974), p. 208.

109. "The prominence of the Logos in our treatise cannot be separated from the repeated 'and God said' of Gen 1" (Runia in *Philo of Alexandria: On the Creation of the Cosmos*, p. 143). *Cosmo-poiesis* has a double meaning, "both material and literary creativity. Philo suggests that for God both aspects are identical" (Niehoff, *Philo on Jewish Identity and Culture*, p. 206). Niehoff considers the instrument of creation to be the "written word" of God: "He creates the world through His written word" (ibid.) But see Feldman on music below.

110. *De opificio mundi* 24.

111. What Philo calls the "archetypal seal, which we call the world which is perceptible only to the intellect, must itself be the archetypal model, the idea of ideas, the Reason of God" (*De opificio mundi* 25).

112. Runia in *Philo of Alexandria: On the Creation of the Cosmos*, p. 142. In Christianity, the Logos theory understands the living being of Christ, hypostatically separate, as the bridging of this gap. Without it, as thematized by immanent philosophers from Heidegger to Derrida, the problem of the relation between the forms and the objects is unresolvable. Derrida discusses this gap in an essay on the *chora* (χῶρα, Derrida spells it *khora*) as it appears in Plato's *Timaeus*. The appearance of the *chora* in Philo is discussed below.

113. Runia notes: "In *Her.* 230–236 Philo goes further and identifies the λογική φύσις τοῦ παντός with the λόγος of God (§239, 234). It is symbolized by the turtle dove, the lover of solitude, because it spends its time in attendance on the One (§234)"; "Logos permeates and holds together the entire cosmos" (Runia, *Philo of Alexandria and the Timaeus of Plato*, p. 214).

114. Runia ignores the musical meaning, and sees the instrument as the tool that stamps the archetype upon matter, in keeping with his reading of the relationship of form to matter in Philo as the same as Aristotle's concept of matter (ὕλη)—God impresses matter with the archetype. He admits that this argument runs into difficulties (Runia, *Philo of Alexandria and the Timaeus of Plato*, p. 144).

115. Philo, *Quis rerum divinarum heres sit* ("Who Is Heir of Divine Things") 15. "[T]he shadow of God is his word, which he used like an instrument when he was making the world" (Philo, *Legum allegoriae III* ["Allegorical Interpretation III"] 96).

116. Martens, Niehoff, and Runia, experts consulted above, give philological privilege to the written text in their dealing with Philonian numerology, with music playing a very minor role.

117. Louis H. Feldman, "Philo's Views on Music," in *Studies in Hellenistic Judaism* (Leiden: Brill, 1996), p. 504. By Feldman's count: "the words 'music' and 'musical' (Greek *mousikē*, *mousikos*) appear no fewer than 98 times . . . the words 'harmony' (*symphōnia*), 'harmonious' (*symphōnos*), and 'to be in harmony' (*symphōneō*) 70 times" (ibid.).

118. Feldman, "Philo's Views on Music," p. 504. Feldman's article, reprinted in this volume, first appeared in the late 1980s; his observation then that there had been "no full-length study" of Philo's views on music still remains the case (ibid.).

119. Feldman, "Philo's Views on Music," p. 515. Feldman's reference is to *De migratione Abrahami* ("On the Migration of Abraham") which speaks of Chaldean astronomers as "adapting the things of heaven to those on earth, and like people who, availing themselves of the principles of music, exhibit a most perfect symphony as existing in the universe by the common union and sympathy of the parts for one another, which though separated as to place, are not disunited in regard of kindred" (*De migratione Abrahami* 178).

120. *De opificio mundi* 48. The full quotation elaborates this musical harmonics: "the principles of the harmonious concords in music, that in fourths, and in fifths, and the diapason, and besides this the double diapason from which sounds the most perfect system of harmonies is produced" (ibid.).

121. *De opificio mundi* 76.

122. *Quis rerum divinarum heres sit* 214.

123. Cited in Feldman, "Philo's Views on Music," p. 512.

124. There is no evidence that the Arabic invention of zero was known to the Hellenic world until Ptolemy's *Almagest* (second century CE).

125. *Quis rerum divinarum heres sit* 213.

126. Hebrew numbers, too, were written in letters.

127. The elements for Philo "are cosmic regions in their intelligible form" (Runia, *Philo of Alexandria and the Timaeus of Plato*, p. 288).

128. The days of creation number six, not because "the Creator stood in need of a length of time . . . but because the things created required arrangement; and number is akin to arrangement; and of all numbers, six is, by the laws of nature, the most productive" (*De opificio mundi* 13).

129. *De opificio mundi* 89.

130. *Legum allegoriae I* 8.

131. The five visible planets, plus sun and moon (the word planet [*planes*/πλάνης] means wanderer).

132. Philo's exegesis of the Creation, among which the seven is "superior to every form of expression" (*De opificio mundi* 90), extends for several pages of description (ibid. 89–128). Exemplary is the following: "And the power of this number [seven] does not exist only in the instances already mentioned but it also pervades the most excellent of the sciences, the knowledge of grammar and music. For the lyre with seven strings, bearing a proportion to the assemblage of the seven planets, perfects its admirable harmonies, being almost the chief of all instruments which are conversant about music. And of the elements of grammar, those which are properly called vowels are, correctly speaking, seven in number" (ibid. 126).

133. *De opificio mundi* 107. "The number seven consists of one, and two and four, numbers which have two most harmonious ratio, the twofold and the fourfold ratio; the former of which affects the diapason harmony, while the fourfold ratio causes that of the double diapason. It also comprehends other divisions, existing in some kind of yoke-like combination" (ibid. 95).

134. *De opificio mundi* 100.

135. Niehoff, *Philo on Jewish Identity and Culture*, p. 259.

136. "Again, this harmony is viewed in musical terms, for Philo . . . regards the ideal, as seen in the personality of Moses, as being a harmony of words and deeds making 'melody together as on a musical instrument'" (Feldman, "Philo's Views on Music," p. 513; he is translating *De vita Mosis I* 29).

137. Hadas-Lebel comments: "the Logos is still compared with the priest's sacrificial knife, since it 'cuts' and 'separates' all things in the universe. This universal divider (*Her.* 130) is the instrument presiding over the separation of contraries in the universe" (*Philo of Alexandria*, p. 187).

138. *De vita Mosis II* 119.

139. This festival is a time for reflection, with men commanded "to keep the seventh holy . . . devoting that day to the single object of philosophizing with a view to the improvement of their morals" (*De opificio mundi* 89). "And the contemplation of the world, and of all the things contained in it, is nothing else but philosophy" (Philo, *Quaestiones et solutiones in Genesin I* ["Questions and Answers on Genesis I"] 41).

140. Feldman, "Philo's Views on Music," p. 513. Feldman is referring to *De specialibus legibus II* 157: "wishing, as if in the case of a musical instrument, to unite the two extremities in harmony."

141. *De specialibus legibus I* 168.

142. Feldman, "Philo's Views on Music," pp. 508–514. "Philo even regards music in the abstract (*De Mutatione Nominum* 21.122, 16.146) as a kind of archetype, a Platonic-like form or idea, which he compares to the forms of the four cardinal virtues (*De Mutatione Nominum* 26.146) and even of the state (*De Mutatione Nominum* 21.122)—the supreme compliment to a Platonist" (ibid., p. 510).

143. Feldman, "Philo's Views on Music," p. 512. Cf: "The honors of virtue belong to no wicked man, but only to him who is a lover of wisdom just as the flute and the lyre and the other instruments of music belong to the musician alone" (Philo, *De sacrificiis Abelis et Cain* ["On the Sacrifices of Abel and Cain"] 18).

144. Feldman, "Philo's Views on Music," p. 517.

145. "Indeed, Philo (*De Somniis* 1.43.256) stresses the need of the soul constantly to proclaim God's blessedness through holy hymns in sweet melodies" (Feldman, "Philo's Views on Music," p. 509). On the male and female choirs, Philo describes the singing of the Therapeutae, a monastic-like Jewish sect: "the treble of the women blended with the bass of the men in harmonious concert, 'music in the truest sense,' each choir responding to the other, note to note and voice to voice" (ibid., p. 524, referring to Philo, *De vita contemplativa* ["On the Contemplative Life or Suppliants"] 83–85).

146. *De opificio mundi* 78.

147. Philo, *De somniis I* ("On Dreams I") 188. This position is distinguished from Spinoza's version of pantheism insofar as the forms are not immanent within nature, but truly transcendent. What is important to note here in the case of Philo is the necessary unity between the Logos and the sensory world that was nonetheless not identical to it. We are not dealing with a Stoic (or Spinoza-like) immanence of forms. Cf. Runia, *Philo of Alexandria and the Timaeus of Plato*, p. 483n.

148. She lived sometime between the third century BCE and the first century CE. This quotation and all of her fragments are known to us through the work of Porphyry. See Barker, "Pythagorean Harmonics," pp. 188–189.

149. John Coltrane, cited in Tommy L. Lott, "When Bar Walkers Preach: John Coltrane and the Crisis of the Black Intellectual," in Leonard L. Brown, ed., *John Coltrane and Black America's Quest for Freedom: Spirituality and the Music* (Oxford: Oxford University Press, 2019), p. 112.

150. Leonard L. Thompson, *Revelation* (Nashville: Abingdon Press, 1998), p. 41. For more on Patmos (and Thompson), see below, chapter 4.

151. The phrase "τρίτον γένος" has another history. It was the word used by second-century Christians to describe themselves as a new lineage, a "third kind," which in modernity became associated with ethnicity/race. It is a sober reminder that what may begin as a self-chosen identity in an act of group solidarity against oppression, as an essentializing discourse excluding others on the basis of shared ancestry, can become a racist tool in the hands of the oppressors. See the revealing study of Denise Kimber Buell, *Why This*

New Race: Ethnic Reasoning in Early Christianity (New York: Columbia University Press, 2005).

152. Plato uses τὸ ὄν (being) and τὸ εἶναι (that which is) to name being-in-itself (τὸ ὄν η ὄν), veridically opposed to "appearance" (φαίνεσθαι), and mutatively opposed to becoming (γίγνεσθαι). For this and other Platonic terminology, see Sean M. McDonough, *YHWH at Patmos: Rev. 1:4 in Its Hellenistic and Early Jewish Setting* (Tübingen: Mohr Siebeck, 1999), pp. 20–27. Additional Platonic names are "essence" (οὐσία) as opposed to existence (ὕπαρξις), and ὅ ἐστι; Sallis clarifies the latter term: "The εἶδος [idea] is what something is. It answers the question: τί ἐστι." John Sallis, *Chorology: On Beginning in Plato's Timaeus* (Bloomington: Indiana University Press, 1999), p. 49.

153. Paul Allen Miller, *Diotima at the Barricades: French Feminists Read Plato* (Oxford: Oxford University Press, 2016), p. 142. Miller's book is an intriguing account of the personal and political contexts of these debates.

154. Sallis gives us the passage (*Timaeus* 49a): "Timaeus asks 'What power (δύναμις) are we to suppose it to have by nature? He answers: 'This, most of all, that it is the receptacle [ὑποδοχή], as it were, the nurse [τιθήνη] of all generation'" (Sallis, *Chorology*, p. 98).

155. Miller, *Diotima at the Barricades*, p. 144 and passim.

156. Miller, *Diotima at the Barricades*, p. 142.

157. Jacques Derrida, "*Khôra*," in *On the Name,* ed. Thomas Dutoit, trans. David Wood, John P. Leavey, Jr., and Ian McLeod (Stanford: Stanford University Press, 1995), p. 93 and passim. Derrida uses a different spelling, and deploys the word as a (feminine) name of address: "*[K]hôra* . . . is neither 'sensible' nor 'intelligible'" (ibid., p. 89); it is "a word" to which no coherence can be ascribed: "there is *khôra*, but *the khôra* does not exist" (ibid., p. 97); it remains "unformed," has to be posited, and yet has no referent: "The thought of the *khôra* exceeds the polarity"; it "would trouble the very order of polarity, of polarity in general, whether dialectical or not" (ibid., p. 92). Miller explains that according to Derrida the *khôra* is not a third space that could be domesticated in Platonic thought, but "the moment in which the Platonic system acknowledges its own outside as always already internal to the system and hence self-deconstructive" (Miller, *Diotima at the Barricades*, p. 146).

158. Miller, *Diotima at the Barricades*, p. 146. Kristeva in her novel *Les Samouraïs* ridicules as "deconstructivist" this praise of "the unsayable femininity lodged in the folds of being and logos" (cited in ibid., p. 145). Her political critique is that Derrida's philosophical practice locks the critical subject within the text, thereby preventing her or him from taking a political stand (ibid., p. 146). "For the practicing analyst, the practical critic, and the pragmatic political revolutionary, discourse cannot simply undo itself *ad infinitum*. Objects ultimately must be stipulated. Things must be done" (ibid., p. 150).

159. A word search with the *Thesaurus Linguae Graecea* gives this result.

160. H. A. Wolfson's interpretation points to Philo's mention of "empty space" (κενή χώρα in *De opificio mundi* 29) as a kind of receptacle that resonates with the discussion of the

χώρα in Plato, and ties this with the wording "unseen and unconstructed" (ἀόρατος καὶ ἀκατασκεύαστο); Runia considers this reading extremely problematic (*Philo and the Timaeus of Plato*, pp. 287–291). He notes (*Philo on the Creation*, p. 65) that Philo translates the first of the words as "invisible" while not commenting on the second, which was a "common epithet of the ideal realm." Runia continues on this topic (in *Philo and the Timaeus of Plato*, pp. 291ff.), writing that the Platonic analogy here, especially Plato's classic description of the transition from chaos to order in *Timaeus* 30a, presumes already existing matter, formless until the demiurge's forming power, an idea that has no place in the Septuagint text. If a Platonic reading is rejected, however, the inescapable problem of the relation between God and matter remains, and a modern reader would then be alert to the problem of a first cause. Runia points to passages in Philo that seem to infer an Aristotelian solution, the Unmoved Mover who imprints matter (ὕλη) with form, at the same time acknowledging, with David Winston, that such a dualistic view runs up against the monotheistic premise of creation: "there can be no question of an active opposition between God and ὕλη resulting in a true dualism" (*Philo and the Timaeus of Plato*, p. 454). Unable to embrace either the *creatio ex nihilo* position (later adopted by Christianity), or the Platonic position of Wolfson, Runia's exhaustive and repeated attempts at clarifying this murky area of Philo's thought are ultimately inconclusive. Philo nowhere tells us the origin of the ὕλη (or of the οὐσία), leaving certain metaphysical questions insufficiently answered (ibid., p. 509). Aristotle rejects Plato's doctrine of ideas "as well as the notion that visible reality could be derived from λογικῶς" (ibid., p. 43); he reinterprets the receptacle according to his own doctrine of matter (ibid., pp. 41–45). For a discussion of Aristotle on *chora*, see Sallis, *Chorology*, esp. pp. 152–153. See also McDonough, *YHWH at Patmos*, pp. 27–31.

161. *De opificio mundi* 20. This passage begins with a comparison: "As therefore the city, when previously shadowed out in the mind of the man of architectural skill had no external place (χώραν ἐκτός), but was stamped solely with the mind of the workman, so in the same manner neither . . . can the world which existed in ideas (τῶν ἰδεῶν κόσμος) have had any other local position (τόπον) except the divine reason (τόν θεῖον λόγον) which made them"; Runia's translation of *De opificio mundi* 17 sharpens the wording: "To state or think that the cosmos composed of ideas exists in some place is not permissible" (commentary in *Philo of Alexandria: On the Creation of the Cosmos*, p. 50) Runia observes that in Philo's description of the creation, rather than a third space where the elements exist, he has God creating the heaven (not fire), the oceans (not water), and dry land (not earth)—that is, in the corporeal sense as "regions of the cosmos"—an approach that "reveals a palpable tension between the contents of the biblical text being explained and the philosophical doctrines being used for that explanation" (ibid., pp. 164–165).

162. Philo explains the reason why humans are the last of God's creations: "in order that when man came into the world he might at once find a feast ready for him" (*De opificio mundi* 78). This is an image found in the Islamic cosmology of Abu Ma'shar. This sense of a gift, the generosity of God, is also in al-Farabi. Indeed, first we fear God, then exchange with God, then see his gift.

163. "In every uncertain and important business it is proper to invoke God, because he is the good Creator of the world, and because nothing is uncertain with him who is possessed of the most accurate knowledge of all things. . . . But since we have on us the marks of folly, and injustice, and of all other vices strongly stamped upon us and difficult to be effaced, we must be content even if we are only able by them to discover some faint copy and imitation of the truth." Philo, *De aeternitate mundi* ("On the Eternity of the World") 1–2.

164. See McDonough, *YHWH at Patmos*, p. 164, for multiple examples of Philo's insistence on this point.

165. Cited in Sallis, *Chorology*, p. 155.

166. The movement across the absolute barrier between God and humans does not prevent the most concrete of descriptions, so much so that "the reader could easily make the mistake of forgetting about their intelligible status altogether" (Philo reminds us in *De opificio mundi* 34). In a sense this pushes the problem down the road (see Runia in *Philo of Alexandria: On the Creation of the Cosmos*, p. 164).

167. "Certainly Philo makes a clear distinction between God as ὁ ὤν and the world of Forms. This is in distinction from Plato himself, who understands τὸ ὄν precisely as this world of Forms" (McDonough, *YHWH at Patmos*, p. 163).

168. We have also conceded to the Christian capitalization of *Logos*. As with our yielding to the translation of *koine*, not consistently as "common" but as "Greek," this situation is unfortunate; but the Christian imperative of "God" is so great that we cannot resist convention without undue complications. It is in reading Philo from later history that the narrative is produced whereby Philo is already Christian. Christianity will make out of the Logos Christ as a living being, hypostatically separate, and will stress the immortality of the soul and punishment for evil actions of humans after death. This is not in Philo, however.

169. In the Septuagint, Exodus 3:14–15. Hence Philo can use *theos* as a term of praise for the emperor Augustus.

170. The exegesis of Exodus 3:14 "has long been the subject of a complex, unfinished debate; it is generally accepted that the Hebrew name of God, the tetragrammaton (YHWH), derives from *hawah*, the verb to be. God's enigmatic answer later became the foundation stone for one aspect of negative theology:—his existence can be known, but his essence cannot." Deirdre Carabine, *The Unknown God: Negative Theology in the Platonic Tradition: Plato to Eriugena* (Louvain: Peters Press/W. B. Eerdmans, 1995), pp. 200–201.

171. This "most important of the 'positive' attributes of God [within Philo's negative theology] is that he is totally and uniquely one. While this concept betrays a Platonic and Pythagorean influence, Philo's insistent emphasis on it is also firmly based on his reading of the Septuagint [Deut 6:4 and Is 44:6]" (Carabine, *The Unknown God*, pp. 202–203).

172. As the "proper name," meaning "essentially existent," ὁ ὤν is, writes McDonough, "perhaps [Philo's] favorite term for deity," although he is "equally comfortable using τὸ ὄν for God"; the two expressions "appear to be interchangeable" (McDonough, *YHWH at Patmos*, p.

162). In Yonge's translation of Philo (used here), the translation for both these words is frequently "the living God."

173. McDonough, *YHWH at Patmos*, p. 162.

174. McDonough, *YHWH at Patmos*, p. 162.

175. "Importantly, the blinding darkness in the cloud at the end of the quest rather than the blinding light of Plato's Sun begins to suggest that the goal of the pursuit of *eudaimonia* [human development; wisdom] is never complete." Brendan Cook, *Pursuing Eudaimonia: Re-Appropriating the Greek Philosophical Foundations of the Christian Apophatic Tradition* (Newcastle upon Tyne: Cambridge Scholars Publishing, 2013), p. 139.

176. *De migratione Abrahami* 52. Cf.: "'My proper name I have not revealed to them'. . . . And, indeed, the living God is so completely indescribable, that even those powers which minister unto him do not announce his proper name to us" (Philo, *De mutatione nominum* ["On the Change of Names"] 13–14). On God's refusal to reveal himself even to Moses see also *De specialibus legibus I* 41–48.

177. "[Moses] is said to have entered into the darkness where God [ὁ θεός] was; that is to say, into the invisible [ἀειδῆ], and shapeless [ἀόρατον], and incorporeal [ἀσώματον] world, the essence, which is the model of all existing things" (*De vita Mosis I* 158). The iteration here of the alpha-prefix qualities of attribution is apophatic (knowledge of God obtained through negation).

178. Hence the equation of τὸ ὄν and ὅ ὤν was "staring Philo in the face" in the Septuagint translation (McDonough, *YHWH at Patmos*, p. 162).

179. "Whatever appellation any one may give Him, will be an abuse of terms; for the living God [τὸ ὄν] is not of a nature to be described, but only to be [ἀλλὰ μόνον εἶναι]. And the proof of this may be found in the oracular answer . . . 'I am that I am.'" Philo, *De somniis I* 230–231. For this "katachrestical" (καταχρῶμενος) misuse and therefore abuse of God's name, see also *De Abrahamo* ("On Abraham") 120–123.

180. "[T]he sound that proceeds from us does not the least resemble the divine organ of voice; for [our] organ of voice is mingled with the air, and flies to a kindred region with itself namely to the ears; but the divine organ consists of unmixed and unalloyed speech, which outstrips the sense of hearing by reason of its fineness, and which is discerned by a pure soul, by means of the acuteness in the faculty of sight." *De migratione Abrahami* 52.

181. Philo, *De Decalogo* ("The Decalogue") 33.

182. Cf. the χώρα as "difficult to catch" (Plato, *Timaeus* 51 a-b), cited in Sallis, *Chorology*, p. 110. Cf.: "[God's Word] is not a beating of the air, being absolutely mingled with nothing else whatever, but it is incorporeal and naked, in no respect different from the unit. But we hear by the number two." Philo, *Quod Deus immutabilis sit* ("On the Unchangeableness of God") 83.

183. "[F]or the prophets are interpreters of God, who is only using their voices as instruments, in order to explain what he chooses" (*De specialibus legibus I* 65). "However, even the name

'I am,' is not to be understood as God's proper name but as a substitute name" (Carabine, *The Unknown God*, p. 209).

184. *De vita Mosis I* 155.

185. On God's refusal to grant Moses' beseeching him to reveal himself, see *De specialibus legibus I* 41–48.

186. Dillon points out the Egyptian equation of Isis with Wisdom, also the "female life principle," suggesting as well a possible correlation with the Pythagorean/Old Academic dyad (Dillon, *The Middle Platonists*, pp. 164 and 204). Dillon says of these gender shifts: "Plainly we are in a marshy area of Philo's thought" (ibid., p. 164n).

187. Runia affirms Nikiprowetzky's warning that we take into account the "*plasticity of the symbols and images*" that Philo uses: "[T]here is no point in *reifying* these symbols and coming to drastic mystical, mythological or philosophical conclusions. The images of mother, daughter, nurse etc. merely record abstract relations" (Runia, *Philo and the Timaeus of Plato*, p. 285n).

188. *Quis rerum divinarum heres sit* 119. "In some cases, Philo links Sophia to a life-giving feminine maternal principle. In union with God, she generates the Logos and the cosmos. . . . On other occasions Sophia is identified with the Logos and has a filial role with respect to God. It is she that takes delight in the father and is the archetype of earthly wisdom. . . . Elsewhere, however, the Logos is the source of Sophia (*Fug.* 97). The fluidity of these schemes reveals the metaphorical orientation of the terminology employed to designate personified Wisdom more than it indicates inconsistency in Philo's theology." Christina Termini, "Philo's Thought within the Context of Middle Judaism," in Kamesar, *The Cambridge Companion to Philo*, pp. 99–100.

189. Cf. *De opificio mundi* 44. See also Philo, *De ebrietate* ("On Drunkenness") 30: "the mother was the knowledge of the Creator. . . . And this knowledge having received the seed of God, when the day of her travail arrived, brought forth her only and well-beloved son, perceptible by the external senses, namely this world."

190. She is called thus by "every wise man . . . [who is] accustomed to say to his mother and nurse, wisdom, 'O mother . . . !'" (*De confusione linguarum* 49).

191. At multiple points in his career, Derrida addressed negative theology; the term became part of the discourse of deconstruction, exemplary of "weak theology," an unconditional claim without force. See *Derrida and Negative Theology*, ed. Harold Coward and Toby Foshay, with contributions by Jacques Derrida (Albany: State University of New York Press, 1992). But while Derrida's negative negates the systemic tendency in Plato, this is not truly negative theology. In contrast, Philo incorporates this negativity into the very core of his affirmation of God.

192. "[I]t is not easy to believe in God on account of that connection with mortality in which we are involved, which compels us to put some trust in money, and glory, and authority, and

friends, and health, and vigour of body, and in numerous other things; but to wash off all these extraneous things, to disbelieve in creation, which is, in all respects, untrustworthy as far as regards itself, and to believe in the only true and faithful God, is the work of a great and heavenly mind" (*Quis rerum divinarum heres sit* 92–93).

193. *De Decalogo* 32 anthropomorphizes God as "Father of the universe who delivered these ten maxims, or oracles, or laws and enactments," at the same time denying any human comparison.

194. *De Decalogo* 32.

195. *De Decalogo* 65.

196. *De Decalogo* 100. Imitation (μίμεσις) of the unknowable God—"forming oneself in the image of the original"—justifies the ruler: "the king is king not by virtue of his place, but by virtue of his actions"; this is the king as "living law," a theme of Middle Platonism, including the discovered Pythagorean fragments that are a part of it: "This κοινωνία [communion/fellowship] among God, the king, and the ruled produces harmony" (Martens, *One God, One Law*, p. 61).

197. *De Decalogo* 106.

198. While God "appointed no punishment for those who would violate" his laws, Philo does not rule out severe "chastisement of sinners" by human authority (*De Decalogo* 176–178).

199. *De Decalogo* 64. The individual is charged with rejecting "impious dishonesty" by "yielding to a desire to please the multitude."

200. "[N]o king or tyrant may ever despise an obscure private individual. . . . [For God] cannot endure to overlook even the meanest of human beings, but has thought even such worthy of being banqueted in sacred oracles and laws. . . . [All are] my equals whose fortunes perhaps are not equal to mine, but whose relationship to me is equal and complete, inasmuch as they are set down as the children of one mother, the common nature of all men" (*De Decalogo* 40–41); "[F]or all created things are brothers to one another, inasmuch as they are created; since the Father of them all is one, the Creator of the universe" (*De Decalogo* 64).

201. *De Decalogo* 38. As with the ancient Greeks, democracy is defined by Philo as equality before the law: the better of two cities "enjoys a democratic government, a constitution which honours equality, the rulers of which are law and justice; and such a constitution as this is a hymn to God" (*De confusione linguarum* 108).

202. Philo, *De plantatione* ("Concerning Noah's Work as a Planter") 36.

203. See Winston, "Philo and Rabbinical Literature," pp. 232–233 (and p. 234n for bibliographical references).

204. See Carabine, *The Unknown God*, esp. chs. 8–11.

205. See Andrew Gibson, *Intermittency: The Concept of Historical Reason in Recent French Philosophy* (Edinburgh: Edinburgh University Press, 2012). Gibson writes of Christian Jambet, a scholar of Islam: "Jambet might appear to be obviously closer to Kojève's Platonic-Christian than to his modern, Hegelian tradition, but this is the case only if we ignore the former's conviction that the later development of the Platonic-Christian tradition in Europe takes place at the expense of another which runs from Plato via Neoplatonism to Islamic Gnosticism. Jambet sees European conceptions of history as having revolved around a problematic staked out for them by what was only one derivative of Platonism. The other derivative . . . [remained] alive in the intellectual culture of Islam" (ibid., pp. 10–11).

206. This term (the plural of λόγος) is sometimes used by Philo to refer to the books of the Septuagint, but also occasionally to divisions of his own books (Runia, "Philo's Reading of the Psalms," p. 68).

207. "This difficult and scarcely explicable perplexity we may escape if we adopt the inner and allegorical explanation" (*De fuga et inventione* 108). Philo's "relentless focus on the allegorical meaning does not always disallow or discredit the literal sense," allowing the latter but "nearly always giv[ing] prime place to the former"; Kamesar lists examples: "that God planted a garden, or a eunuch had a wife" (Adam Kamesar, "Biblical Interpretation in Philo," in Kamesar, *The Cambridge Companion to Philo*, p. 77).

208. "As is well known, allegorical interpretation was developed by Greek scholars primarily as a means of explaining mythical narratives, especially those contained in the Homeric poems and in Hesiod"; here again Philo is "following Greek models." Kamesar, "Biblical Interpretation in Philo," pp. 78–79.

209. Kamesar, "Biblical Interpretation in Philo," p. 85.

210. "In a series of seven *quaestiones* a complex allegory of Noah's ark in terms of the physical structure of the human body is given . . . all manner of physiological and arithmological information is used to demonstrate the persuasiveness of the allegory" (Runia, *Philo of Alexandria and the Timaeus of Plato*, p. 316). For example: "Why does God say, you shall make the ark in nests? (Genesis 6:14). He gives this order very naturally, for the human body is formed of holes like nests; every one of which is nourished and grows like a young bird. . . . Some of the holes and nests are the eyes, in which the faculty of sight has its abode; other nests are the ears, which are the place where hearing is situated. A third class of nests are the nostrils. . . . [T]he fourth nest . . . is the mouth . . . reposing in it, namely, the tongue, which, as Socrates was wont to say, by beating in every direction in various manners, and by touching different parts, composes and forms a word, being, in truth, an instrument under the immediate guidance of reason" (*Quaestiones et solutiones in Genesin II* 3).

211. *De plantatione* 36.

212. Kamesar, "Biblical Interpretation in Philo," p. 86. See also, in *Philo of Alexandria: On the Creation of the Cosmos*, Runia's "Excursus: Philo's Attitude towards Women and Sexuality," pp. 359–361.

213. In *De confusione linguarum* Philo rejects those who interpret the Babel story as an allegory for the origin of languages, urging us "to proceed onward to look at the passage in a figurative way, considering that the mere words of the scriptures are, as it were, but shadows of bodies, and that the meanings which are apparent to investigation beneath them, are the real things to be pondered upon" (*De confusione linguarum* 190). Unlike God's harmonious divisions, "confusion is a name most appropriate to wickedness" (ibid., 198). And the wicked man shares a language of practice with others of his kind: "the fact that identity of language, and the sameness of dialect does not consist more in names and common words than in his participation in iniquitous actions," reflects "the parts of the soul mingled together and in a state of confusion" that he shares with "all his fellow revelers," with whom he "begins to build a city and a tower as a citadel for sovereign wickedness" (ibid., 83–84).

214. *De confusione linguarum* 193. The passage continues: "to put out of sight and extirpate all their powers, to overthrow the might of their dominion, which they had strengthened by fearful lawlessness" (ibid.) As a consequence, "when these [the wicked] are put to rout, then those who have long ago been banished by the tyranny of folly, now, at one proclamation, find themselves able to return to their own country" (ibid., 197). This is a likely reference not only to the periodic purges of philosophers by the Roman emperors, but specifically to the exile of (non-citizen?) Jews from Rome by Tiberius in Philo's lifetime in 19 CE, on the charge of attempting to convert others to Judaic belief.

215. *De confusione linguarum* 196.

216. "A large population of Israelites, living in their own section of the country, did not march out of an Egypt devastated by various plagues and despoiled of its wealth and spend 40 years in the wilderness before conquering the Canaanites." Grabbe, *Ancient Israel*, p. 97.

217. *De Decalogo* 13. Philo gives allegorical interpretations of proper names in the scripture, including the meaning of the name Israel as "seeing God" (*Quis rerum divinarum heres sit* 78).

218. *De Decalogo* 81.

219. *Quis rerum divinarum heres sit* 86–88.

220. *Quis rerum divinarum heres sit* 81–82; on the deceit of cities, see *De Decalogo* 3.

221. *Quis rerum divinarum heres sit* 84.

222. *De confusione linguarum* 79. Philo is citing Gen 23:4.

223. *De mutatione nominum* 152. Abraham is recognized as king "not out of consideration for his resources (for what resources could a man have who was an emigrant and who had no city to inhabit, but who was wandering over a great extent of impossible country?), but because they saw that he had a royal disposition of mind. . . . For in real truth the wise man is king of those who are foolish" (ibid., 152–153).

224. *De confusione linguarum* 77–78. The home of the wise man is the land of "incorporeal wisdom" (ibid. 81).

225. *De vita Mosis I* 157.

226. *De vita Mosis I* 155.

227. *De vita Mosis I* 156.

228. Diogenes Laertius, cited in Catherine Rowett, "The Pythagorean Society and Politics," in *A History of Pythagoreanism*, ed. Carl A. Huffman (Cambridge: Cambridge University Press, 2014), p. 119.

229. Kamesar, "Biblical Interpretation in Philo," p. 85. Philo speaks of the "historical part," but his meaning of history is far from our own. Runia writes: "One is struck, first of all, by his total lack of interest in the 'historical' aspect. His reflections on history have a predominantly abstract quality, similar to the timelessness of his allegories"; "Certainly there is no question of historicity in the modern sense or even consciousness of historical development" (Runia, *Philo of Alexandria and the Timaeus of Plato*, pp. 532 and 532n).

230. Kamesar, "Biblical interpretation in Philo," p. 88.

231. Dillon, *The Middle Platonists*, p. 145. "What the Patriarchs did is plainly what all of us *should* do. Philo is, then, able to embrace both the Stoic definition of the *telos* and the more Pythagorean one, without experiencing any discomfort. Since for him 'Nature' is the *logos* of God in action in the world, 'living in conformity with Nature' is simply 'following God'" (ibid., pp. 145–146). Martens notes that the sage king was called "zealot" (ζηλοτάς), meaning "imitator" of God (Martens, *One God, One Law*, p. 60).

232. Martens focuses on the idea of the patriarchs as "living law" in Philo's texts, and argues the Pythagorean kingship tractates may have been influential here. He makes the case (appendix 1) that these (pagan) texts are Hellenic, a late dating that converges with Philo's own time (Martens, *One God, One Law*, pp. 165–174).

233. Martens, *One God, One Law*, p. 59.

234. Philo connects the symbolic meaning of the patriarchs as divine attributes with God's allowing certain names to be used by humans for himself: "In order that the human race may not be wholly destitute of any appellation, I allow you to use the word Lord (Κύριος) as a name; the Lord God (Κύριος ὁ Θεός) of three natures—of instruction, and of holiness, and of the practice of virtue; of which Abraham, and Isaac, and Jacob are recorded as the symbols" (*De mutatione nominum* 12). The narratives of the patriarchs show how adhering to right conduct in particular cases, when a less principled approach would have appeared to be personally advantageous, in fact wins the respect of others and just rewards. This is the opposite of practice based on instrumental reason. Philo criticizes those who want to use knowledge (as do magicians) for personal gain.

235. "[V]irtue is both theoretical and practical; for it takes in theory, since the road which leads to it is philosophy in three of its parts—the reasoning, and the moral, and the physical part. It also includes action; for virtue is art conversant about the whole of life; and in life all actions are exhibited" (*Legum allegoriae I* 57).

236. Kamesar, "Biblical Interpretation in Philo," p. 90.

237. "Now the prudence which exists in the virtuous man is the authority of himself alone . . . but that which has stretched out this authority is generic prudence, not any longer the authority of this or that person, but absolute intrinsic authority; therefore that which exists only in species will perish at the same time with its possessor, but that which, like a seal, has stamped it with an impression, is free from all mortality, and will remain for ever and ever imperishable" (*De mutatione nominum* 79).

238. Philo, *Quod deterius potiori insidiari soleat* ("That the Worse Is Wont to Attack the Better") 75.

239. Theodor W. Adorno, *Metaphysics: Concept and Problems* (1965), ed. Rolf Tiedemann, trans. Edmund Jephcott (Stanford: Stanford University Press, 2001), p. 20.

240. Immanuel Kant, *Critique of Pure Reason*, A319/B375. "Anyone seeking . . . to draw the concepts of virtue from experience . . . would turn virtue into an ambiguous non-entity, mutable according to time and circumstances, and unusable for any sort of rule" (A315/B371).

241. Kant, *Critique of Pure Reason*, A314/B371.

242. Kant, *Critique of Pure Reason*, A314/B371.

243. Kant, *Critique of Pure Reason*, A315/B372. Such ideas are a consequence of the "natural" need of reason to "exalt itself" and go "much too far" beyond what we can experience (A314/B317).

244. Kant, *Critique of Pure Reason*, A314/B371.

245. Kant, *Critique of Pure Reason*, A315/B372. Philo would agree with Kant that we can never know the whole of justice; it is the "insatiable desire and thirst for knowledge" that impels the "zealous" emulation of virtue (*Quis rerum divinarum heres sit* 97).

246. See, for example, Martin Schuster, "Adorno and Negative Theology," *Graduate Faculty Philosophy Journal* 37, no. 1 (2016): 97–130, here pp. 103ff.

247. "It would be a sign of great simplicity to think that the world was created in six days, or indeed at all in time. But the sun is a portion of heaven, so that one must confess that time is a thing posterior to the world. Therefore it would be correctly said that the world was not created in time, but that time had its existence in consequence of the world. For it is the motion of the heaven that has displayed the nature of time" (*Legum allegoriae I* 2)

248. This is the topic of *De aeternitate mundi*, wherein Philo considers philosophical counterarguments.

249. True practice is harmonious. Remarkably, the most affirmative aspect of the written laws is their number: ten, "containing every kind of number, and ratio connected with number, and every proportion, and harmony, and symphony" (*De Decalogo* 23). In Philo's description of the Ten Commandments, only after fifty paragraphs extoling the virtues of "the ten" does he turn to the laws themselves. The ten "contains the harmonic proportion, in accordance with which that number which is in the middle between two extremities, is exceeded by

the one, and exceeds the other by an equal part; as is the case with the numbers three, four, and six." "The decade also contains the visible peculiar properties of the triangles, and squares, and other polygonal figures; also the peculiar properties of symphonic ratios, that of the diatessaron [perfect fourth] in proportion exceeding by one fourth, as is the ration of four to three; that of fifths exceeding in the ratio of half as much again . . . also that of the diapason, where the proportion is precisely twofold, as is the ration of two to one, or that of the double diapason, where the proportion is fourfold, as in the equal ration of eight to two" (*De Decalogo* 20).

250. Philo, *De praemiis et poenis* ("On Rewards and Punishments") 63.

251. Plato, *Timaeus* 52e. The movement of the *chora* here is thus not only out of balance, but also a form of bringing order (53a).

252. Drunkenness, as excessive, signifies "every extravagance of evil," as "the wicked man within ourselves." *De ebrietate* 15, 29.

253. *De confusione linguarum* 67–68. Philo uses as well τίναγμα (shake; quake); and various forms of σείω (shake; as does Plato).

254. *De confusione linguarum* 198. The passage continues: "of which every foolish man is visible proof, having all his words, and intentions, and actions, incapable of standing an examination and destitute of steadiness" (ibid.).

255. *De vita Mosis II* 14.

256. Kamesar, "Biblical Interpretation in Philo," p. 86.

257. Sandmel cited in Kasemar, "Biblical Interpretation in Philo," p. 86.

258. Kasemar, "Biblical Interpretation in Philo," p. 86.

259. Frank has proposed, as fundamental to understanding Plato's writing down of Socrates' dialogues, that "there is something about Plato's dialogues that requires that they be neither performed nor heard in real time, but read. And reread." Her point is not formal persistence, but rather multiplicities of interpretive possibility. Jill Frank, *Poetic Justice: Rereading Plato's Republic* (Chicago: University of Chicago Press, 2018), p. 1.

260. J. B. Kennedy, *The Musical Structure of Plato's Dialogues* (Durham, UK: Routledge, 2014).

261. The "scale" as the term is used here (but not in our chapter) is explained by Kennedy: "The term 'scale' is often taken to denote a musical structure that remains the same from octave to octave. The 'scale' in Plato's dialogues is not a scale in this sense. For example, the intervals from note 6 to note 12 and again from note 3 to note 6 are both one octave (i.e. they span a 1:2 ratio). Thus the equal intervals of text between each pair of the major notes from 1 to 12 do not correspond to equal musical intervals in the conventional sense." Kennedy, *The Musical Structure of Plato's Dialogues*, p. 255.

262. Kennedy, *The Musical Structure of Plato's Dialogues*, p. 30. He recognizes: "Much further research will be required to clarify how strong this case is, and whether or not the neo-Pythagoreans recognized the musical structure of Plato's dialogues" (ibid., p. 266).

263. See John Z. McKay and Alexander Rehding, "The Structure of Plato's Dialogues and Greek Music Theory," *Apeiron* 44 (October 2011): 359–375. The authors make a strong case against Kennedy's claims due to his ignorance of ancient Greek music theory, and mistaken assumptions about music theory *tout court*.

264. Cited in Kennedy, *The Musical Structure of Plato's Dialogues*, p. 260. Kennedy relies on Theon for providing the insight for his own work. He tells us: "Theon (fl. 100 CE) was a compiler and included long passages from . . . the neo-Pythagorean Thralsyllus (died 36 CE). He is usually identified with the Egyptian Greek who became the court philosopher to the Roman emperor Tiberius and organized Plato's dialogues into the tetrologies still used in some editions today" (ibid.).

265. Theon of Smyrna, cited in Kennedy, *The Musical Structure of Plato's Dialogues*, p. 261. A second work by Theon, concerning the order in which to study Plato's works, has recently been discovered in an Arabic translation.

266. βλαστησάτω, to sprout, is the verb form.

267. Similarly, whereas the first computers imposed themselves as mechanistic allegories for the human brain, now the human brain provides the allegory for computer connectivity.

268. In earlier times, the laboratory had physical boundaries, and mechanical actions could occur in isolation. But genetic mutations cannot be similarly confined, and the alteration of any one gene affects the whole.

CHAPTER 4

1. See, for example, John R. Hall, *Apocalypse: From Antiquity to the Empire of Modernity* (Cambridge, UK: Polity Press, 2009).

2. Eusebius, bishop of Caesarea Maritima and church historian in the early fourth century, whose hagiographic account of the emperor Constantine's conversion at this time became canonical. See H. A. Drake, *In Praise of Constantine: A Historical Study and New Translation of Eusebius' Tricennial Orations* (Berkeley: University of California Press, 1976).

3. For Christopher Columbus's citations from the book of Revelation and other biblical and apocalyptic texts in interpreting his voyages as the divine fulfillment of Christian prophecy, see his journal, *Repertorium Columbianum*, vol. 3: *The Book of Prophecies* (1500–1503), ed. Geoffrey Symcox et al. (Los Angeles: UCLA Center for Medieval and Renaissance Studies, 1997).

4. Luther's words: "I miss more than one thing in this book [of Revelation], and this makes me hold it to be neither apostolic nor prophetic. . . . There is one sufficient reason for me not to think highly of it—Christ is not taught or known in it. . . . I stick to the books which give me Christ clearly and purely." Martin Luther, Preface to Revelation in his 1522 translation of the New Testament, cited in Harry O. Maier, *Apocalypse Recalled: The Book of Revelation after Christendom* (Minneapolis: Fortress Press, 2002), p. 1. For Luther's and

other interpretations, see also Arthur W. Wainwright, *Mysterious Apocalypse: Interpreting the Book of Revelation* (Nashville: Abingdon Press, 1993).

5. For Newton's theological writings, including his mathematical predictions of the end of the world (2060 CE, hence yet to be disproven!), as well as the debates regarding Newtonian thought as science, see the excellent anthology edited by Margaret J. Osler, *Rethinking the Scientific Revolution* (Cambridge: Cambridge University Press, 2000).

6. Friedrich Engels, "The Book of Revelation" (1883), https://www.marxists.org/archive/marx/works/subject/religion/book-revelations.htm. On both Marx's and Engels' treatment of the Bible in general and the theme of apocalypse in particular, separating fact from fiction concerning the convergence of Judaeo-Christian eschatology and Marxist communist politics, see Roland Boer, "Marxism and Eschatology Reconsidered," *Mediations* 25, no. 1 (Fall 2010): 39–59 www.mediationsjournal.org/articles/marxism-and-eschatology-reconsidered (downloaded December 20, 2017).

7. See for Trotsky, Mark Steinberg, *The Russian Revolution 1905–1921* (Oxford: Oxford University Press, 2017), p. 323; and for popular visions of the Russian Revolution in theological terms, Mark Steinberg, *Proletarian Imagination 1911–1930: Self, Modernity and the Sacred in Russia, 1910–1925* (Ithaca: Cornell University Press, 2002).

8. Ernst Bloch, *Geist der Utopie* (1921). On modern messianism, see the excellent article by Anson Rabinbach, "Between Enlightenment and Apocalypse: Benjamin, Bloch and Modern German Jewish Messianism," *New German Critique* 34 (Winter 1985): 78–124.

9. On Patmos, the explicit geographical setting of John's Revelation, as described in texts and visual arts over the centuries (e.g., as place of exile, monastic withdrawal, desert of visions), see Ian Boxall, *Patmos in the Reception History of the Apocalypse* (Oxford: Oxford University Press, 2013). While the island has consistently been accepted as a real place and visited by the faithful, in the modern era the name Patmos has become symbolic of spiritual solitude in hopes of illumination. Hölderlin's poem *Patmos* (1803) reflects on the separation and loss that the poet was experiencing in personal life, while the island symbolizes a liminal space between Graeco-pagan Asia and the Christianity of his youth; Jacob Burckhardt spoke of being banished to academic isolation: "Berlin is my Patmos, and more than one book shall make my belly bitter," a reference to Rev 10:9–10 (Burckhardt, letter to Heinrich Schreiber, 1839, cited in Thomas Albert Howard, *Religion and the Rise of Historicism: W. M. L. de Wette, Jacob Burckhardt, and the Theological Origins of Nineteenth-Century Historical Consciousness* [Cambridge: Cambridge University Press, 2000], p. 141). In contrast, Jacques Derrida, at a Capri conference on the "Post-Secular," commented on the sociable ambiance of the hotel and meeting rooms: "Capri will never be Patmos" ("Faith and Knowledge" [1996; in English 1998], in Jacques Derrida, *Acts of Religion*, ed. Gil Anidjar [New York: Routledge, 2002], p. 48).

10. Even this might be questioned. A crucial source for scholarly work on the book of Revelation is the three-volume study of David E. Aune, comprising volume 52 (a, b, and c) of

World Biblical Commentary (Dallas: World Books, 1997–1998). For the remainder of this book they will be referenced briefly as Aune 52a (or 52b, 52c).

Aune considers pseudo- or multiple authors (52a, pp. xviii–l), and of course the authenticity of the manuscript as it has come down to us has all the usual problems regarding possible tampering. On the status of the text and its variants (in multiple languages), see ibid., pp. cxxxiv–cl. Pagels notes that controversy over the book's place within a Christian canon occurred from the second century to the fourth century CE, "when it barely squeezed into the canon to become the final book in the New Testament"; its defenders "sought to lend it legitimacy by insisting that Jesus' own disciple John wrote its prophecies, in addition to the Gospel of John." Elaine Pagels, *Revelations: Visions, Prophecy, and Politics in the Book of Revelation* (New York: Viking, 2012), p. 2.

11. The most convincing case by a modern scholar for continuing to presume the early date is made by John W. Marshall, *Parables of War: Reading John's Jewish Apocalypse* (Waterloo, Ontario: Wilfrid Laurier University Press, 2001), pp. 88–97, who wants to tie the book immediately to the effects of the Judaean War.

12. This late dating is actually a return to the past, when Irenaeus (late second century) dated it to the final years of Domitian's reign.

13. This approach is in line with contemporary scholarship. Mason writes that emphasis on "social realia over and against purely theological-exegetical motives has become indispensable to the field." Steve Mason, *A History of the Jewish War: A.D. 66–74* (New York: Cambridge, 2016), p. 204.

14. In the late second century CE, this book was a source of controversy, with some desiring to refuse it canonical status. The convert Justin, known as the Philosopher, in defending Christian prophecy against critics within the clergy "insisted that the Book of Revelation was not heretical but had been written when 'a man among us named John, one of Christ's disciples, received a revelation.' Justin was the first, so far as we know, to claim that John of Patmos was none other than *John of* Zebedee, Jesus' actual disciple" (Pagels, *Revelations* [2012], p. 107). For debates in the early church over the role of prophecy generally as a potentially heretical and continuing challenge to the institutional power of the clergy, see ibid., chs. 4–5.

15. Dating the gospels is difficult. No copies survive from the first century. Mark's "little apocalypse" is taken to be the earliest (68–70 CE), about 40 years after Jesus' death and synchronic with the events of Luke-Acts (describing the missionary acts of Paul); the Gospels of Matthew and Luke are now dated 80–90 CE, and John 90–100 CE. Elaine Pagels, *Beyond Belief: The Secret Gospel of Thomas* (New York: Vintage Books, 2004), p. 41. A hypothetical "Q" (*Quelle*/source) manuscript, since lost, has been proposed to account for the similarities between Matthew and Luke.

16. The word ἐκκλεσία was used very generally for a meeting of adult male citizens. Today, "church" is synonymous with a Christian assembly, and is opposed to the Jewish "synagogue" (συναγωγή). But the distinction simply does not hold for the first century, so

that the appearance of both terms in Revelation does not determine separate identities. Marshall explains: "To be sure, ἐκκλεσία may have a different tone, perhaps a slightly more political or civic one, than συναγωγή [literally, a group led together], but if this is a differentiating characteristic, it is a thoroughly problematic characterization of Christianity vs. Judaism. . . . There is nothing in the usage of ἐκκλεσία in the first century that need connote a Christian gathering as opposed to a Jewish gathering," while συναγωγή "was not particularly Jewish" (Marshall, *Parables of War*, pp. 84–85). The reason this is relevant is that John addresses "churches" (i.e., assemblies), but criticizes Pergamon as home of a "synagogue of Satan" (Rev 3:9), leading some interpreters to presume a clear division between Jews and Christians. Modern scholars disagree.

17. Rev 1:9–3:22. As for the "trials and tribulations" to which John refers, the earlier assumption that John was a political exile, indeed prisoner, on Patmos is believed now to be mistaken. Christians in the province of Asia were not persecuted at this time. See below, chapter 5, I.

18. ". . . τῶν λεγόντον Ἰουδαίους καὶ οὐκ εἰσὶν . . ." (Rev 2:9, addressing the church of Smyrna; this phrase is repeated, Rev 3:9, in John's letter to Philadelphia).

19. This has led to the invention of a plethora of what Marshall calls "mediating categories" of identification: Jewish Christians, Christian Gentiles, Jewish Gentiles, proto-Christians, and primitive Christians (the latter term can have anti-Jewish overtones). For a theoretically informed discussion of the use of these terms, relying on insights of Jacques Derrida, Jonathan Culler, and others, see Marshall, *Parables of War*, chs. 1–7.

20. Marshall, *Parables of War*, p. 5.

21. For Aune's discussion of John's evolution, and the possibility that Revelation is a composite of several different apocalyptic tracts composed by a single author over a 20- to 30-year period, see the introduction to Aune 52a, pp. cxviii–cxxxiv. For counterarguments that describe the literary unity of Revelation, see the analysis of its "essential structure" in Richard Bauckham, *The Climax of Prophecy: Studies on the Book of Revelation* (Edinburgh: T&T Clark, 1993); also Adela Yarbro Collins, *Crisis and Catharsis: The Power of the Apocalypse* (Louisville: Westminster John Knox Press, 1984), p. 54.

22. Elaine Pagels, "The Social History of Satan. Part Three: John of Patmos and Ignatius of Antioch: Contrasting Visions of 'God's People,'" *Harvard Theological Review* 99, no. 4 (October 2006): 497. Marshall considers the tendency to "retroject 'Christianity' onto elements of its prehistory" as a manifestation of "Christian interpretive hegemony" (Marshall, *Parables of War*, p. 5).

23. David E. Aune, "The Apocalypse of John and Palestinian Jewish Apocalpytic," in *Apocaplyticism, Prophecy and Magic in Early Christianity: Collected Essays* (Tübingen: Mohr Siebeck, 2006), p. 173. Aune speculates that John was perhaps an "immigrant" from Palestine "in the wake" of the Judaean War. He continues: "Since a close analysis of the Apocalypse of John betrays an intimate knowledge of many apocalyptic sources and traditions, it appears likely that the author read, and perhaps even owned a modest library of Palestinian apocalyptical literature" (ibid., pp. 173–174).

24. "I agree with Collins, Duff, and others that John's target includes followers of Jesus who accept Pauline teaching—teaching already widespread in Asia Minor, especially among Gentiles" (Pagels, "The Social History of Satan. Part Three," p. 496). The present consensus as to the late dating of John's text can be seen to strengthen this speculation.

25. Aune 52a, p. 156. Aune notes the one "major exception" to John's inclusiveness was "the issue of the propriety of eating meat sacrificed to pagan deities" (ibid.) This exception was not one of identity but practice, participation in the communal worship of false gods.

26. She notes that "others among [John's] near contemporaries in Asia" called Paul "simply 'the great apostle' and revered even above 'the twelve'" (Pagels, "Social History of Satan. Part Three," p. 502). In her book *Revelations*, Pagels argues that the lack of mention of Paul is in fact evidence for his presence: "John of Patmos never mentions Paul's name—perhaps, as we shall see, because he remained skeptical of Paul's teaching and kept his distance from those who accepted it" (Pagels, *Revelations*, p. 45). The word "perhaps" comes frequently in this (more popular) text, as Pagels attempts to tell her readers what it is that "John intends to show . . ." (ibid., p. 34). Aune—and historians in this field generally—do likewise. Attributing intention to individuals writing 2000 years ago is not an approach followed here.

27. Pagels, "The Social History of Satan. Part Three," p. 505. "Perhaps it is no accident that Ignatius, himself a Syrian convert writing perhaps ten years after John (depending on how we date his writing) to believers in the same Asian towns, is the first, so far as we know, to aggressively identify himself and his fellow believers as 'Christians' over against what he sees as the adherents of an inferior and obsolete 'Judaism'" (ibid., p. 496). In his "attempt to corral belief into orthodoxy under the nascent Christian hierarchy" Ignatius "goes so far as to accuse those who introduce Ἰουδαϊσμός of introducing αἵρεσις [heresy]"; "Christians have taken over the Jews' identity as God's people" (ibid., pp. 501 and 505).

28. Andrew S. Jacobs, "The Lion and the Lamb," in *The Ways That Never Parted: Jews and Christians in Late Antiquity and the Early Middle Ages*, ed. Adam H. Becker and Annette Yoshiko Reed (Minneapolis: Fortress Press, 2007), pp. 98–100.

29. Alain Badiou, *Saint Paul: The Foundation of Universalism*, trans. Ray Brassier (Stanford: Stanford University Press, 2003). The fantasy of Christian universalism is problematic in the works of Slavoj Žižek and Giorgio Agamben as well. In contrast, this chapter continues the argument of the preceding one that approached Philo's understanding of Judaism as itself universal. For a helpful summary of the enormous complexity of identity-labeling in regard to Paul, see Glen W. Bowersock's review of recent books on Paul (including Karen Armstrong's; see following note), "Who Was Saint Paul?," *New York Review of Books*, November 5, 2015, http://www.nybooks.com/articles/2015/11/05/who-was-saint-paul/.

30. Daniel Boyarin, *A Radical Jew: Paul and the Politics of Identity* (Berkeley: University of California Press, 1994). Cf. Karen Armstrong, *St. Paul: The Apostle We Love to Hate* (Boston: New Harvest, 2015): "Paul never forgot that he was a Jew" (p. 50). Boyarin, in another study, cites Ignatius' anti-Jewish statement: "'It is monstrous to talk of Jesus Christ and to

practice Judaism'. . . . These very monsters were to appear as a heresiological topos of the orthodox Christian writers who almost constantly figured heresy as a hydra. The Rabbis, in those same centuries, produced an analogous response, a discourse as well of the pure and the authentic opposed to the impure, the contaminated, the hybrid, the *min*," states Boyarin, positioning himself as an orthodox Jew: "I speak here, then, for the monsters." Daniel Boyarin, *Borderlines: The Partition of Judaeo-Christianity* (Philadelphia: University of Pennsylvania Press, 2004), p. xxi.

31. This popular interpretation is reductive in its understanding of the genre of apocalypse, for which the Society of Biblical Literature has proposed a definition that is now generally accepted: "'Apocalypse' is a genre of revelatory literature with a narrative framework, in which a revelation is mediated by an otherworldly being to a human recipient, disclosing a transcendent reality which is both temporal, insofar as it envisages eschatological salvation, and spatial, insofar as it involves another, supernatural world, intended to interpret present, earthly circumstances in light of the supernatural world and of the future, and to influence both the understanding and the behaviour of the audience by means of divine authority." *Semeia* 36 (1996): *Early Christian Apocalypticism: Genre and Social Setting*, ed. Adela Yarbro Collins, pp. 2 and 7. Pagels emphasizes the multiple terms that appear in the documents: "although the term 'apocalypse' is used in the Nag Hammadi library more often than terms like 'gospel' or 'apocryphon,' varous terms are used for writings that claim to offer 'revelation'" (Pagels, *Revelations*, p. 180). She refers here to David Frankfurter's article "The Legacy of Jewish Apocalypses in Early Christianity: Regional Trajectories," in *The Jewish Apocalyptic Heritage in Early Christianity*, ed. William Adler and James VanderKam (Assen, Netherlands: Van Gorcum, 1996), pp. 135 and 156.

32. Moderns have expressed an active distaste for John. The writer D. H. Lawrence hated the book of Revelation. The historian Frank Kermode connected it with fascism. "[A]mong the major works of early Christianity included in the New Testament, it remains the Cinderella. It has received only a fraction of the amount of scholarly attention which has been lavished on the Gospels and the major Pauline letters" (Bauckham, *The Climax of Prophecy*, p. 10). This situation has changed in the past several decades, given the resonances of the millennial turn to the year 2000. In July 2020 Google listed over 9,700,000 responses to the search "book of Revelation."

33. A Hebrew, a Pharisee, and a Roman citizen, Paul was a contemporary of Jesus whom he did not know.

34. Rev 22:20. Jesus' name is mentioned at the beginning and end of the text, as well as Rev 19:10: "Worship God! For the testimony of Jesus is the spirit of prophecy." The lack of a major role for Jesus led Martin Luther to complain there was "no Christ" in the book of Revelation: "Christ is not taught or known in it" (see above, note 4).

35. Israel compelled Jordan to hand over the Dead Sea Scrolls after the 1967 war, and the Israel Antiquity Authority maintains control of access. Beginning in 1993, the scrolls were photographed using infrared technology borrowed from the US National Aeronautics and

Space Administration. Much of the material is now available on line in the multilingual Leon Levy Digital Library: http://www.deadseascrolls.org.il/?locale=en_US.

36. These are online: http://gnosis.org/naghamm/nhl.html.

37. A total of 981 manuscripts were discovered in the decade of 1946–1956; 867 of these date from the Second Temple period. The discovery of the scrolls and their contentious reception has been told by John J. Collins in fascinating detail: John J. Collins, *The Dead Sea Scrolls: A Biography* (Princeton: Princeton University Press, 2013).

38. Among the now-canonical books, only Esther is excluded. The Jewish Bible of Hebrew texts was not codified until the second to fourth centuries CE; the Masoretic text, canonical for rabbinical Judaism, was copied and disseminated even later (seventh to eleventh centuries).

39. Jubilees (14 copies of which were found) follows a 364-day solar calendar, dividing time into jubilee periods of 49 years, within which are seven "weeks" of years, at the end of which debts are to be canceled.

40. Josephus mentions the Essenes' "sharing rule" for property (Collins, *The Dead Sea Scrolls*, 53). Philo concurs (*Hypothetica/Apologia pro Iudaeis* 11) and gives a respectful description of the Essenes of "Palestine and Syria" who numbered "more than four thousand in my opinion," and who were "men devoted to the service of God, not sacrificing living animals, but studying rather to preserve their own minds in a state of holiness and purity" (*Quod omnis probus liber* 75). Sharing property is part of this. But so too is song. The words of hymns, songs of praise, Psalms, even Deuteronomy (called a hymn by Philo) are a major part of the Dead Sea Scrolls. Note that Philo also writes of the "Therapeutae," a sect close to Alexandria, who pursued a contemplative life (Collins, *The Dead Sea Scrolls,* p. 40). Pagels discusses this sect in connection with Nag Hammadi documents in *Beyond Belief,* p. 100.

41. It is still the scholarly consensus that the Essene community was situated in the Qumran caves, and that these parchment scrolls were its library. Yet countertheories exist, and they have political implications. (An alleged "scriptorium" of the Essenes at Qumran was later determined to be a pottery factory.) Collins writes: "At least in some cases (e.g., Norman Golb), scholars seem to feel that attribution to the Essenes impugns the authenticity of the Jewish character of the Scrolls, and diminishes their importance"—although many Jewish scholars support the Essene thesis (*The Dead Sea Scrolls*, p. 64). Collins concludes: "The identification of Qumran as an Essene settlement continues to command an overwhelming consensus" (ibid., p. 92). Its relationship to the Temple priests is debated. An early speculation that the Dead Sea caves were a safe place of hiding provided by the Essenes for the Temple manuscripts during the Judaean war has been rejected, insofar as many of the scrolls have a different perspective from that of the Temple priests. This leads to the understanding of diversity within Second Temple Judaism. Still contested is the question of a connection between the Essenes and Christianity; see Simon J. Joseph, *Jesus, the Essenes, and Christian*

Origins: New Light on Ancient Texts and Communities (Waco, TX: Baylor University Press, 2018).

42. "The belief that the community enjoyed present fellowship with the angels is perhaps the most distinctive aspect of the eschatology of the Dead Sea Scrolls," hence the theme of resurrection was "relatively unimportant." John J. Collins, *The Apocalyptic Imagination*, 2nd ed. (Grand Rapids, MI: Eerdmans, 1998), p. 217.

43. See the excellent posting by Loren L. Johns, "The Dead Sea Scrolls and the Apocalypse of John," http://ljohns.ambs.edu/DSS&APJN.htm (downloaded January 4, 2017).

44. The book of 1 Enoch has been found in fragments among the Dead Sea Scrolls in Aramaic; a complete text is extant only in Ge'ez (Ethiopic). Versions of 1 Enoch have been found in widely different languages and sites, suggesting a diversity of readers who escape categorization. Regarding 4 Ezra, the online English translation notes: "Neither the Semitic, apparently Hebrew original nor its ancient Greek translation survives. . . . Complete daughter translations exist in Latin, Syriac, Ethiopic, Georgian, Armenian, and two different ones in Arabic. In addition, fragments of a Coptic version in the Sahidic dialect have been discovered." Pagels relates that a copy of 4 Ezra was found at Nag Hammadi: the Jewish prophet Salathiel, a contemporary of John of Patmos, adopted the pseudonym Ezra to connect to the earlier texts in this name written at the time of the Babylonian destruction: "Like John, Salathiel calls Rome by the code name Babylon" (Pagels, *Revelations*, p. 77). On 2 Baruch: "The author of 2 Baruch wrote in response to the Roman destruction of Jerusalem in 70 CE, though the apocalypse is set fictitiously during and after the Babylonian sacking of Jerusalem in the year 587 BCE. . . . Now it is Baruch who speaks directly with God and is promised to survive the impending eschatological doom in order to be a witness to the divine intention regarding Israel and the nations at the end of days" (introduction to online English translations of both 4 Ezra and 2 Baruch, downloaded June 2019, http://www.augsburgfortress.org/media/downloads/9780800699680Intro.pdf).

45. This is a highly controversial issue, as the War Scroll (*Milhamah*) speaks of holy war as waged not only by God but by human beings. It has been dated to the 60s CE, that is, as a call to arms by zealous Jews in the Judaean War, and contains military strategies for how to wage it. If holy war is a human task in these early Jewish and Christian texts, then Islam is undistinguished in this regard. The Christian Crusades in the eleventh and twelfth centuries were understood as such by their participants. Bauckham agrees with Matthew Black who reads the book of Revelation as a "Christian war scroll" (Bauckham, *The Climax of Prophecy*, 161), and sees the "combat myth" embedded in John's Revelation as a continuation of this theme of "struggle" and an invitation to participate in eschatological war. Bauckham argues, however, that John "reinterprets the holy war traditions and makes the warfare metaphorical rather than literal" so that it lacks "the concern with practical military matters which we find in 1QM [the Dead Sea War Scroll]" (ibid., p. 213).

46. "At stake is the relevance of the Scrolls for mainline Jewish tradition, or the degree to which they should be taken to reflect a marginal form of Judaism, closer to Christianity than to the religion of the rabbis" (Collins, *The Dead Sea Scrolls*, p. xi). The yearly Enoch Seminars,

established in 2001, have focused their work on this issue, publishing a series on what might be called the Jewish Gospels, several of which have been cited below. See the website: http://enochseminar.org.

47. The story has been told by Marvin Meyer in *The Gnostic Discoveries: The Impact of the Nag Hammadi Library* (New York: HarperCollins, 2005). Meyer is general editor of their English translation (with an introduction by Elaine Pagels): *The Nag Hammadi Scriptures: International Edition* (New York: HarperCollins, 2007). Specific Nag Hammadi texts are Pagels' area of expertise. As a graduate student, she worked in Cairo editing and annotating these texts. She describes the experience: "When my fellow students and I investigated these sources, we found that they revealed diversity within the Christian movement that later, 'official' versions of Christian history had suppressed so effectively that only now, in the Harvard graduate school, did we hear about them" (Pagels, *Beyond Belief*, p. 32).

48. The victory of Constantine under the standard of the Christian God came at the battle of the Milvian Bridge in 312 CE. Constantine defeated the rival emperors of the Tetrarchy in a series of civil wars to become the sole ruler of the Roman Empire, which over the course of the fourth century adopted Christianity as the official faith. Constantine's own commitment to Christianity did not prevent his financial support of pagan projects as well.

49. Helmut Koester has proposed that the Gospel of Thomas, "although compiled c. 140 CE, may include some traditions even *older* than the gospels of the New Testament, 'possibly as early as the second half of the first century'" (Elaine Pagels, *The Gnostic Gospels* [1979; New York: Vintage Books, 1989], p. xvii). Based on these speculations, the question has been raised whether the Gospel of Thomas, rather than being a late "Gnostic" gospel, "as many of us first assumed," might be, "on the contrary, an early collection of Jesus' teaching—perhaps even one that Matthew and Luke used to compose their own gospels?" Could it perhaps even be "the so-called Q source, a hypothetical first-century list of Jesus's sayings? . . . At present, however, many do not share the view that the *Gospel of Thomas* is a kind of rough quarry of early Jesus sayings strung together with minimal editorial point of view" (Pagels, "Introduction," in *The Nag Hammadi Scriptures*, p. 9). Meyer writes that "impassioned dispute" as to a first-century date for the Gospel of Thomas has to do with the desire to marginalize its importance, which threatens the basic idea of Protestantism that the canonical four Gospels lead to the pure Christianity (Meyer, *The Gnostic Discoveries*, p. 37).

50. "Jesus in the Gospel of Thomas performs no physical miracles, reveals no fulfillment of prophecy, announces no apocalyptic kingdom about to disrupt the world order, and dies for no one's sins. . . . In the Gospel of Thomas Jesus is proclaimed the living one, and he lives in his sayings" (Meyer, *The Gnostic Discoveries*, pp. 61–62).

51. Einar Thomassen, "Introduction to *The Gospel of Truth*," in *The Nag Hammadi Scriptures*, p. 32. This discourse on the gospel, the "good news about the appearance of the Savior on earth and the message he brought to humanity," describes the Savior as crucified by his enemies, and through a series of images, "evolves into a portrait of the Savior as the Word

that goes forth from the Father and permeates the All"; the Gospel of Truth was used by the Valentinians, Iranaeus (writing ca. 180 CE) tells us, in his polemic *Against Heresies*; it may have been authored by Valentinus himself (ibid., pp. 31–34). Iranaeus' exclusion of heretics was motivated by the desire for a single "catholic" church, as was also true of his teacher Polycarp, bishop of Smyrna.

52. Close to the site of the Nag Hammadi discovery, archaeologists have examined a Pachomian monastery and monastic church at Pbow (there are five monasteries within walking distance of the site [Pagels, *Revelations*, p. 145]). It has been suggested that the Nag Hammadi texts were buried by monks when Athanasius, bishop of Alexandria, issued a festal letter to Egyptian Christians warning generally against books of spiritual wisdom considered heretical (Meyer, *The Gnostic Discoveries*, p. 31; also Pagels: "Athanasius interpreted John's Book of Revelation as condemning all 'heretics,' and then made this book the capstone of the New Testament canon, where it has remained ever since" [*Revelations*, p. 145]).

53. The find indicates that the so-called "Gnostic texts" are unified only by virtue of their being excluded by the evolving church. King writes that Gnosticism is a term "invented in the early modern period to aid in defining the boundaries of normative Christianity"; it is an empty category, a "rhetorical term" that "has been confused with a historical entity": "Gnosticism has been constructed largely as the heretical other in relation to the diverse and fluctuating understandings of orthodox Christianity" (Karen L. King, *What Is Gnosticism?* (Cambridge, MA: Belknap Press of Harvard University Press, 2003), pp. 1–2).

54. King, *What Is Gnosticism?*, pp. 191–217. See also Michael Allen Williams, *Rethinking "Gnosticism": An Argument for Dismantling a Dubious Category* (Princeton: Princeton University Press, 1999).

55. Meyer, *The Gnostic Discoveries*, p. 48.

56. From *Three Forms of First Thought* (NHC XIII,1, in *The Nag Hammadi Scriptures*, p. 729). The "shaking" of the earth and "dawn" of a new age replicate themes found in John of Patmos' text; shaking is a key word as well in Philo's cosmology, as we have seen.

57. Elaine Pagels, *Revelations*, pp. 89–90. The Gospel of Thomas, writes Pagels, "teaches that recognizing one's affinity with God is the key to the kingdom of God" (*Beyond Belief*, p. 75). Likewise the *Dialogue of the Savior* shows "*how* to seek revelation," a process that includes prayer (Pagels, *Revelations*, p. 91). See also her general account, *The Gnostic Gospels*.

58. Marvin Meyer, introduction to "The Gospel of Thomas," NHC II,2, in *The Nag Hammadi Scriptures*, p. 133.

59. Seth, as Philo recounts this figure from Genesis, was the third son of Adam and Eve; when Cain killed Abel, the "seed of Seth" became progenitor of all that followed. For an account of Philo's connections to this tradition (and those of Middle Platonists more generally), see John D. Turner, *Sethian Gnosticism and the Platonic Tradition* (Quebec: Presses de l'Université Laval; Louvain-Paris: Éditions Peeters, 2001), pp. 355–362. On the strain of Gnostic texts that scholars call Sethian, following the terminology of the early Church

fathers, see John D. Turner, "The Sethian School of Gnostic Thought," in the epilogue to *The Nag Hammadi Scriptures,* pp. 784–789. King tells us that the word "Sethian" does not refer to a self-defined community; like the word "gnostic," it was applied by early Christian heresiologists: Karen L. King, *Revelation of the Unknowable God* (Santa Rosa, CA: Polebridge Press, 1995), pp. 34–40.

60. A figure whom Allogenes calls "my son Messos" has led to speculation that this name may be a play on Moses (*The Nag Hammadi Scriptures,* NHC XI,3, p. 682). King cautions, however, that there is in this text "no evidence of any explicitly Jewish or Christian figures or influence" (*Revelation of the Unknowable God,* 42).

61. From "The Secret Book of John," NHC II,1; III,1, IV,1. *The Nag Hammadi Scriptures,* p. 110. See also King, *Revelation of the Unknowable God,* p. 45; Pagels, "God the Father/God the Mother," in *The Gnostic Gospels,* pp. 48–69. For the connection of Sophia with Isis and the theory of *chora* (via Plutarch), see Turner, *Sethian Gnosticism and the Platonic Tradition,* pp. 373–376.

62. *The Nag Hammadi Scriptures,* pp. 680–682. Cf. "The Wisdom [Sophia] of Jesus Christ" speaks as "The One who is ineffable," "without a name" and "with no human form" (ibid., p. 288).

63. "The Prayer of Thanksgiving," Coptic text NHC VI,7, in *The Nag Hammadi Scriptures,* p. 423. The introduction (by Jean-Pierre Mahé) to this document connects it to the Corpus Hermeticum (ibid., pp. 419–420).

64. "Thunder, Perfect Mind," NHC VI,2, *The Nag Hammadi Scriptures,* p. 372. "*Thunder* takes the form of a discourse, composed for the most part of self-predications in the first-person singular (Coptic *anoke pelte,* Greek *egō eimi.* . . . The speaker remains unnamed, but many features in the text show that the person or entity speaking is a feminine being" suggesting the Egyptian goddess Isis as well as "female Wisdom in the Jewish scriptures," although "these parallels remain only partial" (Introduction to "Thunder, Perfect Mind" by Paul-Hubert Poirier, ibid., p. 367).

65. "Thunder, Perfect Mind," NHC VI,2, *The Nag Hammadi Scriptures,* pp. 373–375. Toni Morrison and Leslie Marmon Silko, contemporary African American and Native American authors, have woven the divine, female voice of "Thunder, Perfect Mind" into their writings.

66. Nag Hammadi's desert location, as well as the presumably monastic setting, does not mean that this site was intellectually isolated. Quite the contrary. North of the marvelous Luxor temples on the Nile, it was within access of the great trade routes that, both before and after Egypt's acquisition by the Romans, connected the Nile to the Red Sea ports and thence to Arabia, east Africa, India, and beyond.

67. Pagels, *The Gnostic Gospels,* p. xxi.

68. "Zostrianos," NHC VIII,1, in *The Nag Hammadi Scriptures,* pp. 537–583.

69. Meyer, *The Gnostic Discoveries,* p. 47.

70. *The Nag Hammadi Scriptures*, p. 410.

71. Garth Fowden, *The Egyptian Hermes: A Historical Approach to the Late Pagan Mind* (Princeton: Princeton University Press, 1986), p. 5.

72. Fowden, *The Egyptian Hermes*, p. 27. Fowden, with Jews like Philo in mind, notes that the fact that the Hermetic writers "absorbed Jewish ideas" of creation and other cosmological themes is not surprising given the Jews' long residence in Egypt (ibid., p. 36).

73. King, *Revelation of the Unknowable God*, p. 35. "[O]ne point is assured by the new discoveries: early Christianity was much more diverse and pluriform than anyone could have suspected a century ago. Moreover, historians will have to write a story in which Christian triumph over pagan culture and Christian supersession of Judaism no longer have an unambiguous historical grounding, and in which women are an active presence" (King, *What Is Gnosticism?*, p. vii).

74. Boyarin emphasizes the variability of belief that characterized Jews in the first century, when no line between Jews and Christians could be drawn: "How and why that border was written and who wrote it are the questions that drive this book" (*Borderlines*, p. 2). Study of first-century Judaism cannot help but make one aware of the tension between the present, nation-state form of Israel and the actual history of the Jewish people, whose remarkable and brilliant contributions to humanity have been tied precisely and productively to the condition of diaspora.

75. Contemporary scholars recognize the arbitrariness of the process. Thus when Pagels, whose early scholarship was on these codices, writes on John, she entitles the book *Revelations*, in the plural, and includes several chapters that deal with these other "Apocalypses" that did not become canonical. Pagels considers the Nag Hammadi manuscripts (including the feminine themes [*Revelations*, p. 100]) too esoteric for institution building; given the persecution of Christians in the early years, she recognizes the need for unity, despite the exclusionary effects. Boyarin speaks of the "production of difference" from Christians as the Rabbinical form that developed in the third century CE (*Borderlines*, p. 27). He considers it "at least plausible to imagine that the notion of orthodoxy/heresy that manifests itself at the beginnings of the rabbinic movement in the guise of the Hebrew neologism *minut*, first attested at this time, is itself the appropriation of a Christian notion, a wheelbarrow smuggled across the border, precisely in service of the establishment and naturalization of the border and of the human kinds that it serves to identify" (ibid., p. 29). These delineations served a purpose "in the production of ideology, of hegemony, the consent of a dominated group to be ruled by an elite (hence 'consensual orthodoxy,' that marvelous mystification)" (ibid., p. 27).

76. The word *hairesis* (αἵρεσις) means simply a choice in opinion or belief that one makes: for ancient philosophers it meant a coherent doctrine or school of thought. "But for Christian polemicists, the term 'heresy' was pejorative in a way the Greek usage was not" (King, *What Is Gnosticism?*, p. 23; see also p. 281n). "The power relations implied in the discourse of orthodoxy and heresy are firmly embedded in struggles over who gets to say what truth is: the orthodox are the winners; the heretics, the losers" (ibid., p. 24). "Calling people

heretics is an effort to place them outside those who claim to be on the inside" (ibid.). "The polemicists needed to create sharp lines of differentiation because in practice the boundaries were not so neat" (ibid., p. 30).

77. Judaeo-Christianity is a post-World War II attempt to arrange a *rapprochement* between Judaism and Christianity, criticized by Taubes for not going far enough. He writes: "The magic spell of Christianity's historical success remains, though the church no longer uses the sword to decide her disputes with the synagogue, and this spell still constrains Jewish-Christian dialogues of our time." Jacob Taubes, *From Cult to Culture: Fragments Toward a Critique of Historical Reason*, ed. Charlotte Elisheva Fonrobert and Amir Engel, intro. Aleida Assman et al. (Stanford: Stanford University Press, 2010), p. 46.

78. See Tomoko Masuzawa, *The Invention of World Religions: Or, How European Universalism was Preserved in the Language of Pluralism* (Chicago: University of Chicago Press, 2005).

79. For the spurious method that "links origin with essence," see King, *What Is Gnosticism?*, pp. 11–12 and (citing Masuzawa) 72–73.

80. Daniel Boyarin, "The Ioudaioi in John and the Prehistory of 'Judaism,'" in *Pauline Conversations in Context* (essays in honor of Calvin J. Roetzel), ed. Janice Capel Anderson, Philip Sellew, and Claudia Setzer (London: Sheffield Academic Press, 2002), p. 217.

81. Jonathan Z. Smith, *Imagining Religion: From Babylon to Jonestown* (Chicago: University of Chicago Press, 1982), p. 14.

82. King, *What Is Gnosticism?*, p. 11.

83. The doctrine of *sola scriptura* is highly problematic, beginning with the problem of the status of the Gospels as historically reliable documents, as we do not know definitively when the Gospels were written down. Moreover, the claim of purity of the source opens the text to demagogic manipulation, precisely through the exclusion of heretics.

84. Boyarin is right to insist that the acknowledgment of blurred identities is a precondition for human justice. We concur that the value of first-century texts today is as testimony against the ideology of border construction. He writes that the latter "negates the very meaning of Jewish survival until now. If we have been for only ourselves, what are we? As I write, in occupied Palestine literal physical boundaries of barbed wire and electrified fencing are being raised to separate violently one 'people' from another. . . . The Prophet teaches: Zion will be redeemed only through justice" (Boyarin, *Borderlines*, p. xv).

85. Pagels, *Revelations*, p. 192n.

86. For a sociolinguistic analysis of what we can know as to who in the Roman world used *koine* and why, see Jorma Kaimio, *The Romans and the Greek Language* (Helsinki: Societas Scientiarum Fennica, 1979).

87. "Im Ägypten, Syrien und Kleinasien, muss in jener Zeit eine ähnliche Form von Griechisch, die eigentliche Koine, gesprochen worden sein" ("In Egypt, Syria and Asia Minor at that time a similar form of Greek, the self-same *koine*, must have been spoken"; trans. mine): S. G. Kapsomenos, cited in G. H. R. Horseley's essay "The Fiction of 'Jewish Greek,'" in

New Documents Illustrating Early Christianity, vol. 5: *Linguistic Essays* (Sydney: Macquarie University, Ancient History Documentary Research Centre, 1989), p. 37. Flavius Josephus (*Bellum Judaicum* 7.43) speaks of the Syrian territory in which Jews were "densely interspersed" among pagans. For Jews in Egypt, see the defining scholarship published as the *Corpus Papyrorum Judaicarum*, vol. 1, ed. Victor A. Tcherikover in collaboration with Alexander Fuks (Cambridge, MA: Harvard University Press, with the Magnes Press, Hebrew University, 1957). For Jews in the province of Asia, see Bradley Ritter, "Judeans in Asia Minor and Greece," *Judeans in the Greek Cities of the Roman Empire: Rights, Citizenship and Civil Discord* (Leiden: Brill, 2015), pp. 198–240. The importance to Jews in the diaspora of the Septuagint translation, in order to read their Scripture, has been referenced in chapter 3 above.

88. "We must assume that most language communities of the Roman Empire were diglot or even polyglot, and quite a few of their members in one way or another bilingual or multilingual" (Kaimio, *The Romans and the Greek Language*, p. 14). In the capital, two groups reliably bilingual were at the extremes of social power: slaves who came from the east, and the imperial families whose philhellenic education was the norm (ibid., pp. 317–318 and passim).

89. For the "tenacious" hold of this language well into the Islamic Umayyad dynasty, see G[len] W. Bowersock, "Hellenism and Islam," in *Hellenism and Late Antiquity*, ed. G[len] W. Bowersock (Ann Arbor: University of Michigan Press, 1990), p. 90.

90. "'Atticistic language' and 'Koine' cannot be regarded as opposed to one another in such a way as to make them mutually exclusive phenomena" (J. Frösén, cited in Horseley, *New Documents Illustrating Early Christianity*, vol. 5, p. 44).

91. Horseley, *New Documents Illustrating Early Christianity*, vol. 5, p. 30. The distinction between the written, literary and the spoken, colloquial form of a language is one of register, not dialect (ibid.).

92. Fergus Millar, "Government and Diplomacy in the Roman Empire during the First Three Centuries," in *Rome, the Greek World, and the East*, vol. 2, ed. Hannah M. Cotton and Guy M. Rogers (Chapel Hill: University of North Carolina Press, 2004), p. 216.

93. Discussed above, chapter 2.

94. Horseley, *New Documents Illustrating Early Christianity*, vol. 5, pp. 41, 34.

95. Biblical texts include the Septuagint translation (mid-third century BCE, more than 100 years after Alexander's death), as well as the Gospels and other New Testament books.

96. Horseley, *New Documents Illustrating Early Christianity*, vol. 5, p. 44. See also Horseley's entry on "'Christian' Greek," in *Encyclopedia of Ancient Greek Language and Linguistics*, 2 vols, ed. Georgos K. Giannakis (Leiden: Brill, 2013–2014), vol. 1, pp. 280–283.

97. Horseley, *New Documents Illustrating Early Christianity*, vol. 5, p. 46. Protestant claims of *sola Scriptura*, the infallibility of "Scripture alone," have endorsed this idea on repeated occasions. Catholics, in contrast, have focused on the Latin translation, pieces of which

were made from the Septuagint version, others of the Gospels from *koine*; but the first full translation, the *Biblia Vulgata*, or "Common Bible," was made in the late fourth century by Jerome, who worked with the Hebrew texts.

98. Horseley, *New Documents Illustrating Early Christianity*, vol. 5, p. 44.

99. Horseley writes: "There is nothing in early Christian texts in Greek which stands apart morphologically from contemporary texts" (Horseley, "'Christian' Greek," p. 282).

100. Horseley, *New Documents Illustrating Early Christianity*, vol. 5, pp. 34–36. As to why the books of the New Testament were written in *koine*, Horseley considers it more likely because of the "widespread knowledge of Greek in Palestine specifically" (not only among the educated, upper classes) rather than anticipation of broad missionary success (ibid., p. 19). Given that Jesus is presumed to have spoken Aramaic, the answer is not self-evident (he may have been bilingual, and even have spoken publicly in Greek—or at least used some Greek words); the issue is contested (ibid. pp. 20–22). Horseley's strong argument is not without critics. For a scholarly argument that the language of Revelation is the "most peculiar Greek in the NT," see Aune 52a, p. clxii. All discussions of language are vulnerable to changes that may have been made in transmission from the missing original. The earliest form of the text of Revelation (third century CE) is difficult to restore (see ibid., p. clviii).

101. Horseley, *New Documents Illustrating Early Christianity*, vol. 5, p. 40. On the racialization of philology, whereby theories of linguistic superiority led to ideas of racial superiority, see Martin Bernal, *Black Athena: The Afroasiatic Roots of Classical Civilization*, vol 2: *The Archaeological and Documentary Evidence* (New Brunswick: Rutgers University Press, 1991), pp. 231ff. This theory included the notion of the German Romantic Friedrich Schlegel that only Sanskrit, Greek, Latin, and German were languages suitable for philosophy and religion.

102. *Commentary on the New Testament Use of the Old Testament*, ed. G. K. Beale and D. A. Carson (Grand Rapids, MI: Baker Academic, 2007), p. 1082. Attempts to "tally the total" of John's Old Testament references vary from 226, to 635, to approximately 1,000. "Roughly more than half the references are from Psalms [hymnic practices], Isaiah [eschatological vision of new heaven and new earth], Ezekiel [final battle, last judgment, New Jerusalem], and Daniel," and in proportion to its length, "Daniel yields the most"; this book (written at the time of the Maccabean revolt of Jews in the second century BCE, about the era of the Babylonian exile in the fifth century BCE) "provides a mother lode of material for John"; themes from Daniel include the faithful witness, reign of the saints, and triumph over the beast, while Zechariah provides the "crucial imagery" of the four horsemen (ibid.).

103. Horseley, *New Documents Illustrating Early Christianity*, vol. 5, p. 28. Even words in common may differ in their use.

104. The fact that the wording departs from that of the Septuagint has led experts to suggest John was working with the Hebrew texts, and yet, on the other hand, "the wording departs from the Hebrew at significant points" (Beale and Carson, *Commentary on the New Testament Use of the Old Testament*, p. 1083).

105. This convergence was first observed in the work of the early twentieth-century scholar Adolf Deissmann, who describes a "polemical parallelism between the cult of the emperor and the cult of Christ," when "words from the treasury of the Septuagint and the Gospels happen to coincide with solemn concepts of the Imperial cult which sounded the same or similar." Deissmann, *Light from the Ancient East: The New Testament; Illustrated by Recently Discovered texts of the Graeco-Roman World*, 2nd ed., trans. Lionel R. M. Strachan (London: Hodder & Stoughton, 1910 [first German publication 1908]), p. 346. Horseley writes that Deissmann's reaction in the 1890s "against the isolation of the Greek of the LXX and of the NT from the *Koine* . . . was notable because, instead of looking for literary parallels, he sought evidence in non-literary texts: inscriptions and papyri—the study of the latter particularly being in their infancy at that time" (Horseley, "'Christian' Greek," p. 281).

106. Cf. Rev 3:21: "To him that overcometh [ὁ νικῶν—literally, the victor] will I grant to sit with me in my throne, even as I also overcame [ἐνίκησα—was victorious] and am set down with my Father in his throne."

107. Rev 1:8 and 2:18; the titles κύριος ὁ θεός and ὁ παντοκράτωρ reappear in the final scene in the Heavenly City (Rev 21:22), where—unlike the cities that sponsored emperor cults—no temple appears, "for the Lord God Almighty and the Lamb are the temple of it" (ibid.). The name "master" (*despotis*/δεσπότης) appears in Rev 6:10. The title "King of kings" (Rev 19:16) was insisted upon by the Parthian king when addressed by the Romans.

108. Rev 5:2. Aune considers John's term "sitting on the throne" a circumlocution that avoids direct mention of the name of God (Aune 52b, p. 565). The term "worthy" appears frequently as a description of the Roman emperors or others holding high office: "Since the term has no great importance in the LXX and Jewish literature, interpreting the concept primarily against the Graeco-Roman background is even more justifiable" (Laszlo Gallusz, *The Throne Motif in the Book of Revelation* [London: Bloomsbury, 2014], p. 147).

109. The word ὁ ὤν appears in the text repeatedly in the phrase: "the one who is, was, and is coming," known as the *Dreizeitenformel* ("three times forumulation").

110. Echoing the *imperium sine fin* (empire without end) claimed by Augustus, the elders sing: "The kingdom of this world (ἡ βασιλεία τοῦ κόσμου) has become the kingdom of our lord, and of his anointed one; and he will reign for ever and ever" (καὶ βασιλεύσει εἰς τοὺς αἰῶνας τῶν αἰώνων)—Rev 11:15; cf. Rev 4:8–11; see Robyn J. Whitaker, *Ekphrasis, Vision, and Persuasion in the Book of Revelation* (Tübingen: Mohr Siebeck, 2015), pp. 129ff. On imperial Rome as eternal, see Kenneth J. Pratt, "Rome as Eternal," *Journal of the History of Ideas* 26, no. 1 (January 1965): 25–44. Pratt observes the prevalence of the sun-moon symbol (also in Rev 12:1): "Coins issued by Vespasian, Titus, and Trajan, among others, depict the personification Eternity holding the sun and the moon" (ibid., p. 29).

111. David E. Aune, "The Influence of Roman Imperial Court Ceremonial on the Apocalypse of John" (1983), reprinted in *Apocalypticism, Prophecy and Magic in Early Christianity*, pp. 99–100. The imperial court was not an official institution but an informal extension of

the residence of the emperor that acquired, by the end of the first century, the sense of a "Palace" (*Palatium*).

112. The wording here is important. It is not (*pace* Whitaker) that John's descriptions are a parody of imperial worship but, rather, the reverse: imperial worship is a parody of the worship of the one true God (see Whitaker, *Ekphrasis, Vision, and Persuasion in the Book of Revelation*, pp. 128–129).

113. Zimmermann emphasizes that the use of pagan formulations places John's text (the *Johannes-Offenbarung*) in dialogue with others; it is inclusive in address, yet adamantly "polemical"in its insistence that emperor worship is not justified. Christiane Zimmermann, *Die Namen des Vaters: Studien zu ausgewählten neutestamentlichen Gottesbezeichnungen vor ihrem frühjüdischen und paganen Sprachhorizont* (Leiden: Brill, 2007), p. 265. The imperial term παντοκράτορ is limited in New Testament use almost solely to the book of Revelation (ibid., p. 271); Philo uses it in only three places (ibid., p. 252), and Josephus only once (ibid., p. 254): God is not a competitor ruler to be compared with earthly rulers, who are "precisely not eternal," but rather, as creator of the cosmos, a transcendent force with life-creating and life-renewing power (ibid., pp. 267ff).

114. Jonathan Z. Smith, "Wisdom and Apocalypse," in *Map Is Not Territory: Studies in the History of Religions* (Chicago: University of Chicago Press, 1993), p. 81.

115. See above, chapter 1, pp. 15–18. The *Roman History* of Dio Cassius (b. Anatolia 155 CE) is our source for this information regarding the history of the cults as beginning, by the emperor's permission, in "preeminent cities" in the province of Asia and spreading from there to other Roman provinces, whereas in the Roman "capital itself, and the rest of Italy none of the emperors, no matter how worthy of fame, has dared to do this" (Dio Cassius 51.20.6–9). Yet this distinction has been challenged, and just how widespread was the deification of a living emperor is now a matter of debate. Aune writes: "Even in Rome . . . claims to divinity and the encouragement of divine honors were consistently part of the imperial program beginning with Julius Caesar himself" (Aune, "The Influence of Roman Imperial Court Ceremonial," p. 111). For Italy during the Republic and early Empire, see Ittai Gradel, *Emperor Worship and Roman Religion* (Oxford: Clarendon Press, 2002). Dio Cassius' distinction feeds into the epistemological bifurcations of Greek versus oriental, rational versus emotional, or east versus west, whereas contemporary historians, "rather than separating the two worlds," consider it "more fruitful to find their common features" ("Closing Thoughts," in *More Than Men, Less Than Gods: Studies on Royal Cult and Imperial Worship*, ed. Panagiotis P. Iossif, Andrzej S. Chankowski, and Catharine C. Lorber [Leuven: Peeters, 2011], p. 705).

116. Where archaeological evidence for each city has not been discovered, the depictions on local coinage, as well as documents and inscriptions, provide the proof. Note that John's "letters" were themselves an appropriation of the imperial practice of sending letters to provincial cities, written in *koine* as the official form of address (Aune 52a, p. 126). Certain of these imperial letters (like the imperial promise of the city's "freedom"—see below) were carved into the city's archive wall.

117. The funding for this temple (the archaeological site of which has not been found) was province-wide. Naming Rome a goddess was a provincial invention, in accord with the practice of anthropomorphizing their cities both as divine beings and as protectors (*neokoroi*) of the temples to them. It is worth noting that 30 years earlier, the city had offered to build a "temple and monument" to the philosopher Cicero and his brother Quintus who had been Roman governor of the province: Barbara Burrell, *Neokoroi: Greek Cities and Roman Emperors* (Leiden: Brill, 2004), p. 312. Hence a human ruler's imperial status was not the only prompt for cultic worship. (Cicero refused the honor.)

118. Burrell tells us that eleven cities competed with one another for this provincial honor (Burrell, *Neokoroi*, p. 119). Smyrna had established even before the Caesars a cult to the goddess of Roma, and was the first to do so.

119. An earlier request made by Ephesus was refused, as this port city was already "known throughout the world" with the title "neo-koros" (temple caretaker) as the cult city of the goddess Artemis/Diana: Steven J. Friesen, *Twice Neokoros: Ephesus, Asia and the Cult of the Flavian Imperial Family* (Leiden: Brill, 1993), p. 54. Burrell discusses evidence for construction of an imperial cult in Ephesus: "If that was so, it was a particularly unfortunate time for the establishment of such a temple. Some two years later, in June 68, Nero was declared a public enemy by the Senate and killed himself, after which his name, not to mention his cult, was condemned," although the effect of a *damnatio memoriae* on imperial cults might have varied, as Burrell notes: "Individual cities could be haphazard in their approach to the condemnation, especially in early cases such as Nero's" (Burrell, *Neokoroi*, p. 60 and 60n).

120. Municipal cults did not need imperial or provincial approval. "They could be instituted by local initiative and were funded by local and private sources, rather than a province-wide tax. The city might send notification or even an embassy to Rome to announce the establishment of a temple, but this was not a requirement." Steven J. Friesen, *Imperial Cults and the Apocalypse of John: Reading Revelation in the Ruins* (New York: Oxford University Press, 2001), p. 59. "Towns and individuals may have set up altars or statues to the emperor without even bothering to seek permission of a governor, much less the nod of authorities at Rome" (Burrell, *Neokoroi*, p. 3).

121. See chapter 1. The kingdom of Lydia became a satrap (province) of the Persian Empire in the sixth century BCE. "Sardis's favorable positioning at the crossing of five roadways [connecting, among other cities, Philadelphia, Laodicea, Thyatira, Smyrna, and Ephesus] . . . made it a lively commercial center"; it had as well "a significant Jewish community—the social ingredients for emerging Christianity. Yet Paul makes no reference to a church at Sardis, nor does the writer of Acts, nor does Ignatius." Leonard L. Thompson, *The Book of Revelation: Apocalypse and Empire* (New York: Oxford University Press, 1990), p. 124.

122. "Under Caligula, the Philadelphians called themselves 'Neocaesareia' on their coins" (Friesen, *Imperial Cults and the Apocalypse of John*, p. 157n). Under Domitian, the Philadelphians became part of the network of Ephesus, setting up in that city an inscription which reads: "The demos of the Flavian Philadelphians honored the neokorate demos of the

Ephesians that is devoted to Sebastos and adorns Asia, because of piety toward the Sebastoi, and (because of) kinship to them and ancestral affection" (ibid., p. 157). In (Phrygian?) Laodicea, although no temple ruins have been found, this temple image appears on the coins (ibid., pp. 61–62).

123. Friesen notes: "The third provincial cult of Asia under Domitian was an unprecedented attempt to build a network, rather than a center, of provincial worship" (Friesen, *Twice Neokoros*, p. 155). Philadelphia and Aphrodisias were part of this network.

124. There were several cities in Anatolia bearing that name, which had been given by the Selucid ruler Antiochus II to honor his wife Laodice. Another, the "Phrygian" Laodicea (Laodicea Combusta) was also in the province of Asia, and possessed a major imperial cult and temple (see Burrell, *Neokoroi*, pp. 119–125). It has been assumed, however, that John was writing to the "Lydian" Laodicea in the Lycus river valley; it is known to have possessed a significant Jewish community, hence a potentially Christian one; more important, it was visited by Paul and is a few miles from Colossae, which is thought to have received two letters of Paul, the Colossians (in which Paul mentions sending a letter to the Laodiceans [not extant]) and Philemon, which speaks of a runaway slave who becomes a fellow worker with Paul. Sardis, important for John, is not mentioned by Paul, indicating that such mention alone does not seem determining (Thompson, *The Book of Revelation: Apocalypse and Empire*, pp.120–121). Friesen discusses a coin indicating a municipal cult in "Laodicea" (Friesen, *Imperial Cults and the Apocalypse of John*, p. 61); yet the identification of the coin by the British Museum lists it as Phrygian (BM Phrygia 229). I assume this apparent discrepancy between a Phrygian coin and a Lydian Laodicea has a clarification known to the experts, if not to me.

125. Thyatira (present day Akhisar) was known for its guilds—of bakers, shoemakers, smiths, slave merchants, and especially dyers of fabrics, including the royal purple; guild members shared in communal meals, thereby participating in the rituals of emperor worship. Thompson notes that partaking in such meals would have been idolatrous for a Jewish guild member. Paul visited Thyatira; he would not have insisted on avoidance of this civic practice (Leonard L. Thompson, *Revelation* [Nashville: Abingdon Press, 1998], pp. 74–77). Burton writes: "Caligula was worshipped as the Sun in Thyatira" (Henry Fairfield Burton, "The Worship of the Roman Emperors," *Biblical World* 40, no. 2 [August 1912]: 83–84).

126. Thus the existence of a cult does not explain why John chose these cities to address. Concerning the seven cities, Aune writes that there is "no obvious reason" for John's choice (Aune 52a, p. 130), although there is much speculation, based on the specifics of John's addresses to each of the cities; Aune speculates that sending letters may have been only as a counter to imperial letters, while the number seven, repeated multiple times in Revelation, has symbolic significance, as we have seen in chapter 3. Note that the magical meaning of the number seven was widespread. Herodotus (4.150) provides a story of Cyrene, founded by the city of Thera (on Santorini), after it suffered a seven-year famine in its seven villages for ignoring an oracle telling them to found a colony (Alan M. Greaves, *The Land of*

Ionia: Society and Economy in the Archaic Period [Chichester, UK: Wiley-Blackwell, 2010], pp. 129–130).

127. Price provides a map of the sites of 199 imperial cults identified in Anatolia/Asia Minor: S. R. F. Price, *Rituals and Power: The Roman Imperial Cult in Asia Minor* (Cambridge: Cambridge University Press, 1984), p. xxv. On the provincial cult to Augustus at Ancyra, see Burrell, *Neokoroi*, pp. 166–174. The Galatians were descendants of nomadic Celts migrating southward from the Danubian basin, who devastated Macedonia in the third century BCE. "The Galatian invaders eventually crossed into Asia and settled on the high Anatolian plateau around Ankara, where they continued to cause trouble for generations to come." Peter Thonemann, *The Hellenistic Age* (Oxford: Oxford University Press, 2016), p. 33.

128. Note, again, that modern politics enters into the way one chooses to name the peninsula. Turkey's nationalist claims against Armenia have perverted the ancient term Anatolia, which means "the east," but was used against Armenians to claim "eastern Anatolia" for Turkey. The name "Asia Minor" avoids this problem, but as it was not a term in circulation at the time, we will use instead Anatolia, making no distinctions between eastern and western regions. The modern desire to map the location of ancient cities confronts obstacles: we have no maps and must rely on written sources. Moreover, the provinces were not marked by boundaries. The cities that belonged to a province changed frequently depending on the politics of regional rulers and the outcomes of continuous wars. The boundary demarcation between the province of Asia and that of Galatea to the east of it, for example, cannot be determined definitively.

129. "Equating a city or a people with a temple official is not a far fetched comparison. Greek cities were often personified, usually as females; the title metropolis exalts them as mothers, and a few [at times Ionopolis, Syracuse, Ephesos, Miletos] were even called nurses" (Burrell, *Neokoroi*, p. 6).

130. Burrell has written the definitive account of the *Neokoroi* in the eastern provinces. She explains the word νεωκόρος, comprised of ναος = temple, a built structure or house for a god, while "the '-koros' is more problematic"; it means "'one who nourishes, maintains,' from which the particular meaning 'sweeper' is a secondary derivation. In addition, archaeological finds indicate that '-koros' appears in Greek as early as the Mycenean period: linear B tablets mention a 'da-ko-ro' and a 'da-mo-ko-ro.' Neither is a sweeper; in fact, both appear to be high officials" (Burrell, *Neokoroi*, p. 4). Burrell notes also an expanded use of the term: in Egypt, "the cult of Serapis had neokoroi, both at Alexandria and elsewhere"; "Also in Egypt there were neokoroi of temples of the god Augustus at Alexandria and [the Egyptian port] Canopus" (ibid., p. 5). Moreover, the two authors central to our account, Josephus and Philo, "transferred the term 'neokoros' to the context of their own religion. Philo . . . used it specifically for the tribe of Levi, especially in their functions as priests (under the supervision of the high priest), guardians, gatekeepers, purifiers, and general caretakers of the temple at Jerusalem"; Josephus in his *Jewish Antiquities* "called certain functionaries who were responsible for the purification of the Jerusalem temple

neokoroi," writing about a time, however, when "no temple yet stood, implying that the Jews' ward over their temple (which he indeed called 'naos' elsewhere) was a spiritual one" (ibid., p. 5).

131. Burrell writes: "There is currently a scholarly tug-of-war over whether in Italy and the western provinces the living emperor was rarely, or constantly, treated as a god" (Burrell, *Neokoroi*, p. 359). For the western provinces, see the series *The Imperial Cult in the Latin West: Studies in the Ruler Cult of the Western Provinces of the Roman Empire*, vol. 3: *Provincial Cult*, especially part 1: *Institution and Evolution*, by Duncan Fishwick (Leiden: Brill, 2002). For the Italian mainland, see Gradel, *Emperor Worship and Roman Religion*.

132. "Scholars have always seen the constitution of Rome, where the living emperor, though occupying an exalted position, did not receive state divinity, as the natural model, and the divine worship of the living emperor as the aberration craving explanation," writes Gradel, who sums up in his own work the revisionist position: "I have argued that the divine worship of the ruling emperor of Rome was far from confined to synchophantic Greeks or rude barbarians recently brought under the sway of Rome. The phenomenon was found all over the Roman empire, including Italy and Rome itself; it was absent from one sphere only, namely, the constitutional one of the state cult in Rome. This image rather suggests divine honors as one of the 'normal' responses to imperial power, and their absence from the state cult as the aberration, the exception in need of explaining" (Gradel, *Emperor Worship and Roman Religion*, p. 264).

133. Gradel, *Emperor Worship and Roman Religion*, p. 262; "whether imperial deification fits our mental categories, or the way we accordingly happen to structure our academic disciplines, is not really the point" (ibid.).

134. For this discussion, see Friesen, *Imperial Cults and the Apocalypse of John*, p. 114.

135. Price, *Rituals and Power*, p. 9.

136. Friesen, *Twice Neokoros*, p. 152.

137. Price, *Rituals and Power*, p. 19. He continues: "the preoccupation with a distinction between religion and politics" is "a perpetuation of the perspective engendered by the struggles and eventual triumph of the Christian Church" (ibid.). Price is skeptical of the conventional narrative that Christians rejected emperor worship on rational grounds, as an early chapter in the developmental story that superimposes enlightenment reason on history, privileging Christianity as critical of king-worship, whereas non-Europeans, and especially Africans, were slow to give up traditions of "divine kings" (ibid., pp. 235–236) Price's approach, indebted to anthropological methods, marks a "turning point" in the study of the imperial cults (Gallusz, *The Throne Motif in the Book of Revelation*, p. 280); Burrell states that Price's "observations inform my work everywhere" (*Neokoroi*, p. 1n).

138. Gallusz, *The Throne Motif in the Book of Revelation*, p. 275, who cites as well Friesen and Price. On the necessity of seeing the cults as part of a "multiplex phenomenon," counted "among the various instruments that served the political, social and economic system of the Roman empire," see Fernando Lozano, "The Creation of Imperial Gods: Not Only

Imposition versus Spontaneity," in Iossif et al., *More Than Men, Less Than Gods*, p. 495. Lozano comments on the mediating role of local elites, "who were admired by the masses," in producing affirmation of imperial power generally via the cults (ibid., pp. 483–485).

139. Gallusz notes that to presume that only the upper classes were involved in displays of loyalty to the rulers manifests a "severely limited understanding of the nature of the cults" (*The Throne Motif in the Book of Revelation*, p. 277n). See also Friesen, *Imperial Cults and the Apocalypse of John*, pp. 5–22; Thompson, *The Book of Revelation: Apocalypse and Empire*, p. 159; Price, *Rituals and Power*, pp. 101–114.

140. "Old festivals were transformed by adding a dimension of sacrifices and prayers offered to the emperors," involving "not only the elite, but the whole city" (Gallusz, *The Throne Motif in the Book of Revelation*, p. 277). Ando emphasizes the unifying aspect of the imperial cult as a province-wide practice (Clifford Ando, *Imperial Ideology and Provincial Loyalty in the Roman Empire* [Berkeley: University of California Press, 2000], pp. 23–24 and passim).

141. Augustus was made Pontifex Maximus ("highest priest") in 12 BCE, thereby receiving official responsibility for the Roman calendar. Augustus refined his father's calendar by establishing a leap year every four years; he then arranged for the construction in Rome of a solar meridian (not, as previously believed, a sundial, which measures the hours; the meridian instead tracks the seasons) "so that all could see that the civil calendar stayed in harmony with the progress of the sun throughout the year." Peter Heslin, "Domitian and the So-Called Horologium Augusti," *Journal of Roman Studies* 97 (2007): 6. Pliny the Elder in his *Natural History* (dedicated CE 77–78 to Titus, who by fixing a slight irregularity showed himself the master of time) described it correctly as a meridian, not a sundial (ibid. p. 9).

142. Text 458 1, *Orientis Graeci Inscriptiones Selectae* (hereafter *OGIS*); trans. in Friesen, *Imperial Cults and the Apocalypse of John*, p. 33. Friesen paraphrases: "the world was in disarray and headed for ruin until Augustus restored and transformed" it; "[t]he old world was given a fresh start, a new origin (ἀφορμή)"; hence the celebration "calculating time to have begun with his birth." Friesen was the first to emphasize the significance of this document when reading the book of Revelation. We follow him closely here, and have used his translations of the inscriptions given in *OGIS*.

143. "The mesh between civil and natural time that the reformed calendar provided was one that had never before been seen in the Mediterranean, and never before aimed at. No civil calendar in the Mediterranean world before 1 January 45 BCE had pretended to approximate a harmony with the high degree of astronomical accuracy that scholars had achieved in their construction of observation-based calendars." Denis Feeney, *Caesar's Calendar: Ancient Time and the Beginnings of History* (Berkeley: University of California Press, 2007), p. 193. It was through his liason with Cleopatra that Julius Caesar came to adopt the Egyptian annual solar calendar of 365¼ days.

144. *OGIS*, trans. Friesen, *Imperial Cults and the Apocalypse of John*, p. 33. For the translation of this specific date from the first-century calendar to today's, see Feeney, *Caesar's Calendar*, p. 154. For the backward counting from October to this date, see ibid., p. 152.

145. *OGIS* (text 458.1), trans. Friesen, *Imperial Cults and the Apocalypse of John*, p. 33.

146. The imposition of the Julian calendar produced uniformity, and yet local distinctions persisted, including the names for months (given in Friesen, *Imperial Cults and the Apocalypse of John*, p. 35). Friesen writes: "The calendar reform was not an attempt to replace the calendars of the cities with the Roman calendar. Rather, a uniform system for reckoning time was added to older ones and all appear to have coexisted" (ibid., pp. 35–36). Feeney concurs: "many other civil calendars remained quite happily in place for as long as the Empire lasted"; these included, importantly, the lunar calendars, as well as the seven-day week (Feeney, *Caesar's Calendar*, p. 198).

147. *OGIS* (text 458.1), trans. Friesen, *Imperial Cults and the Apocalypse of John*, p. 33. "Forever" here is *aiōn*/αἰών, connoting eras (or even levels) of historical time, cf. "for ever and ever" (εἰς τοὺς αἰῶνας τῶν αἰώνων) in Rev 10:6. The document concludes: "I will command that the decree, engraved on a stele, be set up in the temple [of Augustus and Roma in Pergamon that was constructed in 29 BCE], having arranged for the edict to be written in both languages [Latin and *koine*]" (cited in Friesen, *Imperial Cults and the Apocalypse of John*, p. 33). Ruins of this temple have not been found; it is known through coins (see illustrations from British Museum in ibid., pp. 29–30). The subsequent decree enacting this winning proposal stated that to honor Augustus, time (*chronos*—i.e., measurable, chronic time as opposed to *kairos*; see *OGIS*, Friesen, p. 55, line 56) was to be calculated to have begun at his birth. Note that the 365¼-day Julian calendar indeed had a high degree of harmony with astronomical accuracy (Feeney, *Caesar's Calendar*, p. 193).

148. "[N]o emperor visited the area in the whole of the first century" (Price, *Rituals and Power*, p. 1). Unlike provincial *ethne* elsewhere, Asia was ruled by no client king.

149. Among the statues of 50 conquered *ethne*, depicted as individual women in the Sebasteion of Aphrodisias, the names of Egypt, Armenia, Britannia, and Judaea are inscribed at the base; the Hellenes of Asia are not represented. R. R. R. Smith, "Simulacra Gentium: The Ethne from the Sebasteion at Aphrodisias," *Journal of Roman Studies* 78 (1988): 50–77.

150. Vergil's poem begins: "Arms, and the man I sing, who, forc'd by fate, / And haughty Juno's unrelenting hate, / Expell'd and exil'd, left the Trojan shore. / . . . / From whence the race of Alban fathers come, / and the long glories of majestic Rome." (Vergil, *Aeneid*, Book I, lines 1–3, 9–10, trans. John Dryden, Internet Classic Library: http://classics.mit.edu/Virgil/aeneid.html.) The *Aeneid* relates the founding of Rome by Romulus and Remus, descendants of Aeneas, who were nursed by a female wolf. Romulus killed Remus, founding Rome through an act of fratricide. The wives of the early Romans were the kidnapped Sabine women.

151. The "Athenocentric" stories of Ionian migration generated in the fifth century BCE are now disputed as having been promoted by Athens as head of the Athens-controlled Delian

League and Athenian Empire and inscribed on the Athenian tribute lists (Greaves, *The Land of Ionia*, p. 11).

152. Greaves notes that whereas Herodotus in the *Histories* (book 5) calls them simply Ionians, he has chosen the term Ionian League "to avoid confusion with the Ionians as an ethnic or cultural grouping" (Greaves, *The Land of Ionia*, p. 219n).

153. The term colony is commonly used, but as Greaves notes, it is problematic: "The Greek language distinguished between two types of colonies: *apoikia* (an away-settlement) and *emporion* (a trading post). It is not always possible to differentiate the two archaeologically. How can one distinguish between a settlement where a farming community also engages in trade and a trading post where the traders also farm? For the purposes of this discussion, the intentionally non-specific English word 'colony' will be used, even though it must be recognized that this term carries some unhelpful meaning in the English language." Greaves, *The Land of Ionia*, p. 120.

154. This (to us) anomalous practice of freedom through submission dates back to Persian protection of Anatolia (the "king's peace"): "This practice is old—the Greeks and the Romans also used the slogans of freedom to play on the internal conflicts of their enemies. They did it specifically for the purpose of weakening and breaking them from within, claiming to act in defense of the 'independence' and 'freedom' of the 'oppressed.' Rome concluded a similar treaty with the Jews, offering them Roman support against the 'oppressing' Selucid kingdom in the 160s [BCE, during the Maccabean revolt]." Sviatoslav Dmitriev, *The Greek Slogan of Freedom and Early Roman Politics in Greece* (Oxford: Oxford University Press, 2011), p. 378 and passim. Dmitriev, only somewhat anachronistically, insists on a modern-day comparison: the cold war logic of the *pax Americana*, like the *pax Romana*, promoted the "common peace" and "mutual protection" in a way that hid imperial pretensions (ibid., p. 377). Dmitriev does not mention its appropriation by the American founding fathers, who praised the Hellenistic *koina* as a model for the federation of American states. Their idealization of this form was based on Polybius' praise of the *koinon* on the Greek mainland known as the Achaean League.

155. This shared culture, described as identifying a Greek *ethnos* (Burrell, *Neokoroi*, p. 344), was produced by origin stories that need to be distinguished from historical fact: "Not only had much time passed between the putative foundation of the earliest Ionian colonies and the later writers who provided their foundation stories, there had also been conscious historical reinvention of those stories by writers and the communities themselves to meet the needs of their immediate political and social context" (Greaves, *The Land of Ionia*, pp. 127–128).

156. Burrell, *Neokoroi*, p. 2.

157. This area, ruled from the city of Sardis, was the farthest outpost of the Selucid ruler Antiochus III, whose empire, which grew from the Hellenic divisions of Alexander the Great, was thenceforth reduced to Syria, Mesopotamia, and western Iran (Thonemann, *The Hellenistic Age*, p. 37). Thonemann emphasizes the lightness of Selucid control. For a discussion of

debates over why the Romans did not annex this wealthy territory outright, see Philip Kay, "What Did the Attalids Ever Do for Us?," in *Attalid Asia Minor: Money, International Relations, and the State*, ed. Peter Thonemann (Oxford: Oxford University Press, 2013), pp. 21–48.

158. See Lionel Casson, *Libraries of the Ancient World* (New Haven: Yale University Press, 2001).

159. "[T]he Attalids systematically devolved the political administration and economic exploitation of their realm to pre-existing local power-holders and semi-independent urban communities; where such cities did not already exist, they were simply created from scratch." Peter Thonemann, "The Attalid State, 188–133 BC," in Thonemann, *Attalid Asia Minor*, pp. 42–43.

160. "In 167 BC, during the war against the Galatians, Eumenes II presented himself to the *koinon* of the Ionians as the 'common benefactor' [κοινός εὐεργέτις] of the Greeks, [who] 'faced many great battles against the barbarians, displaying all zeal and care to make sure that the inhabitants of the Greek cities should always live in peace and enjoy the best state of affairs.'" Selene Psoma, "War or Trade? Attic-Weight Tetradrachms from Second-Century BC Attalid Asia Minor in Seleukid Syria after the Peace of Apameia and Their Historical Context," in Thonemann, *Attalid Asia Minor*, p. 286. Psoma continues: "The king's letter was erected at Miletos, the most significant city of the *koinon*. Miletos was an autonomous city and [citing R. E. Allen, *The Attalid Kingdom* (1983)] it was 'at Miletos that Eumenes was almost certainly called a god in his lifetime'" (ibid., p. 286).

161. Rev 2:13.

162. Pagels, *Revelations*, p. 11. On the imagistic propaganda of the Augustan Roman Empire generally, see Paul Zanker, *the Power of Images in the Age of Augustus* (Ann Arbor: University of Michigan Press, 1990).

163. Price, *Rituals and Power*, p. 27.

164. The find was made by the archaeologist Kenan Erim, who continued his work at the excavation until his death in 1990. His successor was the Oxford classicist R. R. R. Smith. The ongoing work of the project is under the auspices of New York University. See the website: https://www.nyu.edu/projects/aphrodisias/home.ti.htm. "An Aphrodisian by the name of Zoilos, who was perhaps inherited as a slave from the household of [Julius] Caesar and later freed by Octavian, played a major role in keeping the city loyal to the cause of Caesar's family"; thereafter, according to documents inscribed on the city's Archive Wall, the city was granted freedom, non-taxable status and inviolability for the city's sanctuary to Aphrodite, and Zoilos was praised by Octavian as his "esteemed friend" (Kenan T. Erim, *Aphrodisias: City of Venus Aphrodite*, intro. John Julius Norwich [New York: Facts on File Publications, 1986], p. 30).

165. Smith writes: "the attitudes to the Roman emperor found here were common to the other cities of Asia Minor in the first century A.D., but the grand and elaborate manner in which

they are expressed in the Sebasteion is so far unique." R. R. R. Smith, "The Imperial Reliefs from the Sebasteion at Aphrodisias," *Journal of Roman Studies* 77 (1987): 138. Aphrodisias was not a *neokoros* city, as it did not have its own provincial cult, but it contributed financially to the provincial temple of the Sebastoi in Ephesus, at the site of which was inscribed "to the emperor Domitian" (his personal names were later erased following his *damnatio memoriae*). Friesen translates from the inscription: "'The demos of the Aphrodesians, devoted to Caesar, being free and autonomous from the beginning [ʼἀπʼ ἀρχῆς] by the grace [χάριτι] of the Sebastoi, set up (this statue) by its own grace because of its reverence toward the Sebastoi and its goodwill toward the neokorate city of the Ephesians, (because of) Asia's common temple of the Sebastoi in Ephesus'" (Friesen, *Twice Neokoros*, p. 33).

166. "The themes of the reliefs taken together were broadly these: the Roman empire, the Greek world within it, and the imperial family" (Smith, "The "The Imperial Reliefs from the Sebasteion at Aphrodisias," p. 95). This idea was "captured in the phrase of one of the inscriptions which dedicated the building 'to the Olympian god-emperors [tois theois Sebastois Olympiois]" (http://www.nyu.edu/projects/aphrodisias/seb.sculpt.ti.htm). This is the official NYU website for the project (see also note 164). For scholarly publications devoted to the site, see the bilingual book *Afrodisyas Sebasteion/Aphrodisias/Sebasteion*, ed. Mesut Ilgım; and Erim, *Aphrodisias*.

167. Smith, "The Imperial Reliefs from the Sebasteion at Aphrodisias," p. 97.

168. Smith, "The Imperial Reliefs from the Sebasteion at Aphrodisias," p. 97.

169. Smith first presumed this emperor was Augustus, identifying the panel as "Augustus by Land and Sea" (Smith, "The Imperial Reliefs from the Sebasteion at Aphrodisias," p. 104). Subsequent identifications of this figure, on the basis of hair style and portraiture, are of Claudius. The same metaphor is found in Philo of Alexandria (Philo, *Flaccus*, 104): the "house of Augustus" is "ruler over land and sea" (ibid.).

170. "The reasons for the long-term vitality of this fluid and elaborate system of cults lie in its capacity to exploit the competitive values of the urban elite. Within the framework of collective decision-making by the council and people, there was naturally room for initiatives by its prominent individuals . . . [who] could give the city a sum of money for the purpose of the cult" (Price, *Rituals and Power*, p. 62).

171. Rev 21:27: "καὶ οὐ μὴ εἰσέλθῃ εἰς αὐτὴν πᾶν κοινόν καὶ ποιῶνβδέλυγμα καὶ ψεῦδος." Here is the New International Version (NIV) translation: "Nothing impure will ever enter it, nor will anyone who does what is shameful or deceitful." On the difficulties of translation of this word, which appears only once in the text, see Aune 52c, pp. 1174–1175. Aune writes: "The term *koinos* used only here in Revelation, means 'profane' or 'ritually unclean,'" and is a close synonym of "ἀκάθαρτος" (Aune 52c, p. 1174). Aune derives this reading as a reference to the "notion of purity and sanctity of the temple," that "was occasionally extended to include the entire city of Jerusalem as well. Isaiah 52:1 anticipates the day when

"no uncircumcised or unclean person" (LXX: ἀκάθαρτος, which occurs in Rev 16:13; 17:4; 18:2) "can enter Jerusalem" (ibid.) The translation, therefore of *koinon* depends on routing the philological connections through the Hebrew word for impurity (טומאה). Aune notes the alternative interpretation that understands this word in a moral sense, connected to illicit forms of sexual intercourse (ibid., p. 1175).

172. Two terms, *pornai* and *amart*, will be considered in chapter 5 below.

173. "[K]oinon was used to designate all kinds of associations of a number of individuals, from small private clubs to entire states, so that it is basically used for everything that is common to two or more people; it distinguishes in this way between matters concerning the 'community' and those concerning single individuals. The theory that *koinon* was used to designate federal states as opposed to other forms of states finds no support in the ancient sources. . . . [T]he term *koinon* seems rather to have designated the common institutions and could apparently only in a less technical usage mean the 'state' as a whole, but in no case does it serve as an indication of the form of government. . . . [T]he meaning 'state' for *koinon* is probably only a secondary development from the primary meaning of 'common institution/affairs.' . . . [These included] associations centered around the cult of a deity whom they worshipped." Thomas Corsten, "*Koinon*," in *The Encyclopedia of Ancient History*, ed. Roger S. Bagnall et al. (Malden, MA: Wiley-Blackwell, 2012), pp. 3798–3799.

174. This wording is repeated twice, in Rev 20:12 and again in Rev 22:12. That salvation pre-exists a person's life is a Calvinist reading that might find support in Revelation's reference to those who have been "sealed" as the "slaves of God" (Rev 7:1–8); see also, regarding the "slaves of God," that God's name is on their foreheads (Rev 22:4, 6, 9). But even this distinction is not an index of collective identity. In the book of Revelation, the enemies of God are personal (ἐχθροὶ: Rev 11:12), not generic (πολέμιος).

175. See David Frankfurter, "Jews or Not? Reconstructing the 'Other' in Rev 2:9 and 3:9," *Harvard Theological Review* 94: 4 (2001): 403–425, here pp. 410–412.

176. Food is mentioned (Rev 2:14 and 2:20) within the larger meaning of participating in the koinon celebrations: in Rev 2:14, to commit "fornication" (πορνεῦσαι) and "eat idol sacrifices (ϕαγεῖν εἰδωλόθυτα). The equivalence of these terms is discussed below in chapter 5.

177. In the second century, when Christians lived in fear of persecution, chiliast interpretations of John's revelation focused on a belief in Christ's return to reign on earth for a thousand years (χίλια = 1,000, see Rev 20:4); with the Christianization of the Roman Emperor, this shifted. The emperor's task was now to spread the faith, providing time for universal exposure to Christianity and with it, the salvation for all who came to believe.

178. Martin Luther, "Of the Antichrist," *Table Talk*, CCCCXXVI, trans. William Hazlitt (Grand Rapids, MI: Christian Classics Ethereal Library, 2004), http://www.ntslibrary.com/PDF%20Books/Luther%20Table%20Talk.pdf.

179. Rev 10:1–6. I have modified the translation (in NIV) of "ὅτι χρόνος οὐκέτι ἔσται" from "there will be no more delay" to "there shall be time no longer." Elaborations of the imperial image are references to Old Testament imagery.

180. Philo had described Augustus as worthy of the name "god" (*theos*), when he ruled well and order was maintained. Josephus wrote that the victories of Vespasian were proof of God's affirmation of Roman rule.

181. "In John's system, then, there was no legitimate place for earthly empire. His religious criticism was specifically aimed at Roman imperialism, but the character of his critique had broader implications. John was not just anti-Roman; he was anti-empire." Friesen, *Imperial Cults and the Apocalypse of John*, p. 208.

182. Cf. the inscription found in Palaiphalos, Cyprus, of the oath to Tiberius, in which allegiance to this emperor is sworn by "the god Caesar Augustus" and "Roma the everlasting." T. B. Mitford, "A Cypriot Oath of Allegiance to Tiberius," *Journal of Roman Studies* 50 (1960): 75. The oath is to Tiberius' entire family and any sons he might have, reckoning the same friends and foes, and requiring "obedience," loyalty," and "worship . . . alike by land and sea" (ibid., p. 76). Such oaths ended with the *ara/ἀρά*, a curse to fall on the oath-taker and his descendants if the oath was broken. The absolute loyalty to the emperor required by the oath, taken yearly in Rome, was criticized by Tacitus (*Annals* 1.7) as "slavery" (*servitium*; cf. the discussion of *doulos* below), however hypocritical and self-serving such flattery of power may have been. And yet, "strongly linked from the beginning" with the emperor cult, the oath remained "a vital indicator of the perpetuation of the principate" (B. F. Harris, "Oaths of Allegiance to Caesar," *Prudentia* 14, no. 2 [1982]: 112, 122). Harris observes: "It cannot have been easy therefore to disengage oneself openly from all recognition of the temporal power and the divinity of the emperor. . . . Thus the oath of allegiance, like the rites of the imperial cult, remained a yardstick of conformity with the regime" (ibid., p. 122).

183. Modifications in contemporary translations acknowledge this limitation, and have settled on a bifurcation in translation that has its own problems, given the fact that no such distinction exists in Greek, or Hebrew or Latin. The NIV translation of *doulos* in the book of Revelation varies according to context: "servant" or "fellow-servant" of God or the prophets (Rev 1:6; Rev 6:11; Rev 7:3; Rev 11:18; Rev 15:3; Rev 15:10; Rev 22:3, 6, 9) but "slave" when paired with "freemen" (Rev 6:15; Rev 13:16; Rev 19:18). For Paul (Colossians 3:18–4:1; Ephesians 6:5–8; cf. 1 Peter 2:18–25), see Clarice J. Martin's interpretation in "The *Haustafeln* (Household Codes) in African American Biblical Interpretation: 'Free Slaves' and 'Subordinate Women,'" in *Stony the Road We Trod: African American Biblical Interpretation*, ed. Cain Hope Felder (Minneapolis: Fortress Press, 1991), pp. 206–231.

184. Paul, Colossians 3:22, again Ephesians 6:5.

185. In the Septuagint, where the Hebrew word '*ebed* is translated, the Septuagint varies among several terms: *pais* is most common in the Pentateuch; in other Septuagint books, *pais* (which can mean child) and *doulos* (slave/servant) are used interchangeably (in Isaiah and Psalms *doulos* is favored). For a detailed account of these (and other related) terms in multiple languages see Benjamin G. Wright III, "'*Ebed/Doulos*: Terms and Social Status in the Meeting of Hebrew Biblical and Hellenistic Roman Culture," in *Semeia: Slavery in Text and Interpretation,* vol. 84, ed. Allen Dwight Callahan, Richard A. Horsley, and Abraham Smith (Atlanta: Society of Biblical Literature, 1998), pp. 83–151. "Of close to 800 uses"

of '*ebed* in the Septuagint, "almost 770 are rendered either by *doulos* or *pais*" (ibid., p. 92). Wright concludes (*pace* Walther Zimmerli) that a distinction in meanings of these terms "does not hold"; they are "roughly" or "relatively synonymous," specifically in the sense that "to be a 'slave of God' is a good thing" (ibid., p. 93). By the first century, "Jews took over the Greek and Latin vocabulary for slaves" (ibid., p. 84); exemplary are Philo, who speaks critically of being a "slave" (*doulos*) to one's passions, and Josephus, who uses *doulos* in the Masada story, where *pais* means child, but *douleia* means slavery (ibid., p. 100), while to be a "slave of God" still persists in its positive meaning, specifically, as "opposed to servants of human rulers" (ibid., p. 109).

186. This interpretation ignored the fact that the institution of slavery had changed drastically within the capitalist plantation system. See J. Albert Harrill, "The Use of the New Testament in the American Slave Controversy: A Case History in the Hermeneutical Tension between Biblical Criticism and Christian Moral Debate," *Religion and American Culture: A Journal of Interpretation* 10, no. 2 (Summer 2000): 149–186.

187. This interpretation is not new with Protestantism. Matthew (8:17) and Mark (9:12) speak in general terms of Jesus' suffering as a fulfillment of the prophecy of Isaiah (see above, n. 28, citing Pagels, "Social History III" [2006] p. 505).

188. The Dutch Republic was established in 1581 after forming a confederacy (Treaty of Utrecht, 1579) that fought together to secede from Spanish (Catholic) rule.

189. For the Dutch Republic's interpretation of its political liberty as the realization of biblical prophecy, see ch. 2, "Patriotic Scripture," in Simon Schama, *The Embarrassment of Riches: An Interpretation of Dutch Culture in the Golden Age* (Berkeley: University of California Press, 1988); see my critique of Schama in *Hegel, Haiti, and Universal History* (Pittsburgh: University of Pittsburgh Press, 2009), pp. 23–25; on the ambiguities produced by the continuation of a bifurcation in the meanings of *Sklav* and *Knecht*, see ibid., pp. 48–58, esp. 52n90 and 53n91.

190. For the considerable appeal of Islam in Britain that Protestant theology needed to counter, see Nabil Matar, *Islam in Britain: 1558–1685* (Cambridge: Cambridge University Press, 1998).

191. The book of Isaiah contains famously the "suffering servant songs" that explain God's treatment of his chosen people, and provide abundant material for the libretto of Handel's *Messiah* (written by Charles Jennens) which applies the words to the suffering of Christ. For the resonance of anti-Semitic themes with Handel's musical masterpiece see Michael Marissen, *Tainted Glory in Handel's Messiah: The Unsettling History of the World's Most Beloved Choral Work* (New Haven: Yale University Press, 2014). "Traditionally, Christians have considered Isaiah 53 to be among the most important of the O[ld]T[estament] texts on messianic expectation. For centuries the fifteen verses of Isaiah 52:13 to 53:12 have attracted vigorous disagreement among Jewish and Christian interpreters, in particular on the identity of Isaiah's 'servant' (whom the prophet does not explicitly associate with God's 'anointed one'—i.e., messiah)" (ibid., pp. 125–126). The "vigorous disagreement"

continues. While philologically the Jewish interpretation has accuracy on its side, the investment for some Christians is to demonstrate to Jews that their conversion is necessary.

192. The modern interpretation of Isaiah 52:13–53:12 is used today to justify exclusionary practices in the nation of Israel, whereas, as Marissen writes: "Typically in traditional Christian understandings, *we*, Jesus' followers alone 'are healed' (N[ew] T[estament 1 Peter 2:24]. . . . Even if Jesus died for everyone, he did not *save* everyone" (Marissen, *Tainted Glory in Handel's Messiah*, p. 130).

CHAPTER 5

1. Leonard Thompson, *The Book of Revelation: Apocalypse and Empire* (New York: Oxford University Press, 1990), p. 164.

2. "[T]here is no indication of political unrest, widespread class conflict, or economic crisis in the cities of that province [Asia]. . . . The urban setting in which Christians worshiped and lived was stable and beneficial to all who participated in its social and economic institutions" (Thompson, *The Book of Revelation: Apocalypse and Empire*, pp. 166–167). Friesen explains the implications: "In the writings of nineteenth-century New Testament scholars, the atrocities committed by Nero against members of the churches in Rome provided a plausible social setting for Revelation"; but when the dating of Revelation shifted from the end of Nero's reign (i.e., ca. 68–70) to late in Domitian's reign, the theory of a possible "Domitianic persecution of Christians" was ultimately abandoned. Steven J. Friesen, *Imperial Cults and the Apocalypse of John: Reading Revelation in the Ruins* (New York: Oxford University Press, 2001), p. 143. He continues: "The rejection of Domitianic persecutions in recent literature has not caused a return to a Neronic date for Revelation. Rather, there has been a general move away from crisis theories as a way of understanding Revelation" (ibid.)

3. Friesen, *Imperial Cults and the Apocalypse of John*, p. 143. Stephens writes: "The commonly held belief in a systematic, empire-wide persecution under Domitian has almost completely fallen by the wayside." Mark B. Stephens, *Annihilation or Renewal: The Meaning and Function of New Creation in the Book of Revelation* (Tübingen: Mohr Siebeck, 2011), pp. 144–145.

4. "In 12 BCE the provincial assembly [of the *koinon* of Asia] inscribed in the temple at Pergamon Augustus' edict making clear the rights of Jews in Asia" (Thompson, *The Book of Revelation: Apocalypse and Empire*, p. 160). An earlier record exists from Rome in 39 BCE that included the protocol of 44 BCE on privileges of Jews, "the inscribed text of which was viewed and copied by Josephus more than a century later" (Clifford Ando, *Imperial Ideology and Provincial Loyalty in the Roman Empire* [Berkeley: University of California Press, 2000], p. 85). A major synagogue was unearthed in the first-century city of Aphrodisias that lists non-Jewish sympathizers among its donors and patrons (see John Dominic Crossan and Jonathan L. Reed, *In Search of Paul: How Jesus's Apostle Opposed Rome's Empire with God's Kingdom* [New York: HarperCollins, 2004], pp. 23–25). Paul taught in the synagogue in Ephesus (Acts 19:10; 20:31). An important synagogue has been discovered in Sardis (see

Tessa Rajak, "The Gifts of God at Sardis," in *Jews in a Graeco-Roman World*, ed. Martin Goodman [Oxford: Clarendon Press, 1998], pp. 229–239). A document (of uncertain date) from the council of the city of Sardis "opens with an assurance of its long-lasting good will towards the Judeans, who 'have had many great benefits through all time from the people'"; the council and people then grant to Jews "a proper quarter for a synagogue and surrounding residences. The Judeans are given public support and public land. Even more astounding, the tasks of the civic ἀγορανόμοι [market laws] are expanded to include oversight of kosher food imports." Bradly Ritter, *Judeans in the Greek Cities of the Roman Empire: Rights, Citizenship and Civil Discord* (Leiden: Brill, 2015), p. 204.

5. The important exception was the Temple tax, which diaspora Jews now owed to Rome, that has been interpreted as a mark of punishment and humiliation (Ritter, *Judeans in the Greek Cities*, p. 281). Yet Jewish attitudes toward Rome were not monolithic, and Rome was not vengeful against Jews generally. Josephus reports that when in 70 CE Antioch, not wanting to be associated with the Judaean rebels, asked that the rights of Jews in their city be rescinded, Titus refused (*Bellum Judaicum* 7.49–53).

6. As we have noted, John himself does not use the category "Christian," and criticizes "those who say they are Jews and are not" (Rev 2:9 and 3:9). David Frankfurter, holding onto identity categories, puts pressure instead on the new consensus as to the late dating of the text: "Evidence for the late, Domitianic date has become quite shaky since Leonard Thompson's and Christian Wilson's demonstrations of this emperor's rather benign reign" (David Frankfurter, "Jews or Not? Reconstructing the 'Other' in Rev 2:9 and 3:9," *Harvard Theological Review* 94, no. 4 [2001]: 423).

7. Ritter's detailed account of this entire subject concludes that Romans "supported the Judaean local citizenship not only in Alexandria and Antioch but also in Ionia [the province of Asia]" (Ritter, *Judeans in the Greek Cities*, p. 227). Ritter's study relies heavily on the evidence provided in the writings of Philo and Josephus; he argues that not exclusion but inclusion caused resentment among non-Jews, insofar as Jews did not share equally in the financial and practical responsibilities of citizenship. For the contrasting theory of the *politeuma* hypothesis (based on the work of Emil Schürer, Victor Tcherikover, and others), which presumes noncitizenship of Jews but self-governance through their own, separate organization defined as a *politeuma*, see Ritter, *Judeans in the Greek Cities*, ch. 1, pp. 1–11.

8. While sporadic and local violence took place against Christians after Nero, there was no empire-wide persecution of them for two centuries.

9. Cultural conflict in some cities was "serious and long-lasting" (Ritter, *Judeans in the Greek Cities*, p. 199). Josephus felt it necessary to challenge the writings of Apion, an Alexandrian gymnasiarch who wrote disparagingly of Jews and Judaism, which Josephus claims "began in Egypt" (Josephus, *Contra Apionem* 1.223, cited by Daniel R. Schwartz, "Philo, His Family and His Times," in *The Cambridge Companion to Philo*, ed. Adam Kamesar [Cambridge: Cambridge University Press, 2009], p. 19).

10. As emissary to Rome, Philo argued successfully for Flaccus' punishment and for Jews' freedom to be reinstated. See the illuminating chapter (based on Philo's account), "The *Stasis* in Alexandria in 38 CE and Its Aftermath," in Ritter, *Judeans in the Greek Cities*, pp. 132–183.

11. See above, chapter 2. Ritter notes: "*Stasis* best describes the events of 38 CE, which is, in fact, the word used by all ancient writers who wrote on these events. Philo uses the word four times in *In Flaccum* . . . [as well as] once in *Legatio* [*ad Gaium*] to describe the risk of similar events in the cities of Judea" (Ritter, *Judeans in the Greek Cities*, p. 161). The words "in a foreign city" (ἐν ἀλλοτρία πόλει), used to describe Jewish presence, occurs in Claudius' letter to Alexandrians several years after the incident, a detail that has received considerable attention, possibly indicating their non-citizen status. Claudius' letter was written before the destruction of the Second Temple, when the taxes paid by Jews throughout the diaspora to Jerusalem could give the appearance of a double loyalty, "but this is not to be confused with an insistence on their non-citizen status" (ibid., p. 146). After the Temple's destruction, the tax continued to be collected, but it was sent to Rome—which could appear to local citizens in the provinces as a different kind of double loyalty. It could be argued, on the basis of evidence from both eras, that the double community inhabited by Jews in the diaspora was a source of strength. Ritter calls this "double citizenship" (ibid., p. 223). Given the complexities of this history that must always deal with multiple locations, various moments in time, and incomplete evidence (handled with skill by Ritter), neither consistency nor coherence of explanation is to be expected.

12. Monotheistic Jews had lived beside polytheists for centuries, yet not all shared the same earthly fate. Ritter (*Judeans in the Greek Cities*) emphasizes their social diversity: as a cross-section of the population, they played many different roles as supporters of the emperor, rebellious subjects, landless laborers, or members of a landed elite. The same individual could (like Josephus) move from slave status as prisoner of war to Roman citizen under imperial patronage. As urban oligarchs, Jews held local offices and engaged in long-distance trade. They were members of trade guilds that, like the *poleis* in which they were citizens, had patron deities to whom honors were due. Particularly helpful in dealing with the complexities of the question of Jewish identity in the first centuries BCE and CE is the careful study of Shaye J. D. Cohen, *The Beginnings of Jewishness: Boundaries, Varieties, Uncertainties* (Berkeley: University of California Press, 1999).

13. Ritter, *Judeans in the Greek Cities*, p. 279. They were exempt from military service, and from Sabbath court appearances and participation in public business on their festival days (ibid., p. 239).

14. Ritter, *Judeans in the Greek Cities*, p. 220.

15. Ritter, *Judeans in the Greek Cities*, p. 228. Again, there is no need to distinguish here between Jews and Christians, unless we would wish to argue that refusal to participate in these aspects of civic life was the very meaning of a Christian. Price, on this point, is skeptical of the conventional narrative that Christians rejected emperor worship on rational grounds, and considers it an early chapter in the developmental story that superimposes

enlightenment reason on history, privileging Christianity as critical of king-worship, whereas non-Europeans, and especially Africans, were slow to give up traditions of "divine kings." S. R. F. Price, *Rituals and Power: The Roman Imperial Cult in Asia Minor* (Cambridge: Cambridge University Press, 1984), pp. 235–236.

16. When this phrase appears in Revelation chapters 2 and 3, it is plausibly addressed exclusively to everyone in the assemblies, or churches; but when the same phrase appears in chapter 13, the address is explicitly to "all those dwelling on earth" (Rev 13: 8–9).

17. He names followers of "Jezebel," worshipers of "Balaam," and the "Nicolaitans." Jezebel is the name of a queen who incited her husband King Ahab to abandon the worship of Yahweh and worship the false deities of Baal and Asherah (1 Kings 16:31). The Old Testament figure of Balaam (Numbers 22–24) tried to entice Israelites to infidelity; speculations as to the identity of the Nicolaitans have included Paulists, Gnostics, or a pagan sect (see Aune 5.2a, pp. 148–149).

18. Elaine Pagels, *Revelations: Visions, Prophecy, and Politics in the Book of Revelation* (New York: Viking, 2012), p. 39. In supposing John's intention, Pagels is humanizing John's message, which Christians have assumed was sent directly from heaven. As an expert on the multiple revelations included in the Nag Hammadi find, Pagels is fully aware of the other possible and arguably more attractive alternatives to John's revelation, and manifests palpable regret that his text won out over the competition.

19. Pagels, *Revelations*, pp. 39–40.

20. The urban oligarchs who ran the cities were an elite "who competed among themselves to take on offices and services, and often laid out their personal fortunes, in order to be preeminent among their fellow citizens, to stand in the esteem of the Romans, and to rise in power and status, sometimes to the ranks of Roman authority itself." Barbara Burrell, *Neokoroi: Greek Cities and Roman Emperors* (Boston: Brill, 2003), pp. 1–2.

21. Burrell, *Neokoroi*, pp. 351–352. Contemporaries in Rome and elsewhere observed the intensity of competition among Asian cities for recognition as "first" (*proteia*/πρῶτεια) among all others in the koinon. Aelius Aristides is Burrell's source both for the valuing of *philotimia*, and criticizing its practice in Asia cities *at a particular moment*. Burrell notes that Aristides praised "honorable rivalry" leading to "all-important firstness (*proteia*)"; yet this same orator, at a meeting of the koinon at Pergamon (167/8 CE), criticized precisely the three neokoroi cities, Ephesos, Pergamon, and Smyrna, for lapsing into faction (*stasis*) by all three claiming to be foremost: "I am amazed that while you pride yourselves most on the temples and contests you think of as common [i.e., of the *koinon*], it is over these very things that you have become divided. When you even quarrel over what you're proud to hold in common, over what will you ever agree? . . . As if you meant them to be contradictions against divisiveness, you have called your council chambers 'common,' your temples and contests 'common,' pretty much all the most important things 'common.' Don't you have to be wrong one way or the other? For if you're rightly proud of these things being common, why aren't you ashamed to be quarreling over them?" (Aelius Arisitides, cited in

Burrell, *Neokoroi*, p. 351.) Aristides named all three rival cities praiseworthy, each for its own attributes—as did John in addressing assemblies in the seven cities, praising—and criticizing—each differently.

22. Privileges included initiating discussions at *koinon* assemblies, leading festival processions, and receiving donations for public buildings that honored both the imperial family and the city's patron deity.

23. A city's position was enhanced by heroic ancestry and divine patron, size and beauty, as well as strategic position and loyalty to Rome (Burrell, *Neokoroi*, p. 355).

24. "Each koinon was like a web, with cities arranged in various positions on its strands"; honor "was the means of gain in favor and gifts from above, loyalty and obedience form below" (Burrell, *Neokoroi*, pp. 357–358). On koinon-wide payment of the hymnodes, see ibid., p. 312.

25. "[T]hey sang hymns to the imperial family, participated in imperial sacrifices, led celebrations, and hosted banquets" (Friesen, *Imperial Cults and the Apocalypse of John*, p. 105). A city's youth was trained competitively at publicly financed gymnasia not only in athletics, the competitions of which were not part of the cults, but also music, which figured centrally in them. Chaniotis notes that very few hymns from this period survive; for one that does, see Angelos Chaniotis, "The Ithyphallic Hymn for Demetrios Poliorketes and Hellenistic Religious Mentality," in *More Than Men, Less Than Gods: Studies on Royal Cult and Imperial Worship*, ed. Panagiotis P. Iossif, Andrzej S. Chankowski, and Catharine C. Lorber (Leuven: Peeters, 2011).

26. A calendar of their meetings (ca. 41 CE) exists as an inscription parsed by Friesen, *Imperial Cults and the Apocalypse of John*, pp. 105–113. It refers to "god Augustus Caesar, Zeus Patroos, emperor and pontifex maximus, father of the fatherland (πατρίς) and of the whole human race. Since it is appropriate to provide a public display of reverence and of pious consideration toward the imperial household during the year, the hymnodes from all Asia—coming together in Pergamon on the most holy birthday of Sebastos Tiberius Caesar God—complete a great work to the glory of the assembly, making hymns to the imperial house and completing sacrifices to the gods Sebastoi, leading festivals and hosting banquets" (ibid., p. 105).

27. "They met at least once a month, since the first day of each month was a celebration of the birthday of Augustus" (Friesen, *Imperial Cults and the Apocalypse of John*, p. 111).

28. Friesen, *Imperial Cults and the Apocalypse of John*, p. 111.

29. Friesen, *Imperial Cults and the Apocalypse of John*, p.113.

30. Friesen, *Imperial Cults and the Apocalypse of John*, p. 113. "Table-settings" were included—literally a place at the table—and a pecuniary subsidy from public, province-wide funds. On the costumes of participants in the imperial cults as "white robes and crowns," see Robyn J. Whitaker, *Ekphrasis, Vision, and Persuasion in the Book of Revelation* (Tübingen: Mohr Siebeck, 2015), p. 129.

31. See above, chapter 3.

32. Burrell, *Neokoroi*, p. 358.

33. Rev 21:10.

34. See above, chapter 4. In the text: "Then I heard every creature in heaven and on earth and under the earth and on the sea, and all that is in them, singing: 'To him who sits on the throne / and to the Lamb / Be praise and honor and glory and power / For ever and ever!'" (Rev 5:13). Cf: "Then I was told, 'You must prophesy again about many peoples, nations, languages and kings'" (Rev 10:11). Scholars see ambiguity here, as ἐπὶ has multiple meanings: prophesy *about*? *to*? or *against*? (see Aune 52b, p. 573). But Whitaker's interpretation emphasizes the inclusiveness of address: "Not only is the Lamb's worship sung by a universal chorus (5.13) but the kingdom he has brought transcends national borders and cultural groups" (Whitaker, *Ekphrasis, Vision, and Persuasion in the Book of Revelation*, pp. 158–159).

35. Rev 5:6–7, 5:9, 5:13. As we have seen, "worthy" (ἀξίως) appears in Hellenic texts as a public evaluation. Whitaker notes that it is unprecedented as "a form of divine address." In both LXX and the New Testament, "it is not language used to describe God nor in praise of God." Rather, the word was used commonly to connote earthly honor; the discourse of imperial power is "a likely locus for such power." Whitaker, *Ekphrasis, Vision, and Persuasion in the Book of Revelation*, pp. 156–158.

36. See Aune 52a, p. 355.

37. The term *kithara* occurs three times: Rev 5:8, 14:2, 15:2.

38. Rev 4:4, 4:10, 5:9. Whitaker compares this scene with one described by Josephus in the *Judean War*, which depicts "universal goodwill that causes a multitude from Rome to pour out of the city to greet Vespasian as 'τὸν εὐεργέτην καὶ σωτῆρα καὶ μόνον ἄξιον ἡγεμόνα τῆς `Ρώμης' ('the benefactor and savior and only worthy ruler of Rome')" (Whitaker, *Ekphrasis, Vision, and Persuasion in the Book of Revelation*, p. 161). Whitaker notes: "participants in Greco-Roman cults regularly wore white robes and crowns such as those worn by the elders in Revelation to temples and festivals. Aristides records the Greeks throwing their crowns before Alexander in recognition of his greatness and their service to him. Religious and political processions typically included music and hymn-singing as well as the offering of sacrifices and prostration or obeisance before some kind of representation of the emperor or deity. . . . [John's] point is not to teach hearer-readers about earthly practices but to reveal the true nature and focus of worship from a heavenly perspective" (ibid., p. 129).

39. The hymns appear repeatedly in Revelation: 4:8, 4:11, 5:9, 5:13, 7:10, 7:12.

40. Rev 7:9; again 11:9, 13:7.

41. See chapter 4 above.

42. Rev 21:6.

43. Rev 21:26. The city is laid out in a square, and high again as it is wide and long. The walls are jasper; the structures are of gold, pure as glass; the twelve gates are twelve pearls, each gate a single one. No temple is in it, "because the Lord God Almighty and the Lamb" are its temple; the "kings of the earth" will bring "the glory and honor of the nations into it." "The nations will walk by its light and the kings of the earth will bring their splendor to it"; the gates are never shut: "the glory and honor of the nations will be brought into it." (Rev 21:22–26.)

44. Rev 21:26–27, 22:2.

45. Rev 22:17.

46. "And I saw . . ." introduces multiple sentences: Rev 5:11, 6:1, 6:2, 6:5. Cf. "And I heard . . . [Καὶ ἤκουσ . . .]: Rev 6:3; 6:5.

47. John's address distinguishes his book from two forms containing comparable material: book III of the sibylline oracles that speaks directly both to God and to others; and narrative descriptions of Old Testament prophets in books telling the stories of their lives.

48. Sickenberger, while focusing on transcendence rather than critique, recognizes this super-imposition of the future on the present: "Die Apk[alipsis] ist also keine Darstellung der damaligen Zeit, durch die man wie durch ein Transparent die Zukunft erkennen kann, son-dern ein Zukunftsgemälde, das auch mit einzelnen Farben der Gegenwart gemalt worden ist" ["The Apocalypse is, then, not a representation of the contemporary times, through which, as through a transparency, one can know the future, but rather a depiction of the future that is nonetheless painted with singular colors of the present"]. Joseph Sickenberger, *Erklärung der Johannesapokalypse*, 2nd ed. (Bonn: Hanstein Verlag, 1942), p. 28.

49. Whitaker, *Ekphrasis, Vision, and Persuasion in the Book of Revelation*, p. 78.

50. Whitaker surmises intent and motive for this rhetorical manipulation: "The problem for a Jew seeking to compete with and criticize the imperial cult was: how do you compete when you cannot create an image of your own God?" (*Ekphrasis, Vision, and Persuasion in the Book of Revelation*, p. 3).

51. These elements are described in detail in Constellation IV of this chapter.

52. Hoff cites De Certeau: "To believe in what others say is what gives access to a thought of the One [God]. This initial derangement makes theory possible. . . . [T]he infinite is not 'visible'; it is only audible." Johannes Hoff, *The Analogical Turn: Rethinking Modernity with Nicholas of Cusa* (Grand Rapids, MI: Eerdmans, 2013), p. 144.

53. In fact Nicholas of Cusa anticipated by seven years Lorenzo Valla's demonstration that the "Donation of Constantine" was a forgery, allegedly granting to the papal See of Rome supremacy over spiritual and temporal matters (Hoff, *The Analogical Turn*, pp. 15 and 10). He "became increasingly uninterested in the line of demarcation separating pagan from Christian traditions," entertaining ideas (mystical, neo-Platonic) that were considered heretical. As "coenobitic" (derived, via Latin, from *koinos*, common, and *bios*, life), his monastic community was separated from the everyday world, much like the Essenes or

Gnostic communities of John's time (see above, chapter 4). In contrast, John's audience participated in public life. They were asked to see what he says, in the face of a lived reality wherein all those in authority denied it. John was not a mystic. Schüssler Fiorenza is right to say that Revelation is "not an esoteric secret work" (Elisabeth Schüssler Fiorenza, *The Book of Revelation: Justice and Judgment*, 2nd ed. [Minneapolis: Fortress Press, 1998], p. 35).

54. Hoff, *The Analogical Turn*, p. 150. Hoff refers here to De Certeau's thesis "that the Holy Scripture became mute after the sixteenth and seventeenth centuries" (ibid.).

55. Alberti was a contemporary of Cusa, whom he probable knew. Hoff notes that although written documents are lacking, evidences and indications of their acquaintance and collaboration are overwhelming (Hoff, *The Analogical Turn*, p. 61n). However, Cusa (perhaps like Kant? see above, chapter 3) believed mathematics was an invention of human reason, and as such, inadequate for the investigation of the "infinite simplicity" and "oneness" of God (Cusa, cited in Hoff, *The Analogical Turn*, p. 46).

56. Hoff, *The Analogical Turn*, p. 48.

57. "In short, after the fifteenth century, the cultivation of sensual habits turned into a polarized battlefield that focused on the two main capacities of Alberti's 'new Narcissus': first, my oculocentric ability to gain control over my mirror image by putting myself in the position of the eye point of a mathematically generated picture; and, second, my phonocentric ability to gain control over the meaning of the words I have received from the past by putting myself in the position of their historically and philologically reconstructed author" (Hoff, *The Analogical Turn*, p. 151). Hoff explains: "This compositional strategy is consistent with Alberti's teaching. The vanishing lines reflect the invisible eye point of the viewer, putting the latter in the position of a sovereign observer who can control the space of his perception as if it were nothing but a mirror image of his subjective position" (ibid., p. 48). Hoff cites Hans Belting's study (*Florence and Bagdad*) that compares this to contemporary digital images produced by "rigorous mathematical deconstruction, only in order to reconstruct it reliably in the bodiless medium of painting" (cited in ibid.).

58. Hoff, *The Analogical Turn*, p. 57.

59. Hoff, *The Analogical Turn*, p. 162. Hoff turns again to Nicolas of Cusa's critique of the idea that creatures *possess* individuality as a unique property. "Rather, the miracle is that every creature and every person is a singularity, not despite, but exactly because it owes everything it is to a giver whose perfections cannot be owned. Rational calculations about the uniqueness of finite creatures can only devaluate this unique gift" (ibid., p. 163)

60. Hoff, *The Analogical Turn*, p. 164.

61. De Certeau, cited in Hoff, *The Analogical Turn*, p. 46.

62. Hoff, *The Analogical Turn*, p. 30.

63. Hoff, *The Analogical Turn*, p. 30.

64. When Revelation states "there will be time no longer" (Rev 10:6), the word is *chronos*; Aune interprets it as delay. There are specific units of time mentioned in Revelation: a half hour,

an hour, a thousand years, and even 1,260 days (Rev 12:6), and of course "forever and ever" (τοὺς αἰῶνας τῶν αἰῶνον) (Rev 1:6, 4:9, 5:13, 15:7). And yet these cannot be fused within a linear chronology. Schüssler Fiorenza assembles evidence for the impossibility of tracking a chronological sequence legible as history's unfolding in Revelation: "[P]revious attempts to explain the sequence of visions or the total composition of Rev either by a linear or cyclic understanding of time have not succeeded in presenting a convincing interpretation. . . . The central apocalyptic section (4:1–22:5), in particular, creates difficulties for these successive temporal interpretations, because here the author mixes together past, present, and future elements of time. His doublets and his repetition of an entire cycle of visions cannot be satisfactorily explained as a temporal or historical sequence." Schüssler Fiorenza, *The Book of Revelation: Justice and Judgment*, p. 46.

65. Sipiora stresses the convergence of temporal and spatial singularity in kairotic time: Phillip Sipiora, "Introduction," in *Rhetoric and Kairos: Essays in History, Theory, and Praxis*, ed. Phillip Sipiora and James S. Baumlin (Albany: State University of New York Press, 2002), p. 18. The fifth-century BCE philosopher Pythagoras (from the Ionian island of Samos, even closer to the Anatolian mainland than Patmos!) understood *kairos* as therefore an epistemological problem: "For Pythagoras, as well as for Gorgias, *kairos* touches upon the problematic issue of knowledge. To frail human perception, things exist in an uncertain, ultimately unknowable way; a veil of sense separates them, indeed, hides them from us. In accordance with *kairos*, therefore, we are compelled to maintain contrary perceptions, interpretations, and arguments: opposing arguments—the *dissoi logoi* of sophistic rhetoric—remain equally probable, and yet the mystery of *kairos* enables rhetors to choose one *logos* over another, making one and the same thing seem great or small, beautiful or ugly, new or old" (ibid., p. 4). As Sipiora elaborates, the mystical nature of numbers is crucial here: "Aristotle notes in his *Metaphysics* that Pythagoras equates *kairos* to the number 7; all human and cosmic events (birth, gestation, maturity, the orbit of the sun, and so forth) are governed by rhythms of seven and, therefore, of *kairos*"; the critical turning point (*krisis*) of an illness is the seventh day, identifying *kairos* with health (ibid., p. 19n).

66. Carolyn R. Miller, "Foreword," in Sipiora and Baumlin, *Rhetoric and Kairos*, p. xiii. In contrast, as a category of rhetoric rather than metaphysics, *kairos* is decorum, the use of the right word at the right time (ibid., p. xii).

67. In *The Time That Remains: A Commentary on the Letter to the Romans*, trans. Patricia Dailey (Stanford: Stanford University Press, 2005), Giorgio Agamben reads an opposition between *kairos* and *chronos* in Paul's work. His approach is philologically inaccurate in two senses. First, he misreads ancient *chronos* as indistinguishable from the linear, chronological, "empty" time of modernity. Second, he does not recognize that Paul himself does not oppose *chronos* and *kairos*, but sees them as one. In critiquing Agamben, Delahaye clarifies: "It is highly doubtful that Paul himself used this terminological opposition. Paul only uses *kairos* and *chronos* in close proximity to each other in 1 Thessalonians 5:1 and in this context Paul uses both *kairos* and *chronos* together to refer to the time when the messiah will return." See Ezra Delahaye, "About Chronos and Kairos: On Agamben's

Interpretation of Pauline Temporality through Heidegger," *International Journal of Philosophy and Theology* 77, no. 3 (November 2016): 89. In his reading of Paul, Agamben's debt to Heidegger is highly problematic on this point; Heidegger's *ekstasis* is an existential comportment of openness toward life abstracted from the historical particulars, a kind of permanent now-time in relation to the world, indifferent to its contents. This is not the "uniquely timely" "radical particularity" of *kairos* that accords with its meaning in Paul's own time.

68. Romans 13:1–2. Paraphrasing this passage, Cullman writes: "every person must submit to the supreme authorities; there is no authority but by act of God, and the existing authorities are instituted by him; consequently, anyone who rebels against authority is resisting a divine institution"; he comments: "no state, not even a new, Jewish state (zealots desired) could be so very important when judged from the relativizing perspective of the coming end." Oscar Cullman, *Christ and Time: The Primitive Christian Conception of Time and History*, 3rd ed., trans. Floyd V. Filson (Eugene, OR: Wipf and Stock, 2018), pp. 131–132. This end is not of the world, but of the time (*chronos*) of earthly power.

69. Barclay writes: "From Paul's perspective, the Roman empire never was and never would be a significant actor in the drama of history. . . . At the deepest level Paul undermines Augustus and his successors not by confronting them on their own terms, but by reducing them to bit-part players in a drama scripted by the cross and resurrection of Jesus. . . . Paul's theology is political precisely in rendering the Roman empire theologically insignificant." John M. G. Barclay, "Why the Roman Empire was Insignificant to Paul," in *Pauline Churches and Diaspora Jews* (Tübingen: Mohr Siebeck, 2011), p. 387. See also Wei Hsien Wan, *The Contest for Time and Space in the Roman Imperial Cults and 1 Peter: Reconfiguring the Universe* (London: T&T Clark, 2019), p. 9.

70. Eusebius' visual model of universal history "arranged the tables of monarchies to teach one massive lesson. As all the other lists of rulers dwindled away and only the Roman one remained, as the multiple columns that recorded the early history of Greece and the Near East funneled down into one long, packed column devoted only to Rome, the *Chronicle* graphically proved that world history culminated in the contemporary [Christianized] Roman Empire. Significantly, the last rival kingdom to have a column of its own was that of the Jews. This ended, as Eusebius remarked, with the fall of Jerusalem to Vespasian . . . at once a clear sign of providential direction and the last step needed for the whole world to be opened to Christianity." Anthony Grafton and Megan Williams, *Christianity and the Transformation of the Book: Origen, Eusebius, and the Library of Caesarea* (Cambridge, MA: Harvard University Press, 2006), p. 141.

71. Eusebius' work was pivotal as "part of a long-standing Christian project of synchronizing the new sacred history with the old profane history of the pagans, and the old sacred history of the Jews so as to create a new truly universal human history, the plan of God for salvation, one that was regularly interpreted as part of various end-time obsessions." Denis Feeney, *Caesar's Calendar: Ancient Time and the Beginnings of History* (Berkeley: University of California Press, 2007), p. 29. Feeney illustrates with examples of these chronological

tables, wherein "the Jewish column disappears with Titus's capture of Jerusalem, so that for the years 73–78 CE . . . there is only one column on each page, *Romanorum*, the column of Roman time" (ibid., p. 32).

72. Eusebius' "ecclesiastical history was bound to be different from ordinary history because it was a history of the struggle against the devil, who tried to pollute the purity of the Christian Church as guaranteed by the apostolic succession." Arnaldo Momigliano, "Pagan and Christian Historiography in the Fourth Century A.D." (1963), in *Essays in Ancient and Modern Historiography* (Chicago: University of Chicago Press, 2012), p. 116.

73. Omitted from the selection is the reason for Paul's affirmation of living among Romans that contradicts an authoritarian reading: "Love your neighbor as yourself. Love does not harm its neighbor. Therefore love is the fulfillment of the law" (Romans 13:9–10).

74. "On Thursday, Attorney General Jeff Sessions defended the Trump administration's policy of separating immigrant children from their families at the border by referencing the New Testament. 'I would cite you to the Apostle Paul and his clear and wise command in Romans 13,' Sessions said, 'to obey the laws of the government because God has ordained them for the purpose of order.' White House Press Secretary Sarah Huckabee Sanders summed up the same idea: 'It is very biblical to enforce the law.'" Lincoln Mullen, "The Fight to Define Romans 13," *Atlantic*, June 15, 2018. Mullen reminds us of the significance of Romans 13 at multiple points in American history, as it was read selectively by opposing sides, those arguing for submission to the authority of law, and those insisting Paul never intended his letter to be used as a justification of tyranny. Romans 13 was cited in 1850 to defend the Fugitive Slave act that required "all good citizens" to assist in returning to their owners those who escaped slavery, and was used as justification by both sides in the American Revolution (ibid.); https://www.theatlantic.com/ideas/archive/2018/06/romans-13/562916/.

75. "Domitian faced at least two serious attempts on his life (in 87 and 96 CE), the final one successful and mounted by his courtiers and his wife." A. J. Boyle, "Introduction," in *Flavian Rome: Culture, Image, Text*, ed. A. J. Boyle and W. J. Dominik (Leiden: Brill, 2002), p. 43. His son, who had died, was deified by Domitian. According to Suetonius, Domitian's wife (Domitia Longina) was exiled in 83 because of an affair with a famous actor, while the actor was murdered; Domitian took Julia as his mistress, who later died during a failed abortion. "Female political transgression is almost always veiled by Roman authors in the rhetorical topoi of alleged sexual misconduct" (Eric R. Varner, "Portraits, Plots and Politics: 'Damnatio memoriae' and the Images of Imperial Women," *Memoirs of the American Academy in Rome* 46 [2001]: 42). Varner notes that the term *damnatio memoriae* has often been misinterpreted: "The term is not ancient, but it does accurately encompass the Romans' preoccupation with the manipulation of memory and posthumous reputation" (p. 41).

76. Tacitus, *Agricola* 44.5, cited in Marcus Wilson, "After the Silence: Tacitus, Suetonius, Juvenal," in Boyle and Dominik, *Flavian Rome*, p. 527.

77. While some recent historians have provided a more sympathetic evaluation, others warn: "[t]he general and coherent picture of Domitianic oppression to be found in Pliny [the Younger], Tacitus, Suetonius and Juvenal, is not simply to be dismissed as . . . propaganda" by his imperial successors (Boyle, "Introduction," p. 37).

78. Quickly confirming Nerva as emperor, the Senate ordered the removal of Domitian's name and likeness.

79. Here Philo concurred with the Neo-Pythagoreans and Stoics of his time. "The periodic renewal of the world (*metacosmesis*) was a favorite doctrine of Neo-Pythagorean teachings, which, along with Stoicism, dominated Roman thought in the second and first centuries B.C. Unlike the Stoics, the Pythagoreans refrained from postulating any cosmic conflagration, and took recurrence to happen within one continuous historical order." Peter J. Holliday, "Time, History and Ritual on the Ara Pacis Augustae," *Art Bulletin* 72, no. 4 (December 1990): 543.

80. Niehoff writes that the imperial cult under Augustus was "remarkably acceptable to Philo," who praised the emperor for his "more than human nature," considering him, justly, "a source of veneration" in the Egyptian synagogues. "He took for granted that 'gilded shields and crowns, monuments and inscriptions' were set up in Egyptian synagogues" (Maren Niehoff, *Philo on Jewish Identity and Culture* [Tübingen: Mohr Siebeck, 2001], p. 81). "He seems to have expected outstanding rulers [Moses as well as Augustus] would reach divinity by virtue of their beneficence" (ibid., pp. 83–84). At the same time, Philo strongly opposed Gaius Caligula's proposal to place a statue of himself in Jerusalem: "No one before had ever considered desecrating the Jewish temple by a statue dedicated to a human being under the name of Zeus" (ibid., p. 82).

81. Given the harmonious perfection of creation, Philo saw no reason why the world should end. "[T]he created world remains good in his eyes, and, through it, divine illumination should be sought. Learning to live well in the world as it is, also remains among Philo's preoccupations." Mireille Hadas-Lebel, *Philo of Alexandria: A Thinker in the Jewish Diaspora*, trans. Robyn Fréchet (Leiden: Brill, 2012), p. 191.

82. Hadas-Lebel, *Philo of Alexandria*, p. 198. She quotes Lester L. Grabbe, "Eschatology in Philo and Josephus," *Judaism in Late Antiquity* 4: "A messianic savior figure does not fit easily into his theological system" (ibid., p. 199n).

83. For Josephus, *chronos* itself harbored an eschatology, understood as cycles of empires as related in the book of Daniel (cited as well by John). Rajak's close reading of the entirety of Josephus' work discerns nuances in what has been understood as his "realist" argument for accepting Roman rule, based on "the irresistible claims of sheer power"; and even in his rendition of Agrippa II's speech making that claim, the argument is "double-edged," "for there is an underlying critique in terms of exploitation" by Rome of its imperial holdings. Tessa Rajak, "Friends, Romans, Subjects: Agrippa II's Speech in Josephus's Jewish War," in *Images of Empire*, ed. Loveday Alexander (Sheffield: Sheffield Academic Press, 1991), pp. 131–132. Moreover, "there is what might be called an implicit, suppressed apocalypse in

what has been taken as being the most shameless of Josephus' doctrines," i.e., his support of Rome (ibid., p. 132): "For Josephus, as for many rabbis, the conception of a cycle of sin, punishment, and salvation, with an eventual new beginning, lay beneath the doctrine of the transference of god's favour" (ibid., pp. 132–133). Rajak notes "Josephus's curious reticence over the identity and fate of the fourth beast in the visions of the seventh chapter of Daniel," which speaks of four imperial orders, leaving open the possibility of its attribution to Rome (ibid., p. 133).

84. David Andrew Thomas, *Revelation 19 in Historical and Mythological Context* (New York: Peter Lang, 2008), p. 32. The reference is to Josephus, *Bellum Judaicum*, 6.5.4. It should be recalled that the Romans' intervention during the Republic was to defend the Maccabean revolt in Judaea against the Seleucids, so that protection, not domination, was the immediate history of Roman rule.

85. This is Aune's position; he sees John's text as "permeated with the motifs and literary conventions of Palestinian Jewish apocalyptic"; hence his migration to Roman Asia, perhaps carrying "a modest library of Palestinian apocalyptic literature; whether he began his career as a Christian apocalyptist or whether he began as a Jewish apocalyptist who only later became a follower of Jesus of Nazareth, can never be known with certainty, although in my view the latter seems more inherently probable." David E. Aune, *Apocalypticism, Prophecy and Magic in Early Christianity: Collected Essays* (Tübingen: Mohr Siebeck, 2006), pp. 173–174.

86. See Schüssler Fiorenza, *The Book of Revelation: Justice and Judgment*.

87. The time that is "near" begins the book (Rev 1:3) and returns at the close (Rev 22:10).

88. Note also that the idea of silence in the heavens as signaling the moment of a temporal turning point can be found in the *Protevangelium Jacobi* (ca. 145 CE), telling the story of Jesus' birth from the perspective of Joseph who has left Mary to find the midwife, when he sees the heavens stand still and the birds of heaven motionless, and workmen stopped, their faces turned to heaven, and sheep stopped, all immobilized: "'then all things, in one instant, were being on again [sic] by their own impetus'" (cited in François Bovon, "The Suspension of Time in Chapter 18 of the *Protevangelium Jacobi*," in *Studies in Early Christianity* [Tübingen: Mohr Siebeck, 2003], p. 227). The vision, which "must coincide, even if the text does not expressly say so, with the birth of Jesus," is narrated by a change from the third to the first person; Joseph "continues speaking in the first person until he has found the midwife and spoken to her" (ibid., p. 227). The December solstice that reverses the movement of the sun was connected with the date of Jesus' birth in the late second or early third century CE.

89. In the Latin Vulgate: *In principio creavit Deus caelum et terram*—where the word *principio* perpetuates the analogy with Augustus' name for himself, princeps.

90. For debates concerning meanings of ἀρχή (ruler, beginning, origin) as referring to Christ in Rev 3:14: "ἡ ἀρχὴ τῆς κτίσεος τοῦ θεοῦ," translated in NIV as "the ruler of God's creation," see the discussion in Stephens, *Annihilation or Renewal*, p. 201 (and 201n).

91. In his commentary on the Genesis story of creation of the universe, Philo uses the analogy of the architect (ἀρχι-τέκτονος) who has the whole plan of a city in his mind as idea: "Then, having received in his own mind as on a waxen tablet, the form of each building, he carries in his heart the image of a city [πόλιν], perceptible as yet only by the intellect, the images of which he stirs up in memory which is innate in him, and, still further, engraving them in his mind like a good workman, keeping his eyes fixed on his model, he begins to raise the city of stones and wood, making the corporeal substances to resemble each of the incorporeal ideas. Now we must form a somewhat similar opinion of God [περὶ θεοῦ], namely that when he had decided to found the great cosmic city [μεγαλόπολιν], [he] first of all conceived its form in his mind . . . and then completed one visible to the external senses, using the first as a model" (Philo, *De opificio mundi* 18–19, trans. modified of μεγαλόπολιν ["great cosmic city," not "mighty state"]).

92. Josephus speaks of six thousand prisoners from the Judaean War sent by Nero to build a canal across the Isthmus of Corinth. The emperor himself presided over the project's initiation (end of 67 CE), chanting hymns to honor the marine deities and wielding a few strokes with a golden pickaxe (*Bellum Judaicum* 3.10).

93. Philo, *De vita Mosis II* 14, 20.

94. Philo, *De opificio mundi* 25.

95. If Nero was held responsible by historians for the great fire in Rome in 64 CE, a second fire in 80 CE (following Vesuvius's eruption and Titus' death) was seen as a bad omen, the effects of which the building projects of the new emperor Domitian might attempt to erase. Central was his new palace with its roof of gold, "so immense that beyond it only heaven lies." David Fredrick, "Architecture and Surveillance in Flavian Rome," in Boyle and Dominik, *Flavian Rome*, p. 217.

96. Rev 5:6–7; see above, note 35.

97. Rev 9:3–10.

98. Rev 13:1–2.

99. Prodigies were unusual natural occurrences, requiring deciphering as forms of prognostication. See D. S. Potter, "Roman Religion: Ideas and Actions," in *Life, Death, and Entertainment in the Roman Empire*, ed. D. S. Potter and D. J. Mattingly (Ann Arbor: University of Michigan Press, 2010), pp. 168–175.

100. Rev 6:12–14. After the seventh seal is opened, the earth trembles once again: "Then there were lightning and rumbling and thunder, and there was a great earthquake such as has never been since people have been on the earth, so great was the earthquake" (Rev 19:17–18).

101. Isaiah 34:4: "All the stars in the sky will be dissolved, and the heavens rolled up like a scroll; all the starry host will fall like withered leaves from the vine, like shriveled figs from the fig tree." Isaiah refers to the coming slaughter as the Lord's vengeance, his fury leashed upon the armies of all nations who are the enemies of his people: "My sword has drunk its fill in

the heavens. . . . The sword of the Lord is bathed in blood. . . . For the Lord has a day of vengeance" (Isaiah 34:4–8).

102. See Richard Bauckham, "The Eschatological Earthquake in the Apocalypse of John," *Novum Testamentum* 19, no. 3 (July 1977): 229. Twelve cities in all were affected, including Ephesus and Pergamon. Tiberius waived taxes in the afflicted cities for five years, and sent significant financial aid, ten million sesterces to Sardis alone. Pliny the Elder called the 17 CE event the greatest earthquake in human memory (*Natural History/Historia naturalis* 2.86). A coin was struck with the inscription: "cities of Asia restored." The first-century Asia Minor city of Aphrodisias (discussed above, chapter 4) experienced a severe earthquake in the process of its construction.

103. Seneca the Younger (d. 65 CE), "Concerning Earthquakes" (*De terrae motu*), sixth book of *Naturales quaestiones*, which generalizes from this specific earthquake, noting equal or worse disasters elsewhere. Note that Seneca's mode of dating this earthquake included the day, February 5 (set by the Augustan calendar), and the then-ruling "counsulship of Regulus and Verginius," which would date the earthquake to 63 CE. Hine suggests that there were two earthquakes (Harry M. Hine, "The Date of the Campanian Earthquake: A.D. 62 or A.D. 63 or Both?," *Antiquité Classique* 53 [1984]: 266–269)—again, an example of the complexities of dating.

104. Seneca, "Concerning Earthquakes." On Seneca's text see G. D. Williams, "Greco-Roman Seismology and Seneca on Earthquakes in 'Natural Questions 6,'" *Journal of Roman Studies* 96 (2006): 124–146.

105. Rev 6:15–17.

106. Tacitus, *Annals* 15.22.2. On the tsunami: https://camws.org/meeting/2014/abstracts/individual/018.TempestasTsunami.pdf.

107. "At once [Nero] was startled by a shock of earthquake and a flash of lightning full in his face, and he heard the shouts of the soldiers from the camp hard by, as they prophesied destruction for him and success for Galba" (Suetonius, *Life of Nero* 48:2). See *The Lives of the Twelve Caesars* (Loeb Classical Library, 1914), online at http://penelope.uchicago.edu/Thayer/E/Roman/Texts/Suetonius/12Caesars/Nero*.html.

108. Newbold notes that Pliny's "belief in earthquakes as portents is explicit." R. F. Newbold, "Pliny HN 2.199," *Classical Philology* 68, no. 3 (July 1973): 21.

109. Clarification of the dating of the eruption of Vesuvius was reported in *Science* magazine: Pliny's account, written some decades later, recalls the date in ways that we have translated as 24 August 79 CE; but an inscription recently found at Pompeii, "likely made during a building renovation, includes the equivalent of the date 17 October 79 CE. That suggests the explosion that buried the inscription in ash, preserving it, happened in late October; but bio-archaeologists had already guessed this later date from the clothing worn, the fruits and other vegetation found, and the prevailing winds for that season (*Science* 362, no. 6413

[October 26, 2018]: 382 [sciencemag.org]). On Pompeii as a trading city, with a great chasm between rich and poor populations, see Willem Jongman, *The Economy and Society of Pompeii* (Amsterdam: J. C. Gieben, 1988).

110. [Pliny the Younger,] *Pliny: Letters and Panegyricus*, 2 vols., vol. 1, *Letters*, books 1–7, trans. Betty Radice (Cambridge, MA: Harvard University Press, 1968). Pliny's two relevant letters (book 6, letters 16 and 20) were written to Tacitus several decades after the event at the historian's request, containing descriptive detail as to the shape and height of the explosion, as well as the timing and nature of the destruction that lasted over several days.

111. Pliny, letter 20, *Letters*, vol. 1, pp. 443–447. Pliny concludes: "Of course these details are not important enough for history, and you will read them without any idea of recording them" (ibid., p. 447). In fact, his accounts are historically central, and continue to influence the study of volcanoes (we speak today of "Plinian flows").

112. Dio Cassius, *Roman History* 66.23.4.

113. Dio Cassius, *Roman History* 66.24.1–3.

114. Haraldur Sigurdsson and Steven Carey, "The Eruption of Vesuvius in A.D. 79," in *The Natural History of Pompeii*, ed. Wilhelmina Feemster Jashemski and Frederick G. Meyer (Cambridge: Cambridge University Press, 2002), p. 62.

115. Bauckham writes that the eruption of Vesuvius that destroyed Pompeii was an event that "would have included both earthquake and a hail of stones quite adequate to the description in Revelation 16:21" (Bauckham, *The Climax of Prophecy*, p. 206).

116. This has been called the "most studied" volcanic explosion. Yet only a simple mention is made by Friesen, *Imperial Cults and the Apocalypse of John*, p. 137; Pagels, *Revelations*, p. 20; Aune 52b, p. 519. Among the Nag Hammadi texts, the "Revelation of Adam" contains a description: "Fire, pumice and asphalt will be thrown upon these people" (cited in Hans Goedicke, "An Unexpected Allusion to the Vesuvius Eruption in 79 A.D.," *American Journal of Philology* 90, no. 3 [July 1969]: 340–341).

117. The pagan Platonist Plutarch (45–127 CE), as well, proposed that Pompeii's destruction indicated the gods' displeasure (Shelley Hales and Joanna Paul, "Introduction," in *Pompeii in the Public Imagination from Its Rediscovery to Today*, ed. Shelley Hales and Joanna Paul [Oxford: Oxford University Press, 2011], p. 13).

118. Chiliasm (millennialism, from Lat: *millennium*, "thousand") was read later into Revelation's mention of "a thousand years" (τά χίλια ἔτη [Rev 20:2, 7]), referring to the time of the reign of Christ (Χριστός), when the dragon/serpent "who is the devil and satan (διάβολος/σατανᾶς)" is locked up, so that he would no longer "deceive/cause to go astray" (πλανήση) the nations, and was then released "for a little time" (μικρὸν χρόνον [Rev 20:3]); the *next* vision is a thousand years of the reign of Christ (Χριστός [Rev 20:4]) after which satan is released, who does battle (here is the reference to Gog and Magog [also found in 4 Ezra]); those not found recorded in "the book of life" are cast into the "lake of fire" (Rev 19:20, again 20:10). Aune connects these images and their language to the discourse of (Jewish)

magic (52c, pp. 1081–1082), and John's reference to "the second death" (Rev 20:14) to an Egyptian conception (ibid., p. 1092), while various aspects of the events narrated appear related to Qumran documents (i.e., Hebrew texts of the Dead Sea Scrolls). Aune summarizes: "The *literal* interpretation of the thousand-year millennium characterized many of the early fathers of the church (e.g., Justin, Iranaeus, Melito, Tertullian, Hippolytus, Methodius). . . . The second line of interpretation [that the thousand years was poetic metaphor] may be called the *spiritual* view maintained by both Clement of Alexandria and Origen. Augustine popularized th[is] view" (ibid., p. 1089). Biblical dating (*annus mundi*), based on 6,000 years since the creation, was the system of the Byzantine Empire, which kept official chronologists in charge of recalculating years symbolically to prevent running out of time. A linear-chronological reading of John's text first became possible with the acceptance of *Anno Domini* dating (eighth century CE and later). For evidence of the eschatological appeal attributed to the year 1000 CE, see Richard Landes, *Relics, Apocalypse, and the Deceits of History: Ademar of Chabannes, 989–1034* (Cambridge, MA: Harvard University Press, 1995).

119. "If Pompeii had not been disinterred, its trace in the historical record would have been negligible" (Hales and Paul, "Introduction," p. 5).

120. The great Lisbon earthquake of 1755, which destroyed the Portuguese imperial port of long-distance trade, caused Voltaire to doubt there was a God at all concerned with human fate. Kant's response to this earthquake was to find hope in the scientific knowledge it revealed regarding how *not* to build on seismic faults. The Jesuit priest Malagrída declared Lisbon's destruction as divine punishment for the brutal effects of greed on the lives of Indians in Portuguese Brazil. Under the Portuguese prime minister Pombal, Malagrída was accused of treason and later heresy, and punished by *auto da fé* in 1761.

121. The stock elements of this genre of "toga fiction," and subsequent "sword-and-sandals" movies, are described by St Clair and Bautz: "The conventions and clichés that Hollywood adopted from the *Last Days*, and its theatrical and visual companions, are still as they were formalised in 1834 and earlier, including the archaic speech, the brutality, the beasts, the banquets, the baths, the lace-up sandals, the insertion of imaginary Christians, the misreading—and misrepresentation—of the scale and implications of the ruins, the portentous attempts to awe young people and adults into Anglo-American middle-class conformity, and the burlesques which undermined them" (William St Clair and Annika Bautz, "Imperial Decadence: The Making of the Myths in Edward Bulwer-Lytton's *The Last Days of Pompeii*," *Victorian Literature and Culture* 40 [2012]: 389).

122. Bulwer-Lytton followed *Pompeiana*, a tourist manual by William Gell (the first comprehensive guide in English), to whom the novel is dedicated; the description was so vivid that tourists thenceforth asked to visit the homes of the novel's characters.

123. In the modern era, "before the *Last Days*, the idea that the Pompeians had brought their destruction on themselves was not widespread. In Bulwer's novel Pompeii was unequivocally

added to the list of cities, including Sodom, Gomorrah, Babylon, Tyre, and Nineveh that the Judaeo-Christian god had righteously punished" (St Clair and Bautz, "Imperial Decadence," p. 364).

124. St Clair and Bautz, "Imperial Decadence," p. 387 (the word "merciful" is an added modifier in the French translation).

125. Bulwer-Lytton, *The Last Days of Pompeii* (book 5, ch. 7), cited in Margaret Malamud, "*The Last Days of Pompeii* in the Early American Republic," in Hales and Paul, *Pompeii in the Public Imagination*, p. 206. Cf: "Woe! Woe, O great city. . . . In one hour such great wealth has been brought to ruin" (Rev 18:16). The novel found a strong reception in the United States, where evangelical sects believed the Second Coming and Day of Judgment to be immanent. Perhaps 100,000 followers of William Miller gathered on the night of October 21, 1844 to await the world's end (ibid., p. 206 and passim).

126. "The thesis that CIL4, 10062 and two cruciform artifacts in Herculaneum and Pompeii are Christian crosses, which indicate a pre-Vesuvian Christian presence in Campania, cannot be sustained. CIL 4, 10062 most probably portrays a scrawl. The cruciform indentation in a wall of Herculaneum was probably left by the support for a shelf. The bas relief of a bakery in Pompeii likely indicates some kind of baker's tool." See "Abstract," John Granger Cook, "Alleged Christian Crosses in Herculaneum and Pompeii," *Vigiliae Christianae* 72, no. 1 (2018): 1–20.

127. "The *Last Days* had mythologized a provincial town into a great city comparable with Rome itself" (St Clair and Bautz, "Imperial Decadence," p. 368). The belief that the eruption of Vesuvius was punishment for pagan immorality of the local populace was "a nineteenth-century Christian idea" (Mary Beard, *Pompeii: The Life of a Roman Town* [London: Profile Books, 2008], p. 279). In fact, of course, the population was indiscriminately destroyed. But the "speak-across" warning from then to the present was that virtue is rewarded with rescue, and wickedness is punished with physical suffering and death (St Clair and Bautz, "Imperial Decadence," p. 366).

128. St Clair and Bautz, "Imperial Decadence," p. 361. Britain's Slavery Abolition Act of 1833 voted to compensate British slaveholders for loss of property.

129. St Clair and Bautz, "Imperial Decadence," p. 369.

130. "Tragically—but conveniently for the plot, since she too is in love with Glaucus—the slave girl drowns herself," although her suicide is no sin, as she is not a Christian (Beard, *Pompeii*, p. 81).

131. At the time, even London's circulating library charged more for the book than the working classes could pay. But cheaper versions followed, as well as reprints, translations, and adaptations, none of which protected the original author. The visual spectacles of *Last Days* that proliferated reached ten times as many as the book (for details, see St Clair and Bautz, "Imperial Decadence," pp. 368–375). "In the absence of international copyright" "reprints, translations and adaptations proliferated" (ibid., p. 370).

132. Key figures of the "apocalyptic sublime" who engaged in the visualization of Revelation in the nineteenth century were William Blake, J. M. W. Turner, and John Martin. See Morton D. Paley, *The Apocalyptic Sublime* (New Haven: Yale University Press, 1986).

133. See Meilee D. Bridges, "Necromantic Pathos in Bulwer-Lytton," in Hales and Paul, *Pompeii in the Public Imagination*, p. 93.

134. See Francesca Spiegel, "In Search of Lost Time and Pompeii," in Hales and Paul, *Pompeii in the Public Imagination*, pp. 232–233. The title of the central volume of Proust's novel is *Sodom and Gomorrah*, the names of cities mentioned in the Septuagint (Deuteronomy 32:32) that were added as graffiti to a house in Pompeii. Like Pompeii, these biblical cites were producers of wine. Philo explains Deuteronomy's verse allegorically: "that which in word indeed is the land of Sodom, but in real fact is the soul made barren of all good things and blinded as to its reason" (Philo, *De congressu quaerendae eruditionis gratia* ["On Mating with the Preliminary Studies"] 109). Philo describes the moral dangers: wine, of which "nearly everyone is insatiably fond . . . especially those on serious business," affects "those who are the slaves of greediness"; they "start with small cups and move to goblets," drinking wine unmixed with water, "until they vomit. . . . 'For their wine is of the vine of Sodom,' as Moses says, 'and their tendrils are from Gomorrah; their grapes are grapes of gall, and their branches are bitter branches. The rage of dragons is their wine, and the incurable fury of serpents'" (*De ebrietate* 220–222). A whole book could be written on wine and the eastern Mediterranean trade, dry climates and thirst. Christians read the Old Testament book of Deuteronomy as a Christian text, and therefore misread the engraved words Sodom and Gomorrah as evidence for Christian presence in Pompeii. Moormann writes: "That a small Jewish community may have lived in Pompeii is plausible, but most historians and archaeologists today agree that the 'evidence' for Christians is dubious to say the least and provides no basis to admit a clear presence of either religious group" (Eric M. Moormann, "Christians and Jews at Pompeii in Late Nineteenth-Century Fiction," in Hales and Paul, *Pompeii in the Public Imagination*, p. 171).

135. Primo Levi's poem "La bambina di Pompeii" brings a young girl, as victim of Vesuvius, in constellation with Anne Frank and a Hiroshima schoolgirl, of whom not even a plaster cast remains (Joanna Paul, "Pompeii, the Holocaust, and the Second World War," in Hales and Paul, *Pompeii in the Public Imagination*, p. 341). Paul notes that in World War II, over 150 Allied bombs fell on the excavations of Pompeii, breaking the plaster casts of some of the victims, and producing a "grotesque" sense that they had been destroyed a second time (ibid., pp. 351–352). Plaster casts of the victims of Vesuvius were first constructed from the skeletal remains by a technique devised in 1863 by the archaeologist Giuseppe Fiorelli.

136. For a pro-Christian, anti-Hegelian review by a British contemporary, see "Publishing News from Germany," *Foreign Quarterly Review* 28 (1842): 500–502.

137. Bruno Bauer, *The Trumpet of the Last Judgment Against Hegel the Atheist and Antichrist: An Ultimatum*, trans. Lawrence Stepelevich (Lewiston, NY: Edwin Mellen Press, 1989), p. 64.

138. Bauer, *The Trumpet of the Last Judgment*, p. 156.

139. Bauer, *The Trumpet of the Last Judgment*, p. 142. Note that the fundament of anti-Semitism is included in the citations: "Judaism lacks, as Hegel says, a universal purpose . . ." (ibid., p. 154). The translator clarifies that Bauer believed Judaism was a particularly irrational form of religion, "a seemingly indigestible bit of a past that should long ago have vanished. . . . It should be pointed out, however, that Bauer's anti-Semitism was not grounded upon any racial theories, as racial mixing was seen as a positive good, nor was it grounded in any Christian prejudice. In sum, Judaism was condemned principally because it was a source and support of Christianity, which Bauer truly 'hated' as the prime obstacle in the face of human progress" (translator's introduction to Bauer, *The Trumpet of the Last Judgment*, p. 52).

140. Bauer, *The Trumpet of the Last Judgment*, p. 149.

141. Bauer, *The Trumpet of the Last Judgment*, p. 190.

142. Bauer, *The Trumpet of the Last Judgment*, p. 177.

143. Theodor W. Adorno and Max Horkheimer, *Dialektik der Aufklärung: Philosophische Fragmente* (Amsterdam: Querido Verlag, 1947).

144. The division is not between "religious" and "secular" thought, as both can be indifferent to the need for humans to act, and religious leaders (strikingly, Pope Francis I) are not all deniers of the science of climate change. Of the "irreligious" moderns who fight religion, Latour observes that "they have made *negligence* their supreme value. Nothing more can happen to them. They are already and forever in another world. There is no direction except straight ahead; it is as though the option of turning back had been cut off." Bruno Latour, *Facing Gaia: Eight Lectures on the New Climatic Regime*, trans. Catherine Porter (Cambridge, UK: Polity Press, 2017), p. 196.

145. Modernity's forgetfulness of its own effects collectivizes Freud's use of Pompeii as a metaphor for the human psyche as nonconscious sedimentations of the past. The Anthropocene's revelation brings to consciousness the sedimented nature within collective history. Latour criticizes the prejudice of secularism that "modernism is an entitlement that cannot possibly be undone. . . . The news does not sink in, as it were," whereas a Christian articulation of this position is the belief that because the Messiah has already come, "believing will save us." Latour protests against the undifferentiated, globalizing discourse of apocalyptic catastrophe wherein fear of coming disasters leads to paralysis of action, and admires the geoscientists who admit that they too are at a loss as to how to proceed, which is why dialogue with these scientists is necessary for the human sciences to engage. He argues that the true sense of "revelation" is embodied in the 2015 encyclical letter of Pope Francis, who unveils the crucial interrelatedness of apocalypse (which he understands, more accurately, as new knowledge) with the science of ecology and the persistence of poverty. Latour exclaims: "That is dynamite . . . booom!" Bruno Latour, Isabel Stengers, Anna Tsing, and Nils Burbandt, "Anthropologists Are Talking—About Capitalism, Ecology, and Apocalypse," *Ethnos* 83, no. 3 (2018): 600–601.

146. Jashemski and Meyer, *The Natural History of Pompeii*. The contributors are 27 professionals from seven nationalities who have collaborated on this common goal.

147. Philo, *De aeternitate mundi* ("On the Eternity of the World") 146. The created world cannot be destroyed or amended, but rather, containing "the seeds of decay in themselves," regenerates by seeds as well (ibid., 80). When things are wholly destroyed by fire, "it follows of necessity the fire itself must also be extinguished as no longer having any nourishment. . . . But it would be impious, and an impiety of double dye, not only to attribute destruction to the world, but also to take away the possibility of its regeneration; as if God delighted in disorder, and irregularity, and all kinds of evil things" (ibid., 85).

148. Philo writes of this choice of Noah, "since all the rest of mankind has been rejected for their ingratitude, he places the just man in the place of them all, asserting that he had found favour with God, not because he alone was deserving of favour, when the whole universal body of the human race had had benefits and mercies heaped on them, but because he alone had seemed to be mindful of the kindnesses which he had received." *Quaestiones et solutiones in Genesin I* 96.

149. Philo, *De praemiis et poenis* ("On Rewards and Punishments") 156.

150. "[T]he new Jerusalem is not a purely future event tacked on 'at the end' . . . [it] also gives added meaning to that term, *hypomonē*, so central to John's understanding of Christian existence." Leonard L. Thompson, *Revelation* (Nashville: Abingdon Press, 1998), p. 189.

151. Rev 12:1–16. She gives birth to a son, "snatched up to God and his throne" (Rev 12:5).

152. Translated as "clothed," the word περιβεβλημένη is the perfect passive of the verb περιβάλλω which means to embrace, to wrap around, to enclose.

153. Latour notes that it was Eric Voegelin who charted the reversal of meaning from "end times, in the Jewish and Christian traditions alike" as the hoped-for end of suffering "*within* the time that passes," into "the end, the final eruption *of* time that passes," that is, "the expectation of the end of the world." In contrast, Latour clarifies: "'End' means first of all achievement, then finitude, finally revelation, but always in and with time, and especially with the passage of time as its necessary medium" (Latour, *Facing Gaia*, pp. 196–197).

154. Latour points out that neo-Darwinian models of the self-correcting system of evolution are as faith-driven as that of belief in the self-correcting invisible hand of the market (*Facing Gaia*, p. 134).

155. Thompson, *Revelation*, p. 189.

156. Cited in John Dominic Crossan, *God and Empire: Jesus against Rome, Then and Now* (San Francisco: HarperCollins, 2007), p. 230. King's reference is to Rev 21:4–5: "He will wipe every tear from their eyes. There will be no more death, or mourning or crying or pain, for the old order of things has passed away. And the One sitting on the throne said: 'Behold I make all things new.'"

157. Richard Bauckham, "Economic Critique of Rome in Revelation 18," in Alexander, *Images of Empire*, pp. 59–60. Traditionally, this passage has been linked to the Old Testament prototype of the destruction of the flourishing Phoenician trading city of Tyre (in Ezekiel), and its language forms a "remarkable patchwork of skillful allusions" to this earlier precedent, as well as to Babylon's fall in Isaiah and Jeremiah (ibid., p. 53). Bauckham writes that in the context of this intertextual interpretive tradition, "John's list of twenty-eight items of merchandise imported by sea to the city of Rome has not received the attention it deserves" (ibid., p. 58). On the historical specificity of John's list of cargo, see also J. Nelson Kraybill, *Imperial Cult and Commerce in John's Apocalypse* (Sheffield: Sheffield Academic Press, 1996).

158. Myrrh (μύρον) was an aromatic ointment "imported from Yemen and Somalia at great expense" (Bauckham, "Economic Critique of Rome in Revelation 18," p. 69). Wise men from the east bring to Jesus at his birth the treasures of myrrh and frankincense (λίβανος) (Matthew 2:11).

159. Pearl diving was dangerous because of the depths required, and the prices were high: "for the largest and best [Romans] would pay more than for any other piece of jewelry" (Bauckham, "Economic Critique of Rome in Revelation 18," p. 62). For the significance of the pearl trade in the second century, see Katia Schörle, "Pearls, Power, and Profit: Mercantile Networks and Economic Considerations of the Pearl Trade in the Roman Empire," in *Across the Ocean: Nine Essays on the Indo-Mediterranean Trade*, ed. Federico De Romanis and Marco Maiuro (Leiden: Brill, 2015), pp. 43–54.

160. Articles fashioned from ivory included "statues, chairs, beds, scepters, hilts, scabbards, chariots, carriages, tablets, bookcovers, table-legs, doors, flutes, lyres, combs, brooches, pins, scrapers, boxes, bird-cages, floors" (Bauckham, "Economic Critique of Rome in Revelation 18," p. 66). On Πᾶν ξύλον θύϊνον: "the phrase may mean 'all articles made of citrus wood'"; men had an "extravagant mania" for tables made of this wood, which came from northern Africa (ibid.). Other expensive woods included ebony from India (ibid., p. 67).

161. Bauckham gives an expansive description: Silk was "imported at great expense from China, some by the overland route through Parthia, most via the ports of northwest India." Purple, obtained in minute amounts from shellfish "fished in various places around the Mediterranean . . . was much prized"; "Reinhold calls it 'the most enduring status symbol of the ancient world.'" Purple cloth was known to have been produced in Thyatira and Laodicea, two of the cities addressed by John. There was at least since Nero "an imperial monopoly in the purple dye," and an inscription in Miletus indicates that those involved in the purple trade were freedmen of the *familia Caesaris*. Scarlet (κοκκίνον) came from a berry of Anatolia, the best of them from Galatea (Bauckham, "Economic Critique of Rome in Revelation 18," pp. 62–64).

162. See the description of the *Periplus of the Erythraean Sea*, above, chapter 1.

163. The twelve gates of the heavenly city of Jerusalem described in Revelation were fashioned each "by a single pearl," while "the city walls were decorated with every kind of precious stones" and the street was of "pure gold" as clear as glass (Rev 21:20–21).

164. Bauckham, "Economic Critique of Rome in Revelation 18," p. 78. Some of the items on John's cargo list were staples—oil, flour, and wheat, all from Mediterranean trade. Wilson notes that the "facilitation of the eastern luxury trade was an indirect way of ensuring the grain supply to Rome by incentivizing the participation of private shippers in *annona* [grain] transport" (Andrew Wilson, "Red Sea Trade and the State," in De Romanis and Maiuro, *Across the Ocean*, p. 27). Egypt was Rome's granary. Bauckham writes: "There is some evidence of bread riots in the cities of Asia Minor around the time when Revelation was written, and since Rome had first claim on Egyptian wheat, before the other cities of the empire, resentment could well have been directed by the poor against the system of corn supply to Rome" (Bauckham, "Economic Critique of Rome in Revelation 18," p. 72).

165. Rev 18:13. The number of slaves in the Roman Empire in the first century CE is estimated at roughly 10 million, between 16 and 20 percent of the population (see Aune 52c, pp. 1002–1003). According to Bauckham, "Asia Minor was evidently the most important source of those slaves who were not taken in war. Ephesus . . . must have played a major role in exporting slaves from Asia Minor to Rome" (Bauckham, "Economic Critique of Rome in Revelation 18," p. 75). Demand for slaves was "a feature of the growing prosperity of the rich and the increasing size of the city [of Rome]. The demand was by no means met by the offspring of existing slaves. The enslavement of prisoners taken at war . . . continued to be important in the first century CE, but it cannot have been as productive a source as it had been during the period of continuous foreign wars. [W. V.] Harris argues that of the other sources (foundlings, children sold by their parents, adults selling themselves into slavery, slavery through debt, victims of kidnapping, some criminals), much the most important source, because of the common practice of exposing children, must have been foundlings" (ibid., p. 74). "Under strict Roman law, if a slave killed a master in his own house, all of his slaves living in the household were to be crucified," and Tacitus records a first-century CE case where the law was implemented, resulting in the death of 400 slaves including women and children: Keith Hopkins, "Novel Evidence for Roman Slavery," in Potter and Mattingly, *Life, Death, and Entertainment in the Roman Empire*, p. 111.

166. See Richard A. Horsley, "The Slave Systems of Classical Antiquity and Their Reluctant Recognition by Modern Scholars," *Semeia* 83–84 (1998): 19–66. The word for slaves, δυοῦλοι, appears multiple times in Revelation in the positive, metaphorical sense of being "slaves of God" in contrast to a human master (see the discussion of this word in chapter 4). Prostitutes, both male and female, were a category of slaves vulnerable to extreme misuse: Asian DNA has been found in Pompeii in a young female skeleton whose pelvis was deformed it is presumed by abuse as a prostitute. Slavery was not a racially or socially distinct category: in the first-century novel by Chariton of Aphrodisias, Callirhoe, a Syracuse noblewoman, was captured by pirates and sold as slave to a man whom she soon

claimed as the father of her child (having considered, and rejected abortion), resulting in her (surreptitiously bigamist) marriage; the true father, attempting to find her, fell into slavery as a mine worker, and was almost crucified before rescue. Chariton, *Callirhoe*, ed. and trans. G. P. Goold (Cambridge, MA: Harvard University Press, 1995).

167. Mass executions were public spectacles. Heads of defeated enemy leaders were sent on tour to advertise victories. The orator (Marcus Tullius) Cicero was killed and his tongue and hands nailed up on display. His younger brother, the propraetor of the province of Asia in 61–59 BCE, had a man convicted of patricide sewn into a sack with a dog, a snake, a rooster, and a monkey, and thence thrown into a river, a death penalty in Roman law known as *poena cullei* ("punishment of the sack").

168. War was the source of multiple brutalities. Josephus reports (*Bellum Judaicum* 6.418–420) that Titus had 97,000 captives during the Judaean War distributed to the Roman provinces to be slaughtered by sword or beast in the public arenas, presumably as a deterrent against further provincial revolts. Josephus himself, of course, had a different fate: freed from prisoner status he became a Roman citizen and was supported by imperial patronage.

169. Crossan and Reed, drawing on Josephus, speak of the "fiery destruction" of the Galilean towns of Jodefat (Gr: Jotapata) and Gamla where Josephus first fought against and then surrendered to the Romans. "Evidence of the battle is scattered widely across the ruins of both towns"; at Gamla, 1,600 arrowheads have been found. John Dominic Crossan and Jonathan L. Reed, *Excavating Jesus: Beneath the Stones, Behind the Texts* (San Francisco: HarperCollins, 2001), pp. 159–161.

170. "It is safe to assume that many Jewish women were raped by Roman soldiers." Cohen, *The Beginnings of Jewishness*, p. 304.

171. Josephus is our only account of this event; he reports that 956 Jews were killed at Masada (*Bellum Judaicum* 7.257–406). On changing views toward Masada in contemporary accounts, see Yael Zerubavel, "The Death of Memory and the Memory of Death: Masada and the Holocaust as Historical Metaphors," *Representations* 45 (Winter 1994): 72–100; and Honora Howell Chapman, "Masada in the 1st and 21st Centuries," in *Making History: Josephus and Historical Method* (Leiden: Brill, 2007), pp. 82–102. It may be noted that Josephus describes the killings at Masada again and again with the word *sphage* (σφάγη; *Bellum Judaicum* 7.394–397). It means "slaughter," but also throat, the spot where the victim of slaughter—animal or human—was struck, where the blood gushes from the wound, hence the cleansing of blood from the body is most extreme, so that the method is a form of purification (see Nicole Loraux, *Tragic Ways of Killing a Woman*, trans. Anthony Forster [Cambridge, MA: Harvard University Press, 1987], pp. 50–53). It is the manner in which, at Masada, wives and children were slaughtered by their warrior husbands who then in turn "offered their throats" to the ten chosen by lot to execute the act.

172. The emperor Claudius initiated the conquest of Britain (43–47 CE). Roman occupation was brutal; the Druid sacred groves were destroyed, instigating acts of vengeance against

the occupiers, including their wives ("stripped, mutilated and impaled" according to Dio Cassius, *Roman History* 62.7.3). The revolt coalesced around the queen Boudica and her three daughters, whose father Prasutagus (ruler of the Iceni tribe of Celts) had willed that his kingdom be ruled jointly by his family and the Romans. But Romans ignored his will and performed these extreme punishments. Graham Webster, *Boudica: The British Revolt against Rome AD 60*, rev. ed. (London: Routledge, 1993), p. 88.

173. Imperial marriages were arranged for reasons of power and property, and adoption of heirs by emperors was frequent. Given the instrumentalization and premeditation of family construction, oaths of loyalty to the emperor were required to be binding on the entire family. Augustus ensured the death of Julius Caesar's son with Cleopatra, Caesarion, a potential threat to his own imperial claim, as he, in contrast, was only adopted as Julius Caesar's son. Marc Antony's will was (illegally) made public, showing that he had promised the distribution of territories in the east, from Anatolia to Egypt, to Cleopatra's children, a plan denounced in Rome, where the Senate declared war—not on Antony (which would have been civil war), but against Cleopatra. After their deaths, their children were spared, and yet paraded through the streets in disgrace. Violence marked imperial domestic life. Nero arranged the murder of his mother Agrippina (59 CE), and kicked his pregnant second wife Poppaea (his favorite!) down the stairs (62 CE). It must be acknowledged that women, when they had power, were not less brutal in their wielding of it: Agrippina, it was rumored, poisoned her husband the Emperor Claudius, to ensure that her son Nero ascended to the throne.

174. A. J. Boyle, "Introduction," *Flavian Rome*, p. 25. Boyle continues: "Daughters began to be reared for specifically economic reasons: they offered a cheap way of securing advantageous alliances with other families" (ibid., p. 27).

175. Ann E. Hanson, "The Roman Family," in Potter and Mattingly, *Life, Death, and Entertainment in the Roman Empire*, p. 33.

176. This is skeleton ERC 110, described in Sara Bisel and Jane Bisel, "Health and Nutrition at Herculaneum: An Examination of Human Skeletal Remains," in Jashemski and Meyer, *The Natural History of Pompeii*, pp. 465–466. Skeletons ERC 13 and 98 are presumed to be of prostitutes due to a "pelvic abnormality also seen in the bones of a modern American prostitute . . . a deterioration beyond what would be expected from simple aging . . . also a series of small bony outgrowths along the rami" (ibid., p. 466).

177. According to Suetonius, any woman who cohabited with a slave was reduced to slave status (Boyle, "Introduction," p. 25). There were cases when Roman noblewomen chose prostitute legal status to protect themselves from the death sentence for adultery.

178. Augustus' refusal to allow a marriage alliance between his teenage daughter Julia and the Parthian king indicates that giving one's daughter to a foreign leader was a mark of subservience. Augustus sent a concubine named Musa instead, whom King Phraates married, while the latter's sons were sent to Rome to be hosted by the emperor. A corresponding logic guided Marc Antony's strategy when he proposed his son (with Cleopatra) in marriage

to the Armenian royal family (the Armenian king refused). Cleopatra's power devolved to Antony through their relationship.

179. See Sarah Pearce, "Rethinking the Other in Antiquity: Philo of Alexandria on Intermarriage," *Antichthon* 47 (2013): 140–155.

180. The standard translation of the word *ethnos* as "ethnic community" covers over a difficult history of biological/cultural identifications. Most problematically, it fosters the erasure of modern racism for which the benign discourse of ethnicity provides a substitute. The words "Nabatean" or "Sabean" may mean little to the modern reader; but if the term substituted is "Arab," a whole host of (mis)understandings follow. I have not discovered in my research an adequate accounting for the differences between *ethnos* as used in the first century and our usage of ethnicity today. John of Patmos supplies a whole list of collective identifications, implying that their meanings were distinct: ". . . authority over every tribe [φυλὴν] and people [λαὸν] and tongue [γλῶσσαν] and nation [ἔθνος]" (Rev 13:7). The translation (in NIV) reads *ethnos* as nation, but this is a modern rendering that may falsely imply that ethnicities were land-based. Buell's interesting book on *ethnos* or race (*genos*) as an early Christian category examines the fluidity of these terms despite their essentializing claims: Denise Kimber Buell, *Why This New Race: Ethnic Reasoning in Early Christianity* (New York: Columbia University Press, 2005). Shaye J. D. Cohen's book *The Beginnings of Jewishness* covers the issue most extensively. He notes that Philo warned against intermarriage lest the offspring (whom he calls *nothos* [bastard]) "unlearn the honor due to one God" (Philo, *De specialibus legibus III* ["On the Special Laws III"] 29), although "Philo knew many Alexandrian Jews who intermarried or committed other forms of rebellion against the Jewish community" (Cohen, *Beginnings of Jewishness*, p. 245). During the Second Temple period, "A gentile woman 'converted' to Judaism through marriage to a Jewish husband, a procedure presumed by the Bible and still presumed by Josephus" (ibid., p. 306). In the first century, *ethne* was written across women's bodies and moved with the exchange of women, while circumcision was a mark of belonging imposed on the bodies of men. The kingdom of Judaea included non-Jews. Those living within the territorial rule of the Hasmoneans were circumcised as a means of entry into the Jewish community. Whether this requirement was aimed at lapsed ("Hellenized") Jews who had neglected this law, or an imposition of force against non-Jews that, like the practice of inscribing war captives with marks of ownership, served as a rite of domination, or, perhaps, more humanely, as a way of opening membership to non-Jews that gave them equal status in the community, cannot be decisively determined. See Steven Weitzman, "Forced Circumcision and the Shifting Role of Gentiles in Hasmonean Ideology," *Harvard Theological Review* 92, no. 1 (January 2011): 37–59. Historians continue to debate whether circumcision was "forced" or "allowed" or even if it ever took place. All interpretations are based on Josephus (who is not totally trusted), supplemented by 1 and 2 Maccabees (in the latter, the distinction between *Judaismos* and *Hellenismos* first appears). The books of Maccabees were written *ex post facto* to justify the Hasmonean dynasty established by the Maccabean revolt against Seleucid "tyrants" (167–160 BCE), who, they claim, prohibited circumcision in an attempt at forced Hellenization.

181. Historians dealing with the first century CE have attempted to make a distinction in terminology, using "Jewish" to mean what is described in the sources as "following the ancestral laws," i.e., customary practices that were accessible to individuals anywhere in the diaspora (but would be threatened through intermarriage if the children did not follow these laws), and "Judaean" as belonging to the territory of Judaea, which, while changing over the centuries, could and did include non-Jews under the dynastic rule of Jewish kings. For insight into the contentious problems of historical truth in this domain, see the anthology *Can a "History of Israel" Be Written?*, ed. Lester L. Grabbe (Sheffield: Sheffield Academic Press, 1997). Grabbe ends this small volume with a plea, if not for unity of hermeneutic positions, then at least for the acknowledgment that both "biblical history" (which treats Old Testament stories as continuous with the modern state of Israel) and "biblical geography" (which does the same with the archaeology of this region) is "bogus history"—whereas "[t]o write a 'history of Israel' as the history of an *ethnic* identity is simply too question-begging. . . . Even using 'Israel' as a *political* term has its problems" (Grabbe, "Reflections on the Discussion," in *Can a "History of Israel" Be Written?*, p. 189). Grabbe considers first-century Judaism a form of Hellenism: "Some of us are also on record as rejecting the existence of a 'normative Judaism' before 70 CE. Unfortunately, there seems to be a recent countermovement back toward the idea of a Pharisee [priest]-dominated Judaism" (ibid., p. 195). The ethico-political stakes are high, given the fact that the more ancient Judaism is in the land of Israel, the more ideologically convincing the exclusion of Palestinians appears. Grabbe states clearly: "[T]o treat a history of one particular 'nation' as *the* history is mistaken, especially if that history accepts only a chauvinistic ideology which treats other inhabitants of the region as inferior, insignificant, non-existent, or even as worthy only of annihilation" (ibid., p. 189). Grabbe's conclusion supports that of Erich Gruen: "The Jews were not so much permeated by the culture of the Greeks as they were an example of it" (Erich S. Gruen, *Heritage and Hellenism: The Reinvention of Jewish Tradition* [Berkeley: University of California Press, 1998], p. 292). For the role of archaeology since the 1967 war in fostering the ideological use of the past, see Nadia Abu El-Haj, *Facts on the Ground: Archaeological Practice and Territorial Self-Fashioning in Israeli Society* (Chicago: University of Chicago Press, 2001).

182. Thompson asks critically: "Is the continuity between the Bible and Judaism reflective of a chronologically linear development, or is it an aspect of rationalistic anachronism, ideologically motivated: a continuity asserted—like that of Christianity's claim of the *New Testament* and the *Septuaginta*—by theological necessity?" (Thomas L. Thompson, "Defining History and Ethnicity in the South Levant," in Grabbe, *Can a "History of Israel" Be Written?*, p. 186). He proposes: "We might also think of Judaism in the Graeco-Roman period more as an intellectual and philosophical movement of Hellenism itself rather than so conveniently as a reactionary religious movement of Palestine's least Hellenized 'Jews'" (ibid., p. 185). He concludes: "If we will have a critical history, we must deal with the anachronisms we have created" (ibid., p. 186).

183. Strabo says: "'The Idumeans are Nabateans, but owing to a sedition they were banished from there, joined the Judeans and shared in the same customs with them." Strabo, *Geography*

16.2.34, cited in Steven Weitzman, "Forced Circumcision and the Shifting Role of Gentiles in Hasmonian Ideology," *Harvard Theological Review* 92, no. 1 (January 1999): 40–41.

184. Kraybill, *Imperial Cult and Commerce*, p. 185.

185. "The wealth flowing into Herod's treasure and the coffers of his ruling elite funded the construction of a lavish urbanization at Caesarea, and the initial investment of the port paid dividends by realigning trade routes from the East through his kingdom and by tapping into the lucrative Mediterranean sea routes. Herod transformed the Jewish homeland into a commercial kingdom" (Crossan and Reed, *Excavating Jesus*, p. 56).

186. Cohen, *The Beginnings of Jewishness*, pp. 272–273. Cohen writes that the historical Herod "regarded himself, and was regarded by other Jews, as a Jew. . . . Herod invented a blue-blooded Judaean extraction for himself, whereas his opponents (at least those who lived a safe distance after him) invented a non-Judaean extraction for him. In sum, depending on whom you ask, Herod was either a *Ioudaios* (that is, a Judaean and a Jew), a blue-blooded Judaean, an Idumaean and therefore not a Judaean, an Idumaean and therefore also a Judaean, an Idumaean and therefore a half-Judaean, an Ascalonite, a gentile slave, an Arab, or—the Messiah!" (ibid., p. 23). On the passing down of Judaic ethnicity Cohen notes: "full collection of all evidence discussing intermarriage is lacking" (ibid., p. 245n). "Perhaps the matrilineal principle [that all children of Jewish mothers were Jewish, the rabbinic rule, still maintained in Israel today] was already known and regarded as normative in some pre-rabbinic circles of the late second temple period, but none of those circles has left behind any documentation of this fact. The matrilineal principle is first attested in the Mishnah" (ibid., p. 273). Despite this principle, however, rabbinic family law remains patrilineal: "Status, kinship, and succession are determined by the father" (ibid., p. 264).

187. Herod shifted his loyalties from Marc Antony to Augustus, a practice that was not uncommon. In 41–40 BCE, when Antony was wintering with Cleopatra in the Anatolian port of Ephesus, where he was heralded as Dionysus and she as the new Isis, 300 senators traveled there from Rome to pledge their support. Note that Antony was already married to Octavia (sister of the future emperor Augustus) when he lived there with Cleopatra. See Morten Horning Jensen, "Josephus and Antipas: A Case Study of Josephus Narratives on Herod Antipas," in *Making History: Josephus and Historical Method*, ed. Zuleika Rodgers (Leiden: Brill, 2007), pp. 294–295. Regarding the Christian legend that Herod had all infant boys killed in the kingdom out of fear of a rival (taken to be Christ), Josephus, our best historical source, would be expected to have mentioned it, but did not.

188. "In fact, the combination of a distinctively Jewish identity and an explicit support of Roman rule had always dominated the self-conception of the Herodian dynasty and provided the basis of the family's power and status in Roman Judea." Julia Wilker, "Josephus, the Herodians, and the Jewish War," in *The Jewish Revolt against Rome: Interdisciplinary Perspectives*, ed. Mladen Popović (Leiden: Brill, 2011), p. 287.

189. Properly identified, he is "Alexander Lysimachus, arabarch in the reign of Tiberius, brother of Philo and father of Tiberius Julius Alexander (who became prefect of Egypt) . . . a man of

extraordinary wealth who loaned Cypros, the wife of Herod the Great's grandson Agrippa, 200,000 drachmas, and covered the nine gates of the temple in Jerusalem with silver and gold" (Wilson, "Red Sea Trade and the State," p. 26).

190. Josephus, *Antiquitates Judaicae* 20.100. "From a regional governorship of the Thebaïd in Upper Egypt in 42 CE Tiberius went to the Judean governorship in 46–48, to a military role alongside Corbulo in the Parthian war of 63 CE (Tacitus, *Annals* 15.28.3), then to the governorship of Egypt under Nero, and he became Titus' chief of staff in the Judean war (Josephus, *BJ*, 5.45–46, 6.237). Eventually, before dropping out of sight, Tiberius was to serve as praetorian prefect in Rome." Schwartz, "Philo, His Family, and His Times," p. 14.

191. See Josephus, *Bellum Judaicum* 2.487–488 for the rebellion of Alexandrian Jews.

192. Her date of birth is proposed as 28 CE, and she was a widow, therefore, at age 15. Eva Anagnostou-Laoutides and Michael B. Charles, "Titus and Berenice: The Elegiac Aura of an Historical Affair," *Arethusa* 48 (2015): 17–46, here p. 22.

193. This port was critical for trade routes down the coast of Africa and across to India and Sri Lanka, import taxes from which were of central importance for funding the emperor's *fiscus* (private purse) and hence the expenses of the empire. The *Petrie Ostraca* indicate that Marcus Julius Alexander was active in trade for private gain at both Myos Hormos and Berenike from 37 to 43/44 CE, suggesting "that government officials in Egypt, and undoubtedly elsewhere in the empire, could maintain their commercial interests while they served the state. . . . There seems to have been no concern on the part of the Roman state of a conflict of interest of an official serving the government." Steven E. Sidebotham, *Roman Economic Policy of the Erythrean Thalassa 36 BC—A.D. 217* (Leiden: Brill, 1986), p. 85. "M. Iulius Alexander . . . [is] attested on ostraca from the Nikanor archives as being involved in private trading activities at Berenice between 37 and 43/4 CE" (Wilson, "Red Sea Trade and the State," p. 26). Berenike was a frequent Egyptian name, beginning with the first Ptolemy ruler's wife. The naming of cities after women, and women after cities, was common practice. The title "metropolis" exalts such cities as mothers, including Jerusalem, the *metropolis* of Jews.

194. Boyle writes that the remarriage of young widows was a function of their essential role as "breeding machines": "They generally married in their early teens, and remarried, if still of childbearing age, when divorced or widowed. . . . Women's sexual practices were constantly regulated" (Boyle, "Introduction," p. 25).

195. Formal marriage of royal siblings was an *Egyptian*-Ptolemaic practice. Sibling incest was distinct from another form, that of sexual relations between young men and their stepmothers who might well be of their same age, and perhaps widowed—a practice condemned by pagans as well. See Paul Hartog, "'Not Even among the Pagans' (1 Cor 5:1): Paul and Seneca on Incest," in *The New Testament and Early Christian Literature in Greco-Roman Context: Studies in Honor of David G. Aune*, ed. John Fotopoulos (Brill: Leiden, 2006).

196. Josephus, *Antiquitates Judaicae* 20.145–147. Josephus recounts that when Agrippa I died (44 CE), rioters against the king stole the statues of Berenike and her two sisters; the statues

were brought to a brothel in the port city of Caesarea, "where they set them upon the roofs and offered them every possible sort of insult, doing things too indecent to be reported" (ibid. 19.357–358). For Josephus' rendering of such stories that suggest criticism of Berenike and Agrippa II in the *Jewish Antiquities* (presumed to have been written in the later years of Domitian's reign, hence about the time of John's writing of Revelation), and his lack of criticism of these figures in the *Bellum Judaicum* (normally dated between 75 and 79 CE), see Daniel R. Schwartz, "Κατὰ τοῦτον τὸν καιρόν: Josephus' Source on Agrippa II," *Jewish Quarterly Review* 72, no. 4 (April, 1982): 241–268. Schwartz proposes that Josephus found these stories in a source sympathetic to those who protested against the royal family's behavior (rumors of incest; Drucilla, sister of Berenike, seduced away from her husband by the procurator Felix; Berenike herself involved in licentious behavior during her marriage to Polemo), and the family's support of the high priesthood against the common priests, who believed them corrupt for accepting sacrifices from Romans (*Bellum Judaicum* 2.410–411); Schwartz, commenting on this source, ventures the "suggestion that fragments of the same composition may be found in the Babylonian Talmud" (ibid., p. 246). The Babylonian Talmud (a compilation of the "oral Torah" compiled ca. 500 CE) includes as well the legend that Titus had sex with a whore on a Torah scroll inside the Temple during its destruction.

197. Berenike's third husband and his two sons converted to Judaism. We do not know the details of Berenike's own pregnancies, if she had them, or whether her status was sufficient to provide access to power for those she married and their offspring, as it appears these sons were adopted as her own. Berenike was not only Judaean royalty but a freeborn Roman citizen, "derived from a grant of Julius Caesar to Antipater of Judaea in 47 BCE, hence the 'Julia' component of her name" (Anagnostou-Laoutides and Charles, "Titus and Berenice," p. 22).

198. Josephus, *Bellum Judaicum* 2.293–309. In her brother's absence (to attend Tiberius Juius Alexander's promotion to prefect of Egypt), she pleaded to Florus for mercy toward the rioters; he refused; captives were tortured and put to death as she watched. I am following here the reconstruction of events in the Honors Project 1 of Michael S. Vasta, Department of Classics, Illinois Wesleyan University, 2007, "Titus and the Queen: Julia Berenice and the Opposition to Titus' Succession," posted since September 2008: https://digitalcommons .iwu.edu/grs_honproj/1. See also Ilan Tal, Jewish Woman's Archive "Berenice" https://jwa .org/encyclopedia/article/berenice.

199. Rajak, "Friends, Romans, Subjects," p. 122. Berenike was visible "in the attire of a Naririte with her head shaven and (perhaps as a suppliant) with her feet bare" (ibid.). But it is only Agrippa II who spoke, according to Josephus (*Bellum Judaicum* 2.345–401).

200. Berenike was "blatantly ignored by the governor" and "hardly managed to escape and was nearly victimized by the soldiers; she thus shared the horrible experiences of her fellow-countrymen of being harassed and humiliated" (Wilker, "Josephus, the Herodians, and the Jewish War," p. 275).

201. Josephus, *Bellum Judaicum* 6.312–313.

202. Josephus, *Bellum Judaicum* 7.38.

203. Michael S. Vasta, "Flavian Visual Propaganda: Building a Dynasty," *Constructing the Past* 8, no. 1 (2007): 109 (citing Josephus, *Bellum Judaicum* 7.96). The act of self-humiliation was repeated by Jewish captives at the victory celebration in Rome. The Temple of Jupiter Optimus Maximus, the chief Roman god, had been damaged during the civil war of 68–69 by Vespasian's defeated rivals, and its rebuilding was an opportunity to "demonstrate his endorsement by the king of the gods through restoration of his chief temple" (ibid., p. 120). Vasta argues that the Flavians attempted to stage themselves as a continuation of the "good" Augustan emperors: "The rewriting of history in order to disparage Nero and promote Flavian restoration appears again and again throughout the reigns of Vespasian and Titus" (ibid., p. 121).

204. The event's symbolism was carefully staged, beginning at the Temple of Isis, Egyptian goddess of rebirth and eternal life, and ending at the restored Temple of Jupiter Optimus Maximus, as "a reenactment of the Flavian rise to power" from Alexandria, to victory in Judaea, to Rome (Vasta, "Flavian Visual Propaganda," p. 112).

205. Josephus's description is in *Bellum Judaicum* 7.124–168. The loot of war included portraits and gems (*Bellum Judaicum* 7.135–136) and statues of gods, animals, and prisoners (*Bellum Judaicum* 7.136–138). The execution of the rebel leader Simon bar Giora, "who had just figured in the pageant among the prisoners," was announced to the crowd (*Bellum Judaicum* 7.153–160).

206. Josephus writes: "almost all objects which men who have ever been blessed by fortune have acquired one by one—the wonderful and precious productions of various nations—by their collective exhibition on that day displayed the majesty of the Roman empire" (*Bellum Judaicum* 7.132–134).

207. Vasta, "Flavian Visual Propaganda," citing *Bellum Judaicum* 7.148–152.

208. Penwill relates that the exiled "Diogenes and Heras, two Cynic philosophers, had managed to sneak back to Rome and publicly criticized Titus' relationship with Berenice. Diogenes was flogged, Heras beheaded (the ultimate mind-expulsion)." John L. Penwill, "Expelling the Mind: Politics and Philosophy in Flavian Rome," in Boyle and Dominik, *Flavian Rome*, 356n.

209. "Titus visited Memphis and participated in the consecration of the sacred bull Apis, wearing a diadem, the symbol of a Hellenistic monarch. Augustus himself had declined participation in the ritual, and it seems that the act of accepting a diadem caused some controversy and suspicion of conspiracy at Rome" (Vasta, "Flavian Visual Propaganda," p. 108). There were rumors that he planned to stay in the east, against his father's wishes.

210. Vasta considers her Jewishness a significant obstacle, yet given the fact she was a Roman citizen there was no legal impediment to marriage. Married twice before, Titus followed "a long-standing Roman tradition of choosing wives to advance one's ambitions" (Anagnostou-Laoutides and Charles, "Titus and Berenice," p. 21). Perhaps he was attempting to redeem his earlier reputation for debauchery and brutality (reported by Tacitus, *Annals* 2.2.1).

211. The latter is particularly intriguing, as the golden table and menorah were placed in the Temple of Peace, suggesting "the ancient ritual of *evocation*, in which the Romans invited an enemy god to abandon his city and join the Roman side." This is the speculation of Vasta, who notes that the holy objects taken to Rome from the Temple were not destroyed but, rather, housed in a new "Temple of Peace" where, according to Josephus (*Bellum Judaicum* 7.159–162), they were displayed in lieu of a cult statue that, of course, Yahweh lacked (Vasta, "Flavian Visual Propaganda," p. 127). On the importance given to the Judaean temple treasures installed in the Temple of Peace, where Josephus and pilgrims (religious tourists) would have viewed them, see Honora Howell Chapman, "What Josephus Sees: The Temple of Peace and the Jerusalem Temple as Spectacle in the Text," *Phoenix* 63, no. 1–2 (Spring 2009): 107–130.

212. Corneille produced *Tite et Bérénice* that same year. Mozart's last opera, *La clemenza di Tito* which premiered in Prague in 1791, also mentions Berenike's dismissal; in some performances she also appears, but in silence, having no speaking or singing role.

213. Titus dismissed Berenike from Rome immediately upon his succession, although sources claim that both sides regretted it. "A colonnade was erected in Titus' honour by his former mistress in Beirut" (Boyle, "Introduction," p. 59n).

214. Samson writes: "The Romans accused Cleopatra of being a harlot, because of the descriptions of the riches of the East." Julia Samson, *Nefertiti and Cleopatra: Queen-Monarchs of Ancient Egypt* (New York: Barnes and Noble, 1985), p. 12.

215. Bauckham, "Economic Critique of Rome in Revelation 18," p. 56. In Isaiah 23:17, the city of Tyre's commercial contacts are called prostitution (in the Hebrew text, Tyre "fornicated with all the kingdoms of the earth"), and the profits of such trade are "the price of the prostitute" (Aune 52c, p. 988). The Septuagint translates this passage more mildly: Tyre "will be a market for all the kingdoms of the earth."

216. Rev 17:9. Aune describes stumbling on the coin image of the goddess Roma reclining on seven hills, and being stunned by its correlations with the imagery in Revelation—only to discover that other scholars—"about 3,741 (slight exaggeration)"—had noticed it before him, although "they had failed to exploit the identification in any meaningful interpretive sense." David E. Aune, "Revelation 17," in *Apocalypticism, Prophecy and Magic in Early Christianity*, p. 243.

217. "It is not that the people of Israel were obsessed with sexual ethics. Rather, the metaphor of 'whoring' stood for the selling out of the radical message of YHWH to the practices of the people who lived around them. . . . Whoring also stood for infidelity in the sphere of foreign relations." Wes Howard-Brook and Anthony Gwyther, *Unveiling Empire: Reading Revelation Then and Now* (Maryknoll, NY: Orbis Books, 1999), p. 167.

218. Kathy L. Gaca, *The Making of Fornication: Eros, Ethics, and Political Reform in Greek Philosophy and Early Christianity* (Berkeley: University of California Press, 2003), p. 165.

219. Philo, *De specialibus legibus* 1.124 (quoted in *The Cambridge Companion to Philo*, p. 11); cf. Rev 2:14, 20.

220. Frankfurter, "Jews or Not?," p. 415.

221. "Thus it appears that the Thyatiran prophetess, who was encouraging her followers to participate without qualms of conscience in the thriving commercial life of the city, was, so to speak, the local representative of the harlot of Babylon within the church at Thyatira" (Bauckham, "Economic Critique of Rome in Revelation 18," pp. 85–86). Bauckham argues that the "kings" with whom the harlot commits adultery "need not be literally kings. It will refer not just to the client kings who put their kingdoms under the umbrella of the Roman empire, but more generally to the local ruling classes whom, throughout the empire, Rome co-opted to a share in her rule," including the local aristocracy (ibid., p. 80). Pagels writes that John "borrows the sexual metaphor for idolatry" by associating the Thyatiran priestess "with the infamous Canaanite queen who induced her husband, Israel's king, to worship idols and even tried to kill the prophet Elijah" (Pagels, *Revelations*, p. 49). John of Patmos accuses "Balaam" (the biblical name of an evil prophet who tries to deceive Israel) and "Jezebel" of inducing people to eat food sacrificed to idols and practice fornication—becoming sexually involved with Gentiles or worse, marrying them (ibid., pp. 48–50).

222. Aune 52c, p. 931. Aune's "reasonable" speculation continues: "that [John] has universalized his outrage on the basis of his experiences and historical legacy as a Palestinian Jew who may have known Roman violence firsthand" (ibid.). A connection to Berenike has been read in Revelation's description of the harlot's fate: "how much she hath glorified herself and lived deliciously. . . . In her heart she boasts, 'I sit as queen: I am not a widow, and I will never mourn.' Therefore one day her plagues will overtake her . . . death and sorrow and famine, repaying her in kind for what she has done" (Rev 18:7).

223. Thomas L. Thompson, "Defining History and Ethnicity," in Grabbe, *Can a "History of Israel" Be Written?*, p. 181.

224. Bauckham's "Economic Critique of Rome in Revelation 18" is representative of class analysis. For postcolonial criticisms see Howard-Brook and Gwyther, *Unveiling Empire*. See also David L. Barr, ed., *The Reality of Apocalypse: Rhetoric and Politics in the Book of Revelation* (Atlanta: Society of Biblical Literature, 2006).

225. Schüssler Fiorenza counters feminist critics: "It must not be overlooked, however, that such female imagery for cities utilizes conventional language because then, as today, cities and countries were grammatically construed as feminine. . . . [T]he images of the heavenly woman, the bride, or the harlot symbolize cities as the places of human culture and political institutions and do not tell us anything about the author's understanding of actual women." Elisabeth Schüssler Fiorenza, *Revelation: Vision of a Just World* (Minneapolis: Fortress Press, 1991), pp. 95–96. Smith sees the figure of the whore of Babylon as both imperial city *and* a woman: "As an African American woman who is both a victim and participant in empire, . . . I embrace both [readings]: The figure of Babylon is a city because she reminds me of the imperial structures by which I and my ancestors have been victimized, and the very same structures from which I benefit. (I am torn.) The figure of Babylon is also a woman because I resonate with the violence that *she* experienced as a female. . . . John's text reminds me

of what my female ancestors endured at the whim of their slavemasters. (I am incensed.)" Shanell T. Smith, *The Woman Babylon and the Marks of Empire: Reading Revelation with a Postcolonial Womanist Hermeneutics of Ambiv*eilence (Minneapolis: Fortress Press, 2014), pp. 91–92.

226. "As Pippin suggests, the prostitute of revelation becomes a scapegoat for the evils of society. . . . The author of Revelation creates a new world where women embody purity and danger. Those in the most favored position, close to the Lamb hold that position because they 'have not defiled themselves with women, for they are virgins' (Rev 14:4)." Joan M. Sakalas, "The Whore of Babylon Metaphor—Permission to Erase Evil?," *Journal of Religion and Abuse* 5, no. 4 (2003): 8. Sakalas concludes: "a theology or governmental vision that posits absolute 'good' in a particular people or nation or faith tradition and absolute 'evil' in others is both arrogant and dangerous. . . . [W]e are in danger of becoming the 'beast' we condemn" (ibid., p. 11).

227. Smith, *The Woman Babylon and the Marks of Empire*, p. 91. "And the ten horns that you saw, and the beast will hate the harlot; they will maker her desolate and naked; they will devour her flesh and burn her up with fire" (Rev 17:16–17).

228. Tina Pippin, "The Heroine and the Whore: The *Apocalypse of John* in Feminist Perspective," in *From Every People and Nation: The Book of Revelation in Intercultural Perspective*, ed. David Rhoads (Minneapolis: Fortress Press, 2005), p. 137. Pippin, who grew up in a fundamentalist Christian textile mill town where the book of Revelation was "mostly ignored" (ibid., p. 127), develops this argument in a book-length study, *Death and Desire: The Rhetoric of Gender in the Apocalypse of John* (Louisville: Westminster John Knox Press, 1992).

229. Pippin refuses the tradition of upholding the patriotic "authority and God-givenness of this final biblical text," and "the belief that God is ultimately 'on our side'" (Pippin, "The Heroine and the Whore," pp. 141–142). Nathaniel Hawthorne's historical novel *The Scarlet Letter* (1850) thematizes adultery and rejection by the community, turning Revelation into a tale of sin and redemption. Representations of the adulterous woman reach a dystopian frenzy in Margaret Atwood's futurist (and feminist) novel *The Handmaid's Tale* (1986), that tells of state enslavement of women, divided into slaves and whores. "Womanist" readings insist on the convergence of these categories: slaves were sexually abused, and Roman prostitutes were slaves.

230. "There's a whole heap of them kinda by-words. . . . They all got a hidden meanin' jus' like de Bible. Everybody can't understand what they mean. Most people is thin-brained. They's born wid they feet under de moon. Some folks is born wid they feet on de sun and then kin seek out de inside meanin' of words." Zora Neale Hurston, *Mules and Men*, cited in Clarice J. Martin, "Polishing the Unclouded Mirror: A Womanist Reading of Revelation 18:13," in Rhoads, *From Every People and Nation*, p. 92.

231. Martin, "Polishing the Unclouded Mirror," p. 95. Martin's citations are from John Lowe, *Jump at the Sun: Zora Neale Hurston's Cosmic Comedy* (Urbana: University of Illinois Press,

1997), pp. 206–209, 249–250. The quotation "tilt the hermeneutic mirror" is in ibid., p. 87.

232. "This is my conclusion as a womanist biblical interpreter who, in Hurston's words, 'seeks the inside meaning' of John's words—the nuanced significance of the words limned and blanketed within his text" (Martin, "Polishing the Unclouded Mirror," p. 95). Cf. Benjamin: "Universal histories are not inevitably reactionary. But a universal history *without* a structural [*konstruktiv*] principle is reactionary. The structural principle of universal history allows it to be represented in partial histories" (Walter Benjamin, *Selected Writings*, vol. 4: 1938–1940, ed. Michael W. Jennings [Cambridge, MA: Harvard University Press, 2003], p. 404).

233. Cited in Martin, "Polishing the Unclouded Mirror," p. 83.

234. Cited in Renita J. Weems, "Reading *Her Way* through the Struggle: African American Women and the Bible," in *Stony the Road We Trod: African American Biblical Interpretation*, ed. Cain Hope Felder (Minneapolis: Fortress Press, 1991), p. 61. Thurman's maternal grandmother, Nancy Ambrose, had been a slave on a plantation in Madison County, Florida. Both she and Thurman's mother Alice were members of Mount Bethel Baptist Church in Waycross, Daytona Beach, Florida, established in 1885.

235. Weems, "Reading *Her Way* through the Struggle," p. 62. Slaves develop an "aural hermeneutics" in listening to the Bible that enables them to measure the text against "what they have experienced of God and reality" (ibid., p. 66).

236. Walter Benjamin, "On the Concept of History" (1940), in *Selected Writings*, vol. 4, p. 391. Benjamin clarifies: "The danger threatens both the content of the tradition and those who inherit it. For both, it is one and the same thing: the danger of becoming a tool of the ruling class" (ibid.).

237. Walter Benjamin, "Paralipomena to 'On the Concept of History'" (1940), in *Selected Writings*, vol. 4, p. 406. That such silencing is particularly true of women, indeed biblical women, whose violation is reduced to the sound of a cry, or to the Hebrew demonstrative "*this*," is the protest of Elizabeth J. A. Siwo-Okundi in her article "Violence against Women and Girls: Where Is God in 'This'?," *Journal of Religion and Abuse* 8, no. 4 (2008): 7–14.

238. The emperor Domitian took as his mistress Julia, his brother Titus' daughter, who, to Domitian's displeasure, became pregnant; she died painfully due to a forced, and failed abortion. In the first-century novel by Chariton of Aphrodisias, the heroine, Callirhoe, contemplates an abortion, but decides to lie instead about the child's paternity (Chariton, *Callirhoe*, pp. 119–131).

239. Nero and Chariton's hero both kick their wives downstairs; in the novel Callirhoe appears dead from the violence of her husband, is buried, then robbed still alive from her tomb, and sold by a pirate as slave (Chariton, *Callirhoe*, pp. 47ff.).

240. Harris writes that abandoned babies were the source of replenishing the slave population. W. V. Harris, "Slavery: Towards a Study of the Roman Slave Trade," in *Rome's Imperial Economy* (Oxford: Oxford University Press, 2010).

241. Martin, "Polishing the Unclouded Mirror," p. 96.

242. Benjamin, "Paralipomena," p. 407.

243. Benjamin, "Paralipomena," p. 402. (Translation modified: *endlich* is translated "finally," not "ultimately").

244. Ginzburg writes that the historian's method is to follow clues and traces, much like the detective, or hunter, or even the inquisitor, turning these details into narratives. Carlo Ginzburg, *Clues, Myths and the Historical Method*, trans. John Tedeschi and Anne C. Tedeschi (Baltimore: Johns Hopkins University Press, 1989).

245. See Thomas Albert Howard, *Religion and the Rise of Historicism: W. M. L. de Wette, Jacob Burckhardt, and the Theological Origins of Nineteenth-Century Historical Consciousness* (Cambridge: Cambridge University Press, 2000). Howard's account is helpful in clarifying the "crisis of historicism" that emerged in nineteenth-century Germany when the study of history went from being the handmaiden of theology to becoming the dominant form of humanistic scholarship. The consequent historicization of religion robbed theology of its legitimation as a source of transcendent truth without replacing it with an alternative. Philosophy was forced to deal with the historical and cultural contingency of truth and the contextual limits of its claims. Heidegger's solution to this epistemological crisis was to shift the focus to the ontological question, the meaning of existence, attempting to preserve permanence for truth by transforming history into historicality. It should be noted that Heidegger's ontology made it unnecessary for him to take a stand against fascism or any other specific historical situation. In this sense, Thurman's grandmother Nancy Ambrose was the superior philosopher.

246. Barbara Burrell, *Neokoroi: Greek Cities and Roman Emperors* (Boston: Brill, 2003), p. 1.

247. Cited in Pieter Willem Van der Horst, "*Philosophia Epeisaktos*: Some Notes on Josephus, *A.J.* 18.9," in Popović, *The Jewish Revolt against Rome*, p. 312.

248. "Truth is undoubtedly the sort of error that cannot be refuted because it was hardened into an unalterable form in the long baking process of history." Michel Foucault, with reference to Nietzsche's *Gay Science*, "Nietzsche, Genealogy, History," in *The Foucault Reader*, ed. Paul Rabinow (New York: Pantheon Books, 1984), p. 79.

249. See G. K. Beale, *The Use of Daniel in Jewish Apocalyptic Literature and in the Revelation of St. John* (Lanham, MD: University Press of America, 1984). Beale and McDonough trace the myriad references that privilege not only Daniel but also Ezekiel and Isaiah: G. K. Beale and Sean M. McDonough, "Revelation," in *Commentary on the New Testament Use of the Old Testament*, ed. G. K. Beale and D. A. Carson (Grand Rapids, MI: Baker Academic, 2007), pp. 1081–1161.

250. "Then one of the elders said to me, 'Do not weep! See, the Lion of the tribe of Judah, the Root of David has triumphed. . . . Then I saw a Lamb, looking as if it had been slain, standing in the center of the throne" (Rev 5:5–6). Humphrey interprets the polysemy: "things are *not* as they seem": "The Lamb is a Lion, the fugitive is a queen, and the dragon is

already judged. . . . In the words of Leonard Thompson, with the Apocalypse, the boundary markers are 'soft,' and so the question of identity is an ever-present one." Humphrey affirms the text: "Rejoice in spite of death, for death implies life"; "the authority of God is secure, despite appearances." Edith M. Humphrey, "To Rejoice or Not to Rejoice?," in Barr, *The Reality of Apocalypse*, p. 124.

251. Rev 7:17.

252. Rev 1:20; again: "The one who holds the seven stars in his right hand and walks among the seven golden lampstands . . ." (Rev 2:1).

253. Rev 5:6.

254. Rev 15:6.

255. "The angel swung his sickle on the earth, gathered its grapes and threw them into the great winepress of God's wrath" (Rev 14:19).

256. "For the lamb in the midst of the throne will shepherd them and will lead them to the springs of waters of life. And God will wipe away every tear from their eyes" (Rev 7:17).

257. In fact, the word "antichrist" does not appear in Revelation to describe the deceiving beast who rules and fulfills this role (Rev. 13:11–14). The figure of the antichrist gains popularity in the Middle Ages, but it becomes hermeneutically determining in the Protestant Reformation as fitting the historical figure of the pope.

258. Rev 12:9.

259. Rev 13:11, 14.

260. Not knowing when the deception will be exposed heightens the insecurity: "But if you do not wake up, I will come like a thief, and you will not know at what time I will come to you" (Rev 3:3).

261. Rev 14:5.

262. "In the Hebrew Bible, as in mainstream Judaism to this day, Satan never appears as Western Christendom has come to know him, as the leader of an 'evil empire,' an army of hostile spirits who make war on God and humankind alike. . . . Satan is not necessarily evil, much less opposed to God. . . . The root *ŝṭn* means 'one who opposes, obstructs, or acts as adversary.' (The Greek term *diabolos*, later translated 'devil,' literally means 'one who throws something across one's path.')" Elaine Pagels, *The Origin of Satan* (New York: Vintage Books, 1995), p. 39.

263. Rev 10:9.

264. Rev 19:12.

265. Rev 22:4.

266. Whitaker, *Ekphrasis, Vision, and Persuasion in the Book of Revelation*, p. 180.

267. Rev 18:4.

268. Rev 17:9.

269. Rev 13:18, again 17:9.

270. Rev 17:9–11.

271. Aune, 52a, p. lxi.

272. For intricate if inconclusive arguments regarding the literary structure of the text, see Aune 52a, pp. xc–cv. For source-critical theories of the evolution of the text in John's hands, see ibid., pp. cv–cxxiv. For the history of surviving texts/fragments of the book of Revelation, see ibid., p. cxxxiv.

273. This event is dated 605–c. 562 BCE; it leads to the exile of Jews known as the Babylon captivity.

274. "[T]here are 337 sentences in Revelation. Of these, 245 sentences (73.79 percent) begin with *kai*" (Aune 52a, p. cxci).

275. Rev 20:12–13.

276. Rev 18:10.

277. Michel de Certeau, *The Writing of History*, trans. Tom Conley (New York: Columbia University Press, 1988), p. 47.

278. De Certeau, *The Writing of History*, p. 27.

279. Aune 52a, pp. cxxxvi: The "most original form of the text" is third century CE. "Revelation is missing from most 'complete' minuscule copies of the N[ew] T[estament], and where it is found it has often been added at a later time" (ibid., p. clviii). Nonetheless, in the past century, "a great deal of progress" has been made in NT textual criticism generally," and "more is known about the textual tradition of Revelation today than about any other book of the NT" (ibid., cxxxvi). The myth of Semitic idiosyncrasies of language emerges here, with the original "awkwardness" of John's Greek "softened" by later copyists (ibid., pp. clix, cxcix).

280. De Certeau, *The Writing of History*, p. 47. "The prejudices of history or of historians disappear when the situation to which they referred is modified. The formerly living organization of a society invested within their point of view is changed into a *past* that can be placed under observation. Its status is transformed: no longer being present within authors as the frame of reference of their thought, it is now situated within the object that we, as new authors, have to render thinkable" (ibid., p. 34).

281. Quentin Skinner, *Visions of Politics*, vol. 1: *Regarding Method* (Cambridge: Cambridge University Press, 2002), p. 63. Skinner continues: "Sometimes even the pretense that this is history is laid aside, and the writers of the present are simply praised or blamed according to how far they seem to have aspired to the condition of being ourselves" (ibid.).

282. Skinner, *Visions of Politics*, vol. 1, p. 59. Concepts become "reified" and at the same time "animated," "hypostasized into an entity" that is "all too easily" spoken about by historians,

as if, after their historical "birth," they were treated as a "growing organism"—the idea of progress, for example, "as if the developed form of the doctrine has always in some sense been immanent in history" (ibid., p. 72). Skinner would resolve the problem by turning to the question of the past author's intent. More on this below.

283. De Certeau, *The Writing of History*, p. 21.

284. This is the position of Koselleck, one of the most accomplished practitioners of the history of ideas—a method that Skinner criticizes for presuming that concepts have a line of descent that animates history in its entirety. In contrast, Skinner historicizes concepts while insisting on the contingency of their historical transformations. But Koselleck is right to insist that the radical historicism as practiced by Skinner cannot be the whole answer.

285. Reinhart Koselleck, *Futures Past: On the Semantics of Historical Time* (in German, 1979), trans. and intro. Keith Tribe (New York: Columbia University Press, 2004), p. 11.

286. Rev 16:7: "true and righteous are your judgments" (ἀληθιναὶ καὶ δίκαιαι αἱ κρίσεις σου). The plural κρίσεις and verb form κρίνω are found repeatedly. See Rev 11:18, 16:5, 16:7, 18:10, 18:20, 19:2, 19:11, 20:12.

287. Reinhart Koselleck, "Crisis," trans. Michaela W. Richter, *Journal of the History of Ideas* 67, no. 2 (April 2006): 370.

288. Friedrich Schiller, from the poem "Resignation" (1784–1785). On Schiller's poem and its influence on others, including Hegel, see the article by Michael Rosen, "Die Weltgeschichte ist das Weltgericht," in *Internationales Jahrbuch des deutschen Idealismus*, ed. Fred Rush and Jürgen Stolzenberg (Berlin: De Gruyter, 2014), 256–272. *Weltgericht* is, literally, "judgment of the world," or "world tribunal" (Koselleck, "Crisis," p. 371).

289. It is relevant here to recall that in this Enlightenment context, the life of Jesus becomes a task of the historian who can establish its empirical verity. Jesus as a *historical* figure takes on the role of empirical "beginning." Christian belief is rescued in secular modernity by grounding its origin in historical fact. History dethrones theology by making theology its content. And yet "belief in history" itself "must be sacrificed to history," as there is "no privileged observer status" that would be impervious to the relativism implied (Howard, *Religion and the Rise of Historicism*, p. 16).

290. Koselleck, "Crisis," p. 371. The concept of crisis "has now entered into a dimension of the philosophy of history that was to become ever more significant in the course of the 18th century" (Koselleck, "Crisis," p. 363).

291. Koselleck, "Crisis," pp. 370ff. By delineating different interpretations of "crisis," not only the eschatological one that becomes in modernity a philosophy of history but also the older medical understanding of the crisis of an illness, he turns the tables on presumptions of historical progress, implying that the second meaning as soberly scientific is to be preferred.

292. *Verweltlichung* means literally making worldly. Koselleck comments in a way that clarifies his approach to the history of concepts: "For the historical treatment of words, parallel

expressions like *Verweltlichung* (secularization) and *Verzeitlichung* (temporalization) must be introduced; the domain of church and constitutional law must be taken into account historically; and in terms of intellectual history, the ideological currents that crystallized around the expression must be examined—all before the concept of *Säkularisation* is sufficiently worked up as a factor in and indicator of the history to which it relates." Koselleck, *Futures Past*, p. 87.

293. "Hence revolution became a metahistorical concept, completely separated, however, from its naturalistic origins," that is, those cyclical revolutions of nature captured in the ancient meaning of *chronos*. Koselleck, *Futures Past*, p. 50.

294. Rev 1:4, again 1:8. Also Rev 11:17: "we thank thee o Lord god Almighty, the one who is and who was . . . [εὐχαριστοῦμέν σοι, κύριε ὁ θεὸς ὁ παντοκράτορ. ὁ ὢν καὶ ὁ ἦν . . .]". For the Philonic understanding of "the one who is" (ὁ ὢν), see above, chapter 3. On the *Dreizeitenformel* found in Hellenic sources which takes on a messianic dimension in Revelation, see Sean M. McDonough, *YHWH at Patmos: Rev. 1:4 in Its Hellenistic and Early Jewish Setting* (Tübingen: Mohr Siebeck, 1999).

295. For *chronos* as the synchrony of apparently unrelated moments in time that account for events seemingly miraculous, see the article by Schwartz, "Κατὰ Τοῦτον Τὸν Καιρὸν: Josephus' Source on Agrippa II."

296. τὸ κατέχον, "that which withholds," or ὁ κατέχων, "the one who withholds," are words that do not appear in the book of Revelation. McQueen has demonstrated convincingly that this conservative function of apocalyptic thought finds a counterpart where it might least be expected, that is, among the tradition of political realists who, while seemingly opposed to nonempirical modes of argumentation, have historically constructed their theories as a way of warding off apocalyptic final days: for Machiavelli, Savanorola's predictions of Florence's tribulations and renewal; for Hobbes, Cromwell's antimonarchial zealous reformism; for Morgenthau, national defense in the thermonuclear age. The goal of such realists has been to hold back the *eschaton* (ἔσχατος = last). Alison McQueen, *Political Realism in Apocalyptic Times* (Cambridge: Cambridge University Press, 2018). The "Savanarolan moment," she argues, is not as antithetical to Machiavelli's own as usually understood in regard to their anticipation of the redemptive transformation of history. In the cases of Hobbes and Morgenthau, she describes their political theories as "fighting apocalypse with apocalypse," as "redirection," using "hopes and fears about the end of the world to secure adherence to political orders that promise perpetual peace" (ibid., p. 14).

297. Koselleck, *Futures Past*, p. 11.

298. Koselleck, *Futures Past*, p. 140. Koselleck describes Johann Albrecht Bengel's reading (in *Erklärte Offenbarung* [Stuttgart: Erhard, 1740; republished in 1773 and 1834]) as a "genuinely historical interpretation," a one-way street of progress in the realization of truth that "implied the irreversible singularity of historical events." Former interpretations of the Apocalypse were viewed not only as a collection of errors but also as historical progress: "The clearing away of past errors was at the same time made possible by the course

of history. And in this way, the [Hegelian] Phenomenology of Spirit is outlined" (ibid., 140). "Revelation disclosed itself . . . in the progressive coincidence of empirical events and salvational interpretation." Event and interpretation progressively converged, but only in the medium of a genuine historical temporality. With progress, "it was natural that all past examples lost their force," "clearing away" past errors, including the error of interpreting Revelation itself. Here is where the history of reception turns into a theory of the correct reading of the text. Koselleck, like most Western historians, does not enter into a discussion of Islamic apocalypse. (See, however, Michael Cook, *Studies in Muslim Apocalyptic* [Princeton: Darwin Press, 2002].)

299. Judith Kovacs and Christopher Rowland, in collaboration with Rebekah Callow, *Revelation: The Apocalypse of Jesus* (Malden, MA: Blackwell, 2004), p. 121.

300. The telling of time in one Islamic apocalyptic text (ca. 780 CE) adheres to early Judaic and Christian models, albeit in a more historically positivistic vein, by including the chronicled time of the historic Byzantine, Umayyad, and Abbasid Empires. The seven-day week is the unit, given the Islamic lunar calendar. See Michael Cook, "An Early Islamic Apocalyptic Chronicle," *Journal of Near Eastern Studies* 52, no. 2 (January 1993): 25–29.

301. See Souleymane Bachir Diagne, *Open to Reason: Muslim Philosophers in Conversation with the Western Tradition*, trans. Jonathan Adjemian (Dakar, Senegal: CODESRIA, 2016); also Irfan Ahmad, *Religion as Critique: Islamic Critical Thinking from Mecca to the Marketplace* (Chapel Hill: University of North Carolina Press, 2018).

302. Jacob Taubes, *From Cult to Culture: Fragments toward a Critique of Historical Reason*, ed. Charlotte Elisheva Fonrobert and Amir Engel (Stanford: Stanford University Press, 2010), p. 46.

303. Skinner, *Visions of Politics*, vol. 1, p. 62. In studying context, Skinner acknowledges the ambiguities and multiplicities in the function of words in use. What a historian selects to narrate as history's meaning, then, will inevitably project present concerns.

304. De Certeau locates here "the very problem of historiographical work: the relations between the 'meaning' which has become an object, and the 'meaning' which today allows it to be understood as such" (De Certeau, *The Writing of History*, p. 34).

305. Hans Blumenberg, *Paradigms for a Metaphorology*, trans. Robert Savage (Ithaca: Cornell University Press, 2010), pp. 1–2. He continues: "Seen from the ideal of its definitive terminology, the value of a history of concepts can only be a critical and destructive one, a role it ceases to perform upon reaching its goal: that of demolishing the diverse and opaque burden of tradition, summarized by Descartes under the second of his fundamental critical concepts, prévention (corresponding to Francis Bacon's 'idols'). History is here nothing other than pre-cipitancy (*précipitation*) and anticipation (*prévention*), a failing of that actual presence whose methodical recuperation renders historicity null and void" (ibid., p. 2).

306. "Vico proceeded from the assumption that the clarity and distinctness called for by Descartes were reserved solely for the creator in his relationship of insight to his work: *verum ipsum factum*. What remains for us mortals? Not the 'clarity' of the given, but solely that of

whatever we have made for ourselves: the world of our images and artifacts, our conjectures and projections—in short, the universe of our 'imagination', in the new, productive sense of the term unknown to antiquity" (Blumenberg, *Paradigms for a Metaphorology*, p. 2).

307. Nietzsche, without Hegel's belief in historical progress, sensed a dissolution of his own person in the process of absorbing his time. See in this regard Foucault, "Nietzsche, Genealogy, History," pp. 82–83.

308. "The matters of true philosophical interest at this point in history are those in which Hegel, agreeing with tradition, expressed his disinterest. They are nonconceptuality, individuality, and particularity—things which ever since Plato used to be dismissed as transitory and insignificant, and which Hegel labeled 'lazy Existenz.'" Theodor W. Adorno, *Negative Dialectics*, trans. E. B. Ashton (London: Continuum, 1973), p. 8.

309. Greek philosophy "goes to ground," continuing to nourish the advance of philosophy that returns to it in the act of supersession: "Thus the beginning of philosophy is the ever-present and self-preserving foundation of all subsequent developments, remaining everywhere immanent in its further determinations" (Hegel, *Logic*, "Doctrine of Being" 21.58).

310. "For Hegel to move beyond Kant one must first move beyond positivity. 'Kantianism,' Derrida writes provocatively [in *Glas*, 1986, p. 34], 'is, in this respect [i.e., as an ethics of positivity], structurally a Judaism.' . . . Despite the antipathy to Judaism that marks Kant's own writings, in Hegel's scheme Kant becomes a 'Jew' by virtue of the 'positivity' of his ethics. In stripping Christianity of its formal and abstract morality, Hegel simultaneously expels the specter of Judaism from world history and the specter of Kant from his moral philosophy. . . . For Christianity to realize its Hellenism, Hegel must first emancipate himself from the 'Jewish' Kant." Miriam Leonard, *Socrates and the Jews: Hellenism and Hebraism from Moses Mendelssohn to Sigmund Freud* (Chicago: University of Chicago Press, 2012), p. 77.

311. Theodor W. Adorno, *History and Freedom: Lectures 1964–65*, ed. Rolf Tiedemann, trans. Wieland Hoban (Cambridge, UK: Polity, 2006), p. 39.

312. Benjamin, letter to Gershom Scholem, January 31, 1918, in *Walter Benjamin, Briefe*, 2 vols., ed. Gershom Scholem and Theodor W. Adorno (Frankfurt am Main: Suhrkamp, 1966), vol. 1, p. 171, trans. in Anson Rabinbach, "Between Enlightenment and Apocalypse: Benjamin, Bloch and Modern German Jewish Messianism," *New German Critique*, no. 34 (Winter 1985): 112.

Bibliography

Adorno, Theodor W. *History and Freedom: Lectures 1964–1965*. Edited by Rolf Tiedemann. Translated by Wieland Hoban. Cambridge, UK: Polity, 2006.

———. *Metaphysics: Concept and Problems*. Edited by Rolf Tiedemann. Translated by Edmund Jephcott. Stanford: Stanford University Press, 2001.

———. *Negative Dialectics*. Translated by E. B. Ashton. New York: Continuum, 1973.

Adorno, Theodor W., and Max Horkheimer. *Dialektik der Aufklärung: Philosophische Fragmente*. Amsterdam: Querido Verlag, 1947.

Agamben, Giorgio. *Stasis: Civil War as a Political Paradigm*. Stanford: Stanford University Press, 2015.

———. *The Time That Remains: A Commentary on the Letter to the Romans*. Translated by Patricia Dailey. Stanford: Stanford University Press, 2005.

Ahmad, Irfan. *Religion as Critique: Islamic Critical Thinking from Mecca to the Marketplace*. Chapel Hill: University of North Carolina Press, 2018.

Alesse, Francesca. *Philo of Alexandria and Post-Aristotelian Philosophy*. Leiden: Brill, 2008.

Allison, June W. *Word and Concept in Thucydides*. Atlanta: Scholar's Press, 1997.

Anagnostou-Laoutides, Eva, and Michael B. Charles. "Titus and Berenice: The Elegiac Aura of an Historical Affair." *Arethusa* 48 (2015): 17–46.

"Ancient Inscription Shifts Date of Pompeii's Destruction." *Science* 362, no. 6413 (October 26, 2018): 382.

Ando, Clifford. *Imperial Ideology and Provincial Loyalty in the Roman Empire*. Berkeley: University of California Press, 2000.

Ariel, Donald T. "Identifying the Mints, Minters and Meanings of the First Jewish Revolt Coins." In *The Jewish Revolt against Rome: Interdisciplinary Perspectives*, edited by Mladen Popović, 373–398. Leiden: Brill, 2011.

Armstrong, Karen. *St. Paul: The Apostle We Love to Hate*. Boston: New Harvest, 2015.

Aune, David E. *Apocalypticism, Prophecy and Magic in Early Christianity: Collected Essays*. Tübingen: Mohr Siebeck, 2006.

———. *Prophecy in Early Christianity and the Ancient Mediterranean World*. Grand Rapids, MI: Eerdmans, 1983.

———. *Revelation*. 3 vols. World Biblical Commentary 52a (Revelation 1–5), 52b (Revelation 6–16), 52c (Revelation 17–22). Dallas: World Books, 1997–1998.

Badiou, Alain. *Saint Paul: The Foundation of Universalism*. Translated by Ray Brassier. Stanford: Stanford University Press, 2003.

Barclay, John M. G. *Pauline Churches and Diaspora Jews*. Tübingen: Mohr Siebeck, 2011.

Barker, Andrew. "Ptolemy's Pythagoreans, Archytas, and Plato's Conception of Mathematics." *Phronesis* 39, no. 2 (1994): 113–135.

———. "Pythagorean Harmonics." In *A History of Pythagoreanism*, edited by Carl A. Huffman. Cambridge: Cambridge University Press, 2014.

Barr, David L., ed. *The Reality of Apocalypse: Rhetoric and Politics in the Book of Revelation*. Atlanta: Society of Biblical Literature, 2006.

Barton, Carlin A., and Daniel Boyarin. *Imagine No Religion: How Modern Abstractions Hide Ancient Realities*. New York: Fordham University Press, 2016.

Bauckham, Richard. *The Climax of Prophecy: Studies on the Book of Revelation*. Edinburgh: T&T Clark, 1993.

———. "Economic Critique of Rome in Revelation 18." In *Images of Empire*, edited by Loveday Alexander, 122–135. Sheffield: Sheffield Academic Press, 1991.

———. "The Eschatological Earthquake in the Apocalypse of John." *Novum Testamentum* 19, no. 3 (July 1977): 224–233.

Bauer, Bruno. *The Trumpet of the Last Judgment against Hegel the Atheist and Antichrist: An Ultimatum*. Lewiston, NY: Edwin Mellen Press, 1989.

Beale, G. K. *The Use of Daniel in Jewish Apocalyptic Literature and in the Revelation of St. John*. Lanham, MD: University Press of America, 1984.

Beard, Mary. *Pompeii: The Life of a Roman Town*. London: Profile Books, 2008.

———. "The Triumph of Flavius Josephus." In *Flavian Rome: Culture, Image, Text*, edited by A. J. Boyle and W. J. Dominik. Leiden: Brill, 2002.

Benjamin, Walter. *The Arcades Project*. Translated by Howard Eiland and Kevin McLaughlin. Cambridge, MA: Belknap Press of Harvard University Press, 1999.

———. *Gesammelte Schriften*. With collaboration of Theodor W. Adorno and Gershom Scholem, edited by Rolf Tiedemann and Hermann Schweppenhäuser. 7 vols. Frankfurt am Main: Suhrkamp Verlag, 1972–1989.

———. "On the Mimetic Faculty." In *Selected Writings*, edited by Michael W. Jennings et al., translated by Rodney Livingston, vol. 2. Cambridge, MA: Harvard University Press, 1999.

———. "Paralipomena to 'On the Concept of History.'" In *Selected Writings*, edited by Marcus Bullock, Michael W. Jennings, Gary Smith, and Howard Eiland, vol. 4. Cambridge, MA: Harvard University Press, 2003.

———. "The Task of the Translator." In *Selected Writings*, edited by Marcus Bullock and Michael W. Jennings, translated by Harry Zohn, vol. 1. Cambridge, MA: Harvard University Press, 1996.

Bernal, Martin. *Black Athena: The Afroasiatic Roots of Classical Civilization*, vol. 1: *The Fabrication of Ancient Greece 1785–1985*. New Brunswick: Rutgers University Press, 1987.

———. *Black Athena: The Afroasiatic Roots of Classical Civilization*, vol. 2: *The Archaeological and Documentary Evidence*. New Brunswick: Rutgers University Press, 1991.

Bielik-Robson, Agata. "Marrano Universalism: Benjamin, Derrida, and Buck-Morss on the Condition of Universal Exile." *Telescope* (blog), Telos: Critical Theory of the Contemporary, June 8, 2015. http://www.telospress.com/marrano-universalism-benjamin-derrida-and-buck -morss-on-the-condition-of-universal-exile/.

Bisel, Sara, and Jane Bisel. "Health and Nutrition at Herculaneum: An Examination of Human Skeletal Remains." In *The Natural History of Pompeii*, ed. Wilhelmina Feemster Jashemski and Frederick G. Meyer (Cambridge: Cambridge University Press, 2002).

Blumenberg, Hans. *Paradigms for a Metaphorology*. Translated by Robert Savage. Ithaca: Cornell University Press, 2010.

Bond, Helen K. "Josephus and the New Testament." In *Companion to Josephus*, edited by Honora Howell Chapman and Zuleika Rodgers. Malden, MA: John Wiley & Sons, 2016.

Bovon, François. *Studies in Early Christianity*. Grand Rapids: Baker Academic, 2005.

Bowersock, Glen W. *Hellenism in Late Antiquity*. Ann Arbor: University of Michigan Press, 1990.

———. "Who Was Saint Paul?" *New York Review of Books*, November 5, 2015. https://www .nybooks.com/articles/2015/11/05/who-was-saint-paul/.

Bowman, Steve. "Josephus in Byzantium." In *Josephus, Judaism, and Christianity*, edited by Louis H. Feldman and Gohei Hata. Detroit: Wayne State University Press, 1987.

Boyarin, Daniel. *Border Lines: The Partition of Judaeo-Christianity*. Philadelphia: University of Pennsylvania Press, 2006.

———. "The Ioudaioi in John and the Prehistory of 'Judaism.'" In *Pauline Conversations in Context*, edited by Janice Capel Anderson, Philip Sellew, and Claudia Setzer. London: Sheffield Academic Press, 2002.

———. *A Radical Jew: Paul and the Politics of Identity*. Berkeley: University of California Press, 1994.

Boyle, A. J. "Introduction." In *Flavian Rome: Culture, Image, Text*, edited by A. J. Boyle and W. J. Dominik. Leiden: Brill, 2002.

Bridges, Meilee D. "Necromantic Pathos in Bulwer-Lytton." In *Pompeii in the Public Imagination from Its Rediscovery to Today*, edited by Shelley Hales and Joanna Paul. Oxford: Oxford University Press, 2012.

Buck-Morss, Susan. *The Dialectics of Seeing: Walter Benjamin and the Arcades Project*. Cambridge, MA: MIT Press, 1989.

Buell, Denise Kimber. *Why This New Race: Ethnic Reasoning in Early Christianity*. New York: Columbia University Press, 2005.

Burrell, Barbara. *Neokoroi: Greek Cities and Roman Emperors*. Boston: Brill, 2003.

Burton, Henry Fairfield. "The Worship of the Roman Emperors." *Biblical World* 40, no. 2 (August 1912): 80–91.

Butler, Judith. *Antigone's Claim*. New York: Columbia University Press, 2002.

"Calendar Era: Ancient Dating Systems." Wikipedia, January 21, 2020. https://en.wikipedia .org/w/index.php?title=Calendar_era&oldid=936796523.

Carabine, Deirdre. *The Unknown God: Negative Theology in the Platonic Tradition: Plato to Eriugena*. Louvain: Peters Press/W. B. Eerdmans, 1995.

Carson, D. A., and G. K. Beale, eds. *Commentary on the New Testament Use of the Old Testament*. Grand Rapids, MI: Baker Academic, 2007.

Cassin, Barbara, ed. *Vocabulaire européen des philosophies: Dictionnaire des intraduisibles* (Paris: Éditions du Seuil, 2004). English trans., *Dictionary of Untranslatables: A Philosophical Lexicon*. Edited by Emily Apter, Jacques Lezra, and Michael Wood; translated by Steven Rendall, Christian Hubert, Jeffrey Mehlman, Nathanael Stein, and Michael Syrotinski. Princeton: Princeton University Press, 2014.

Casson, Lionel. *Libraries in the Ancient World*. New Haven: Yale University Press, 2002.

Certeau, Michel de. *The Writing of History*. Translated by Tom Conley. New York: Columbia University Press, 1988.

Chancellor, Gary. "Hölderlin, Brecht, Anouilh: Three Versions of Antigone." *Orbis Litterarum* 34, no. 1 (1979): 87–97.

Chaniotis, Angelos. "The Ithyphallic Hymn for Demetrios Poliorketes and Hellenistic Religious Mentality." In *More Than Men, Less Than Gods: Studies on Royal Cult and Imperial Worship*, edited by Panagiotis P. Iossif, Andrzej S. Chankowski, and Catharine C. Lorber. Leuven: Peeters, 2011.

Chapman, Honora Howell. "'By the Waters of Babylon': Josephus and Greek Poetry." In *Josephus and Jewish History in Flavian Rome and Beyond*, edited by Joseph Sievers and Gaia Lembi. Boston: Brill, 2005.

———. "Masada in the 1st and 21st Centuries." In *Making History: Josephus and Historical Method*. Leiden: Brill, 2007.

———. "What Josephus Sees: The Temple of Peace and the Jerusalem Temple as Spectacle in the Text." *Phoenix* 63, no. 5 (2009): 77–78.

Chariton. *Callirhoe*. Edited and translated by G. P. Goold. Cambridge, MA: Harvard University Press, 1995.

Cohen, Shaye J. D. *The Beginnings of Jewishness: Boundaries, Varieties, Uncertainties*. Berkeley: University of California Press, 1999.

Collins, Adela Yarbro. *Crisis and Catharsis: The Power of the Apocalypse*. Louisville: Westminster John Knox Press, 1984.

———, ed. *Semeia 36: Early Christian Apocalypticism: Genre and Social Setting*. Missoula, MT: Society of Biblical Literature, 1986.

Collins, John J. *The Apocalyptic Imagination: An Introduction to Jewish Apocalyptic Literature*. 2nd ed. Grand Rapids, MI: Eerdmans, 1998.

———. *The Dead Sea Scrolls: A Biography*. Princeton: Princeton University Press, 2012.

Columbus, Christopher. *Repertorium Columbianum*, vol. 3: *The Book of Prophecies (1500–1503)*. Edited by Geoffrey Symcox et al. Los Angeles: UCLA Center for Medieval and Renaissance Studies, 1997.

Cook, Brendan. *Pursuing Eudaimonia: Re-Appropriating the Greek Philosophical Foundations of the Christian Apophatic Tradition*. Newcastle upon Tyne: Cambridge Scholars Publishing, 2013.

Cook, David. *Studies in Muslim Apocalyptic*. Princeton, NJ: Darwin Press, 2002.

Cook, John Granger. "Alleged Christian Crosses in Herculaneum and Pompeii." *Vigiliae Christianae* 72, no. 1 (2018): 1–20.

Cook, Michael. "An Early Islamic Apocalyptic Chronicle." *Journal of Near Eastern Studies* 52, no. 2 (January 1993): 25–29.

Cooley, Alison E. *Res gestae divi Augusti: Text, Translation, and Commentary*. Cambridge: Cambridge University Press, 2009.

Corsten, Thomas. "Koinon." In *The Encyclopedia of Ancient History*, edited by Roger S. Bagnall, 3798–3799. Malden, MA: Wiley-Blackwell, 2012.

Çoruh, Shulamit Bruckstein. *House of Taswir: Doing and Un-doing Things: Notes on Epistemic Architecture(s) = Zur Umordnung der Dinge: Notizen zur epistemischen Architektur*. Paderborn: Wilhelm Fink, 2014.

Crossan, John Dominic. *Excavating Jesus: Beneath the Stones, behind the Texts*. San Francisco: HarperCollins, 2001.

———. *God and Empire: Jesus against Rome, Then and Now*. San Francisco: HarperCollins, 2007.

Crossan, John Dominic, and Jonathan L. Reed. *In Search of Paul: How Jesus' Apostle Opposed Rome's Empire with God's Kingdom*. New York: HarperCollins, 2005.

Cullmann, Oscar. *Christ and Time: The Primitive Christian Conception of Time and History*. Translated by Floyd V. Filson. 3rd ed. Eugene, OR: Wipf and Stock, 2018.

Declercq, Georges. *Anno Domini: The Origins of the Christian Era*. Turnhout, Belgium: Brepols, 2000.

Deissmann, Adolf. *Light from the Ancient East: The New Testament; Illustrated by Recently Discovered Texts of the Graeco-Roman World*. Translated by Lionel R. M. Strachan. 2nd ed. London: Hodder & Stoughton, 1910.

Delahaye, Ezra. "About Chronos and Kairos: On Agamben's Interpretation of Pauline Temporality through Heidegger." *International Journal of Philosophy and Theology* 77, no. 3 (November 2016): 85–101.

Den Hollander, William. *Josephus, the Emperors, and the City of Rome: From Hostage to Historian.* Leiden: Brill, 2014.

De Romanis, Federico, and Marco Maiuro, eds. "Introduction." In *Across the Ocean: Nine Essays on Indo-Mediterranean Trade.* Leiden: Brill, 2015.

Derrida, Jacques. "The Eyes of Language: The Abyss and the Volcano." In *Acts of Religion*, edited by Gil Anidjar. New York: Routledge, 2001.

———. *On the Name.* Edited by Thomas Dutoit. Translated by David Wood. Stanford: Stanford University Press, 1995.

Deutsch, Robert. "Coinage of the First Jewish Revolt against Rome: Iconography, Minting Authority, Metallurgy." In *The Jewish Revolt against Rome: Interdisciplinary Perspectives*, edited by Mladen Popović, 361–372. Leiden: Brill, 2011.

Diagne, Souleymane Bachir. *The Ink of the Scholars: Reflections on Philosophy in Africa.* Translated by Jonathan Adjemian. Baltimore: CODESRIA, 2016.

———. *Open to Reason: Muslim Philosophers in Conversation with the Western Tradition.* Translated by Jonathan Adjemian. Dakar, Sengal: CODESRIA, 2016.

Dillon, John M. *The Middle Platonists: 80 B.C. to A.D. 220.* Rev. ed. Ithaca: Cornell University Press, 1996.

Dines, Jennifer M. *The Septuagint.* Edited by Michael A. Knibb. London: Continuum, 2004.

Dio Cassius. "Roman History." Vol. VIII of Loeb Classical Library Edition, 1925. http://penelope.uchicago.edu/Thayer/E/Roman/Texts/Cassius_Dio/66*.html.

Dionysius of Halicarnassus. *On Thucydides.* Translated by W. Kendrick Pritchett. Berkeley: University of California Press, 1975.

Dittenberger, Willhelm. *Orientis Graeci Inscriptiones Selectae: Supplementum Sylloges Inscriptionum Graecarum.* New York: Georg Olms Verlag, 1986.

Dmitriev, Sviatoslav. *The Greek Slogan of Freedom and Early Roman Politics in Greece.* Oxford: Oxford University Press, 2011.

Drake, H. A. *In Praise of Constantine: A Historical Study and New Translation of Eusebius' Tricennial Orations.* Berkeley: University of California Press, 1976.

Dyson, S. L. "Native Revolts in the Roman Empire." *Historia* 20 (1971): 239–274.

Eck, Werner. "Flavius Iosephus, Nicht Iosephus Flavius." *Scripta Classica Israelica* 19 (2000): 381–383.

El-Haj, Nadia Abu. *Facts on the Ground: Archaeological Practice and Territorial Self-Fashioning in Israeli Society.* Chicago: University of Chicago Press, 2002.

Eluard, Paul. *Répétitions, dessins de Max Ernst*. Paris: Au Sans Pareil, 1922.

Erim, Kenan T. *Aphrodisias: City of Venus Aphrodite*. New York: Facts on File, 1986.

Etman, Ahmed. "A Light from Thucydides on the Problem of Sophocles' 'Antigone' and Its Tragic Meaning." *Antiquité Classique* 70 (2001): 147–153.

Fallahzadeh, Mehrdad. *Persian Writing on Music: A Study of Persian Musical Literature from 1000 to 1500 AD*. Uppsala: Uppsala Universitet, 2005.

Feeney, Denis. *Caesar's Calendar: Ancient Time and the Beginnings of History*. Berkeley: University of California Press, 2007.

Feldman, Louis H. "Hellenizations in Josephus' *Jewish Antiquities*: The Portrait of Abraham." In *Josephus, Judaism, and Christianity*, edited by Louis H. Feldman and Gohei Hata. Detroit: Wayne State University Press, 1987.

———. "The Influence of the Greek Tragedians on Josephus." In *The Howard Gilman International Conferences I: Hellenic and Jewish Arts*, edited by A. Ovadiah. Tel Aviv: Ramot Publishing House, 1998.

———. *Josephus and Modern Scholarship, 1937–1980*. Berlin: De Gruyter, 1984.

———. "Philo's Views on Music." In *Studies in Hellenistic Judaism*. Leiden: Brill, 1996.

Finley, M. I. *The Use and Abuse of History*. New York: Viking, 1975.

Fishwick, Duncan. *The Imperial Cult in the Latin West*, vol. 3: *Provincial Cult*, part 1: *Institution and Evolution*. Leiden: Brill, 2002.

Forum Ancient Coins. "Forum Ancient Coins." Accessed February 6, 2020. https://www.forumancientcoins.com/.

Foucault, Michel. *The Foucault Reader*. Edited by Paul Rabinow. New York: Pantheon, 1984.

Fowden, Garth. *Before and after Muḥammad: The First Millennium Refocused*. Princeton: Princeton University Press, 2014.

———. *The Egyptian Hermes: A Historical Approach to the Late Pagan Mind*. 2nd ed. Princeton: Princeton University Press, 1986.

Frank, Jill. *Poetic Justice: Rereading Plato's "Republic."* Chicago: University of Chicago Press, 2018.

Frankfurter, David. "Jews or Not? Reconstructing the 'Other' in Rev 2:9 and 3:9." *Harvard Theological Review* 94, no. 4 (2001): 403–425.

———. "The Legacy of Jewish Apocalypses in Early Christianity: Regional Trajectories." In *The Jewish Apocalyptic Heritage in Early Christianity*, edited by William Adler and James VanderKam. Assen, Netherlands: Van Gorcum, 1996.

Fredrick, David. "Architecture and Surveillance in Flavian Rome." In *Flavian Rome: Culture, Image, Text*, edited by A. J. Boyle and W. J. Dominik. Boston: Brill, 2002.

Frey, Jörg. "The Relevance of the Roman Imperial Cult for the Book of Revelation." In *New Testament and Early Christian Literature in Greco-Roman Context: Studies in Honor of David E. Aune,* edited by John Fotopoulos. Leiden: Brill, 2006.

Friesen, Steven J. *Imperial Cults and the Apocalypse of John: Reading Revelation in the Ruins.* Oxford: Oxford University Press, 2001.

———. *Twice Neokoros: Ephesus, Asia, and the Cult of the Flavian Imperial Family.* Leiden: Brill, 1993.

Gaca, Kathy L. *The Making of Fornication: Eros, Ethics, and Political Reform in Greek Philosophy and Early Christianity.* Berkeley: University of California Press, 2003.

Gallusz, Laszlo. *The Throne Motif in the Book of Revelation.* London: Bloomsbury, 2015.

Gibson, Andrew. *Intermittency: The Concept of Historical Reason in Recent French Philosophy.* Edinburgh: Edinburgh University Press, 2011.

Ginzburg, Carlo. *Clues, Myths, and the Historical Method.* Translated by John Tedeschi and Anne C. Tedeschi. Baltimore: Johns Hopkins University Press, 1989.

Goedicke, Hans. "An Unexpected Allusion to the Vesuvius Eruption in 79 A.D." *American Journal of Philology* 90, no. 3 (July 1969): 340–341.

Goldhill, Simon. "Representing Democracy: Women at the Great Dionysia." In *Ritual, Finance, Politics: Athenian Democratic Accounts Presented to David Lewis*, edited by Robin Osborne and Simon Hornblower, 347–369. Oxford: Oxford University Press, 1995.

Goodman, Martin. "Coinage and Identity: The Jewish Evidence." In *Coinage and Identity in the Roman Provinces*, edited by Christopher Howgego, Volker Heuchert, and Andrew Burnett, 163–166. Oxford: Oxford University Press, 2005.

Gordon, Bertram M. "The 'Vichy Syndrome' Problem in History." *French Historical Studies* 19, no. 2 (1995): 495–518.

Grabbe, Lester L. *Ancient Israel: What Do We Know and How Do We Know It?* Rev. ed. London: T&T Clark, 2007.

———, ed. *Can a "History of Israel" Be Written?* London: Sheffield Academic Press, 1997.

Gradel, Ittai. *Emperor Worship and Roman Religion.* Oxford: Clarendon Press, 2002.

Grafton, Anthony, and Megan Williams. *Christianity and the Transformation of the Book: Origen, Eusebius, and the Library of Caesarea.* Cambridge, MA: Belknap Press of Harvard University Press, 2006.

Graham, Daniel W. "Philolaus." In *A History of Pythagoreanism*, edited by Carl A. Huffman. Cambridge: Cambridge University Press, 2014.

Gray, Jeremy. *Plato's Ghost: The Modernist Transformation of Mathematics.* Princeton: Princeton University Press, 2008.

Greatrex, Geoffrey. "Roman Frontiers and Foreign Policy in the East." In *Aspects of the Roman East: Papers in Honour of Professor Fergus Millar FBA*, edited by Richard Alston and Samuel N. C. Lieu. Turnhout, Belgium: Brepols, 2007.

Greaves, Alan M. *The Land of Ionia: Society and Economy in the Archaic Period.* Chichester, UK: Wiley-Blackwell, 2010.

Griswold, Eliza. "John Chau's Death on North Sentinel Island Roils the Missionary World." *New Yorker*, December 8, 2018. https://www.newyorker.com/news/on-religion/john-chaus-death -roils-the-missionary-world.

Gruen, Erich S. *Diaspora: Jews amidst Greeks and Romans.* Cambridge, MA: Harvard University Press, 2004.

———. *Heritage and Hellenism.* Berkeley: University of California Press, 2002.

Hadas-Lebel, Mireille. *Philo of Alexandria: A Thinker in the Jewish Diaspora.* Translated by Robyn Frechet. Boston: Brill, 2012.

Hales, Shelley, and Joanna Paul, eds. *Pompeii in the Public Imagination from Its Rediscovery to Today.* Oxford: Oxford University Press, 2012.

Hall, John R. *Apocalypse: From Antiquity to the Empire of Modernity.* Cambridge, UK: Polity, 2009.

Hansen, Mogens Herman. "The 'Autonomous City-State': Ancient Fact or Modern Fiction?" In *Studies in the Ancient Greek Polis (Papers from the Copenhagen Polis Centre, Vol. 2)*, edited by Mogens Herman Hansen and Kurt Raaflaub. Stuttgart: F. Steiner Verlag, 1995.

———. "Kome. A Study in How the Greeks Designated and Classified Settlements Which Were Not Poleis." In *Studies in the Ancient Greek Polis (Papers from the Copenhagen Polis Centre, Vol. 2)*, edited by Mogens Herman Hansen and Kurt Raaflaub. Stuttgart: F. Steiner Verlag, 1995.

Hanson, Ann E. "The Roman Family." In *Life, Death, and Entertainment in the Roman Empire*, edited by D. S. Potter and D. J. Mattingly. Ann Arbor: University of Michigan Press, 2010.

Harrill, J. Albert. "The Use of the New Testament in the American Slave Controversy: A Case History in the Hermeneutical Tension between Biblical Criticism and Christian Moral Debate." *Religion and American Culture: A Journal of Interpretation* 10, no. 2 (Summer 2000): 149–186.

Harris, B. F. "Oaths of Allegiance to Caesar." *Prudentia* 14, no. 2 (1982): 109–122.

Harris, William Vernon. "Slavery: Towards a Study of the Roman Slave Trade." In *Rome's Imperial Economy.* Oxford: Oxford University Press, 2010.

Hartog, Paul. "'Not Even among the Pagans' (1 Cor 5:1): Paul and Seneca on Incest." In *The New Testament and Early Christian Literature in Greco-Roman Context. Studies in Honor of David G. Aune.* Edited by John Fotopoulos. Brill: Leiden, 2006.

Hata, Gohei. "Is the Greek Version of Josephus' 'Jewish War' a Translation or a Rewriting of the First Version?" *Jewish Quarterly Review* 66, no. 2 (October 1975): 89–108.

Heller-Roazen, Daniel. *The Fifth Hammer: Pythagoras and the Disharmony of the World*. New York: Zone Books, 2011.

Heslin, Peter. "Domitian and the So-Called Horologium Augusti." *Journal of Roman Studies* 97 (2007): 1–20.

Hicks, Andrew. *Composing the World: Harmony in the Medieval Platonic Cosmos*. New York: Oxford University Press, 2017.

———. "Pythagoras and Pythagoreanism in Late Antiquity and the Middle Ages." In *A History of Pythagoreanism*, edited by Carl A. Huffman. Cambridge: Cambridge University Press, 2014.

Hine, Harry M. "The Date of the Campanian Earthquake. A.D. 62 or A.D. 63 or Both?" *Antiquité Classique* 53 (1984): 266–269.

Hoff, Johannes. *The Analogical Turn: Rethinking Modernity with Nicholas of Cusa*. Grand Rapids, MI: Eerdmans, 2013.

Holliday, Peter J. "Time, History and Ritual on the Ara Pacis Augustae." *Art Bulletin* 72, no. 4 (December 1990): 542–557.

Holtgrefe, Jon Mark. "The Characterization of Civil War: Literary, Numismatic, and Epigraphical Presentations of the 'Year of the Four Emperors.'" PhD dissertation, University of Oregon, 2011.

Honig, Bonnie. *Antigone, Interrupted*. Cambridge: Cambridge University Press, 2013.

Hopkins, Keith. "Novel Evidence for Roman Slavery." In *Life, Death, and Entertainment in the Roman Empire*, edited by D. S. Potter and D. J. Mattingly. Ann Arbor: University of Michigan Press, 2010.

Horkheimer, Max, and Theodor W. Adorno. *Dialectic of Enlightenment*. Edited by Gunzelin Schmid Noerr. Translated by Edmund Jephcott. Stanford: Stanford University Press, 2002.

Hornblower, Simon. "The Religious Dimension to the Peloponnesian War, or, What Thucydides Does Not Tell Us." *Harvard Studies in Classical Philology* 94 (1992): 169–197.

Horseley, G. H. R. "'Christian' Greek." In *Encyclopedia of Ancient Greek Language and Linguistics*, edited by Georgios K. Giannakis, 2 vols. Leiden: Brill, 2013–2014.

———. *New Documents Illustrating Early Christianity*, vol. 5: *Linguistic Essays*. Sydney: Macquarie University, Ancient Documentary Research Centre, 1989.

Horsley, Richard A. "The Slave Systems of Classical Antiquity and Their Reluctant Recognition by Modern Scholars." *Semeia* 83–84 (1998): 19–66.

Horst, Pieter Willem van der. "Philosophia Epeisaktos: Some Notes on Josephus, A.J. 18.9." In *The Jewish Revolt against Rome: Interdisciplinary Perspectives*, edited by Mladen Popović. Leiden: Brill, 2011.

Hourani, George F. "Did Roman Commercial Competition Ruin South Arabia?" *Journal of Near Eastern Studies* 11, no. 4 (October 1, 1952): 291–295.

Howard, Thomas Albert. *Religion and the Rise of Historicism: W. M. L. de Wette, Jacob Burckhardt, and the Theological Origins of Nineteenth-Century Historical Consciousness*. Cambridge: Cambridge University Press, 1999.

Howard-Brook, Wes, and Anthony Gwyther. *Unveiling Empire: Reading Revelation Then and Now*. Maryknoll, NY: Orbis Books, 1999.

Humphrey, Edith M. "To Rejoice or Not to Rejoice?" In *The Reality of Apocalypse: Rhetoric and Politics in the Book of Revelation*, edited by David L. Barr. Atlanta: Society of Biblical Literature, 2006.

Ihrig, Stefan. *Atatürk in the Nazi Imagination*. Cambridge, MA: Belknap Press of Harvard University Press, 2014.

Ilan, Tal. "Berenice." In *Jewish Women: A Comprehensive Historical Encyclopedia*. Jewish Women's Archive, February 27, 2009. https://jwa.org/encyclopedia/article/berenice.

Ilgım, Mesut, ed. *Aphrodisias Sebasteion [Sevgi Gönül Salonu]*. Ankara: Yarı Kredi Yayınları, 2008.

L'inaugurazione dell'Ara Pacis nel nuovo assetto urbanistico. Rome: Istituto Luce Cinecittà, 1938. https://www.youtube.com/watch?v=CILr3dV3hxI.

Iossif, Panagiotis P., Andrzej S. Chankowski, and Catharine C. Lorber, eds. *More Than Men, Less Than Gods: Studies on Royal Cult and Imperial Worship*. Leuven: Peeters, 2011.

Jacobs, Andrew S. "The Lion and the Lamb." In *The Ways That Never Parted: Jews and Christians in Late Antiquity and the Early Middle Ages*, edited by Adam H. Becker and Annette Yoshiko Reed. Minneapolis: Fortress Press, 2007.

Jashemski, Wilhelmina Feemster, and Frederick G. Meyer, eds. *The Natural History of Pompeii*. Cambridge: Cambridge University Press, 2002.

Jensen, Morten Horning. "Josephus and Antipas: A Case Study of Josephus Narratives on Herod Antipas." In *Making History: Josephus and Historical Method*, edited by Zuleika Rodgers. Leiden: Brill, 2007.

Johns, Loren L. "The Dead Sea Scrolls and the Apocalypse of John." In *The Bible and the Dead Sea Scrolls: The Princeton Symposium on the Dead Sea Scrolls*, vol. 3: *The Scrolls and Christian Origins*, edited by James H. Charlesworth, 255–279. Waco, TX: Baylor University Press, 2006.

Jones, Christopher P. "Multiple Identities in the Age of the Second Sophistic." In *Paideia: The World of the Second Sophistic*, edited by Barbara Borg. Berlin: Walter de Gruyter, 2004.

Jongman, Willem M. *The Economy and Society of Pompeii*. Amsterdam: J. C. Gieben, 1988.

Joseph, Simon J. *Jesus, the Essenes, and Christian Origins: New Light on Ancient Texts and Communities*. Waco, TX: Baylor University Press, 2018.

Kaimio, Jorma. *The Romans and the Greek Language*. Commentationes Humanarum Litterarum, 64. Helsinki: Societas Scientiarum Fennica, 1979.

Kamesar, Adam. "Biblical Interpretation in Philo." In *The Cambridge Companion to Philo*, edited by Adam Kamesar. Cambridge: Cambridge University Press, 2009.

Kant, Immanuel. *Critique of Pure Reason*. Translated by Werner S. Pluhar, introduction by Patricia W. Kitcher. Indianapolis: Hackett, 1996.

———. *Lectures on Logic*. Translated by J. Michael Young. Cambridge: Cambridge University Press, 1992.

Kay, Philip. "What Did the Attalids Ever Do for Us?" In *Attalid Asia Minor: Money, International Relations, and the State*, edited Peter Thonemann. Oxford: Oxford University Press, 2013.

Kennedy, J. B. *The Musical Structure of Plato's Dialogues*. Durham, UK: Routledge, 2014.

King, Karen L. *Revelation of the Unknowable God*. Santa Rosa, CA: Polebridge Press, 1995.

———. *What Is Gnosticism?* Cambridge, MA: Belknap Press of Harvard University Press, 2003.

Klawans, Zander H. *Reading and Dating Roman Imperial Coins*. 4th ed. Racine, WI: Western Publishing, 1977.

Koselleck, Reinhart. "Crisis." Translated by Michaela W. Richter. *Journal of the History of Ideas* 67, no. 2 (2006): 357–400.

Koselleck, Reinhart, and Keith Tribe. *Futures Past: On the Semantics of Historical Time*. New York: Columbia University Press, 2004.

Kovacs, Judith, and Christopher Rowland. *Revelation: The Apocalypse of Jesus*. Malden, MA: Blackwell, 2004.

Kraybill, J. Nelson. *Imperial Cult and Commerce in John's Apocalypse*. Sheffield: Sheffield Academic Press, 1996.

Kushnir-Stein, Alla. "City Eras on Palestinian Coinage." In *Coinage and Identity in the Roman Provinces*, edited by Christopher Howgego, Volker Heuchert, and Andrew Burnett, 157–161. Oxford: Oxford University Press, 2005.

Landes, Richard. *Relics, Apocalypse, and the Deceits of History: Ademar of Chabannes, 989–1034*. Cambridge, MA: Harvard University Press, 1998.

Latour, Bruno. *Facing Gaia: Eight Lectures on the New Climatic Regime*. Translated by Catherine Porter. Cambridge, UK: Polity, 2017.

Latour, Bruno, Isabelle Stengers, Anna Tsing, and Nils Bubandt. "Anthropologists Are Talking—About Capitalism, Ecology, and Apocalypse." *Ethnos* 83, no. 3 (2018): 587–606.

Lee, Chonghwa, ed. "Afterthoughts, 'Afterlife,' on the Occasion of Translation." In *Still Hear the Wound: Toward an Asia, Politics, and Art to Come—Selected Essays*, Pap/DVD edition. Ithaca: Cornell University, Cornell East Asia Series, 2016.

Lehoux, Daryn. *What Did the Romans Know? An Inquiry into Science and Worldmaking*. Chicago: University of Chicago Press, 2012.

Leonard, Miriam. *Athens in Paris: Ancient Greece and the Political in Post-war French Thought*. Oxford: Oxford University Press, 2005.

———. *Socrates and the Jews: Hellenism and Hebraism from Moses Mendelssohn to Sigmund Freud*. Chicago: University of Chicago Press, 2012.

Leoni, Tommaso. "The Text of Josephus Corpus." In *A Companion to Josephus*, edited by Honora Howell Chapman and Zuleika Rodgers. Malden, MA: John Wiley & Sons, 2016.

Lewis, R.G. "An Alternative Date for Sophocles' Antigone." *Greek, Roman, and Byzantine Studies* 29 (1988): 35–50.

Liverani, Mario. *Israel's History and the History of Israel*. London: Equinox, 2007.

Lo Cascio, Elio. "Afterword." In *Across the Ocean: Nine Essays on Indo-Mediterranean Trade*. Leiden: Brill, 2015.

Long, A. A. "Law and Nature in Greek Thought." In *The Cambridge Companion to Ancient Greek Law*, edited by Michael Gagarin and David Cohen. London: Cambridge University Press, 2005.

Loraux, Nicole. *The Divided City: On Memory and Forgetting in Ancient Athens*. Translated by Corinne Pache and Jeff Fort. New York: Zone Books, 2006.

———. "Thucydides and Sedition among Words." In *Thucydides*, edited by Jeffrey S. Rusten. Oxford University Press, 2009.

———. *Tragic Ways of Killing a Woman*. Translated by Anthony Forster. Cambridge, MA: Harvard University Press, 1987.

Lozano, Fernando. "The Creation of Imperial Gods: Not only Imposition versus Spontaneity." In *More Than Men, Less Than Gods: Studies on Royal Cult and Imperial Worship*, edited by Panagiotis P. Iossif, Andrzej S. Chankowski, and Catharine C. Lorber, 475–519. Leuven: Peeters, 2011.

Luther, Martin. *Table Talk*. Translated by William Hazlitt. Grand Rapids, MI: Christian Classics Ethereal Library, 2004. http://www.ntslibrary.com/PDF%20Books/Luther%20Table%20Talk.pdf.

Mader, Gottfried. *Josephus and the Politics of Historiography: Apologetic and Impression Management in the Bellum Judaicum*. Leiden: Brill, 2000.

Malamud, Margaret. "The Last Days of Pompeii in the Early American Republic." In *Pompeii in the Public Imagination from Its Rediscovery to Today*, edited by Shelley Hales and Joanna Paul. Oxford: Oxford University Press, 2012.

Manchester, Paula. "Kant's Conception of Architectonic in Its Historical Context." *Journal of the History of Philosophy* 41, no. 2 (April 25, 2003): 187–207.

Marissen, Michael. *Tainted Glory in Handel's Messiah: The Unsettling History of the World's Most Beloved Choral Work*. New Haven: Yale University Press, 2014.

Marshall, John W. *Parables of War: Reading John's Jewish Apocalypse*. Waterloo, Ontario: Wilfrid Laurier University Press, 2001.

Martens, John W. *One God, One Law: Philo of Alexandria on the Mosaic and Greco-Roman Law*. Boston: Brill, 2003.

Martin, Clarice J. "The Haustafeln (Household Codes) in African American Biblical Interpretation: 'Free Slaves' and 'Subordinate Women.'" In *Stony the Road We Trod: African American Biblical Interpretation*, edited by Cain Hope Felder, 206–331. Minneapolis: Fortress Press, 1991.

———. "Polishing the Unclouded Mirror: A Womanist Reading of Revelation 18:13." In *From Every People and Nation: The Book of Revelation in Intercultural Perspective*, edited by David M. Rhoads, 82–109. Minneapolis: Fortress Press, 2005.

Marx, Karl. "Grundrisse." Translated by Martin Nicolaus. Accessed February 6, 2020. https://www.marxists.org/archive/marx/works/1857/grundrisse/.

Mason, Steve. "Figured Speech and Irony in Josephus." In *Flavius Josephus and Flavian Rome*, edited by Jonathan Edmondson, James Rives, and Steve Mason. Oxford: Oxford University Press, 2005.

———, ed. *Flavius Josephus, Translation and Commentary*. Translated and commentary by Steve Mason. Vol. 1B: Judean War 2. Leiden: Brill, 2008.

———. *History of the Jewish War: A.D. 66–74*. New York: Cambridge University Press, 2016.

———. "Jews, Judaeans, Judaizing, Judaism: Problems of Categorization in Ancient History." *Journal for the Study of Judaism in the Persian, Hellenistic, and Roman Period* 38, no. 4/5 (2007): 457–512.

———. *Josephus and the New Testament*. 2nd ed. Peabody, MA: Hendrickson Publishers, 2002.

———. "PACE: Project on Ancient Cultural Engagement." *AWOL—The Ancient World Online* (blog), February 4, 2018. http://ancientworldonline.blogspot.com/2010/10/pace-project-on-ancient-cultural.html.

"Masoretic Text." Wikipedia, January 19, 2020. https://en.wikipedia.org/w/index.php?title=Masoretic_Text&oldid=936480632.

Masuzawa, Tomoko. *The Invention of World Religions: Or, How European Universalism Was Preserved in the Language of Pluralism*. Chicago: University of Chicago Press, 2005.

Matar, Nabil. *Islam in Britain, 1558–1685*. Cambridge: Cambridge University Press, 1998.

McDonough, Sean M. "Revelation." In *Commentary on the New Testament Use of the Old Testament*, edited by G. K. Beale and D. A. Carson, 1081–1161. Grand Rapids, MI: Baker Academic, 2007.

———. *YHWH at Patmos: Rev. 1:4 in Its Hellenistic and Early Jewish Setting*. Tübingen: Mohr Siebeck, 1999.

Mckay, John, and Alexander Rehding. "The Structure of Plato's Dialogues and Greek Music Theory: A Response to J. B. Kennedy." *Apeiron* 44 (October 2011): 359–375.

McLaughlin, Raoul. *The Roman Empire and the Silk Routes: The Ancient World Economy and the Empires of Parthia, Central Asia and Han China*. Barnsley, UK: Pen & Sword Books, 2016.

McQueen, Alison. *Political Realism in Apocalyptic Times*. Cambridge: Cambridge University Press, 2018.

Mendels, Doron. "The Formation of an Historical Canon." In *Josephus and Jewish History in Flavian Rome and Beyond*, edited by Joseph Sievers and Gaia Lembi. Boston: Brill, 2005.

"Messiah." Wikipedia, January 13, 2020. https://en.wikipedia.org/w/index.php?title=Messiah&oldid=935647631.

Meyer, Marvin W. *The Gnostic Discoveries: The Impact of the Nag Hammadi Library*. San Francisco: HarperCollins, 2005.

Millar, Fergus. *Rome, the Greek World, and the East*, vol. 2: *Government, Society, and Culture in the Roman Empire*. Edited by Hannah M. Cotton and Guy M. Rogers. Chapel Hill: University of North Carolina Press, 2004.

Miller, Carolyn R. "Foreward." In *Rhetoric and Kairos: Essays in History, Theory, and Praxis*, edited by Phillip Sipiora and James S. Baumlin. Albany: State University of New York Press, 2002.

Miller, Paul Allen. *Diotima at the Barricades: French Feminists Read Plato*. New York: Oxford University Press, 2016.

Mitford, T. B. "A Cypriot Oath of Allegiance to Tiberius." *Journal of Roman Studies* 50 (1960): 75–79.

Momigliano, Arnaldo. "Pagan and Christian Historiography in the Fourth Century A.D." In *Essays in Ancient and Modern Historiography*. Chicago: University of Chicago Press, 2012.

Moore, Stephen D. *Empire and Apocalypse: Postcolonialism and the New Testament*. Sheffield: Sheffield Phoenix Press, 2006.

Moormann, Eric M. "Christians and Jews at Pompeii in Late Nineteenth-Century Fiction." In *Pompeii in the Public Imagination from Its Rediscovery to Today*, edited by Shelley Hales and Joanna Paul. Oxford: Oxford University Press, 2012.

Morris, Ian. "The Athenian Empire 478–404 BC." Princeton/Stanford Working Papers in Classics, December 2005.

Mullen, Lincoln. "The Fight to Define Romans 13." *Atlantic*, June 15, 2018. https://www.theatlantic.com/ideas/archive/2018/06/romans-13/562916/.

Murison, Charles L. *Galba, Otho and Vitellius: Careers and Controversies*. New York: G. Olms Verlag, 1993.

"Museum of the Ara Pacis." Wikipedia, September 3, 2019. https://en.wikipedia.org/w/index.php?title=Museum_of_the_Ara_Pacis&oldid=913884352.

Newbold, R. F. "Pliny HN 2.199." *Classical Philology* 68, no. 3 (1973): 211–213.

Niehoff, Maren R. *Philo on Jewish Identity and Culture*. Tübingen: Mohr Siebeck, 2001.

Ober, Josiah. "The 'Polis' as Society: Aristotle, John Rawls and the Athenian Social Contract." In *The Ancient Greek City-State. Symposium on the Occasion of the 250th Anniversary of the Royal Danish Academy of Sciences and Letters, July, 1–4 1992*, edited by Mogens Herman Hansen, 129–160. Copenhagen: Munksgaard, 1993.

———. "Thucydides Theōrētikos/Thucydides Histōr: Realist Theory and the Challenge of History." In *Thucydides*, edited by Jeffrey S. Rusten. Oxford University Press, 2009.

Osborne, Peter, and Matthew Charles. "Walter Benjamin." In *The Stanford Encyclopedia of Philosophy*, edited by Edward N. Zalta. Winter 2019 Edition. Accessed February 6, 2020. https://plato.stanford.edu/archives/win2019/entries/benjamin/.

Osler, Margaret J. *Rethinking the Scientific Revolution*. Cambridge: Cambridge University Press, 2000.

Pagels, Elaine. *Beyond Belief: The Secret Gospel of Thomas*. New York: Vintage Books, 2004.

———. *The Gnostic Gospels*. New York: Vintage Books, 1989.

———. *The Origin of Satan*. New York: Vintage Books, 1995.

———. "Introduction." In *The Nag Hammadi Scriptures: The International Edition*, edited by Marvin Meyer. New York: HarperCollins, 2007.

———. *Revelations: Visions, Prophecy, and Politics in the Book of Revelation*. New York: Viking, 2012.

———. "The Social History of Satan. Part Three: John of Patmos and Ignatius of Antioch: Contrasting Visions of 'God's People.'" *Harvard Theological Review* 99, no. 4 (October 2006): 487–505.

Paley, Morton D. *The Apocalyptic Sublime*. New Haven: Yale University Press, 1986.

Paul, Joanna. "Pompeii, the Holocaust, and the Second World War." In *Pompeii in the Public Imagination from Its Rediscovery to Today*, edited by Shelley Hales and Joanna Paul. Oxford: Oxford University Press, 2012.

Pearce, Sarah. "Rethinking the Other in Antiquity: Philo of Alexandria on Intermarriage." *Antichthon* 47 (2013): 140–155.

Penwill, John L. "Expelling the Mind: Politics and Philosophy in Flavian Rome." In *Flavian Rome: Culture, Image, Text*, edited by A. J. Boyle and W. J. Dominik. Leiden: Brill, 2002.

Philo of Alexandria. *Philo's Flaccus: The First Pogrom*. Translated by Pieter Willem Van Der Horst. Leiden: Brill, 2003.

———. *The Works of Philo*. New updated edition. Translated by C. D. Yonge. Peabody, MA: Hendrickson Publishers, 1993.

"Allegorical Interpretation I" (*Legum allegoriae I*).
"Allegorical Interpretation III" (*Legum allegoriae III*).
"Concerning Noah's Work as a Planter" (*De plantatione*).
"Every Good Man is Free" (*Quod omnis probus liber*).
"On Abraham," (*De Abrahamo*).
"On Dreams" (*De somniis. I*).
"On Drunkenness" (*De ebrietate*).
"On Flight and Finding" (*De fuga et inventione*).
"On Rewards and Punishments" (*De praemiis et poenis*).
"On Mating with the Preliminary Studies" (*De congressu quarendae erutionis gratia*).
"On the Change of Names" (*De mutatione nominum*).

"On the Confusion of Tongues" (*De confusione linguarum*).

"On the Contemplative Life or Suppliants" (*De vita contemplativa*).

"On the Creation of the World" (*De opificio mundi*).

"On the Eternity of the World" (*De aeternitate mundi*).

"On the life of Moses I" (*De vita Mosis I*).

"On the Life of Moses II" (*De vita Mosis II*).

"On the Sacrifices of Abel and Cain" (*De sacrificiis Abelis et Cain*).

"On the Special Laws I" (*De specialibus legibus I*).

"On the Special Laws II" (*De specialibus legibus II*).

"On the Special Laws III" (*De specialibus legibus III*).

"On the Migration of Abraham" (*De migratione Abrahami*).

"On the Unchangeableness of God" (*Quod Deus immutabilis sit*).

"Questions and Answers on Genesis I" (*Quaestiones et solutiones in Genesin I*).

"Questions and Answers on Genesis II" (*Quaestiones et solutiones in Genesin II*).

"That the Worse is Wont to Attack the Better" (*Quod deterius potiori insidiari soleat*).

Who is Heir of Divine Things" (*Quis rerum divarum heres*).

"The Decalogue" (*De Decalogo*).

Philo of Alexandria and David T. Runia. *Philo of Alexandria: On the Creation of the Cosmos According to Moses*. Introduction, translation, and commentary by David T. Runia. Leiden: Brill, 2001.

Pippin, Tina. "The Heroine and the Whore: The Apocalypse of John in Feminist Perspective." In *From Every People and Nation: The Book of Revelation in Intercultural Perspective*, edited by David Rhoads. Minneapolis: Fortress Press, 2005.

Pliny the Younger. *Pliny: Letters and Panegyricus*. Translated by Betty Radice. Vol. 1: Letters, Books 1–7. Cambridge: Harvard University Press, 1969.

Poschenrieder, Thomas. "Material Constraints in Thucydides' Representation of History." In *Thucydides, a Violent Teacher? History and Its Representation*, edited by Georg Rechenauer and Vassiliki Pothou. Göttingen: Vandenhoeck and Ruprecht Unipress, 2011.

Potter, D. S. "Roman Religion: Ideas and Actions," in *Life, Death, and Entertainment in the Roman Empire*, edited by D. S. Potter and D. J. Mattingly. Ann Arbor: University of Michigan Press, 2010.

Potter, D. S., and D. J. Mattingly, eds. *Life, Death, and Entertainment in the Roman Empire*. Ann Arbor: University of Michigan Press, 2010.

Prager, Brad. *Aesthetic Vision and German Romanticism: Writing Images*. Rochester, NY: Camden House, 2007.

Pratt, Kenneth J. "Rome as Eternal." *Journal of the History of Ideas* 26, no. 1 (January 1965): 25–44.

Price, Jonathan J. *Jerusalem under Siege: The Collapse of the Jewish State, 66–70 C.E.* Leiden: Brill, 1993.

———. "Josephus' Reading of Thucydides: A Test Case in the Bellum Iudaicum." In *Thucydides, a Violent Teacher? History and Its Representation*, edited by Georg Rechenauer and Vassiliki Pothou. Göttingen: Vandenhoeck and Ruprecht Unipress, 2011.

———. "The Provincial Historian in Rome." In *Josephus and Jewish History in Flavian Rome and Beyond*, edited by Joseph Sievers and Gaia Lembi. Boston: Brill, 2005.

———. *Thucydides and Internal War*. Cambridge: Cambridge University Press, 2001.

Price, S. R. F. *Rituals and Power: The Roman Imperial Cult in Asia Minor*. Cambridge: Cambridge University Press, 1984.

Psoma, Selene. "War or Trade? Attic-Weight Tetradrachms from Second-Century BC Attalid Asia Minor in Seleukid Syria after the Peace of Apameia and Their Historical Context." In *Attalid Asia Minor: Money, International Relations, and the State*, edited by Peter Thonemann. Oxford: Oxford University Press, 2013.

"Publishing News from Germany." *Foreign Quarterly Review* 28 (1842): 500–502.

Rabinbach, Anson. "Between Enlightenment and Apocalypse: Benjamin, Bloch and Modern German Jewish Messianism." *New German Critique*, no. 34 (1985): 78–124.

Rajak, Tessa. "Friends, Romans, Subjects: Agrippa II's Speech in Josephus's Jewish War." In *Images of Empire*, edited by Loveday Alexander, 122–135. Sheffield: Sheffield Academic Press, 1991.

———. "The Gifts of God at Sardis." In *Jews in a Graeco-Roman World*, edited by Martin Goodman. Oxford: Clarendon Press, 1998.

———. *Josephus: The Historian and His Society*. 2nd ed. London: Duckworth, 2002.

———. *Translation and Survival: The Greek Bible of the Ancient Jewish Diaspora*. Oxford: Oxford University Press, 2009.

Rappaport, Uriel. "Who Were the Sicarii?" In *The Jewish Revolt against Rome: Interdisciplinary Perspectives*, edited by Mladen Popović, 323–342. Leiden: Brill, 2011.

Rhoads, David, ed. *From Every People and Nation: The Book of Revelation in Intercultural Perspective*. Minneapolis: Fortress Press, 2005.

Ritter, Bradley. *Judeans in the Greek Cities of the Roman Empire: Rights, Citizenship and Civil Discord*. Leiden: Brill, 2015.

Roberts, Neil. *Freedom as Marronage*. Chicago: University of Chicago Press, 2015.

Robinson, Chase F. *'Abd al-Malik*. Oxford: Oneworld Academic, 2007.

"Roman Imperial Coins—Free Online Resource for Collectors." Accessed February 6, 2020. http://www.ancientcoins.ca/RIC/.

Rose, Steve. "When in Rome . . ." *Guardian*, May 1, 2006, sec. Travel. https://www.theguardian.com/travel/2006/may/01/travelnews.museums.

Roselli, David Kawalko. *Theater of the People: Spectators and Society in Ancient Athens*. Austin: University of Texas Press, 2012.

Rosen, Michael. "'Die Weltgeschichte ist das Weltgericht.'" In *Internationales Jahrbuch des Deutschen Idealismus*, edited by Fred Rush and Jürgen Stolzenberg. Berlin: De Gruyter, 2014.

Rowett, Catherine. "The Pythagorean Society and Politics." In *A History of Pythagoreanism*, edited by Carl A. Huffman. Cambridge: Cambridge University Press, 2014.

Runia, David T. "Philo and the Early Christian Fathers." In *The Cambridge Companion to Philo*, edited by Adam Kamesar. Cambridge: Cambridge University Press, 2009.

———. *Philo in Early Christian Literature: A Survey*. Assen: Van Gorcum; Fortress Press, 1993.

———. *Philo of Alexandria and the Timaeus of Plato*. Leiden: Brill, 1986.

———. "Philo's Reading of the Psalms." *Studia Philonica Annual* 13 (2001): 102–121.

Rzepka, Jacek. "Ethnos, Koinon, Sympoliteia and Greek Federal States." In *Εὐεργεσίας χάριν: Studies Presented to Benedetto Bravo and Ewa Wipszycka by Their Disciples*, edited by Tomasz Derda, Jakub Urbanik, and Marek Węcowski, *Journal of Juristic Papyrology*, Supplement 1. Warsaw: Fundacaja im. Rafała Taubenschlaga, 2002.

Sakalas, Joan M. "The Whore of Babylon Metaphor—Permission to Erase Evil?" *Journal of Religion and Abuse* 5, no. 4 (2003): 3–14.

Sallis, John. *Chorology: On Beginning in Plato's Timaeus*. Bloomington: Indiana University Press, 1999.

Samson, Julia. *Nefertiti and Cleopatra: Queen-Monarchs of Ancient Egypt*. New York: Barnes and Noble, 1985.

Sartre, Jean-Paul, Benny Lévy, and Ronald Aronson. *Hope Now: The 1980 Interviews*. Translated by Adrian van den Hoven. Chicago: University of Chicago Press, 1996.

Schama, Simon. *The Embarrassment of Riches: An Interpretation of Dutch Culture in the Golden Age*. Berkeley: University of California Press, 1988.

Schmitt, Carl. *The Nomos of the Earth in the International Law of Jus Publicum Europaeum*. Translated by G. L. Ulmen. New York: Telos Press, 2006.

Schörle, Katia. "Pearls, Power, and Profit: Mercantile Networks and Economic Considerations of the Pearl Trade in the Roman Empire." In *Across the Ocean: Nine Essays on Indo-Mediterranean Trade*, edited by Federico De Romanis and Marco Maiuro. Leiden: Brill, 2015.

Schürer, Emil. *History of the Jewish People in the Age of Jesus Christ (175 B.C.–A.D. 135)*. Edited and revised by Geza Vermes and Fergus Millar. 5 vols. Edinburgh: T&T Clark, 1973.

Schüssler Fiorenza, Elisabeth. *The Book of Revelation: Justice and Judgment*. 2nd ed. Minneapolis: Fortress Press, 1998.

———. *Revelation: Vision of a Just World*. Edited by Gerhard Krodel. Minneapolis: Fortress Press, 1991.

Schuster, Martin. "Adorno and Negative Theology." *Graduate Faculty Philosophy Journal* 37, no. 1 (2016): 97–130.

Schwartz, Daniel R. "From Masada to Jotapata." In *A Companion to Josephus*, edited by Honora Chapman and Zuleika Rodgers. Malden, MA: John Wiley & Sons, 2016.

———. "Introduction: Was 70 CE a Watershed in Jewish History? Three Stages of Modern Scholarship, and a Renewed Effort." In *Was 70 CE a Watershed in Jewish History? On Jews and Judaism before and after the Destruction of the Second Temple*, edited by Daniel R. Schwartz and Zeev Weiss. Leiden: Brill, 2011.

———. "Κατὰ Τοῦτον Τὸν Καιρὸν: Josephus' Source on Agrippa II." *Jewish Quarterly Review* 72, no. 4 (April 1982): 241–268.

———. "Philo, His Family, and His Times." In *The Cambridge Companion to Philo*, edited by Adam Kamesar. Cambridge: Cambridge University Press, 2009.

———. *Studies in the Jewish Background of Christianity*. Tübingen: Mohr Siebeck, 1992.

Schwartz, Daniel R., and Zeev Weiss, eds. *Was 70 CE a Watershed in Jewish History? On Jews and Judaism before and after the Destruction of the Second Temple*. Leiden: Brill, 2011.

Sharon, Nadav. "Setting the Stage: The Effects of the Roman Conquest and the Loss of Sovereignty." In *Was 70 CE a Watershed in Jewish History? On Jews and Judaism before and after the Destruction of the Second Temple*, edited by Daniel R. Schwartz and Zeev Weiss. Leiden: Brill, 2011.

Sickenberger, Joseph. *Erklärung der Johannesapokalypse*. Rev. ed. Bonn: Hanstein Verlag, 1942.

Sidebotham, Steven E. *Roman Economic Policy of the Erythrean Thalassa 36 BC–A.D. 217*. Leiden: Brill, 1986.

Sievers, Joseph, and Gaia Lembi, eds. *Josephus and Jewish History in Flavian Rome and Beyond*. Boston: Brill, 2005.

Sigurdsson, Haraldur, and Frederick G. Meyer. "The Eruption of Vesuvius in A.D. 79." In *The Natural History of Pompeii*, edited by Wilhelmina Feemster Jashemski and Frederick G. Meyer. Cambridge: Cambridge University Press, 2002.

Sipiora, Phillip. "Introduction." In *Rhetoric and Kairos: Essays in History, Theory, and Praxis*, edited by Phillip Sipiora and James S. Baumlin. Albany: State University of New York Press, 2002.

Siwo-Okundi, Elizabeth J. A. "Violence against Women and Girls: Where Is God in 'This'?" *Journal of Religion and Abuse* 8, no. 4 (2008): 7–14.

Skinner, Quentin. *Visions of Politics*, vol. 1: *Regarding Method*. Cambridge: Cambridge University Press, 2002.

Smith, Jonathan Z. *Imagining Religion: From Babylon to Jonestown*. Chicago: University of Chicago Press, 1982.

———. *Map Is Not Territory: Studies in the History of Religions*. Chicago: University of Chicago Press, 1993.

Smith, Morton. "Terminological Boobytraps and Real Problems in Second-Temple Judaeo-Christian Studies." In *Studies in the Cult of Yahweh*, vol. 1: *Studies in Historical Method, Ancient Israel, Ancient Judaism*, edited by Shaye J. D. Cohen. Leiden: Brill, 1995.

Smith, R. R. R. "Simulacra Gentium: The Ethne from the Sebasteion at Aphrodisias." *Journal of Roman Studies* 78 (1988): 50–77.

———. "The Imperial Reliefs from the Sebasteion at Aphrodisias." *Journal of Roman Studies* 77 (1987): 88–138.

Smith, Shanell T. *The Woman Babylon and the Marks of Empire: Reading Revelation with a Postcolonial Womanist Hermeneutics of Ambiveilence.* Minneapolis: Fortress Press, 2014.

Sowerby, Robin. "Thomas Hobbes's Translation of Thucydides." *Translation and Literature* 7, no. 2 (1998): 147–169.

Spahn, Peter. "Between Office and Tyranny, Internal and External Rulership: Archē in Herodotus and Thucydides." In *Thucydides and Political Order: Concepts of Order and the History of the Peloponnesian War*, edited by Christian R. Thauer and Christian Wendt, 59–85. New York: Palgrave Macmillan, 2015.

Spiegel, Francesca. "In Search of Lost Time and Pompeii." In *Pompeii in the Public Imagination from Its Rediscovery to Today*, edited by Shelley Hales and Joanna Paul. Oxford: Oxford University Press, 2012.

Spilsbury, Paul S. "Reading the Bible in Rome: Josephus and the Constraints of Empire." In *Josephus and Jewish History in Flavian Rome and Beyond*, edited by Joseph Sievers and Gaia Lembi. Boston: Brill, 2005.

St Clair, William, and Annika Bautz. "Imperial Decadence: The Making of the Myths in Edward Bulwer-Lytton's The Last Days of Pompeii." *Victorian Literature and Culture* 40 (2012): 359–396.

Steinberg, Mark. *Proletarian Imagination 1911–1930: Self, Modernity and the Sacred in Russia, 1910–1925.* Ithaca: Cornell University Press, 2002.

Stephens, Mark B. *Annihilation or Renewal: The Meaning and Function of New Creation in the Book of Revelation.* Tübingen: Mohr Siebeck, 2011.

Swain, Simon. *Hellenism and Empire: Language, Classicism, and Power in the Greek World, AD 50–250.* Oxford: Clarendon Press, 1998.

Taubes, Jacob. *From Cult to Culture: Fragments toward a Critique of Historical Reason.* Edited by Charlotte Elisheva Fonrobert and Amir Engel. Stanford: Stanford University Press, 2010.

Tcherikover, Victor A., ed. *Corpus Papyrorum Judaicarum: 1.* Cambridge: Harvard University Press, 1957.

Termini, Christina. "Philo's Thought within the Context of Middle Judaism." In *The Cambridge Companion to Philo*, edited by Adam Kamesar. Cambridge: Cambridge University Press, 2009.

Thackery, H. St. J., trans. Josephus, *The Jewish War Books (Bellum Judaicum).* 8 vols. London: William Heinemann, 1927.

———, trans. *The Letter of Aristeas.* Oxford: Clarendon Press, 1917.

Thomas, David Andrew. *Revelation 19 in Historical and Mythological Context.* New York: Peter Lang, 2008.

Thompson, Leonard L. *The Book of Revelation: Apocalypse and Empire.* New York: Oxford University Press, 1990.

———. *Revelation.* Nashville, TN: Abingdon Press, 1998.

Thompson, Thomas L. "Defining History and Ethnicity." In *Can a "History of Israel" Be Written?*, edited by Lester L. Grabbe. London: Sheffield Academic Press, 1997.

Thonemann, Peter, ed. *Attalid Asia Minor: Money, International Relations, and the State.* Oxford: Oxford University Press, 2013.

———, ed. "The Attalid State, 188–133 BC." In *Attalid Asia Minor: Money, International Relations, and the State,* edited by Peter Thonemann. Oxford: Oxford University Press, 2013.

———. "A Copy of Augustus' Res Gestae at Sardis." *Historia: Zeitschrift für alte Geschichte* 61, no. 3 (2012): 282–288.

———. *The Hellenistic Age.* Oxford: Oxford University Press, 2016.

Thucydides. *The War of the Peloponnesians and the Athenians.* Edited and translated by Jeremy Mynott. Cambridge: Cambridge University Press, 2013.

Tranquillus, C. Suetonius. "Life of Nero: The Lives of the Twelve Caesars." Loeb Classical Library, 1914. http://penelope.uchicago.edu/Thayer/E/Roman/Texts/Suetonius/12Caesars/Nero*.html.

Turner, John D. *Sethian Gnosticism and the Platonic Tradition.* Quebec: Presses de l'Université Laval; Louvain-Paris: Éditions Peeters, 2001.

Tuval, Michael. "Doing without the Temple: Paradigms in Judaic Literature of the Diaspora." In *Was 70 CE a Watershed in Jewish History? On Jews and Judaism before and after the Destruction of the Second Temple,* edited by Daniel R. Schwartz and Zeev Weiss. Leiden: Brill, 2011.

"2,000 Years of Josephus: The Wars of the Jews; or The History of the Destruction of Jerusalem." Accessed January 8, 2015. http://preteristarchive.com/JewishWars/Josephus/index.html.

Tyrrell, William Blake, and Larry J. Bennett. *Recapturing Sophocles' Antigone.* Lanham, MD: Rowman & Littlefield, 1998.

Varner, Eric R. "Portraits, Plots, and Politics: 'Damnatio Memoriae' and the Images of Imperial Women." *Memoirs of the American Academy in Rome* 46 (2001): 41–93.

Vasta, Michael S. "Flavian Visual Propaganda: Building a Dynasty." *Constructing the Past* 8 (2007): 107–138.

———. "Titus and the Queen: Julia Berenice and the Opposition to Titus' Succession." Honors project, Illinois Wesleyan University, 2007. https://digitalcommons.iwu.edu/grs_honproj/1.

Veltri, Giuseppe. *Eine Tora für den König Talmai. Untersuchungen zum Übersetzungsverständnis in der judisch-hellenistischen und rabbinistischen literatur.* Tübingen: Mohr Siebek, 1994.

Vernant, Jean Pierre. "The Polis: Shared Power." In *Ancestor of the West: Writing, Reasoning, and Religion in Mesopotamia, Elam, and Greece,* translated by Teresa Lavender Fagan. Chicago: University of Chicago Press, 2000.

Volk, Katharina. *Manilius and His Intellectual Background.* Oxford: Oxford University Press, 2009.

———. "Manilius' Cosmos of the Senses." In *Synaesthesia and the Ancient Senses,* edited by Shane Butler and Alex C. Purves. Durham, UK: Routledge, 2013.

Wainwright, Arthur W. *Mysterious Apocalypse: Interpreting the Book of Revelation.* Nashville: Abingdon Press, 1993.

Wallace-Hadrill, Andrew. "The Imperial Court." In *The Cambridge Ancient History,* Vol. 10. Cambridge: Cambridge University Press, 1996.

Wan, Wei Hsien. *The Contest for Time and Space in the Roman Imperial Cults and 1 Peter: Reconfiguring the Universe.* London: T&T Clark, 2019.

Wasserstein, Abraham, and David J. Wasserstein. *The Legend of the Septuagint: From Classical Antiquity to Today.* New York: Cambridge University Press, 2009.

Weber, Samuel. *Benjamin's -abilities.* Cambridge, MA: Harvard University Press, 2010.

Webster, Graham. *Boudica: The British Revolt against Rome AD 60.* London: Routledge, 2000.

Weems, Renita J. "Reading Her Way through the Struggle: African American Women and the Bible." In *Stony the Road We Trod: African American Biblical Interpretation,* edited by Cain Hope Felder, 206–331. Minneapolis: Fortress Press, 1991.

Weitzman, Steven. "Forced Circumcision and the Shifting Role of Gentiles in Hasmonian Ideology." *Harvard Theological Review* 92, no. 1 (January 1999), 37–59.

Whitaker, Robyn J. *Ekphrasis, Vision, and Persuasion in the Book of Revelation.* Tübingen: Mohr Siebeck, 2015.

Wilker, Julia. "Josephus, the Herodians, and the Jewish War." In *The Jewish Revolt against Rome: Interdisciplinary Perspectives,* edited by Mladen Popović, 373–398. Leiden: Brill, 2011.

Williams, G. D. "Greco-Roman Seismology and Seneca on Earthquakes in 'Natural Questions 6." *Journal of Roman Studies* 96 (2006): 124–146.

Williams, Margaret H. *Jews in a Graeco-Roman Environment.* Tübingen: Mohr Siebeck, 2013.

Williams, Michael Allen. *Rethinking "Gnosticism": An Argument for Dismantling a Dubious Category.* Princeton: Princeton University Press, 1999.

Wilson, Andrew. "Red Sea Trade and the State." In *Across the Ocean: Nine Essays on Indo-Mediterranean Trade,* edited by Federico De Romanis and Marco Maiuro. Leiden: Brill, 2015.

Wilson, Marcus. "After the Silence: Tacitus, Suetonius, Juvenal." In *Flavian Rome: Culture, Image, Text,* edited by A. J. Boyle and W. J. Dominik. Leiden: Brill, 2002.

Winston, David. "Philo and Rabbinical Literature." In *The Cambridge Companion to Philo,* edited by Adam Kamesar. Cambridge: Cambridge University Press, 2009.

Wright, Benjamin G., III. "*Ebed/doulos*: Terms and Social Status in the Meeting of Hebrew Biblical and Hellenistic Roman Culture." *Semeia: Slavery in Text and Interpretation* 84 (1998): 83–151.

Zanker, Paul. *The Power of Images in the Age of Augustus*. Translated by Alan Shapiro. Ann Arbor: University of Michigan Press, 1990.

Zanker, Paul, and Henry Heitmann-Gordon. *Roman Art*. Los Angeles: J. Paul Getty Museum, 2012.

Zerubavel, Yael. "The Death of Memory and the Memory of Death: Masada and the Holocaust as Historical Metaphors." *Representations* 45 (Winter 1994): 72–100.

Zimmermann, Christiane. *Die Namen des Vaters: Studien zu ausgewählten neutestamentlichen Gottesbezeichnungen vor ihrem frühjüdischen und paganen Sprachhorizont*. Leiden: Brill, 2007.

Index

Aristotle, 19, 68, 91, 266n, 267n, 274n, 276n, 281n, 328n

Asia (Roman province), 17–18, 26, 120–123, 131, 133, 139–144, 146, 147, 154, 161, 162, 164, 180, 206, 216, 233n, 294n, 295n, 304n, 307n, 309n, 310n, 313n

Attalid, 146, 315n

Augustine, saint, 73, 243n, 336n

Augustus Caesar (Gaius Octavius, r. 27 BCE–14 CE), x, 1–4, 6, 12–15, 17–19, 23, 24, 94, 133, 135, 138–140, 143–144, 146–147, 164, 172, 175, 227n, 228n, 229n, 231n–234n, 235n, 282n, 306n, 310n, 312n, 313n, 316n, 318n, 320n, 324n, 329n, 331n, 332n, 344n, 347n, 350n

Aune, David, 121–123, 136, 166, 207, 292n–295n, 306n, 307n, 309n, 316–317n, 323n, 325n, 327n, 332n, 335n–336n, 342n, 351n, 352n, 357n

axios/ἀξίως (worthy), 178, 255n, 312n, 325n

axiosis/ἀξίωσις (evaluation), 58–60, 325n
   in *Antigone*, 65, 70
   as divine judgment, 216

Badiou, Alain, 38, 122, 295n

Barker, Andrew, 83, 270n, 271n, 274n, 279n

Bar Kochba revolt, 250n

Bauckham, Richard, 180, 196, 206, 294n, 296n, 298n, 334n, 335n, 341n, 342n, 351n, 352n

Bauer, Bruno, 186, 188, 339n

Beard, Mary, 39, 43, 241n, 244n, 337n

Being (τὸ ὄν / ὅ ὦν), 61, 90, 91, 93, 101–104, 108, 255n, 280n, 361n. *See also* Philo of Alexandria

bellum civile (civil war; Rome, 68–69 CE), 3, 20, 47, 181, 202, 246n, 350n

Bellum Judaicum (Flavius Josephus), 39–43, 45, 47, 50, 53, 56, 60, 202, 204, 242n–246n, 248n–250n, 254n, 304n, 321n, 332n, 333n, 343n, 348n–350n. *See also* Flavius Josephus; Judaean War

Benjamin, Walter, xii, xiii, 30–32, 35–37, 46, 58, 70, 93, 210–211, 224, 227n, 237n–240n, 262n, 276n, 292n, 318n, 354n, 361n, 364n–366n, 378n, 380n, 385n

Berenike (sister of Agrippa II of Judaea, mistress of Titus), 73, 200–204, 207, 348n–352n

Berenike (Red Sea port), 24, 201, 235–236n, 348n

Bernal, Martin, 240n, 305n

biblical dating (*annus mundi*), 1, 336n

Bielik-Robson, Agata, 34, 239n

Blake, William, 194, 338n

Bloch, Ernst, 119, 292n

Blumenberg, Hans, 223, 360n, 361n

Boudica, 198, 343–344n

Bowersock, Glen W., 295n, 304n

Boyarin, Daniel, 57, 122, 123, 129, 254n, 255n, 263n, 295–296n, 302n, 303n

Boyle, A. J., 241n, 330n, 331n, 333n, 344n, 348n, 351n

Buell, Denise Kimber, 279–280n, 345n

Bulwer-Lytton, Edward, *The Last Days of Pompeii*, 184, 189, 337n

Burrell, Barbara, 146, 164, 212, 308n–311n, 314n, 323n–325n, 355n

Butler, Judith, 260n, 261n

Caesar, Augustus. *See* Augustus Caesar

Caesar, Gaius Julius, 2, 3, 143, 307n, 312n, 315n, 344n, 349n

Cairo
   Coptic Museum, 123, 298n
   Geniza documents, 74

calendar, 3, 4, 64, 97, 142, 143, 154, 164, 228n–231n, 297n, 312n, 313n, 324n, 334n, 360n

Caligula (Gaius Caesar Augustus Germanicus, r. 37–41 CE), 2, 6, 73, 139, 269n, 308n, 309n, 331n

Carabine, Deirdre, 282n, 284n, 285n

Cassin, Barbara, 238n

Chapman, Honora Howell, 45, 242n–248n, 343n, 351n

Chariton of Aphrodisias (author of the novel *Callirhoe*), 342n, 343n, 354n, 366n

chiliasm (millennialism), 317n, 335n

choral/χώρα ([third] space), 26, 100, 101, 103, 105, 108, 111, 276n, 281n, 290n, 301n

Christian. *See* identity

Christianity, vii, 10, 41, 48, 72, 73, 79, 107, 112, 121–122, 129–130, 153, 156, 160, 172, 184, 188, 220, 222, 247n, 266n, 276n, 281n, 282n, 292n, 294n, 296n–300n, 302n–304n, 308n, 311n, 317n, 323n, 329n, 339n, 346n, 361n

christos/χριστός ("the anointed one"), 120, 171

chronos/χρόνος (chronic, predictable time), 142, 153, 154, 170–172, 175, 176, 195, 220, 313n, 327n–329n, 331n, 359n

Cicero, Marcus Tullius, 5, 78, 267n, 268n, 308n, 343n

civil war, 7, 47, 50–52, 54–56, 62–64, 69, 70, 77, 146, 162, 181, 202, 246n, 254n, 256n–258n, 299n, 344n. *See also bellum civile*; *stasis/στάσις*

Claudius (Tiberius Claudius Caesar Augustus Germanicus, r. 41–54 CE), 2, 6, 152, 197, 316n, 322n, 343n, 344n

Clement of Alexandria, 73, 82, 270n, 336n

Cohen, Shaye J. D., 263–264n, 322n, 343n, 345n, 347n

coins, 2–3, 7–11, 96, 138, 147, 164, 206, 227n–230n, 235n, 306n–309n, 313n, 322n, 334n, 351n

Collins, Adela Yarbro, 294n, 296n

Collins, John J., 297n–299n

Coltrane, John, viii, 98, 99, 279n

Columbus, Christopher, 119, 220, 291n

common. *See koine/κοινή*

Common Era (CE), 12, 231n, 236–237n, 263n

concept, critique of the, vii, 9, 32, 33, 47, 53, 58, 80, 81, 91, 129–132, 217–219, 222–225, 228n, 237n, 251n

and Aristotle, 276n

and Benjamin, 32, 237n, 240n

and Derrida, 106

of empire, 217

and Hegel, 29, 68, 77

and Islam, 286n

and Kant, 267n, 272n, 289n

of patriarchy, 198

of politics, 142, 254n

and Skinner, 357n–361n

and Thucydides, 248n

of universality, 169

Constantine (Flavius Valerius Constantinus, r. 306–337 CE), 119, 171–173, 221, 253n, 291n, 299n, 326n

constellation as method, x, 26, 89, 100, 130, 159–160, 198, 209, 216, 224n, 236n, 336n

Cooley, Alison E., 20, 231n–233n

Çoruh, Shulamit Bruckstein, 26, 27, 236n, 275n

Crossan, John Dominic, 320n, 340n, 343n, 347n

damnatio memoriae (condemnation of memory), 175, 308n, 316n, 330n

Daniel, book of, 72, 124, 174–175, 254n, 257n–258n, 264n, 305n, 331n, 332n, 355n

Dead Sea Scrolls, 26, 123–125, 128, 296n, 297n, 298n, 336n

de Bary, Brett, 259n

de Certeau, Michel, 216, 217, 326n, 327n, 357n, 360n

Delahaye, Ezra, 328n–329n

Derrida, Jacques, viii, 39, 67, 91, 101, 106, 113, 224, 239n, 241n, 260n, 276n, 280n, 284n, 292n, 294n, 361n

Descartes, René, viii, 80, 106, 169, 223, 360n

Dessalines, Jean-Jacques, 9, 230n

Hellenes, 44, 68, 313n. *See also* identity

Hellenic, 18, 20, 39, 46, 72–74, 77, 83, 130–133, 141, 144, 146, 148, 184, 230n, 233n, 244n, 277n, 288n, 304n, 314n, 325n, 350n, 359n

Hellenism/*Hellenismos*, vii, 67, 79, 112, 233n, 240n, 246n, 250n, 345n, 346n, 361n

Heller-Roazen, Daniel, 238n, 271n

Hermetic Corpus, 128, 301n

Hicks, Andrew, 83, 270n

Hijra dating, 10, 12, 231n

historical image, 31, 80, 115, 117, 126, 130, 153, 160, 184, 212

versus mirror image, 10, 169, 209, 211, 218, 327n, 353–354n

historical materialist, 30, 32, 239n, 240n

history, vii, x, xiii, 10, 12, 15, 20, 24, 29, 30, 33–37, 39–46, 52–54, 60–68, 72, 73, 75, 79–81, 119, 121, 128–130, 141, 155, 157, 160, 183–185, 188, 198, 212–215, 217–225, 237n, 240n, 246n, 260n, 264n, 286n, 299n, 311n, 322n, 329n, 345n, 355n, 357n, 358n. *See also* natural history; philosophy

and Christian/Western hegemony, 119, 120, 141, 286n, 294n, 299n, 311n, 323n, 329n, 330n

civilizational overlaps in, 120

in common, xi, 339n

and complexity, 322

of concepts, 360n

as constellation, 160

critical history, 264n, 346n, 361n

in its entirety, 185, 213, 220, 221, 354n, 358n, 361n

as epistemological schema, x, xiii, 9, 33, 34, 36

fragments of, xiii, 25, 30

hard-baked, 214

and humanity's childhood, 36, 240n

of ideas, 239n

and Islam, 231n, 237n, 286n

as judgment of the world, 219

against linear continuum, 34, 48, 155, 219, 311n, 322n, 328n

and modernity, xi, 9, 111, 217, 220–223, 225, 279n, 323n

and/as myth, 147, 213, 217, 218, 269n

against ontology, 59

and ownership, viii, 12, 20, 39, 43, 53, 54, 128, 129, 141, 162, 172, 241n, 250n, 263n, 302n, 346n

and Philo's meaning, 282n, 288n

and remembrance, 70

secularization of, 359n

within the text, 12, 34, 91, 120, 144, 157, 218, 222, 237n, 355n

and truth, xii, 37, 81, 130, 157, 212, 355n

universal, 329n, 330n, 354n

and victors, 41, 92, 172, 210, 213, 330n, 354n

Hobbes, Thomas, 54–55, 67, 114, 251n–253n, 359n

Hoff, Johannes, 168–170, 326n, 327n

Homer, 19, 45, 100, 145, 246n, 261n, 286n

Honig, Bonnie, 261n

Horkheimer, Max, 115, 188, 240n, 272n, 339n

Horseley, G. H. R., 132, 303n–306n

Hourani, George, 234n

Howard, Thomas Albert, 237n, 292n, 355n, 358n

Hurston, Zora Neale, 353n

hymnodes, 164–165, 324n

hymns, 124, 136, 142, 154, 165, 166, 180, 279n, 285n, 297n, 305n. *See also* Revelation, book of

Thanksgiving hymns (Dead Sea Scrolls), 124, 325n

identity, xiii, 26, 38, 40, 41, 44, 48, 53, 60, 73, 76, 77, 80, 82, 86, 109, 121, 124, 128, 129, 151, 154, 155, 157, 161–163, 169, 193, 200, 207, 240n, 246n, 250n,